HEROES

of

IRELAND'S GREAT HUNGER

To front-line workers, then and now.
You are true heroes.

HEROES

of

IRELAND'S GREAT HUNGER

Edited by

CHRISTINE KINEALY,
JASON KING
and **GERARD MORAN**

QUINNIPIAC UNIVERSITY PRESS
CORK UNIVERSITY PRESS

Published by:
Quinnipiac University Press
275 Mount Carmel Ave
Hamden, CT 06518–1908
www.quinnipiac.edu
for

Ireland's Great Hunger Institute:
www.qu.edu/institutes-and-centers/irelands-great-hunger-institute/
Cork University Press:
www.corkuniversitypress.com

Copyright: IGHI 2021
ISBN: 978-1-7361712-0-2

Cover design by the Office of Integrated Marketing Communications

Interior design and typesetting by Marsha Swan
Printed in Villatuerta, Spain, by GRAPHYCEMS

Contents

MEDICAL HEROES

ROLE OF RELIGIOUS ORDERS

CONTENTS

INTRODUCTION

Christine Kinealy, Jason King and Gerard Moran

The recent COVID-19 pandemic has highlighted the heroic, and often unsung, efforts and contributions of first responders in coming to the aid of not only those who contracted the virus, but also to the general public by providing necessities. During emergencies such as famines, natural disasters and pandemics, the contributions of people who risk their lives and assist those in danger and distress are often overlooked or marginalized as society attempts to understand and deal with the crisis. In recent times, organizations and individuals are alerted quickly when a calamity occurs enabling prompt intervention to take place when required. Charities such as *Trócaire* and *Concern*, as well as international agencies such as *Médecins Sans Frontières*, the *Red Cross* and *Red Crescent*, have been instrumental in intervening in war zones, famines and natural disasters. These are the often unsung heroes in times of crisis.

Throughout the nineteenth century, Ireland encountered perennial famines, subsistence crises, food shortages and crop failures, most notably in 1821-1823, 1861-1863, 1879-1882 and 1885-1886, which necessitated both internal and external intervention.[1] Among those organizations who assisted the starving Irish were the Mansion House Relief Committee, the Duchess of Marlborough Relief Committee, the Society of Friends, the First Nations in the United States and Canada, the American Catholic hierarchy, as well as many individuals. It was during the Great Irish Famine of 1845-1852 that the role of the international community was most evident as has been documented by Christine Kinealy in her work, *Charity and the Great Hunger in Ireland: The Kindness of Strangers*.[2] While the international community provided the funding for relief operations, it was left to individuals and organizations to distribute this aid, which was often just a drop in the ocean compared to what was required.

Since the sesquicentenary commemoration of the Great Hunger in 1995, the British government's role in relief operations has been examined and analysed by historians, and the overwhelming consensus is that the government reneged on its responsibilities to a nation that had been part of the Union since 1801. It was not until 1997 that the then British Prime Minister, Tony Blair, acknowledged that the administrations of Sir Robert Peel and, in particular, Lord John Russell, had failed in its responsibilities to the Irish people during the Great Famine.[3] The failure to provide adequate relief compared to the British government's intervention in the Scottish Famine during the same period and in the economic crisis caused by the Cotton Famine in Lancashire in 1862, indicated that the authorities regarded Ireland as a separate entity and that the Irish should look after its starving poor from its own resources. Throughout the nineteenth century, the government's response to famine and food crises in Ireland was minimalistic and it was left to private relief organizations and international charity to fill this void.[4] This was especially evident during the Great Hunger and was commented on by many of those heroes who engaged in relief operations, such as James Hack Tuke.[5] It was left to individuals and organisations in Ireland and beyond to come to the aid of the starving Irish—even if several did so reluctantly—and their service at the front-lines providing relief created numerous unsung heroes of *An Gorta Mór*.

This publication evolved out of the Great Famine Voices Roadshow "Famine Heroes" in the summer of 2020—a season of short films and online post-show discussions hosted by the National Famine Museum in Strokestown Park and the Irish Heritage Trust, with funding from the Government of Ireland Emigrant Support Programme.[6] The purpose of these "Famine Heroes" films, as well as this book, is to provide uplifting stories about coping with epidemics and to pay tribute to caregivers, both in the mid-nineteenth century and today. It is ironic that had COVID-19 not occurred, these lectures would probably not have taken place. During the post-show discussions for the "Famine Heroes" films and in discussions with other colleagues, it became clear that there were numerous heroes—far too many to fit into one volume. The historiography of the Great Famine has traditionally focused on victims and, in the words of Cormac Ó Gráda, "famine villians."[7] It is also true that any time of crisis can bring out the darker side of human nature and Ireland in the 1840s was no different. Breandán Mac Suibhne has identified examples of the "brutal callousness" and numerous "gray zones" that existed throughout Irish society as suffering intensified, but they are only part of a larger and more complex story of how desperate people sought to survive seven years of famine and disease.[8] Nevertheless, there are remarkable stories of those who often made the ultimate sacrifice in coming to the aid of the Famine Irish in Australia, Canada, the United States, Britain and Ireland itself, and their legacies resonate more powerfully and should inspire gratitude to the heroes of today's COVID-19 pandemic. The stories of these Famine caregivers are gathered for the first time in this volume.

The role of Irish elites who did come to the aid of their poorer fellow country men and women is sometimes forgotten. A case in point is Stepney St. George (1791-1847) of Castle Headford in County Galway. As the town's most prominent landlord, St George became chairman of its famine relief committee, and he made extraordinary efforts to alleviate the suffering of his tenants. Shortly before he perished, St. George observed in an unpublished letter on 22 April 1847 that "even on this very day I have seen several persons actually die in the streets of this small village and fever is commencing its attack on us."[9] John Caldwell Bloomfield (1823-1897), who inherited the Castlecaldwell estate in County Fermanagh in 1849, was even more successful in aiding the poor. He "expended much money and effort on attempts to foster local industry and to increase employment in Fermanagh."[10] The Belleek Pottery was created in 1857 from a famine relief project initiated by Bloomfield. In 1883, he recollected how his own endeavors contrasted with most famine relief measures in the 1840s:

> I can testify myself to the expenditure of seven-hundred pounds on half-a-mile of road in 1847, which remained for years without the slightest utility, a monument of the 'stirabout works,' as they were contemptuously called, where many a poor creature died from dragging himself on his swollen limbs to get his name entered on this bogus work.[11]

Shortly thereafter, Bloomfield founded "the Irish pottery which I had the honour of originating and producing." Indeed, he recalled the very moment when:

> on a hill in Fermanagh, I first found kaolin and felspar, and then and there registered a vow that I would, if I lived, have a china manufacture in the village of Belleek, one of the poorest hamlets in Ireland, filled with ragged children, whose maximum of art lay in the making of mud pies in the streets ... Whatever may become of "Belleek" in the future, it has taken its place as a special ware.[12]

Belleek Pottery Limited is "Ireland's oldest working pottery" and recorded annual turnover in 2019 of more than £9.6 million.[13] Yet the Visitor Centre does not acknowledge the company's origins as a famine relief project. Indeed, reminiscences of famine relief stress bogus "stirabout works" and roads to nowhere rather than this iconic global brand.

The figure of Father Theobald Mathew (1790-1856) of Cork, the famous "apostle of temperance," resisted the predations of less salubrious Irish merchants. He kept up a steady stream of correspondence with officials in the British government asking that more be done to help the poor of Ireland. In December 1846, he informed Charles Trevelyan of the Treasury that "men, women, and children, are gradually wasting away. They fill their stomachs with cabbage-leaves, turnip-tops &c. &c., to appease the cravings of hunger." To increase the profits of the local merchants, food prices were artificially inflated, and the result was 100 people a week were dying in the city. In the face of government inertia, Mathew responded by opening soup kitchens throughout the city "to supply the poor with nutritious and cheap cooked food." As the Famine progressed, Mathew kept a number of these kitchens open and paid and funded them through a combination of charity and his own personal income.[14] This philanthropy continues in the city today with Cork Penny Dinners on Little Hanover Street, the successor to the soup kitchen established by the Society of Friends in 1847. As one of Cork's oldest charitable organizations, it has provided food and meals to those in need during the recent pandemic.[15]

A Famine hero who has achieved belated renown because of his famous descendant is Edward Blewitt of Ballina in County Mayo, the great-great-great-grandfather of President Joe Biden. Like Captain Arthur Edward Kennedy, featured elsewhere in this volume, Blewitt worked within a system that was inherently unsympathetic to those it was intended to relieve. Both Blewitt and Kennedy worked in poor law unions that were amongst the poorest in the country. The Ballina Union also had the disadvantage of being large—60 miles by 30 miles—with some people living 40 miles away from the local workhouse. In February 1848, the year that Blewitt was employed by the poor law authorities, a new project was undertaken in the union to improve the system of the cultivation of the soil. It was an initiative of the Society of Friends, who so often filled the vacuum left by the government's relief initiatives. The work was done entirely by spade-labour, and over 1,000 people were employed. The wages were paid in task-work, that is, by the amount of work done, but it was also recognized that:

> as the persons employed were very generally chosen from among those whose strength had been greatly reduced by previous starvation, the rates of payment were necessarily considerably higher than would have been required, if none but strong, able-bodied labourers had been employed.[16]

It was Blewitt's job, with his background in public works, to oversee the drainage works on this and similar projects, essential work if the cultivation was to be improved.[17] The Blewitt family emigrated from Ireland in 1851, on the SS *Excelsior*. They settled in Scranton, Pennsylvania.[18] Their emigration is a reminder that it was not only the poor who left Ireland as a result of the Famine, skilled workers also believed that their future lay in North America. Historian Ciarán Reilly claimed that Blewitt's work in Ireland, on the public works and then as an overseer for the Poor Law, "saved thousands of lives during the Famine."[19]

The experiences of Blewitt continue to inform the philosophy of his famous descendant. On 25 March 2021, at Joe Biden's first press conference as President of the United States, he was asked repeatedly about the plight of migrants at the U.S./ Mexico border, most particularly that of unaccompanied children. Displaying his trade-mark empathy, he told one reporter that no child who arrived at the border would be allowed to "starve to death and stay on the other side." He explained that it was necessary to understand why they left: "It's because of earthquakes, floods. It's because of lack of food. It's because of gang violence. It's because of a whole range of things ... People don't want to leave." The actions of Biden's Irish ancestors in the mid-nineteenth century were clearly on his mind during this discussion:

> When my great grandfather got on a coffin ship in the Irish Sea, expectation was: Was he going to live long enough on that ship to get to the United States of America? But they left because of what the Brits had been doing. They were in real, real trouble. They didn't want to leave. But they had no choice.

Encapsulating the actions of many Famine and front-line heroes, Biden added, "I can't guarantee we're going to solve everything, but I can guarantee we can make everything better. We can make it better. We can change the lives of so many people."[20]

Other countries contributed to the Irish relief effort, with individuals and communities in the United States, South America, Canada, Asia, Australasia, and Europe sending donations and aid to the starving Irish. Despite these generous interventions, over one million people died in Ireland from disease and starvation, and another 2.1 million left Ireland between 1845 and 1855, more than had emigrated from Ireland over the previous two-and-a-half centuries. An estimated one-and-a-half million went to the United States, 300,000 to Canada or, as it was then known, British North America, and an estimated 300,000 went to Britain. Many arrived in a diseased and emaciated condition, especially during "Black' 47." Places including Grosse Île, Montreal, Liverpool and Boston saw an influx of Famine refugees that overwhelmed the resources of these cities. Tellingly, although Liverpool was in Britain and Canada was part of the British Empire, the government in London felt that the primary responsibility for financing this additional burden was on local taxpayers and not on government resources. In the case of Liverpool, which was a staging post for longer overseas journeys, initial sympathy for the Irish poor dissipated as poor rates and deaths from disease continued to rise. By 1847, the city was overwhelmed, but virtually no support came from the British government. Again, the contribution of individuals in these destinations cannot be understated.

The most destitute Famine Irish emigrants crossed the Atlantic in "coffin ships" and arrived in the British North American colonies of New Brunswick, Canada East (Quebec) and Canada West (Ontario) during the spring and summer of 1847. The Famine migration to New Brunswick, in particular, is often overlooked, although the quarantine stations on Partridge Island, Saint John and Middle Island in the Miramichi River received a disproportionate number of emigrants and were places of intense suffering. Among the very worst of the coffin ships was the *Loosthauk,* which arrived on the Miramichi on 3 June 1847. The *Loosthauk* had left Liverpool on 17 April with 462 passengers, but 146 perished during the transatlantic voyage after an outbreak of typhus, and another 100 on board were gravely ill.[21] So badly stricken was the *Loosthauk* that it had to change course and make landfall in the town of Chatham. Local residents "immediately set about collecting necessaries, and to the credit of the inhabitants of the town, the appeal to their humanity was spontaneously responded to," according to the *New Brunswick Standard.*[22] Nevertheless, the *Loosthauk* was so afflicted that its captain had the corpses moved from the deck to the hold before a pilot could be brought on board to help bring the ship ashore. Shortly thereafter, its fever-stricken passengers were quarantined on Middle Island (now the Middle Island Irish Historical Park in Miramichi), where temporary fever sheds had been erected, but 40 emigrants immediately perished and 96 more died within a few days.[23] Despite the obvious risk, 26-year-old Dr. John Vondy volunteered to take charge and almost single-handedly cared for the Irish fever victims. He toiled almost by himself without adequate facilities, shelter or even food to alleviate the emigrants' suffering. Vondy fell ill on the 22 June 1847 and lay dying for a week, nursed by his sister, before he finally perished on 29 June. According to *The Miramichi Gleaner*:

> He fell, a sacrifice to that alarming disease with which the passengers of the ill-fated ship *Loosthauk* were visited ... His remains were placed in a double coffin, made perfectly airtight, and conveyed from Middle Island to Coulson's slip, and from thence to St. Paul's Churchyard, followed by an immense concourse of people.[24]

Dr. John Vondy was one of many Canadian caregivers of the Famine Irish who fell victim to infectious disease in 1847.

Mark McGowan's chapter explores the role of Bishop Michael Power, but a number of other high-ranking ecclesiastics were involved in relief in Canada. This includes Joseph Signay, Archbishop of Quebec who, with the unenviable reputation of being inactive in church matters, proved more responsive in relation to Irish suffering.[25] In June, he sent £1,021-13-3 to the Central Relief Committee in Dublin for the use of Bishop Daniel Murray.[26] He was also monitoring with alarm the deteriorating situation in Grosse Île.[27] On 9 June, approximately three weeks after the arrival of the first Famine immigrants, Signay issued a Circular Letter to the Catholic archbishops and bishops of Ireland, which opened with a warning about "the dismal fate that awaits thousands of the unfortunate children of Ireland who come to seek in Canada an asylum from the countless evils afflicting them in their native land."[28] His words had little impact as wave after wave of diseased Irish continued to arrive on the shores of Canada. Signay played his part as, according to one biography, "during the ship fever of 1847 and 1848, he rivaled his priests in his personal sacrifices for the victims."[29]

Sacrifice was evident elsewhere. The Sisters of Mercy in St John's in Newfoundland lost one of the two sisters residing there. Sister Mary Joseph Nugent had moved to the convent from Ireland in 1842. She was a teacher and a translator of Italian religious texts. Nugent died in May 1847 of "malignant typhus fever," which she caught while tending to a sick immigrant from Ireland.[30] Other deaths include that of Dr. Bernard McGale, aged 45, who contracted typhus in the fever sheds in Griffintown, and Dr. Alfred Malhiot, aged 24, who had only recently graduated from medical school, the obituary stating that, "his life is the forfeit of his zeal."[31] The most detailed and evocative eyewitness accounts of the suffering of both the emigrants and those who cared for them can be found in the unpublished, but recently digitized, diaries of Stephen de Vere and in the annals of the Sisters of Charity, or Grey Nuns, of Montreal.[32] In April 1847, de Vere, from Curragh Chase in County Limerick, risked his life traveling in steerage with former tenants to bear witness to harrowing conditions on the coffin ships and campaign for Passenger Act reform.[33] His eyewitness account would become the most widely cited description of the Famine voyage. In de Vere's own words:

> Before the emigrant has been a week at sea he is an altered man. How could it be otherwise? Hundreds of poor people men, women, and children of all ages ... huddled together without light, without air, wallowing in filth and breathing a fetid atmosphere, sick in body, dispirited in heart.[34]

De Vere's harrowing testimony shocked a House of Lords Select Committee on Colonisation from Ireland, chaired by his uncle Lord Monteagle, into recommending comprehensive Passenger Act reform.[35] Years later, his younger brother, the poet Aubrey de Vere, recalled that Stephen had risked his life when:

he took passage for Canada with a considerable number of those who had been employed ... under his supervision, and conducted them to Quebec, sharing with them all the sufferings and perils which then belonged to a crowded steerage passage. Those who escaped fever on their sea-passage frequently caught it on landing, the dormant seeds of disease becoming rapidly developed by the stimulus of better air and food, and by infection. It was so on this occasion. They reached Quebec in June of 1847, and in a short time nearly all of those whom he had taken with him and lodged in a large, healthy house were stricken down in succession, during a period covering about eight months, and received from him personally all the ministrations which they could have had from a hospital nurse ... His letter describing the sufferings of emigrants was read aloud in the House of Lords by Earl Grey, then Secretary for the Colonies, and the Passengers Act was amended, due accommodations of all sorts being provided in the emigrant vessels. Most of those emigrants who on reaching Quebec went into the crowded and infected hospitals died there. It is impossible to guess how many thousands of emigrants may have been saved by this enterprise.[36]

Such was de Vere's influence, contends Historian Oliver MacDonagh, that "it is scarcely too much to regard it as the basis of most of their future legislation for ship life."[37]

Despite his influence, the fact that de Vere kept copious journals and wrote extensive letters during his voyage to Canada in 1847-1848 remains little known. He recorded scenes of the heroism and self-sacrifice of Canadian caregivers in the fever sheds on Grosse Île and in Montreal where approximately 6,000 Irish emigrants lie buried in mass graves. On 16 June 1847, de Vere wrote in his red leather-bound journal:

Arrived at Grosse isle quarantine about 7 am. Detained waiting for doctor till evening, when he inspected & gave us clean bill of health – abt. 40 ships detained there – villages of white tents on shore for the sick. Daily mortality about 150. One ship, Sisters of Liverpool, in with all passengers & crew in fever. Of this ship, all but the Cap'n and one girl died.

Laid alongside of 'Jessy' in which many ill. Water covered with beds, cooking utensils, refuse of the dead. Ghastly appearance of boats full of sick going ashore never to return. Several died between ship and shore. Wives separated from husbands, children from parents. Ascertained by subsequent enquiry that funds in agents' hands altogether insufficient for care. Medical attention bad. Exemplary conduct of Catholic Clergy.[38]

When he reached Montreal on 24 June, de Vere observed "frightful mortality in the Emigrant Sheds hospitals & generally throughout the town."[39] "Great mortality amongst the Catholic clergy," he added in a cross-hatched entry in his journal on 11 July: "It is impossible to find nurses. Grey Nuns undertake it all not knowing how many dead! 48 now ill. Blessed nuns able to leave convent to take charge of sick orphans of Quebec and Montreal steamers ill of fever."[40]

Nearer to Ireland, front-line workers in Liverpool were honored with a monument erected in 1898 to the ten Catholic priests "who, attending the sick caught typhus fever and died in 1847."[41] It was not only the clergy who assisted the Famine Irish. A name well known to the people of Liverpool was William Rathbone, a wealthy merchant and noted philanthropist. In addition to many initiatives on behalf of the city's poor, he introduced washhouses to Liverpool in 1840—an initiative that proved invaluable in saving lives a few years later. During the late 1840s, up to 10,000 persons per week were making use of these facilities where they could wash both themselves and their clothes.[42] Liverpudlians might not be as familiar with his work during the Great Famine, but both Rathbone and his wife, Elizabeth, were friends of Father Mathew in Cork and provided financial assistance for his soup kitchens and other relief schemes.[43] When the U.S.S. *Jamestown* made her famous landing in the city, William traveled there to assist Captain Robert Bennet Forbes in the distribution of relief.[44] Not only did donors in New England trust Rathbone with the distribution of their relief in Cork, but a number of other societies in America chose to work through Rathbone.[45] Rathbone was also entrusted with the proceeds of a collection made in Providence in Rhode Island, on behalf of the Galway Industrial Society.[46] He continued this philanthropy in the 1880s when he played a major role in the Tuke Emigration Scheme, which saw nearly 10,000 people from the west of Ireland assisted to emigrate to North America.[47]

The chapters that follow examine the contributions of 15 individuals and two groups of people who helped to alleviate the suffering of the Irish poor during the Great Famine. It commences with a chapter by Gerard Moran on James Hack Tuke. In Famine historiography, the role and endeavors of the Society of Friends have been well documented and acknowledged.[48] The innovative contribution of a community that numbered only 3,000 people in Ireland is evident in that not only were they responsible for setting up soup kitchens in the autumn of 1846, but they also sent representatives to the most remote parts of the country to distribute aid and to document the levels of starvation and deaths they witnessed. These reports were subsequently published in the aftermath of the calamity.[49] Whereas many others who engaged in relief work were accused of being biased and subjective in their reporting, these criticisms could not be leveled at the Quakers. While Irish Quakers like Jonathan Pim and Joseph Bewley were to the forefront in the relief efforts, they were assisted by their fellow religionists from Britain such as William Bennett, William F. Forster and James Hack Tuke, who all responded to the call for assistance. Among the Quakers in America who played a prominent role was Irish-born Jacob Harvey of New York. Tuke's role is the focus of Moran's essay, which argues that his experience during the Great Hunger laid the foundation for his long-term commitment to the Irish during subsequent famines in the west of Ireland, including his endeavors to promote the economic development of the region to improve the living standards of its people.

The role of private charity is highlighted in several chapters. The British Association for the Relief of Distress in Ireland and the Highlands of Scotland was one of a number of organizations that came into existence in the wake of the second appearance of potato blight. Founded and run by bankers in London, it proved highly effective at raising funds, recording over 15,000 separate donations from all over the world. This included one from a young American lawyer with political ambitions, who donated £5.[50] His name was Abraham Lincoln. Due to the dedication of the associations' agents in Ireland—notably the remarkable Paul de Strzelecki and his small team of volunteers—the association proved effective at saving lives. The chapter by Christine Kinealy outlines the contribution of this intrepid Polish man who proved to be a true friend of the Irish poor.

While private relief to Ireland came from all over the world, in the spring of 1847, one of the most celebrated charitable interventions took place; it was the voyage of the U.S.S. *Jamestown*—a sloop of war that sailed from Boston to Cork. Symbolically, the process of loading the ship with foodstuffs commenced on 17 March. The members of the crew were volunteers, as was the captain, Robert Bennet Forbes. In response to criticism of allowing a warship to be used for such a purpose, Forbes responded, "It is not an everyday matter to see a nation starving."[51] In Cork, Forbes was assisted in distributing the 800 tons of supplies by Father Mathew and William Rathbone of Liverpool, two men, as mentioned earlier, noted for their philanthropy.[52] Their efficiency was praised by a newspaper in Cork, for dispensing the relief "in less time than it would take to get an intelligible answer from the Board of Works or to take the initiatory steps into carrying them into action."[53] Catherine Shannon's chapter tells the story of Forbes' role in bringing relief from the people of New England to Ireland, and she explains how this modest man refused to accept any official honors for his "mission of mercy" to the Irish poor.

History has not been kind to Irish landowners whose response during the Great Hunger was inadequate or inhumane. Some took their responsibilities to their tenants seriously by working with relief committees, by bringing food to feed not only their own tenants, but also to those on neighbouring estates, and by not collecting rents from their tenants. However, there were many proprietors who cleared their properties of bankrupt and insolvent tenants and made no provision for them. After 1847, many availed of the Quarter Acre Clause, also known as the Gregory Clause, to clear their estates of tenants. It is estimated that between 250,000 and 500,000 people were evicted, with the most notorious instances occurring on the Vandeleur estate in County Clare, the Lucan estate in County Mayo and the Lansdowne property in County Kerry.[54] Owners of smaller estates also adopted this approach as on Mrs Marcella Gerrard's estate in County Galway and on John Walsh's land in the Mullet in County Mayo.[55] A number of landowners were prepared to pay their tenants' passage fares to North America, including Major Dennis Mahon in County Roscommon, Lord Palmerston in County Sligo and Earl Fitzwilliam in County Wicklow.[56] The outcome was sometimes disastrous.[57] While landowners have been held responsible for the large scale clearances, in many instances the impetus came from their agents as with the Mahon and Lansdowne estates, and the Bath estate in County Monaghan. However, not all landed proprietors adopted a cavalier and uncaring approach toward their desperate and starving tenants and their benevolent actions have been largely overlooked or forgotten. These included Sir Robert Gore Booth in County Sligo and George Henry Moore in County Mayo who not only forgave rents from their tenants, but also purchased food for distribution among the poor.[58] In also included the Sligo family of Westport House in County Mayo, whose diverse role is examined in the chapter by Sandy Letourneau O'Hare. The recent discovery of Lady Sligo's letters, many relating to the 1840s, allows a rare insight into how a privileged woman residing in the Big House responded to the plight of her tenants. Her chapter highlights that, due to the longevity of the Famine, the response changed over time as the impact of a reduced income from rents and the increasing burden of poor rates took their toll on Irish landlords. The response of the Sligo family is in marked contrast with the way in which a number of Irish landowners responded to the crisis, including Colonel Vandeleur of Kilrush, examined in a later chapter.

Mary Ann McCracken also had a privileged upbringing but endeavored to alleviate poverty. Her adult life spanned many significant events in Irish history—the 1798 Uprising (when she lost her beloved brother, Henry Joy), the Act of Union, Catholic Emancipation, the Great Famine, and the ending of slavery in both the British Empire and America. Throughout all, her humanitarianism and commitment to social change were evident. The McCrackens were part of the radical Presbyterian tradition that was strongest at the end of the eighteenth century. Her spirit of inclusivity was evident during the Famine when McCracken helped found the Belfast Ladies' Association for the Relief of Irish Destitution, which promised to "sink all doctrinal distinctions" and provide relief without regard to religion.[59] This commitment was in marked contrast to the proselytism, or "souperism," evident amongst a minority of relief givers. Peter Murphy's chapter recovers the memory of this remarkable woman as a hero not only of the Famine, but of the poor and suffering whatever their religion and wherever they were located.

The American missionary Asenath Nicholson was very critical of the response of landlords and the government to the unfolding crisis. As Maureen Murphy's chapter shows, Nicholson had first visited Ireland in 1844 and she returned following the appearance of the blight, thus becoming among the first foreign visitors to provide relief from a base in Cork Street in Dublin. Following this, she traveled extensively throughout those areas where there was widespread starvation and death, especially along the western seaboard. She often stayed in the homes of people who were trying to provide relief and visited those who endured the greatest hardship. Her writings provided important, forthright, eye-witness testimony of the divergent responses to the suffering of the Irish poor. She praised the work of respondents like the Ladies' Relief Association in Belfast and the Quakers, which included the intrepid Mary Ann McCracken and James Hack Tuke, respectively.

An examination of the role of doctors and other medical personnel during the Great Hunger has been largely neglected. One of these was Dr. Richard Grattan from Carbury, County Kildare, who was also a landowner and chairman of the Edenderry Board of Guardians and the subject of Ciarán Reilly's essay. A prolific writer on social, medical and political affairs, Grattan was heavily involved in various nationalist movements throughout his career and sought ways of improving the condition of the poor. Grattan provided relief works for the tenants and medical assistance for the sick and elderly, despite the handicap of losing a hand in a farming accident. He used his medical expertise to provide information on infectious diseases such as cholera. To counteract the loss of the potato he purchased Indian corn for his tenants, but they remained skeptical about cooking it. Grattan also established a working farm so that the inmates in Edenderry workhouse could be employed.

The contribution of Irish artist James Mahony in providing a visual record of the suffering in west Cork in 1847 is explored in a later chapter. Mahony's route through the county had been partly inspired by the publication of Dr. Daniel Donovan's diary in *The Cork Southern Reporter*, starting in December 1846. Extracts of these powerful narratives were included in Mahony's reports in *The Illustrated London News* in 1847.[60] Marita Conlon-McKenna explores Dr. Donovan's harrowing experiences in Skibbereen as recounted in his diary. Skibbereen and its surrounding areas became synonymous with the suffering of the Irish poor during the Famine, and Donovan's devotion to the Skibbereen people is sensitively retold by Conlon-McKenna. As with many of the heroes in this volume, Donovan's eyewitness testimony offered a powerful rebuttal to some claims that the suffering caused by the Famine had been exaggerated.

A number of chapters provide reminders that not all of the heroes of the Famine resided in Ireland. The Port of Liverpool in the north-west of England was the major recipient of many emigrants after 1846. Between 1846 and 1847, over half a million Famine emigrants arrived in the city and, while North America was the intended final destination for many, the majority arrived with few resources and in an emaciated and diseased state. These unwell emigrants put tremendous pressure on the city. The chapter by Christine Kinealy, on the role of Dr. William Duncan, highlights the dilemmas faced by the people of Liverpool who were in the front-line of coping with the Famine refugees, while receiving minimal support from the government. Even before 1845, Duncan was a leading figure in public health reform, showing the link between poverty and disease the importance of recognizing and treating the underlying causes. His response to the Irish influx provides an insight into the conflict between science and supposition in informing medical practices. This chapter also provides a powerful reminder that, despite Ireland being part of the United Kingdom and the British Empire, the Irish poor had no legal right to receive relief. Consequently, they could be, and they were, deported back to Ireland. Nor was Liverpool the only city who responded in this way: "British poor law unions in areas heavily affected by the refugee crisis adopted rigorous removal policies."[61]

Most emigration during the Famine was a flight of desperation, done with little thought as to the conditions on board the ships or the reception in the place of destination. An exception to this was the highly organised Earl Grey Irish Orphan Assisted Emigration Scheme to Australia, where there was little disease or death amongst the young women who participated. The scheme was suggested in 1847 by authorities in Australia who were concerned with the imbalance between men and women in the colony. Initially, it was proposed that young female orphans from British workhouses should be given the chance to volunteer for this scheme, but as the Famine worsened in Ireland, the British government changed the focus. From their perspective, the fact that it would be financed by the colony made it particularly attractive. Thus, between 1848 and 1850, 4,114 girls between the ages of 14 and 18 were sent from Irish workhouses to Australia.[62] Regardless of the careful planning that accompanied this scheme, it was soon beset with scandals, including accusations that the young women were dirty and incapable of housework and, more shockingly, that several of the girls from the Belfast workhouse were former prostitutes.[63] The scheme was brought to a premature end. The chapter by Rebecca Abbott shows that in the midst of accusations and counter-accusations, the scheme had a number of notable successes. She examines the role of Dr. Strutt, the surgeon who accompanied the young women on board the *Thomas Arbuthnot*, and then into the interior of Australia to find employment. Strutt brought humanity to a scheme that took orphaned teenage girls on a journey of over 9,000 miles, with little chance of ever returning to Ireland. Strutt is largely forgotten today, but at the time, he was regarded as a hero of the emigration scheme for the "healthy, cleanly, and orderly" condition of those in his care.[64]

Stephen de Vere was inspired by numerous Canadian caregivers, a number of whom are included in this volume. Indeed, he worked alongside Toronto Emigrant Agent Edward McElderry, "boarding with him every steamer filled with the wretched cargoes, and transmitting to the 'proper authorities' the result of his laborious experience."[65] On 6 November 1847, de Vere wrote that "I regret to hear of poor McElderry's death of fever at Toronto."[66] McElderry had also worked closely with Dr George Robert Grasett, the medical superintendent of Toronto's temporary Emigrant Hospital, who perished on 16 July 1847. "Since his appointment as hospital superintendent," eulogized *The British Colonist*, "he knew no other duty than that of staying disease and alleviating the sufferings of those who, driven from their own land by famine and pestilence, sought a refuge among us, their brethren in Canada."[67]

Yet Dr. Grasett's sacrifice was by no means unique. As Laura J. Smith and Robert G. Kearns note in their chapter, his story is emblematic of eight other lesser-known medical personnel from Toronto's Emigrant Hospital who did not survive that summer; namely, Head Nurse Susan Bailey, nurses Sarah Duggan, Anne Slocomb and Catherine Doherty, orderlies Richard Jones and John McNabb and physician Dr. Joseph Hamilton. They acknowledge that these men and women paid the ultimate price in caring for the Famine Irish. The doctors, nurses and orderlies overcame sectarian and class divisions and the rudimentary medical infrastructure of the colonial city to respond to the needs of newcomers amidst the chaos of an unprecedented migration season. Moreover, they have all been honored with the opening of the Dr. George Robert Grasett Park in downtown Toronto on the site of the former Emigrant Hospital. The park commemorates not only the heroism of Dr. Grasett, but also of the individuals who died while caring for the sick and dying Irish emigrants in Toronto in the summer of 1847.

Priests, ministers and nuns, in addition to providing spiritual succour, during the Famine often were on the frontlines of providing relief. It was not only in Canada that many died performing these duties, although no systematic recording was made. Historian Donal Kerr estimated that 40 Catholic priests died in Ireland.[68] In his 1848 publication *The Irish Crisis*, Charles Trevelyan named seven priests who lost their lives in Lancashire—six in Liverpool and one in Manchester of the "Irish fever."[69] A memorial unveiled in St. Patrick's Church in Liverpool in 1898 listed ten local priests who had perished from fever in 1847, "in the discharge of their duties."[70] It is likely that there were dozens more members of religious orders who died while tending to the sick. This publication examines the role of two Catholic bishops who lost their lives, like so many Irish poor, from typhus fever. One lived in Donegal in Ireland, the other in Toronto in Canada. Edward Maginn, the Bishop of Derry, was an uncompromising defender of "Catholic Ireland," supporting Daniel O'Connell's Repeal movement and promoting tenants' rights. He was also an outspoken critic of the British government's relief policies, which he regarded as "murderous." Turlough McConnell, a Donegal man himself whose family lives in Maginn's former home in Buncrana, explores Maginn's growing national status as a champion of his people before his untimely death in January 1849.

Stephen de Vere continued to record scenes of heroism in his journal as he traveled from Montreal to Toronto in 1847. He was in Toronto on 1 October when its bishop, Michael Power, passed away. De Vere recorded this in a very moving private obituary:

> Rev. Michael Power Catholic bishop of Toronto died this morning. He was a man of great generosity and nobleness, most kindly and charitable in a true and most extended kindly sense, a humble Christian. By his example, his justice, his unfailing attention to the duties of his high station, & the strictness of his discipline, he brought into perfect order a diocese which he found almost in anarchy. His death is attributable, under providence, to the noble and devoted zeal with which, since the illness of so many of his clergy, he has visited the beds of every sick and dying emigrant. He did not spare himself, but God has spared him a longer sojourn on earth. He was a man of no political party, of no religious bigotry. He was too strong-minded to be a bigot, & too wise to be a partisan. He was therefore respected and beloved by men of all creeds and parties. May Almighty God have Mercy on his soul.[71]

De Vere paid tribute to Bishop Power again several years later when he returned to Limerick. He recalled that "when in Toronto, disease had so thinned the ranks of the priesthood that none but the Bishop remained to do the duty of visiting the sick, that excellent man instantly undertook it. He labored unremittingly and died of fever within a fortnight."[72] The full story of Bishop Power's sacrifice is recounted in Mark G. McGowan's chapter, as well as in his biography of the bishop, *Michael Power: The Struggle to Build the Catholic Church on the Canadian Frontier* (2005). As McGowan notes, Power was one of the few Canadian leaders who experienced the Irish tragedy from both sides of the Atlantic. He had travelled to Ireland in the spring of 1847 to recruit Loretto Sisters to serve in his diocese. Bishop Power witnessed harrowing scenes while travelling in the Irish countryside and observed thousands of migrants waiting to depart from the Port of Dublin in the hope of finding a better life. McGowan contends that this experience seared into Power's mind the need to marshal aid for Ireland and to prepare his colleagues at home for what he thought would be a crush of Irish refugees. Ultimately, Bishop Power played a leading role in ameliorating the suffering of Irish emigrants in Toronto. His funeral was the largest in the city's history, and he is now on a pathway to canonization.

The important role of Stephen de Vere has been described above and his praise for caregivers in Canada, most notably his commendation of the work of the Grey Nuns. Amongst those cared for by the Grey Nuns in Montreal were orphans George (age 10), Bridget (age 9) and Rose Brown (age 7) from County Galway whom Jason King examines in his chapter in this volume. As he notes, the Brown family was one of thousands from Ireland tended to by the Grey Nuns, yet unlike most, the Brown family's surviving members joined the ranks of their rescuers and helped shelter emigrant orphans in turn. King contends that their story attests to the Grey Nuns' courage, compassion and devotion, as well as to their extraordinary vulnerability to "ship's fever" or typhus which afflicted both Irish emigrants and their caregivers alike. More specifically, King examines the Brown family story as a case study that brings together and breaks down ethnic, linguistic, and social barriers between Irish emigrants and their Canadian caregivers whose lives became increasingly intertwined in the aftermath of the catastrophe. He also suggests that their ultimately uplifting story of endurance and survival throws into sharp relief the recurrent "mortuary spectacles"[73] found in the Grey Nuns' annals which compress countless Irish emigrants into an anonymous mass of stricken fever victims and stacks of corpses. King argues that tracing these stories can help put a face on the figure of the individual Famine migrant and inspire a sense of resilience in the midst of latter crises.

Captain Arthur Edward Kennedy has been immortalized in history through James Mahony's 1849 illustration of his daughter, Elizabeth, distributing relief to the starving poor in west Clare—this image appears on the front cover of this publication. Kennedy was employed as a poor law official in the Kilrush Union and, as Ciarán Ó Murchadha shows, while Kennedy initially conformed to the regulations stipulated under the Poor Law, his approach changed in the aftermath of "Black' 47," as he witnessed increased mortality levels and widespread evictions. It led him to criticize publicly both landlords and the workings of the Poor Law in providing relief. His public criticisms resulted in the establishment of a parliamentary inquiry which provides a highly detailed account of the suffering in one of the most distressed parts of the country, where population loss was as high as 50 percent. Local landlords, including the now-notorious Colonel Vandeleur, emerged in a poor light. Kennedy's position did not endear him to his superiors, and his testimony resulted in him being transferred out of west Clare.

At the time of the Irish Famine, photography was in its infancy, and topics such as hunger, poverty and starvation were regarded as inappropriate subjects for classically trained artists. *The Illustrated London News* broke boundaries not only by providing graphic images of the suffering but by complementing it with a narrative that gave the victims a voice. The man responsible for this was himself Irish, from Cork. In February 1847, readers were informed that James Mahony was visiting Skibbereen and its vicinity, which had become "the seat of extreme suffering."[74] Only two months later, Mahony's services would again be called upon when he was commissioned to design a silk banner from the people of Cork to the people of Boston as a thank you for the magnificent gift of the *Jamestown*.[75] It was presented to Captain Forbes, the subject of an earlier chapter. Niamh Ann Kelly explores the significance of both Mahony and *The Illustrated London News* in providing searing visual and written eye-witness accounts of the Famine. The power of both remains undiminished with the passage of time.

We end this collection with two reflections. The first retells the powerful story of the Choctaw Nation's gift to Ireland of $170, made in 1847, but retold through the contemplations of two people today—one Irish and one Choctaw. It is a story that has particular resonance during the COVID-19 pandemic as it reunited these two peoples, this time with multiple donations being sent to Native Americans from Ireland and the Irish diaspora.

The volume concludes with comments by Caroilin Callery whose family has done so much to keep the memory of the Famine alive, not least with the opening of the National Famine Museum in Strokestown in 1994 and the launch of the National Famine Way in 2019.

As this volume took shape, and people adjusted to the restrictions imposed by COVID-19 and the untold suffering it was inflicting throughout the world, it was hard not to make comparisons not only with Ireland in the 1840s, but also with other periods of pandemic and famine. Throughout the nineteenth century, Ireland encountered perennial famines, food shortages and crop failures, with an estimated 29 being recorded.[76] The authorities in London refused to accept the severity and extent of these crises, maintaining that the Irish were prone to exaggerate, often leading to famine intervention being minimal or, as in the case of public works, inappropriate. Fortunately, there were private individuals and groups, both within and outside Ireland, who took their responsibilities to their fellow man seriously and played major roles in providing aid to the Irish poor. The chapters that follow highlight the work of a number of these benefactors. While some names might be familiar due to the large body of research undertaken on the Great Famine since 1995, a number will be less so. Individually and collectively, their contributions to saving people from starvation and death and giving them hope cannot be understated, nor should the personal and professional sacrifice they made on behalf of the Irish poor be forgotten.

NOTES

1. Christine Kinealy and Gerard Moran (eds), *Famines before and after the Great Hunger* (Cork University Press, 2020).

2. Christine Kinealy, *Charity and the Great Hunger in Ireland: The Kindness of Strangers* (London & New York: Bloomsbury, 2013).

3. *The Irish Times*, 2 June 1997.

4. See Gerard Moran, "'Giving a Helping Hand': International Charity during the Forgotten Famine of 1879-82" in *Irish Studies Review*, 24:2 (Samhraidh/Summer, 2020), pp 132-149.

5. James Hack Tuke, *A Visit to Connaught in the Autumn of 1847* (London: C. Gilpin, 1848), p. 25.

6. All of the "Famine Heroes" short films and post-show discussions from the Great Famine Voices Roadshow can be viewed at http://greatfaminevoices.ie/famine-heroes/ They are funded by the Government of Ireland Emigrant Support Programme.

7. This was the title of a review of Peter Duffy's publication on the murder of Major Denis Mahon, "Famine Villians," *New York Times,* 9 December 2007.

8. Breandán Mac Suibhne, *Subjects Lacking Words? The Gray Zones of the Great Famine* (Quinnipiac University, Hamden: 2017), Famine Folio Series 4.

9. Stepney St. George to Relief Commissioners in Dublin, unpublished letter, 22 April 1847, National Archives of Ireland, RLFC/3/2/11/29.

10. Linde Lunney, "Bloomfield, John Caldwell" in *Dictionary of Irish Biography*, at: https://dib.cambridge.org/viewReadPage.do?articleId=a0746

11. John Caldwell Bloomfield, "The Development of Irish Industries", *Journal of the Society for Arts*, vol. 31, no. 1582 (16 March 1883), 432-439, p. 433.

12. Ibid.

13. *The Irish Times*, 29 November 2019. www.irishtimes.com/business/manufacturing/belleek-pottery-boss-john-maguire-to-step-down-1.4099650

14. Father Theobald Mathew to Charles Trevelyan, Cork, 16 December 1846, reprinted in John Francis Maguire, *Father Mathew: a Biography* (London: Longman and Green, 1863), p. 419.

15. See http://corkpennydinners.ie/

16. *Transactions of the Central Relief Committee of the Society of Friends* (Dublin: Hodges and Figgis, 1852), pp 86-87.

17. Ciarán Reilly, "How Joe Biden's Irish ancestor saved thousands of lives during the Famine," at: www.rte.ie/brainstorm/2020/1020/1172761-joe-biden-ancestor-edward-blewitt-mayo-ireland-great-famine/

18. Laura Carroll, "Vice-President Joe Biden's Irish Family History," at: www.irishfamilyhistorycentre.com/article/vice-president-joe-bidens-irish-family-history-1

19. Reilly, "Joe Biden's Irish ancestor."

20. Remarks by President Biden in Press Conference, 25 March 2021, The White House, at: www.whitehouse.gov/briefing-room/speeches-remarks/2021/03/25/remarks-by-president-biden-in-press-conference/

21. Caroline Daley and Anna Springer, *Middle Island: Before and After the Tragedy* (Miramichi, New Brunswick: Middle Island Irish Historical Park, 2002), p. 67.

22. *New Brunswick Standard*, 16 June 1847.

23. Daley and Springer, *Middle Island*, p. 67.

24. *The Miramichi Gleaner,* 6 July 1847.

25. Sonia Chassé in Dictionary of Canadian Biography says by 1846 Signay was accused by Ignace Bourget, Bishop of Montreal, of 'inertia as an administrator, the low level of respect and confidence he inspired, his inability to deal with important matters, and his lack of close relations with the suffragan bishops," quoted at: www.biographi.ca/en/bio/signay_joseph_7E.html. It was Bourget who oversaw the work of the Grey Sisters and other religious orders, catching typhus fever, but surviving.

26. "General Central Relief. Donations received since April," *The Sun* (London), 29 July 1847.

27. Marianna O'Gallagher and Rose Masson Dompierre, *Eyewitness Grosse Isle, 1847* (Quebec: Livres Carraig, 1995), Letter of Rev. Bernard McGauran to Archbishop Joseph Signay Outlining the Condition of the Irish Famine Emigrants Who Arrived at Grosse Isle in May 1847, pp 50–51.

28. *Circular letter to the Catholic Archbishops and Bishops of Ireland, dated 9 June 1847* [S.l.: s.n.]. Available online at: https://babel.hathitrust.org/cgi/pt?id=aeu.ark:/13960/t1xd1rn8f&view=1up&seq=5

29. James Grant Wilson and John Fiske, *Appleton's Cyclopaedia*, p. 525.

30. "Died," *Royal Gazette*, 15 June 1847.

31. "Fever in the City of Montreal,' *The Lancet,* 1847, vol. 2, p. 414.

32. See Stephen De Vere's digitized journals from his voyage to Canada in 1847-1848 at Jason King (2021): https://dev.irishfaminestories.ca/en/bearing_witness#diary; the digitized annals of the Sisters of Charity, or Grey Nuns, can be found at Jason King (2015), Irish Famine Archive, http://faminearchive.nuigalway.ie/eyewitness-accounts/grey-nuns

33. For recent studies of Stephen de Vere, see Jason King, *Irish Famine Migration Narratives: Eye-Witness Testimonies,* vol. II. *The History of the Irish Famine*, 4 vols. Eds. Christine Kinealy, Jason King, and Gerard Moran (London & New York: Routledge, 2019), pp 12-19; Jason King, "'The Atrocious Avarice of the Irish Landlords': Canadian Public Sentiment and the Irish Famine Migration of 1847", *The Great Irish Famine and Social Class: Conflicts, Responsibilities, and Representations* (eds), Marguérite Corporaal and Peter Gray (Oxford: Peter Lang, 2019), pp 237-256; Jason King, "The Famine Irish Migration to Canada in 1847–48: Assisted Emigration, Colonization, and the unpublished Famine Diaries of Stephen de Vere", *John Mitchel, Ulster, and the Great Irish Famine* (eds), Patrick Fitz-Gerald and Anthony Russell (Dublin: Irish Academic Press, 2017), pp 30-45.

34. Stephen de Vere, *Minutes of Evidence before Select Committee on Colonisation from Ireland, letter to the Select Committee* (30 November 1847) in *British Parliamentary Papers, Emigration,* vol. 5 (Shannon: Irish University Press, 1968), p. 45.

35. Oliver MacDonagh, *A Pattern of Government Growth: The Passenger Acts and their Enforcement, 1800-1860* (London: MacGibbon & Gee, 1961), pp. 194-199.

36. Aubrey de Vere, *Recollections of Aubrey De Vere* (London: Edward Arnold, 1897), p. 253.

37. MacDonagh, *A Pattern of Government Growth*, p. 191.

38. Stephen de Vere, 1847-1848 America Journals, vols. I. Trinity College Library Dublin. Manuscripts Department, MSS 5061, pp 2-3.

39. Ibid., p. 7.

40. Ibid., p. 12.

41. See, "Memorial to the Martyr Priests," at: www.liverpoolmonuments.co.uk/pat01.html

42. "The Health Committee," *The Liverpool Standard and General Commercial Advertiser,* 5 December 1848.

43. Father Mathew to Mrs. Rathbone, Cork, 5 May 1848, Maguire, *A Biography*, p. 451. The Rathbones had sent £50 for the purchase of seed potatoes.

44. See chapter by Catherine Shannon.

45. "Life and Labours of William Rathbone," *Liverpool Mercury*, 18 February 1868.

46. "Galway Industrial Society," *The Galway Mercury, and Connaught Weekly Advertiser*, 8 May 1847.

47. See Gerard Moran, *Fleeing from Famine in Connemara: James Hack Tuke and his Assisted Emigration Scheme in the 1880s* (Dublin: Four Courts Press, 2018).

48. See Helen Hatton, *The Largest Amount of Good: Quaker Relief in Ireland, 1654-1921* (Kingston and Montreal: McGill-Queens University Press, 1993), chapters 5-9.

49. *Transactions of the Central Relief Committee.*

50. Kinealy, *The Kindness of Strangers,* p. 209.

51. *The Cork Examiner*, 16 April 1847.

52. *Liverpool Mercury,* 10 April 1847.

53. *Cork Advertiser*, 15 April 1847.

54. James S. Donnelly, *The Great Irish Potato Famine* (Stroud: Sutton Publishing 2001), pp 138-40; Matthew Lynch, *The Mass Evictions in Kilrush Poor Law Union during the Great Famine* (Milltown Malbay: Old Kilfarboy Society, 2013); Donald E. Jordan*, Land and Popular Politics in Ireland: County Mayo from the Plantation to the Land War* (Cambridge University Press, 1994), pp 112-113; Gerard J. Lyne, *The Lansdowne Estate in Kerry under W.S Trench, 1849-72* (Dublin: Geography Publications, 2001), pp 25-48.

55. Tom Crehan, *Marcella Gerrard's Galway Estate, 1820-70* (Dublin: Four Courts Press, 2013); Rita Nolan, *Within the Mullet* (Belmullet, 1998), pp 121-122.

56. Reilly, *Strokestown and the Great Irish Famine;* Lyne, *The Lansdowne Estate in Kerry;"* Patrick Duffy, "Assisted Emigration from the Shirley Estate, 1843-54" in *Clogher Record*, xiv (1992).

57. Ciarán Reilly, *Strokestown and the Great Irish Famine* (Dublin: Four Courts Press, 2013), pp 65-78; Thomas Power, "The Palmerston Estate in County Sligo; Improvement and Assisted Emigration before 1850" in Patrick J. Duffy & Gerard Moran (eds), *To and from*

Ireland: Planned Migration Schemes, c. 1600-2000 (Dublin: Geography Publications, 2004), pp 105-138; Fidelma Byrne, "The Mechanics of Assisted Emigration: From the Fitzwilliam Estate in Wicklow to Canada" in Ciarán Reilly (ed.), *The Famine Irish: Emigration and the Great Hunger* (Dublin: The History Press, 2016), pp 41-54.

58. Gerard Moran, *Sir Robert Gore Booth and his Landed Estate in County Sligo 1814-1876: Land, Famine, Emigration and Politics* (Dublin: Four Courts Press, 2006), pp 21-48; Joseph Hone, *The Moores of Moorehall* (London: J. Cape, 1939).

59. *First Report of the Belfast Ladies' Committee,* 6 March 1847 (Belfast: s.n., 1847), p. 1.

60. Ibid.

61. The Laws of Settlement were part of the English and Welsh, and Scottish, Poor Laws. Irish immigrants fleeing the famine were not entitled to relief in those countries. See, Lewis Darwen, Donald Macraild, Brian Gurrin and Liam Kennedy, "'Unhappy and Wretched Creatures': Charity, Poor Relief and Pauper Removal in Britain and Ireland during the Great Famine," *The English Historical Review*, vol. 134, issue 568, June 2019, pp. 589–619. At: https://doi.org/10.1093/ehr/cez137.

62. For more see, Christine Kinealy, *This Great Calamity. The Irish Famine, 1845-52* (Dublin: Gill and Macmillan, 2006), pp 315-326.

63. H.E. Young, Adelaide, to Colonial Office, 8 March 1850, BPP, *Ninth general report of Colonial Land and Emigration Commissioners,* 1849 [1082], xxii; Poor Law Inspector to Board of Belfast Union, Minutes of Belfast Board of Guardians, 31 May 1849, PRONI (Belfast), BG/7/A.

64. E. Thomson, New South Wales Colonial Office, 8 February 1850, quoted in "Emigration to Australia," *The Advocate: or, Irish Industrial Journal*, 7 August 1850.

65. Trinity College Library, Dublin, Manuscripts, 5073; *British Canadian*, (May 20, 1848), 1.

66. Trinity College Library, Dublin, Manuscripts, 5061, 49.

67. *The British Colonist*, 20 July 1847.

68. Donal A. Kerr, *A Nation of Beggars. Priests, People, and Politics in Famine Ireland, 1846-1852* (Oxford: Clarendon Press, 1994).

69. Charles Trevelyan, *The Irish Crisis* (London: Longman, Brown, Green & Longmans, 1848), p. 140.

70. For more, see "Memorial to the Martyr Priests," at: liverpoolmonuments.co.uk/pat01.html

71. Ibid. 40-41.

72. Trinity College Library, Dublin, Manuscripts 5074/3, 15-16.

73. See Jason King, "Mortuary Spectacles: The Genealogy of the Images of the Coffin Ships and Fever Sheds" in Marguérite Corporaal, Oona Frawley, Emily Mark-FitzGerald (eds), *The Great Irish Famine: Visual and Material Cultures* (Liverpool: Liverpool University Press, 2018), pp 88-109.

74. "Sketches in the West of Ireland", *The Illustrated London News*, 13 February 1847.

75. "The Jamestown in Cork," *The Dublin Evening Post*, 24 April 1847.

76. This statement was made during a debate in the House of Commons in March 1901, see *Hansard,* Parliamentary Debates, fourth series, xc, Feb. to March 1901, c. 1436.

The Kindness of Strangers

CHAPTER ONE

JAMES HACK TUKE (1819–96)

An English Quaker Philanthropist and "Ireland's Greatest Benefactor"[1]

Gerard Moran

While there were many heroes during the Great Famine of 1845 to 1852, few played a more long-term role, not only in providing and distributing relief, but also in attempting to offer solutions for the underlying vicissitudes which contributed to perennial starvation, hunger, poverty and destitution. One person who stands out is the English Quaker and philanthropist, James Hack Tuke, whose experiences in Ireland in 1846 and 1847 led him to adopt a more holistic approach in the 1880s and 1890s to the underlying causes of these problems, especially in the west of Ireland. Unfortunately, historians have neglected or downplayed Tuke's contribution to the poor of Ireland and his benevolence has not been sufficiently acknowledged. It was left to friends and colleagues to highlight his endeavors in Ireland immediately after his death in 1896 and only recent historiography has acknowledged his role during recurring famines in Ireland.[2]

Quaker involvement in relief operations during the Great Famine commenced in autumn 1846, when soup kitchens were opened in Cork, Youghal, Clonmel and Waterford in response to the almost total destruction of the potato crop.[3] The reaction of the new Whig administration of Lord John Russell was inadequate, especially given the extent of the subsistence crisis. On 13 November 1846, the Society of Friends established the Central Relief Committee in Dublin with the objective of gathering as much information as possible and initiating a fund-raising campaign to alleviate distress. As was pointed out in the introduction to the *Transactions of the Central Relief Committee of the Society of Friends during the Famine in Ireland in 1846 and*

1847, published in 1852, "we have no private objects to serve, or no interests, other than the general welfare of the community."[4] It highlighted the Quaker philosophy that the love of God was not an abstract ideal, but had to be actualized in practical compassion for the vulnerable and impoverished. There was an awareness that the Irish Quaker community was limited in what they could achieve because they were few in numbers, totalling about 3,000 members, and were confined mainly to the east and south of the country.

Increasing reports of death and starvation encouraged members of the English Quaker community to travel to Ireland to provide assistance and report on the distress. This suggested that the Quakers were not prepared to accept the reports in British newspapers that largely followed the government's policy in relation to the Famine. In December 1846, James Hack Tuke arrived in Ireland having received reports on the Famine from his friend, William E. Forster, who had been stationed in Galway since the previous summer. Tuke volunteered his services to the Central Relief Committee for the duration of the Famine. He soon became a champion of the Irish poor. When visiting Carrick-on-Shannon with Forster, they found that workers on the relief works were being paid for only one week out of three, and that families were starving; in Donegal, families were surviving on sea weed with corpses being buried in graveyards without sheets or coffins.[5] At the same time that the world was being informed of the tragedies and deaths in Skibbereen and elsewhere through reports in *The Illustrated London News* and the *Times* of London, Tuke and Forster highlighted the deplorable conditions in Donegal and the west of Ireland, which remained largely unknown because of their remoteness and inaccessibility. In his first report on famine conditions from Dunfanaghy, County Donegal in December 1846, Tuke declared, "nothing, can indeed, describe too strongly the dreadful conditions of the people."[6] He came across 17 people in one cabin in a wretched condition, one an old woman whom the family had taken in and shared the little resources they had. In Killybegs, he encountered a poor farmer who was unable to get relief because he owned a cow, but this would have to be sold to secure food which would only last two weeks and, after that, the family would have nothing. From Clifden, he described a 14-year-old boy who had begged for food: "The ghastly livid face and emaciated form, wasted with hunger and sores, of his breathing skeleton, told me that to him this world would soon pass away."[7] Tuke and Forster quickly realized that immediate action was required to alleviate the widespread distress. They handed out relief gratuitously much to the annoyance of the Central Relief Committee who wanted it distributed at cost price. This indicated that Tuke was prepared to act independently when he felt it was necessary and not

4

accept directives being imposed by those who did not witness the extent of the distress first-hand.[8]

Tuke's correspondence and pamphlets inform us more about conditions in the west of Ireland than the communications from government because the Society of Friends insisted that these reports were published unedited or uncensored. The Quakers during the Famine provided compelling eye-witness testimony regarding the depth and extent of the suffering. This ensured that the opinions of those on the ground who witnessed the direct impact of famine were conveyed to the general public and provided an impartial portrayal of what was happening, in particular in the more remote parts of the west of Ireland. Were it not for the writings of Tuke, Forster and other Quakers, the true extent of the devastation in some of the poorest and most inaccessible parts of the country would not have been recorded. The reports are detailed and show the extent of the crisis in places like Dunfanaghy, Erris and Clifden. The Society of Friends was more aware of conditions in these areas than government officials in London and, to a lesser extent, the administration in Dublin. Agents were sent on fact-finding missions to assess the level of starvation and destitution. Tuke was given such an assignment in the autumn of 1847. One of his main conclusions was that the poor law unions in the west were unable to provide adequate relief to the poor and starving because of the enormous area that they covered. The Ballina workhouse was 60 miles from the people of the Mullet where, Tuke stated, "human wretchedness seems concentrated in Erris, the culminating point of man's physical degradation seems to have been reached in the Mullet."[9] Tuke was clearly moved by the scenes that he witnessed with at least half of the people of Erris starving, many only surviving by stealing turnips from their neighbors, writing "It is doubtful whether any other people would have endured their late terrible privations with equal patience."[10]

Tuke not only commented on the Famine situation but highlighted the social conditions which the people endured. He was deeply moved by the position of the people in Erris and their endeavors to survive. He observed the state of their houses, many comprising banks of turf which acted as walls, with roofs so low it was difficult to enter. There, Tuke encountered families of six to eight persons "kneeling or squatting, round the peat fire, or lying on the damp ground," with only one or two broken stools and "a boiling pot."[11] He had visited the United States in 1845 and observed slavery, but in comparing the position of the inhabitants in this part of Mayo he said: "Never have I seen misery so intense, or physical degradation so complete, as among the dwellers in the bog holes of Erris."[12] Tuke's philanthropic attitude and exasperation at the scenes he witnessed can be seen in his statement after the government had stopped the public relief works: "It is impossible for any charitable association to supply the vacuum caused by the expiration of the 'Temporary Relief Act'." He reproached the government for its inaction: "... if the duty of a good Government be the protection of life and property, is not legislative interference called for to prevent the misery, disease and death, from those wholesale evictions?"[13] This attitude contrasted with the official government approach. While the Russell administration and, in particular, the Secretary of the Treasury, Charles Trevelyan, adopted a *laissez faire* approach, even suggesting that the calamity was "Divine Intervention" to teach the Irish a lesson, Tuke argued that more government involvement was urgently required. Charity alone was inadequate "to meet the real necessities of the miserable people of Connaught."[14] As Ireland had been part of the United Kingdom since 1801, Britain should provide aid and investment to develop fishing and a better transport infrastructure.

While the government maintained that Irish landowners were not doing enough to help their tenants, Tuke showed that many landlords who resided on their estates were doing everything that was humanely possible, but several were bankrupt because they were not receiving their rents.[15] Others did not take their responsibilities seriously, in particular, absentees. Sir Roger Palmer and John Walsh were castigated for evicting their tenants in Erris. Palmer, one of the largest landowners in County Mayo and an absentee, was condemned for his treatment of his tenants, doing little for those who were starving while carrying out widespread evictions.[16] Walsh had evicted 140 tenants just before Christmas 1847. Tuke arrived in Erris in February 1848 and provided a detailed account of what he witnessed, with the houses knocked down and the people having no place to go.[17] Tuke's criticisms of Sir Richard O'Donel of Newport House, for the eviction of 150 families in Keel on Achill Island, where O'Donel was the nominal owner but the rents were paid to the Achill Church Mission Society, led to a prolonged public debate. Those evicted did not have the safety-net of a workhouse as the nearest was in Westport, 40 miles away. Blaming O'Donel may have been harsh, as he claimed to have been unaware of the evictions. What Tuke highlighted though, was that O'Donel had a responsibility for his tenants. The criticisms of O'Donel were an embarrassment for the Central Relief Committee as the landlord was working with the Quakers in a flax-growing operation in the Newport area. O'Donel took Tuke's criticisms personally. He stated that they were "taken without affording me an opportunity of refuting his charges," and he was annoyed that the Quakers had published them.[18] O'Donel was so incensed that he threatened to go to York to horsewhip Tuke, "but was stopped by his and my [Tuke's] friends." However, he threatened to shoot Tuke if he ever returned to the west of Ireland.[19]

The Central Relief Committee, unhappy that Tuke had named O'Donel, acted as an intermediary in the attempt to reach a compromise: Tuke agreed to withdraw the original allegations, and, when the report was re-released, it contained explanatory footnotes, corrections and additions.[20] Tuke was willing to make concessions, but not in relation to his basic allegations, showing that he was prepared to highlight injustices whether by the government or landlords.

A Visit to Connaught in the Autumn of 1847 was published in November 1847, with an appendix afterwards included of his tour of the Mullet in February 1848. The appendix featured the Walsh evictions, and highlighted the starvation and suffering in the more remote areas of the province. It counteracted the statements of government officials and administrators in London that the Irish exaggerated the extent of the crisis. This could not be levelled at Tuke, because he had no Irish connections and his family was held in high esteem by the British establishment because of their philanthropic work in York. Tuke and the other Quaker relief workers concluded that the distribution of relief was only part of the overall solution and that government intervention was required to ensure the economic long-term viability of the poorer regions. He suggested there was abundant waste land in Mayo that could be reclaimed, that fishing and textile work could be promoted and a better transport infrastructure developed. When the calamity ended, the same zeal for the moral and social improvements would have to be put in place.[21] Tuke was deeply affected by what he witnessed during the Great Hunger and it impacted on him for the rest of his life, influencing his subsequent involvement in Ireland in the 1880s and 1890s. The 1847 pamphlet showed his empathy with the suffering that the poor endured and highlighted the misrepresentations being put forward by the government and many landlords.

While Tuke's involvement in relief work was as part of the Society of Friend's operations, the Great Hunger not only affected Ireland, but also Britain and North America as tens of thousands fled from death and hunger. Nearly all major urban centers in Britain, including Tuke's hometown of York, saw an influx of famine emigrants who arrived without money or resources, many on the verge of death. Most of the officials and the population in York were hostile towards these arrivals, but the Tuke family were to the forefront in giving assistance and shelter, providing a shed on their land where the Famine Irish could be looked after.[22] At a public meeting in York in January 1847, Tuke related his first-hand experiences in Ireland and said the Irish "ought to be considered as our fellow countrymen."[23] As a result of his engagement with famine emigrants in York, Tuke contracted typhus, or "Famine Fever," which had a debilitating effect on his health for the rest of his life. He later said:

"I got the Irish fever in 1848, and have had it with more or less severity ever since."[24]

The Great Famine brought about major economic, social and demographic changes in most of Ireland, but it failed to have the same impact in the poorer parts along the western seaboard. These areas recorded a major population decline in the late 1840s, the result of high mortality levels, but in the following decades the population increased leading to regular famines and food crises. In 1862, over two-thirds of the potato crop in Errismore in the Clifden Poor Law Union was devastated by blight. In 1867, the Clifden Board of Guardians informed the Poor Law Commissioners in Dublin that the situation in the union was "bordering on famine" with the people relying on Indian meal to survive, which was becoming so expensive that it was beyond the reach of the poor.[25]

Throughout his association with Ireland, Tuke was prepared to take an alternative view to the country's problems. His writings repeatedly expressed sympathy and empathy with the suffering poor: "I regret that I feel so incompetent to express or describe the state of total helplessness that these gentle, suffering people are reduced to," he attested.[26] This compassion continued throughout his life. In criticizing officials who described the Irish poor as paupers, Tuke stated that in places like Connemara they were "the rank and file of the poorer classes of the district."[27] During all his visits to Ireland, Tuke dispelled many of the myths circulating in England that the Irish peasant was lazy and lived a life of idleness and leisure in winter. He emphasized the compassion that Irish people had for each other, explaining, "... the poor Irishman cannot be accused of indifference to the claims of his helpless neighbour."[28] He was prepared to employ the methods that the Quakers used during the Great Hunger—pamphlets, publicity, parliamentary pressure and patience—to highlight the deplorable conditions that were endemic in the west of Ireland. Just like in the late 1840s, he published extensively in contemporary journals and newspapers to highlight what he witnessed during his travels in the west. His writings on the famines and crises of the 1880s also were published in *Irish Distress and its Remedies: A Visit to Donegal and Connaught in the Spring of 1880* and *Report of the Distribution of the Seed Potato Fund in the Spring of 1886*.

Tuke visited Ireland on five further occasions, at times of widespread famine and food shortages due to the failure of the potato crop, namely in 1880, 1885-6, 1887, 1889 and 1891. He was able to compare conditions that he observed on each occasion. During his tour of Donegal and the west of Ireland in the spring of 1880, he was asked by the Society of Friends in England to "provide some reliable information with regard to the famine crisis" and to recommend what should be done.[29] After visiting those areas that he had written about in 1847, Tuke concluded that conditions were worse than during the Great Famine period. When he visited Kilcar, County Donegal, on 27 February 1880, along with the Parish Priest, Father Logue, he wrote, "Kilcar we think is, as a whole, the most destitute parish we have seen. The faces of the people are more like 'Famine' faces than those in any other place."[30] He realised that the scene that he witnessed was not an emergency, but how these people existed, on the brink of perpetual disaster. This was confirmed by the Poor Law Inspector, Henry Robinson, who stated that the journalists who wrote about famine conditions in the west of Ireland did not understand that this was the norm in these areas.[31] Government policies and inaction only exacerbated this condition and suffering. During these crises the authorities relied on the Poor Law and, in more extreme cases, looked to private charities, like the Mansion House Relief Committee, to intervene. Poverty, famine and destitution would continue until substantial changes were made, but this would not happen under existing government policies.

While many who assisted Ireland during the Great Hunger did so out of an immediate need, Tuke took a more long-term approach to Ireland's problems. From his experiences in 1846 and 1847, Tuke was aware of the limits of philanthropy and private relief. He was prepared to look beyond the entrenched political philosophy on how to deal with Irish poverty and distress. Unless there were fundamental economic and social changes in the west of Ireland, famine would continue and devour the funds and charitable donations that were forwarded to alleviate these crises. Again, his empathy with the people was evident from the pamphlet, *A Visit to Donegal and Connaught in the Spring of 1880*, when he wrote from Camus in Connemara on 2 April 1880: "I wish I could produce that rocky coast and wild miserable village, or rather introduce it into England for a while, so that English people might realise how, in these remote places, so many thousands of people are living."[32] While Tuke's experience during the Great Famine had a profound effect on him both emotionally and health wise, it was his visit to the west of Ireland in the spring of 1880 that had the most dramatic impact as he concluded that the condition of the poor had not improved. As he stated in 1882, this experience changed his life and "began the chapter of my Irish work of which this work will be a continuation ... and all the more so as I had never looked for or thought of it."[33] He was undertaking a painstaking investigation into the causes of the region's endemic poverty and concluded after his visit in 1880 that the only remedy to the famines and food crises "appears to be emigration, or migration to other districts in Ireland." He concluded that the only viable means of relief in the absence of employment was "emigration" or "scattering."[34] Yet Tuke felt that all avenues for emigration were closed to the poor, thus exacerbating their wretchedness and forcing them to continue their subsistence existence.[35]

Tuke's response to the famine and destitution in 1880 differed to that of the Great Hunger. While he and others provided relief and aid to the starving poor in 1846 and 1847, his 1880 visit to the west of Ireland reinforced the need for a more long-term approach to counteract the perennial and underlying problems. While the Land League agitation advocated peasant proprietorship, he realized that this was not the panacea to the crisis in places like Donegal, Connemara and Mayo. Tuke stated: "It must I think be admitted, there are a very large number of tenants in the west of Ireland for whose circumstances no land legislation of the nature adverted to can be considered a remedy."[36] He supported the concept of the tenants owning their farms, but was aware of its limitations for the small farmers along the western seaboard who eked out an existence on holdings that were uneconomical and on land that was sterile. Even if the small farmers had the land rent free, they would be unable to survive. "It must not be forgotten," he contended, "that peasant proprietorship, whether peasant or otherwise, necessarily involves possession of sufficient means to become a proprietor in addition to the requisite capital required for the cultivation of the land."[37] Even when the Ashbourne Land Purchase bill was being debated in the House of Commons in March 1886, Tuke maintained that it would have little impact on the living standards of the small farmers of the west. "Should we not merely be face to face with 300,000 impoverished owners instead of 300,000 impoverished tenants?" he asked, "Truly wrote the wise man of old, 'the destruction of the poor is his poverty.'"[38]

The majority of tenants in the poorer poor law unions supplemented their income from non-agricultural activities such as the earnings from seasonal migration labor in Britain, the manufacture of kelp, or remittances sent home from relatives in North America as the land was too barren to support them. As Father Patrick Greally, the Catholic Administrator of Carna, said: "If the small farmers of Connemara had the land for nothing they could not live. The holdings are too small, the land so sterile, that the people will always be steeped in poverty."[39] Having witnessed the conditions under which the tenants lived, Tuke concluded that a radical approach was required to deal with the perennial problems of famine, poverty and destitution. He advocated a system of assisted emigration to be introduced where families would have their passage paid to North America. Emigration would relieve the pressure on those families who remained as the vacated land could be distributed creating viable, economic holdings. However, assisting families to leave created its own difficulties for there had to be sufficient breadwinners in each group, otherwise they would be exchanging poverty in Ireland for a similar state in North America. During his trip to the United States in 1845, Tuke had seen how Irish emigrants sent money back to friends and relations in Ireland to help them survive and concluded that those assisted from places like Connemara and Mayo would continue this process.

Throughout the nineteenth century, emigration was a constant feature of Irish life, but the majority had the funds to emigrate or the passage fare was forwarded from friends and relatives who were living in North America. However, there was a cohort who did not have the means to leave but were prepared to avail of any assistance which would allow them to start a new life in the United States. This was evident from the nearly 22,000 young females who applied to Vere Foster for the vouchers he provided towards their passage. Applicants from Connemara totaled 1,900, 400 also came from Clifden parish and 360 from Ross.[40] Individual clergymen and others were prepared to assist these young girls to leave so they could remit money back to their families in Ireland; others disapproved, arguing it created a demographic imbalance as fewer females remained for marriage.[41] Family emigration would have a greater impact as the whole group would leave, avoiding the heart- rending scenes of parents seeing their children depart and the likelihood of never meeting again.

Tuke's emigration proposals to counteract poverty in the west of Ireland were radical, but not original. During the Great Hunger, assisted emigration schemes were utilized by the Poor Law and landowners such as Lord Palmerston, Lord Lansdowne, Major Denis Mahon and Sir Robert Gore-Booth.[42] Even during the early 1880s, schemes were organized by Rev. James Nugent and Vere Foster to North America.[43] While most of the previous schemes were undertaken for economic reasons, Tuke's motives were philanthropic. He believed that the removal of the surplus population was the only immediate remedy to counteract famine and poverty. Unlike the landlords' schemes in the late 1840s, Tuke's project was well planned, co-ordinated and organized. Following his travels in the west of Ireland in 1880, Tuke held discussions with W.E. Forster, Sir Alexander Galt, the Resident Minister in Ireland for the Dominion of Canada, and others to debate the feasibility of sending emigrants to North America before he traveled to the mid-western states in the United States and Canada with two of his daughters. He also met with Bishop John Ireland of St. Paul, Canadian Prime Minister John A. McDonald, U.S. President Hayes, and others to determine the most suitable locations for families and where there was a demand for labor. He concluded that the emigrants would have better prospects in rural areas than in the large eastern industrial cities. Tuke's preference was that the emigrants should proceed to Canada rather than the United States because the Canadian authorities were prepared to look after them from the time of their arrival in Quebec and forwarded them to their allotted destinations. He was aware that most emigrants wanted to go the United States to join friends and relations who were already settled there. Those assisted had to prove that their friends and relations would support them and envelopes had to be produced with an American stamp to validate the relationship. Tuke arranged with friends in Boston to meet these new arrivals and send them to their destinations. He ensured the emigrants were dispersed throughout Canada and the United States and not clustered in areas which could lead to hostility with the local population. Only two families were sent to each location in North America. Employment was also secured for many families as with Pat Monaghan from Tallagh, Belmullet, who went to the mills in Warren, Rhode Island, while those departing from Clifden in 1882 went to industries and manufacturers in Pennsylvania where there was a major demand for labour.[44] Arrangements were also made with the local Catholic clergy to support the emigrant families as with the Gaughans and Duceys from Belmullet, who were sent to Richmond, Indiana and cared for by the local pastor, Rev. McMullen.[45]

Tuke was always aware of the responsibilities and challenges that lay ahead of him when dealing with the poor in Ireland. Before leaving Ireland to commence his emigration scheme in Connemara in April 1882, he stated: "A feeling akin to dread, a feeling engendered by the magnitude of the task naturally sobers my rejoicing."[46] To deliver on his proposals he was prepared to abandon his business concerns in England during "the Forgotten Famine," when he travelled to Connemara in early April 1882, days after the Tuke Fund had been established in the London home of the Duke of Bedford on 31 March 1882, and again during the crisis of 1885-6.[47] Once Tuke committed himself, as with the emigration scheme, or his involvement with the Congested Districts Board in the early 1890s, he was prepared to give unwavering time and commitment. Despite concerns about his health, he and his wife, Georgina, who often accompanied him, worked from dawn until after midnight. They traveled from Letterfrack, where they based their headquarters, to places like Cleggan, Clifden, Rosmuc, Carna and Roundstone to interview the applicants, make the selections, and organize clothing for those who were leaving. They also had to help make arrangements for emigrant sailings and complete numerous forms for the committee in London and those meeting the emigrants in Quebec and Boston, which involved much time and energy. When the Tukes arrived in Carna on 27 February 1883, they were met by between 300 and 400 people who wanted to be assisted and each had to be interviewed.[48] It often took over four hours to complete the interviews and, as few applicants spoke English, the local relieving officer, doctor or parish priest had to act as interpreter. Within seven weeks of his arrival in Connemara in April 1882, Tuke had organized and sent 1,276 people to North America on three ships from the Clifden Poor Law Union. This led Georgina to state: "Hard, anxious work this selecting is, and we have so many applicants that could be granted for the steamer on the 23rd [March]."[49] Even when problems arose, Tuke was not disheartened, as when the Clifden Board of Guardians withdrew their grant application for emigration in April 1882, shortly after his arrival in Connemara, or when 30 candidates from Carna, who were to sail on the *Manitoban* from Galway on 3 May 1883, failed to show up.[50] This indicated that Tuke saw his work as a mission to improve the lives of those who left and those who remained in the west of Ireland. In total, 9,500 were assisted by Tuke from Connemara and the Belmullet, Newport and Swinford Poor Law Unions between 1882 and 1884.

Tuke remained cognizant that long-term remedial measures were needed for the advancement of those who remained along the western seaboard. While emigration dealt with the immediate problem, it was not the long-term panacea for the region's difficulties. Being aware of the crises and solutions was important. Between 1880 and 1882, Tuke visited the west of Ireland on seven occasions before initiating the emigration scheme from Clifden in 1882.[51] Throughout the period that Tuke worked in the west of Ireland, whether during the emigration scheme of 1882-4 or the distribution of seed potatoes during the crisis of 1885-6, he consistently consulted those with local knowledge and expertise such as government officials, the local clergy and doctors, to minimize difficulties that could arise. He was always prepared to work with any group or individual who would improve the lives of the poor. Prior to leaving for Clifden in April 1882, he held meetings with Vere Foster, Rev. James Nugent and John Sweetman about their experiences with their emigration schemes. While in North America during the summer of 1882, he visited Graceville, Minnesota, to see how the Connemara emigrants sent out by Nugent were faring.

The view that emigration was a panacea for Irish problems incurred hostility and opposition from certain quarters. Nationalists condemned the Nugent and Foster schemes maintaining that they drained the country of its population and urged people not to contribute financially to such projects.[52] Initially, opposition to Tuke's scheme came from shopkeepers in Clifden who had local political influence and were largely responsible for the local board of guardians rescinding their application for a loan for emigration in late April 1882. Their motives were economic. They feared that the removal of families would have a negative impact on their businesses, and they objected to individuals emigrating because of the debts they owed.

In order to achieve his objective of improving the lives of the poor in the west of Ireland, Tuke used his political, business and religious contacts and friendships to secure support and financial aid for his schemes. After his article "Irish Emigration" was published in *The Nineteenth Century* in spring 1882, his friends, William Rathbone, a Liverpool philanthropist, and Samuel Whitbread, organized a meeting which led to the establishment of the Tuke Committee on 31 March 1882. One hundred politicians were invited and £8,000 was subscribed for the emigration scheme.[53] Tuke used these contacts again in June 1882 after he realized that the demand for emigration in the west was beyond the resources of a private company. It resulted in the British Government providing £150,000 for emigration purposes in 1883 and 1884, with the Tuke Committee administering the scheme in Connemara, Mayo and Aranmore Island off the Donegal coast. Again in 1885, Tuke secured £5,100 from friends and supporters, many of whom had contributed to his emigration scheme between 1882 and 1884, including the Duke of Bedford, W.H. Smith, W.E. Forster, William Rathbone, Samuel Whitbread and John Morley, for the purchase and distribution of seed potatoes in Connemara and the coastal areas of Mayo after the potato crop was devastated by blight.[54]

By the 1880s, Tuke was regarded as an expert on conditions in the west of Ireland. He was asked by the Irish Chief Secretary, John Morley in January 1886, and his successor, Arthur Balfour in 1887, 1889 and 1891, to visit the western seaboard and write reports when the potato crop failed again. In late 1885, the Local Government Board Inspector, Henry Robinson, pleaded with Tuke to provide assistance on Achill Island when the potato crop was destroyed by storms. The islanders were unable to borrow money because of the high levels of debt they had accrued over the previous years, while returns from seasonal migration to Britain were very low. Tuke feared he would be unable to raise public funds because of the hostility in Britain towards Ireland over the Home Rule debate and approached individuals who had previously subscribed to his relief and emigration operations. Despite the reservations of Georgina, who was concerned about the impact the work would have on his health, Tuke decided to take on the relief project in Achill stating, "I cannot let them [the people] starve."[55] As he distributed seed potatoes to the local population, Tuke recalled his visits to the island in 1847 and 1880. "Here we are once more," he recollected, "about to visit the same places with more or less the same needs and wants in the condition of the people."[56] When he arrived in Achill, Tuke was informed that 750 of the 1,100 families were in need of relief, but he quickly concluded that 954 families were destitute. In a letter to the *Times* of London looking for donations, he stated that "the island is like a besieged city in a state of semi-famine, the people relieved by fortnightly doles of meal barely half the required amount." He added that unless assistance was provided, 80 percent of the families would have no seed potatoes to plant while the remainder would have insufficient supplies.[57] Tuke quickly realized that the crisis was not only confined to Achill Island. The problem was more widespread than he had envisaged, with many communities in Connemara and Mayo in need of relief. From Lettermullen, he wrote, "the poverty is unspeakable —and what misery and suffering are borne which can never be revealed until some stranger comes poking into those out of way corners."[58] Over the three months he was in the west, the work was onerous and consuming, often not ending till one or two in the morning. Tuke distributed 1,425 tons of Champion seed potatoes including 420 tons to the Clifden Poor Law Union, 370 tons to Achill, and 140 tons to Belmullet, Rossport and the Inishkea Islands.[59] This resulted in 6,000 families, numbering between 30,000 and 40,000 people, being assisted. Without his intervention many would have suffered greater distress and the crisis would have lasted longer. According to Rev. Thomas Flannery of Carna, hundreds of families would have died of starvation if this relief had not been provided. Father Lynskey of Clifden told Tuke in June 1886 that the people "frequently come to tell how grateful they have reason to be to you." "They gladly will give you and her [Tuke's wife] a 'cead mile failte' when you next do them a favour of a visit," he added.[60] Tuke's intervention resulted in his relief being called "the Tuke potatoes," but it led him to conclude "emigration and colonisation are after all the only remedies."[61]

After his trip in 1886, Tuke issued recommendations regarding relief and economic development in the west of Ireland including the encouragement of fisheries, the extension of the tramways and emigration or colonization. He believed that a separate body should be established and relief operations should not be left to the local authorities such as the boards of guardians. He was convinced that such funding was squandered and did little for the overall improvement of the region.[62] There was a realization that the problems of the west needed to be addressed and special provisions were required. When Arthur Balfour was appointed Irish Chief Secretary in 1886, he consulted with Tuke at all times in relation to projects for the region and asked him to write reports which subsequently resulted in legislation being enacted. Balfour trusted Tuke and this led to the proposals which he had long advocated being brought to fruition. In 1887, he was asked to conduct a study into the feasibility of a light railway system, and, as early as October 1889, the Chief Secretary informed him of his proposals which resulted in the establishment of the Congested Districts Board in 1891.[63] When asked by Balfour in June 1891 to become one of the board's commissioners, Tuke was ambivalent. "I could not reject but I felt anxious in many ways about it," he wrote. This indicated that his devotion to the poor of the west since the Great Hunger was recognized.[64] Tuke was aware that the board was a long-term project that would lead to economic development but it would not have an immediate impact.

While Tuke was always prepared to publicize the conditions which the poor endured, he did not seek publicity for his work in Ireland. This had important advantages as it allowed him from an early stage to develop his emigration and seed distribution schemes without media and political scrutiny. The 220 families assisted from the Clifden Poor Law Union in 1882 were not even mentioned in the Irish newspapers. It was only when the government sanctioned £100,000 for emigration purposes in July 1882 that the Tuke project gained national attention with members of the Irish Parliamentary Party inquiring in the House of Commons who Tuke was, evidently not aware of his philanthropic work with the Society of Friends during the Great Hunger.[65] Again, during his time in Ireland in 1885-86, his work went largely unnoticed largely because of the debate on Gladstone's first Home Rule Bill. Only when he visited areas in Connemara and Mayo that needed assistance was his charitable work acknowledged. As a result of his endeavors, he was able to gain the trust of the people and their leaders.

Throughout his dealings with Ireland, largely influenced by his work during the Great Famine, Tuke showed great organizational skills, determination and a strong conviction in what he was doing and what he wanted to achieve. He took pains to acquire practical knowledge of the questions that he desired to deal with and had the gift of being forceful and lucid in expressing his views. As a result, he was largely able to influence and shape the social policies of successive governments in improving the position of the poor in the west of Ireland. He used his political contacts in pursuing these objectives and had a close association with both the Liberal and Conservative parties in the years after "the Forgotten Famine" of 1879-82, in particular with successive Irish Chief Secretaries, W.E. Forster, George Trevelyan and Arthur Balfour. Consequently, he achieved his goals, including the assisted emigration scheme and the development of the west through the Congested Districts Board. The British political establishment engaged with him and accepted his advice because he was objective and had no political agenda to further. There is little doubt that Tuke's activities and foresight brought about a transformation in the social and economic conditions of the west of Ireland. As Helen Hatton has pointed out, Tuke was "one of the most innovative of the Friends working in Ireland."[66] As early as the 1840s, he had realized that major change needed to be implemented to stop the perennial famines and subsistence crises. Tuke argued that government investment was required for local landowners who had neither the capital nor inclination to provide this. By advocating for state investment in infrastructure and the local economy, he challenged the economic philosophy of the period, that of *laissez faire*. While others urged for a similar approach at various stages during the nineteenth century, they had neither the influence nor the persistence to achieve this. It was Tuke's experiences during the Great Hunger which led to this conversion, but he remains an unsung hero.

NOTES

1. Sir William Gregory, the former Governor General of Ceylon and husband of Lady Augusta Gregory, described Tuke as "Ireland's greatest benefactor" in March 1883; diary of Georgina Kennedy Tuke, entry dated 17 March 1883 (NLI, Ms 49,529/90, John Pitt Kennedy papers).
2. The only biography of Tuke was written by his friend, Edward Fry, *James Hack Tuke: A Memoir* (London: Macmillan & Co., 1899).
3. Helen Hatton, *The Largest Amount of Good: Quaker Relief in Ireland, 1654-1921* (Kingston and Montreal: McGill-Queens University Press, 1993), p. 84.
4. *Transactions of the Central Relief Committee of the Society of Friends during the Famine in Ireland in 1846 and 1847* (1852, rep. Dublin: Edmund Burke, 1995), p. 4.
5. Hatton, *Largest Amount of Good*, pp 96-98.
6. Fry, *James Hack Tuke*, p. 14
7. Christine Kinealy, *This Great Calamity: The Irish Famine, 1845-52* (Dublin: Gill and Macmillan, 1994), pp 125-26; Fry, *James Hack Tuke*, pp 14, 47-48.
8. Kinealy, *Great Calamity*, pp 159-60.
9. Fry, *James Hack Tuke*, pp 54-55; James Hack Tuke, *A Visit to Connaught in the Autumn of 1847* (London: C. Gilpin, 1848), pp 25, 43. The temporary Poor Law Inspector, R. Hamilton, corroborated the scenes in Binghamstown in November 1847, writing, "many have nothing to subsist on but the roots of weeds." Ivor Hamrock, *The Famine in Mayo: A Portrait from Contemporary Sources, 1845-1850* (Castlebar: Mayo County Council, 1998), pp 48-49.
10. Fry, *James Hack Tuke*, pp 54-55; Tuke, *A Visit to Connaught ... 1847*, pp 25, 43.
11. Tuke, *A Visit to Connaught in ... 1847*, p. 22.
12. Ibid., p. 26. Asenath Nicholson who was distributing relief in Erris confirmed this distress stating, "...here was a place which justly be called the fag-end of misery," Maureen Murphy (ed), *Asenath Nicholson, Annals of the Famine in Ireland* (Dublin: Lilliput Press, 1998), p. 91.
13. Hatton, *Largest Amount of Good*, p. 182; Tuke, *A Visit to Connaught in ... 1847*, p. 25.
14. Tuke, *A Visit to Connaught in ... 1847*, p. 28.
15. Hatton, *Largest Amount of Good*, p. 99.
16. For an account of the Palmer estate see David Byrne, *The Impact of the Great Famine on Sir William Palmer's Estate in Mayo, 1840-69* (Dublin: Four Courts Press, 2021). In 1848, Palmer conducted extensive evictions in Erris. The *Tyrawley Herald* stated on 7 September 1848, "Such conduct at any time should be considered heartless, but at present, when wanton deaths are decimating the poor people we look upon it as monstrous, and the promoters of it less humanised than savages." R. Hamilton, the temporary Poor Law Inspector, stated: "There is no proprietor or person of respectability who takes the least interest in the welfare of the unfortunate poor in this district." Hamrock, *The Famine in Mayo*, p. 49.
17. Tuke, *A Visit to Connaught in ... 1847*, pp 61-68. Walsh's estate comprised 800 acres in the Mullet and had an annual rental of £160, Brian Dornan, *Mayo's Lost Islands: The Inishkeas* (Dublin: Four Courts Press, 2000), p. 155-6; *Donald E. Jordan, Land and Popular Politics in Ireland: County Mayo from the Plantation to the Land War* (Cambridge University Press,

1994), p. 111. For a detailed account of the Walsh evictions see Rita Nolan, *Within the Mullet* (Belmullet, 1998), pp 121-122.

18. Hatton, *Largest Amount of Good*, p. 187. While Nicholson described O'Donel as "humane," she was scathing of his "driver" who engaged in evictions and throwing down the peasants' houses without any pity or compassion for the evicted, Murphy, *Asenath Nicholson*, pp 115-116.

19. James Hack Tuke to Meta Tuke, 13 August 1893 (Tuke papers, University of Limerick). It is ironic that in August 1893, while on his way from Achill to Westport, Tuke stopped at Newport House to have lunch with O'Donel's granddaughter.

20. Hatton, *Largest Amount of Good*, p. 188.

21. Tuke, *A Visit to Connaught in ... 1847*, p. 60. Nicholson held similar views, Murphy, *Asenath Nicholson*.

22. Tuke, *A Visit to Connaught in ... 1847*, p. 182.

23. Frances Finnegan, *Poverty and Prejudice: A Study of Irish Immigrants in York, 1840-1875* (Cork: Cork University Press, 1982), p. 181.

24. Fry, *James Hack Tuke*, p. 73.

25. Henry Coulter, *The West of Ireland: Its Existing Condition and Prospects* (Dublin, Hodges & Smith; 1862), p. 85; Clifden Poor Law Union Archive collection, 1849-1921 (Galway County Library), p. xi.

26. Quoted in Kinealy, *Great Calamity*, p. 126.

27. *Second Report of the Select Committee of the House of Lords on Land Law (Ireland), together with the proceedings of the committee, minutes of evidence and appendix*, HC 1882 (359), xi, p. 259.

28. Tuke, *A Visit to Connaught in ... 1847*, p. 29. Another Quaker, William J. Bennett, stated similar opinions during his tour of the Erris area in 1847 when he encountered families with very few resources taking in orphans "for these poor people are kind to one another to the end." William J. Bennett, *Narrative of a Recent Journey of Six Weeks in Ireland* (London & Dublin, 1847), p. 28.

29. *Second Report of the Select Committee of the House of Lords on Land Law,* p. 257, q. 7649.

30. Tuke, *A Visit to Connaught in ... 1847*, p. 17.

31. Brendan O'Donoghue, *Activities Wise and Otherwise: The Career of Sir Henry Augustus Robinson* (Dublin: Irish Academic Press, 2015), pp 17-18.

32. James Hack Tuke, *Irish Distress and its Remedies: A Visit to Donegal and Connaught in the Spring of 1880* (London: W. Ridgeway, 1880), p. 76.

33. Tuke to Frances and Meta Tuke, dated 22 Jul. 1882 (Tuke papers, UL).

34. Tuke, *A Visit to Donegal and Connaught in ... 1847*, pp 92, 110.

35. J. H. Tuke, "Ought emigration from Ireland to be assisted?" *Contemporary Review* (April 1882), pp 702-703.

36. Tuke, *A Visit to Donegal and Connaught in ... 1880*, p. 109.

37. Ibid., p. 108.

38. Carla King, "'Our destitute countrymen on the western coast': relief and development strategies in the congested districts in the 1880s and '90s" in Carla King & Conor

McNamara (eds), *The West of Ireland: New Perspectives on the Nineteenth Century* (Dublin: History Press, 2011), p. 170.

39. *Second Report of the Select Committee of the House of Lords on Land Law*, p. 300.

40. Ibid., p. 247, q. 7545.

41. Ibid., pp 263-264, q. 7701.

42. See Gerard Moran, *Sending Out Ireland's Poor: Assisted Emigration to North America in the Nineteenth Century* (Dublin: Four Courts Press; 2004), pp 35-69; idem., *Sir Robert Gore Booth and his Landed Estate in County Sligo, 1826-1876: Land, Famine, Emigration and Politics* (Dublin: Four Courts Press, 2006), pp 33-8; Thomas Power, "The Palmerston estate in County Sligo: improvement and assisted emigration before 1850" in Patrick Duffy & Gerard Moran (eds), *To and From Ireland: Planned Migration Schemes, c. 1600-2000* (Dublin: Geography Publications, 2004), pp 105-36.

43. Jane Kennedy, "The Connemaras: despair in the heartland" in Christine Kinealy & Gerard Moran (eds), *Irish Famines before and after the Great Hunger* (Hamden: Quinnipiac University Press; 2020), pp 213-24; Ruth-Ann Harris, "'Where the poor man is not crushed down to exalt the aristocrat': Vere Foster's programmes of assisted emigration in the aftermath of the Irish Famine" in Patrick O'Sullivan (ed.), *The Irish World Wide: History, Heritage, Identity, vol 6, The Meaning of the Famine* (London: Leicester University Press, 1997), pp 172-194.

44. *Second Report of the Select Committee of the House of Lords on Land Law*, p. 219, q. 7663.

45. *Report and Papers relating to the Proceedings of the Committee of "Mr Tuke's Fund" for Assisted Emigration from Ireland, during the years 1882, 1883 and 1884* (London, 1889), p. 117.

46. Sydney Buxton, "Mr Tuke and his work", *Contemporary Review*, 69 (June 1896), p. 866.

47. For the background to the Tuke Fund, see Gerard Moran, *Fleeing from Famine in Connemara: James Hack Tuke and His Assisted Emigration Scheme, 1882-1884* (Dublin: Four Courts Press, 2018), pp 26-27.

48. Georgina Tuke diary, 27 February 1883 (NLI, Ms 49,529/90, John Pitt Kennedy papers).

49. Ibid., 22 February 1883.

50. Ibid., 4 May 1883.

51. *Second Report of the Select Committee of the House of Lords on Land Law*, p. 257, q. 7650.

52. See Gerard Moran, "'In search of the promised land': the Connemara colonization scheme to Minnesota, 1880," *Eire/Ireland*, 31:3 (1996), pp 139-140.

53. *Report from the Select Committee on Colonization*, p. 202, q. 3417.

54. *Report ... relating to the Proceedings of "Mr. Tuke's Fund,"* pp 208-213.

55. Fry, *James Hack Tuke*, p. 236.

56. Tuke to his daughters, August 1886 (Tuke papers, UL).

57. London *Times*, 23 March 1886.

58. Tuke to Meta Tuke, 15 April 1886 (Tuke papers, UL)

59. *Report ... relating to the Proceedings of "Mr. Tuke's Fund"*, p. 207.

60. *Poor Relief (Ireland) Inquiry Commission, report and evidence with appendices*, HC 1887, xxxviii (c-5043), p. 145; *Report ... relating to the Proceedings of "Mr. Tuke's Fund"*, p. 12.

61. Tuke to Frances Tuke, dated 25 April 1886 (Tuke papers, UL).

62. Ciara Breathnach, *The Congested Districts Board of Ireland, 1891-1922: Poverty and Development in the West of Ireland* (Dublin: Irish Academic Press, 2005), p.23.
63. Fry, *James Hack Tuke*, pp 263-266.
64. Tuke to Meta Tuke, Whit Monday, June 1891 (Tuke papers, UL).
65. Ibid., Tuke to Frances and Meta Tuke, undated 1882.
66. Hatton, *Largest Amount of Good*, p. 9.

CHAPTER TWO

COUNT PAWEL DE STRZELECKI (1797–1873)

A Polish Count in County Mayo

Christine Kinealy

A political exile from Poland who found fame and fortune as an explorer in Australia and then became a naturalized British citizen might seem an unlikely hero of the Irish Famine, but Count Pawel (Paul) de Strzelecki proved to be a relentless and compassionate champion of the Irish poor, putting his own life at risk on their behalf. This chapter provides a brief overview of his remarkable life and multiple contributions in bringing relief and compassion to marginalized people in Ireland and beyond.

Pawel Edmund de Strzelecki was born in 1797 in the *Poznań* region of Poland, to an old, but impoverished, noble family. At the time of his birth, Europe was in the midst of war and *Poznań* was occupied by Prussian troops.[1] The conclusion of the Napoleonic Wars in 1815 resulted in Poland being divided between two of the victors, Prussia and Russia, with *Poznań* returning to Prussian control. Strzelecki left Poland finally in the wake of the failed rising of 1830, which had sought Polish independence.[2] He made London his new home and, by 1832, his name was appearing in the fashionable news columns of the British press.[3] He was referred to as a Polish Count, although he himself never signed or referred to himself as such. The handsome—and eligible—Strzelecki moved within high society, but he had another calling, as a talented scientist. Strzelecki, the geographer, geologist and mineralogist, chose to explore the world, keeping detailed journals as he went.[4] Wherever he found himself, he showed compassion for the poor and down-trodden. In 1836, when he visited a captured slave ship in Brazil, he commented, "No sooner had I looked over the ship's bulwarks than I felt that the chain that attached me to civilization had been broken."[5]

From 1839 to 1843, Strzelecki explored Australia and Van Diemen's Land. During this time, he climbed Australia's highest mountain and named it after the Polish patriot Tadeusz Kosciusko. He explored and charted the Gippsland district, and even discovered gold, but was persuaded not to make his finding public, the British government fearing it would prove too disruptive to the convict population. In total, he covered 7,000 miles on foot, often only accompanied by a convict as an assistant.[6] Strzelecki's physical fitness, intrepid spirit and resourcefulness as an explorer were to prove invaluable during his time in the west of Ireland during the Famine. Strzelecki's findings were published in May 1845 in the well-received "Physical descriptions of New South Wales and Van Diemen's Land."[7] Both the publication and its' author were widely praised:

> Mr. de Strzelecki is, to say the least, is an indefatigable traveller. For twelve years he was moving about the globe and visiting in their turns, the two Americas, part of the West Indies, the South Sea Islands, New Zealand, New South Wales, Van Diemen's Land, the Javanese Islands, part of China and the East Indies and Egypt. We know not how far his practical mind has engaged itself in the investigation of the soils, climates and productions, animal and vegetable and fossil, of the majority of those lands; but if he has bestowed upon a quarter of them a hundredth part of the time and labour expended upon the countries of whose physical condition the present volume treats he is a pioneer of whose useful and laborious exertions some mention should be made.[8]

The book was also reviewed in the Irish press, where it was described as a work, "of the highest authority."[9]

Apart from the scientific content, what was impressive and unusual about the publication was the compassion that Strzelecki used when describing the indigenous people that he had encountered. Regarding the Aborigines of New South Wales, he pointed out that "oppression and cruel persecution ... have signally failed." Instead, he appealed to the British government to "listen and attend to the last wishes of the departed, and to the voice of the remaining," when they asked:

> Leave us to our habits and customs; do not embitter the days which are in store for us by constraining us to obey yours; nor reproach us with apathy to that civilisation which is not destined for us; and if you can still be generous to the conquered, relieve the hunger which drives us in despair to slaughter your flocks, and the men who guard them. Our fields and forests, which once furnished us with abundance of vegetable and animal food, now yield us no more; they and their produce are yours. You prosper on our native shore, and we are famishing.[10]

His words were equally applicable to Ireland. In 1846, Strzelecki was awarded the Founders' Gold Medal by the Royal Geographic Society for his "distinguished service" to geography and discovery.[11] Shortly after the book's publication, he applied for British citizenship. One of his main sponsors was Samuel Jones-Loyd, a prosperous English banker. At this stage Strzelecki, regardless of his achievements, had no regular income.[12]

At the same time that Strzelecki's book was published, a new form of potato blight was appearing in many parts of Europe, including England and Scotland. On 13 September, a leading horticultural newspaper announced:

> We stop the presses with great regret to announce that the potato Murrain has unequivocally declared itself in Ireland. The crops about Dublin are suddenly perishing. Where will Ireland be in the event of a universal potato rot?[13]

By November, newspapers in the west of Ireland were carrying regular reports of the spread of the disease.[14] Because the blight had appeared relatively late in the harvest season, approximately 60 percent of the crop was sound. Moreover, the British government under the premiership of Sir Robert Peel put in place a variety of comprehensive relief measures. These measures, combined with the actions of the people themselves, who were familiar with periodic food shortages, proved effective, with few cases of excess mortality in the year following the first appearance of disease.[15] However, many of the poor, especially in remote parts of the west, had suffered severe deprivation in the spring and summer months, leaving them with few resources to face a second year of shortages.

The reappearance of blight in 1846, earlier in the season and more destructive than in the previous year, was reported in the press as early as July 1846. Apprehensions about the loss were compounded by the small oat and barley crop.[16] The government in London, under the new administration of Lord John Russell, responded to the impending shortfall in provisions by making public works available as the main form of relief. However, the system proved to be bureaucratically cumbersome, expensive, and an inappropriate test of destitution on a people who were already hungry and weak. As reports of suffering and death in Ireland appeared in newspapers throughout the world, a massive fund-raising project got under way, with even people who had no connection to Ireland, wanting to donate. In 1845, there had been a few isolated responses to the food shortages, but the second, more devastating, failure prompted a larger and more organized charitable response that was unprecedented in its geographic range.

The largest of the various charitable societies created to respond to the unfolding crisis in Ireland was founded by wealthy English bankers. The idea of creating a fund-raising association based in London had been formulated at the end of 1846, but the first official meeting of the British Association for the Relief of Distress in Ireland and the Highlands of Scotland did not take place until 1 January 1847.[17] As its name suggested, a portion of its funds (one-sixth) was to be used to help the Scottish poor in areas where the potato had also failed. The British Relief Association was largely the idea of the Anglo-Jewish banker, Lionel de Rothschild, and he and his brother, Meyer, played active roles in its day-to-day administration. They were joined by some of the leading merchants and bankers in London, together with a small number of MPs. The chairman was Samuel Jones-Loyd, a friend and sponsor of Strzelecki. At their first meeting, it was agreed that they would assist people who were beyond the reach of government aid and provide, "food, clothing and fuel, but in no case money ... to the parties relieved."[18] However, as the extent of suffering in Ireland became apparent, their approach became far more flexible, and money grants were sometimes given. What distinguished the Association from the other relief organizations was that they worked closely with the British government, in order to make the most efficient use of their resources. This arrangement proved to be particularly beneficial to government officials who, on numerous occasions, relied on the resources of the Association to financially support their own, inadequately-funded, relief measures.[19] Within days of being formed, the Association achieved a major publicity coup when they were informed that Queen Victoria was to give a donation of £2,000. They were also the beneficiary of the proceeds of a "Queen's Letter" that was read in Anglican churches in Britain, calling for prayers and donations for Ireland.[20] The Association proved adept at fund-raising and within 12 months had received approximately 15,000 individual donations from all parts of the world. In total, they raised over £470,000, which was far more than any other relief organization.

On 20 January, Jones-Loyd informed the committee that Count Strelitzski [sic] "a Polish gentleman of extensive travel had offered his personal services gratuitously to Ireland with a view of being useful to the committee.:[21] Strzelecki was thanked "for his tender of service," and asked to meet with the committee.[22] They accepted his offer and Strzelecki immediately left for Dublin, to meet Sir Randolph Routh, chairman of the Relief Commission. The process had taken less than a week. Strzelecki then proceeded to the west, to report on the condition of people in counties Donegal, Mayo and Sligo and to distribute a cargo of food on behalf of the Association.[23] Strzelecki's journey was not an easy one. The extreme weather of the winter of 1846-47—snow, rain, hail, frost and bitter cold—hampered his movements. Undaunted though, when, as occurred on several occasions, his carriage became stranded due to snow drifts, he proceeded to his next destination on foot.[24] In County Mayo, Strzelecki chose the town of Westport as his base. Westport, which was part of the estate of the Marquis of Sligo, was at the heart of some of the poorest and most remote famine-stricken areas. As he had promised, he immediately wrote to the London committee:

> No pen can describe the distress by which I am surrounded. It has actually reached such a degree of lamentable extreme that it becomes above the power of exaggeration and misapprehension. You may now believe anything which you hear and read, because what I actually see surpasses what ever read of past and present calamities.[25]

The testimonies of Strzelecki and other volunteers who traversed Ireland in 1846 and 1847, including James Hack Tuke and Asenath Nicholson, provided a powerful counter-balance to suggestions in sections of the British and conservative Irish press that the suffering of the Irish had been embellished.

It was not only Strzelecki who experienced weather-related problems. Heavy snow falls, which continued as late as April 1847, hampered the progress of both government and private relief officials, while impeding the output of those employed in the public works, many of whom were inadequately clothed. The coming of warm weather proved to be problematic also. On 25 March 1847, Strzelecki reported from Westport that:

> The sudden warmth of the weather and the rays of a bright sun accelerate prodigiously the forthcoming end of those whose constitutions are undermined by famine or sickness. Yesterday, a countrywoman, between this and the harbour (one mile distance), walking with four children, squatted against a wall on which the heat and light reflected powerfully; some hours after, two of her children were corpses, and she and the two remaining ones taken lifeless to the barracks. Today, in Westport, similar melancholy occurrences took place.[26]

When travelling in other parts of Mayo, Strzelecki quickly realized that the relief measures put in place by the government were failing:

> ... in the locality of Ballina, Foxford, Swineford [sic], Castlebar, the desolate aspect of the country is more fearful still. The population seems as if paralyzed and helpless, more ragged and squalid; here fearfully dejected, there stoically resigned to death; there, again, as if conscious of some greater forthcoming evil, they are deserting their hearths and families ... Of the fate, gloomy and awful, which overhangs the whole population, that of the poor children, and the babies at the breasts of their emaciated and enervated mothers, excites the deepest feelings of commiseration.[27]

He was particularly moved by the suffering in remote parts of Erris, home to 25,000 people spread over 400 square miles. In Belmullet, the local Relief Committee was inefficient, forcing people who were weak and hungry, including those employed on the public works, to walk up to 30 miles in order to obtain food.[28] In 1838, when the Poor Law divided the country into 130 unions, it had been decided to make those in the west larger than elsewhere, to reflect population density. The five unions in County Mayo—Ballina, Ballinrobe, Castlebar, Swinford and Westport—were particularly sprawling. For example, the distance from Binghamstown on the Mullet Peninsula to the Ballina workhouse was 42 English miles.[29] Strzelecki responded to the problem by immediately appointing a "Special Committee" consisting of the two Protestant clergymen, a Catholic Priest and the local Coast Guard, to oversee the distribution of relief.[30] Moreover, he realized that food alone would not save the people, they were also suffering from a lack of clothing, especially warm and clean clothing.[31] He immediately arranged for a cargo of clothing to be sent to Belmullet.[32]

Regardless of the bad weather and poor infrastructure, by 1 March 1847, Strzelecki had provided relief in 65 localities, including 30 bales of clothing, 1,020 bags of rice and 1,905 barrels of Indian meal. To ensure efficient and prompt distribution, he employed two constables as his assistants, informing the London committee that the expense was "unavoidable."[33] By 1 April, Strzelecki had spent £2,953 in County Mayo, £1,740 in County Donegal, and £1,193 in County Sligo. As the public works started to be summarily closed by the British government, the demands on the Association's funds would increase.[34] In the Westport Union, income from the poor rates was proving inadequate to meet the demands on the workhouse, and so, by mid-April, an estimated 8,000 persons were being fed weekly from Association grants, and this amount was expected to triple.[35] Even at this early stage, government officials were unequivocal about their debt to the Strzelecki and the British Relief Association. The Poor Law Officer in Westport informed Strzelecki that:

> To them [the BRA] this union owes a debt of gratitude, for this as well as the many grants made to them during the last three months; and to you I am personally under great obligation, for putting at my disposal so effective a stimulant to the several Committees to commence the new system of relief. Pray convey my acknowledgement to your truly benevolent Association.[36]

It was not only the poor in County Mayo who were relying on grants from Strzelecki. Within weeks of being formed, the Association was receiving applications from all parts of Ireland, including one on behalf of the Claddagh fishermen, from Daniel O'Connell on behalf of the parish priest of the small village of Tracton in Cork, from Sir Robert Ferguson, MP for Derry, on behalf of the people of the north, and several from the Dublin Ladies' Committee, who were providing clothing to all parts of Ireland.[37] To cope with what was clearly a nationwide crisis, the Association appointed more agents to travel to Ireland, while making Strzelecki their Executive Director. The first of these volunteers was Lord Robert Clinton who was put in charge of counties Galway, Clare, Limerick and Kerry.[38] A few weeks later, he was joined by Lord James Butler.[39] Like Strzelecki, these agents offered their services for free.

In mid-March, the writer Matthew Higgins offered the Association his services, specifically for the purpose of proceeding to Belmullet, an area gaining the same grim notoriety as Skibbereen in the British press, largely through the appeals of Strzelecki.[40] Higgins's family was landed gentry from Benown Castle, County Meath.[41] Like Strzelecki, he was an author, writing in the London press using various pen names, particularly *Jacob Omnium* (or JO). In this capacity, he had been critical of the government's response to the famine.[42] Before travelling to Ireland, Higgins was advised by the British Relief Association:

> The experience of the Count Strzelecki will be most useful to you, and he has therefore been requested to furnish you with all the information in his power, as to the districts adjacent to Belmullet, and, if possible, to communicate with you personally.[43]

Despite having written about famine in Ireland, when he arrived in Belmullet Higgins was appalled by what he witnessed: "The streets are full of people in a dying state; at every corner one hears horrible accounts of bodies found in ditches and on dung heaps." He believed deaths and disease in the district, "equal the worst details from Skibbereen."[44] Like Strzelecki, Higgins was particularly touched by the plight of the children:

> I cannot express to you how painful it is to witness the wretched children, actually expiring in the streets, and to be debarred from assisting them; but if I were to do so once, I could not walk about the town.[45]

Higgins immediately arranged for food and clothing to be provided gratuitously in the remote coastal districts of Ballyglass, Dulock, Tullaghan and Berwick. In doing so, he was contravening his instructions, but he justified his intervention on the grounds that, "the destitution of the people in these districts is so utter, that I feel I am but acting as you would wish."[46] Like many involved in private relief, Higgins realized that the poor required more than just food and clothing. Dead bodies were putrefying in the streets because their relatives could not afford to bury them. Higgins arranged for numerous coffins to be made. This included two coffins from his own money, out of sympathy for a woman whose children had died.[47] As was the case nationally, no official or systematic records of mortality were kept.

During the week ending 28 February 1847, 13 deaths from starvation were reported in County Mayo by local constabulary officers.[48] Eye-witness reports from Higgins and Strzelecki, however, suggest that the official statistics regarding mortality were gross under-estimates.

Higgins was based in Letterbrick, a small townland in Mayo, which had no dispensary and was 31 miles away from the nearest workhouse. Like other voluntary relief givers, Higgins despaired of the response of many of the local elites. In his case, he was critical of the three local Protestant clergymen, claiming, "one is insane; the other two are not on speaking terms and will not 'act' together in any way." In contrast, the three Catholic clergy were "good, simple men – poor, ignorant and possessing little influence over their flocks."[49] Although in advance of Higgin's arrival the local soup kitchen had been given money by Strzelecki, no food had been provided because the vicar and the curate had quarreled and, "preferred seeing the parishioners starve than make soup for them in concert."[50] There were only two large resident landlords and Higgins was scathing about the one known as, "The Mulligan," but praised "Mr Black," who had been distributing relief. Overall, widespread landlord apathy meant that the main food available was that provided by the British Relief Association.[51] Higgins left Erris on 4 May. During his short stay, he had established soup kitchens throughout the district as well as providing clothing and coffins.[52] Despite all that he had done, his final letters to the Association were dejected, pleading that Erris should "be made an exception to the general relief measures."[53] Higgins received neither compensation nor lasting recognition for his time in County Mayo, but, like Strzelecki, not only had he saved lives, he had given a voice and dignity to people who had been forsaken by their government, their landlords and their ministers.

The role of Strzelecki and his fellow agents was continually adapting to the various changes in government policy. In January 1847, it had been announced that the public works would be closing and that in autumn an extended Poor Law would be made responsible for both ordinary and extraordinary relief. In the intervening summer months, a national network of soup kitchens would be opened. In the weeks following this announcement the numbers on the public works increased, regardless of low wages, inclement weather and harsh working conditions. To prevent further increases, the Treasury announced that, on 20 March, the workforce had to be reduced by 20 per cent, regardless of whether or not soup kitchens were operative. This harsh directive left many people without any relief. At the recommendation of Strzelecki, the British Relief Association informed their agents that they could provide immediate assistance, "with more than the previous freedom to whatever district they find to be under severe pressure."[54] It was a stark, if unintended, admission that government policies were not saving lives in Ireland.

Regardless of the difficulties during the transition period, the opening of government soup kitchens in 1847 was generally successful. Despite some reports of watery soup, of low nutritional quality, the move from the public works to the soup kitchens, proved beneficial. Strzelecki, writing from Westport, reported:

> The great recommendation of the present system, independently of its comparative merits, is, that besides being more systematic, and capable of contracting and extending its issues from fortnight to fortnight, and thus of adjusting and adapting itself to circumstances, it is more effective; for, since it came into operation, the afflicting and heart-rending crowds of destitute have disappeared, and Westport, the receptacle of misery, assumes daily a more cheering aspect.[55]

After the soup kitchens closed in August 1847, the Poor Law was to become responsible for all government relief in Ireland. In recognition of the unwieldy size of the five Poor Law Unions in County Mayo, four new ones unions were to be created—in Belmullet, Claremorris, Killala and Newport. Their formation was indicative of the limitations of the previous system to cope with extensive distress. Just as the new Poor Law was becoming operative, many charities were ceasing to operate as their funds were exhausted and most donations had dried up. The exceptions were the Society of Friends and the British Relief Association who, with straightened budgets, continued their involvement into early 1848.

Following the move to Poor Law relief, the role of Strzelecki changed. He was the only agent remaining in Ireland on behalf of the Association and was solely in charge of distributing their residual funds. In this capacity, he worked closely with the newly-appointed Poor Law Inspectors, using the remaining funds of the Association to support the 22 Poor Law Unions that had been officially declared "distressed." The Association, aware that the change-over to Poor Law relief would create some hardships, had offered Strzelecki's services on the grounds that, "the transition from the one system to the other, it was obvious, would be attended with considerable difficulty, out of which much additional pressure of a temporary character might probably arise."[56] To fulfill his new responsibilities, Strzelecki relocated to Dublin where he could work with, and advise, the restructured Irish Poor Law Commission. Again, private charity was providing essential relief when the government was failing, and a Polish count was the foremost expert on Irish famine relief.

Even when the extended Poor Law was fully operational, it still proved unable to cope with the demands placed on it. In County Mayo and elsewhere, the condition of the poor deteriorated further. In 1848, the geographic impact of the distress was changing, with it becoming mostly confined to the unions of Ballina, Belmullet, Castlebar, Ballinrobe, Westport and Clifden. The distress was exacerbated by the spread of typhus fever, the appearance of cholera in coastal districts, and by the poor weather. In 1848, Strzelecki reported that the condition of the poor in parts of Connaught and Munster was worse than in the previous two years.[57] He estimated that 99,000 people had been evicted and were homeless. Many did not want to take shelter in the workhouse due to "domestic separation," that is the splitting up of families, leaving them to accept outdoor relief, even if they had no home.[58] Relief from the British Relief Association was called on repeatedly to fill this gap. In spring 1848, when Poor Law Inspector Bourke found the state of fishermen in Boffin Island to be "desperate," he appealed to Strzelecki for biscuits on their behalf. It was immediately granted. Bourke reported that "this benevolence has been attended with the best results."[59] Regardless of assistance that he was giving, the usually discreet Strzelecki reported to the Association that, "The Inspectors of Ballina and Belmullet write to me that, notwithstanding all their efforts, this district is a disgrace to any civilized country."[60]

An abiding concern of Strzelecki was how children would fare as the family unit and other social structures broke down. In addition to providing financial support to the newly-extended Poor Law, therefore, Strzelecki continued with his personal scheme of giving direct relief to the children, a project commenced in the previous year. Strzelecki believed that separate provision needed to be made for children, who in the "general run and scramble for food have been left behind." Moreover, children, especially young girls, needed protection "from the afflicting scenes in which they have been partly spectators, partly actors."[61] In the spring of 1847, Strzelecki had pioneered a system of feeding schoolchildren in the Westport Union. He had placed 600 girls under the care of the Sisters of Mercy, 700 boys under the local Catholic Dean, and 160 children in the Protestant schools in Westport and Louisburg under the protection of their ministers, with each child receiving clothing and one meal a day, at a daily cost of one-third of a penny. The children thus helped were aged between 5 and 14. Before receiving the meal, they were required to wash their face and hands and to comb their hair.[62] Whatever the motivation for this stipulation, it was a rare, but important, acknowledgement of the importance of personal hygiene at a time of rampant disease. Apart from aiding the children, the parents also benefitted from not having to share their scant resources. The scheme was widely praised. The Westport Board of Guardians, under the chairmanship of Lord Sligo, passed a vote of thanks to the British Relief Association and to Strzelecki on behalf of the children, for, "not alone relieving their physical wants, but extending the blessings of education, so necessary for the well-being of society."[63] Strzelecki's efforts were also applauded in the local press, the *Tyrawly Herald* saying of the children: "Their pure hearts should glow with gratitude at this fresh proof of the concern entertained for their comforts by their generous benefactors."[64] The success of the scheme encouraged Strzelecki to ask the committee in London if he could extend his scheme to other unions. His appeals became more urgent with the transfer to the new Poor Law. In October 1847, he "begged" the London committee to consider his request, adding that he feared for poor children and "the actual and future effects which the physical and moral degradation to which they are exposed, through hunger and nakedness, has and will have on the country."[65] In the winter of 1847, the scheme was extended to the 22 distressed unions. By January 1848, at a cost of less than $4d$ a week, 58,000 children in the poorest parts of the country were being fed daily. By March, this had risen to over 200,000 children, spread across 27 Poor Law unions.[66] This incredible act of charity was the result of the vision and persistence of one man.

In anticipation that the funding of the Association would finally dry up in summer 1848, Strzelecki made a personal request that the government continue the work in the schools until the harvest.[67] The Prime Minister agreed, issuing a Memorandum saying that feeding school-children should be maintained, paid for by the Treasury. Charles Trevelyan, the Secretary of the Treasury, however, refused to do so, on the grounds that this fell outside the scope of government relief provision.[68] It was a telling insight into the control exerted by the Treasury over relief provision. It also meant that Strzelecki's attempts to have the government finance the scheme failed. Consequently, relief to the schools ended in August 1848.

In July 1848, the British Relief Association formally suspended its work in Ireland due to its funds being exhausted. Since October 1847, they had provided £150,000 to supplement the Poor Law, with almost £46,000 spent in June 1848 alone. Additionally, they had, at the urging of Strzelecki, fed the children of the poor. The ending of the involvement of Strzelecki and the British Relief Association was lamented by many. The Poor Law Commissioners, whose work after 1847 would not have been possible without the financial support of the Association and the practical guidance of Strzelecki, keenly felt the loss, informing him:

> It must be a source of true and refined pleasure to your benevolent mind, to know that your exertions on behalf of the poor children have been attended with even more than that measure of success which could have been anticipated.[69]

Before he left Dublin, the Viceroy, landlords and clergy thanked Strzelecki with a public address, and the 40 Poor Law officers with whom he had worked presented him with a silver plate, on which their names were engraved.[70] He was also praised in the Irish press, one Dublin newspaper noting:

> The readers of this journal are well acquainted with the noble exertions and untiring philanthropy of the Count de Strzelecki, in superintending the measures of relief adopted by the British Association, during the whole period of the famine in this country. For more than eighteen months has this distinguished Pole devoted himself, heart and soul, to the work of benevolence, in feeding the destitute, and particularly in providing food and clothing for the multitudes of poor children at the various schools in wide districts of this country.[71]

Praise for Strzelecki from the committee in London, on whose behalf he had worked so tirelessly in Ireland, was fulsome. They acknowledged that his duties had required "great labour and anxiety, and a considerable degree of personable risk."[72] Jones-Loyd, Chairman of the Association and a long-standing friend of Strzelecki, wrote a personal letter, which opened with, "I feel it difficult to confine myself to the cold and measured language of official form," adding, "You have indeed established the strongest claim upon the gratitude of the country which you have adopted."[73] Strzelecki was presented by the Association with a silver tea service, contained in two rosewood chests, upon which the names of the committee appeared.[74] Strzelecki had achieved a virtually impossible feat: being equally admired in both Ireland and England for his work during the Irish Famine.

In 1848, it was announced, with little fanfare, that Charles Trevelyan, in addition to his usual civil service salary, had received a bonus of £2,500 for his "extraordinary labors during that trying time."[75] He was also knighted. Trevelyan responded to these accolades by informing the Prime Minister that, "he could not conceive how he had continued to outlive the extreme mental and bodily exertion of that crisis."[76] When Strzelecki was honored some months later by being made a first Civil Companion of the Bath,[77] the *Morning Chronicle* noted:

> The labour, the ability and the deserts of Count Strzelecki were, to say the least, in no degree inferior to those of Mr Trevelyan. Moreover, they were voluntary and gratuitous, and they involved much personal danger and discomfort'.[78]

For them, the recognition had come "somewhat tardily."[79] Strzelecki continued to refuse to accept any payment for the work he had undertaken.

In 1849, regardless of extreme suffering in the west of Ireland, the government remained unwilling to commit further Treasury funds to alleviate the situation. Instead, they sought to re-activate the role of private charity. To encourage donations, a private subscription was opened with MPs being asked to donate £100, while

the Queen gave £500. Strzelecki agreed to return to Ireland to oversee the distribution of these funds, which amounted to £6,400.[80] It was a pitifully small amount
given the extent of misery. Moreover, when Strzelecki arrived in the west of the
country he was dismayed by what he found as, "the distress of these ill-fated districts
presented in June a character of suffering greatly exceeded in severity that which I
witnessed there in the fatal winter of 1846-'47."[81] He reported that those receiving
outdoor relief from the Poor Law were:

> in a state of emaciation, sickness and nudity hardly credible, crowding together
> and crouching under heaps of rotten straw of their unroofed cabins, under bridges,
> burrowing on the roadside, or in the ditches of the cold and wet bogs'.[82]

Strzelecki spent four months in Ireland, travelling 2,700 miles to help those whom
the Poor Law did not reach.[83] Again, his work was noted and praised in the local
press, Thomas O'Dowd, the Catholic curate averring that the Polish Count, "may
be truly styled one of the best and most disinterested friends of the Irish poor."[84]
The on-going suffering in the west of Ireland in 1849, most particularly in County
Clare, prompted the *Illustrated London News* to ask artist, James Mahony, to reprise
the journey he had undertaken in 1847 and capture the wretchedness with his pencil
and pen.[85]

   In 1849, Strzelecki also gave evidence before a select committee on the Poor
Laws. His responses were unequivocal, stating that, "the calamity which has befallen
to Ireland is an Imperial calamity." He believed that it was beyond the powers of
either local powers or the Poor Law to alleviate it.[86] In his opinion, "people in the
British Empire, as long as that empire possesses any means, should not be allowed to
die from starvation."[87] When the questioner suggested that the money spent on Irish
relief had been, "wasting funds upon the mere support of the people," Strzelecki
responded that, "You cannot reason in an abstract way when you see men dying in
the streets,"[88] adding, "the first thing you have to do is to keep the soul and body
together of the starving; there is justice and humanity concerned in it."[89] Overall,
Strzelecki's responses to being grilled by the select committee highlighted the fact
that the view of famine in London, compared with the reality of famine in the west of
Ireland, was based on more than simply geographical distance, but deeply grounded
in an ideology that deemed the Irish poor to be unworthy of relief.

   When his work with the poor ended in Ireland, Strzelecki returned to London
where he again moved within British high society and resumed his work with the
Royal Geographic Society. His philanthropic work continued, including overseeing
the safe emigration of single women to Australia.[90] In this, he was reunited with

Matthew Higgins, they both serving on a committee to raise funds for this purpose.[91] Strzelecki returned to Ireland in 1850, seemingly, acting on his own initiative, a London paper noting, "The Count de Streletzski [sic] arrived in Limerick last week, upon his benevolent mission for the relief of the Irish poor."[92] At this stage, famine was still raging in parts of the west, but, for the most part, Ireland was still being left to its own resources. While there, Strzelecki made a financial contribution to alleviate the suffering in Clare.[93] This visit marked the end of his direct association with Ireland but not of his work with the poor and distressed, he serving on various philanthropic committees including the Nightingale Fund, on behalf of soldiers wounded in the Crimean War.[94] Strzelecki received multiple awards and distinctions during the remainder of his life. These included receiving an Honorary Doctorate in Civil Law from the University of Oxford in 1860.[95] In 1869, he was made a Knight Commander of the Order of St Michael and St George (KCMG) in honour of his explorations in Australasia.[96] He was honored further afield with various geographical features being named after him in Canada, Tasmania and Australia, and a statue being erected to him in New South Wales.[97]

Unlike a number of famine heroes and front-line relief givers, Strzelecki did make it through those traumatic and dangerous years. Yet, working so closely with the poor took its toll on Strzelecki's health and he did contract typhoid fever. Although he survived, he never returned to full health.[98] In 1873, Strzelecki died at his home in Saville-Row, London. He was aged 77. His death was noted in newspapers in Britain, Poland and Australia, but passed with little notice in Ireland.[99] According to an early historian of the Famine, William O'Brien, Strzelecki was not forgotten in Ireland, and within the west, "the name of this benevolent stranger was then, and for long afterwards, a familiar one if not a household word, in the homes of the suffering poor."[100] Strzelecki was buried in Kensal Green Cemetery in London. In 1943, on the 70th anniversary of his death, a memorial plaque was placed at his grave by the Australian and Polish governments, to honour his work as an explorer.[101] In 1997, his remains were transferred to his birth-place, *Poznań*.[102]

Regardless of the work of the Association and other relief agencies, the suffering of the Irish poor during the Famine remains unimaginable. As Strzelecki said when he arriving in Westport, no pen could describe the scenes of misery he witnessed first-hand. In monetary terms, the British Relief Association was the charitable organization that raised the largest amount of money. What this meant in terms of saving lives and providing comfort to a desperate people cannot be numerically measured. Despite Strzelecki's untiring efforts, people continued to suffer and die. The reduction in population, however, provides only one measure of the human cost of this tragedy, exacerbated by inadequate and often inappropriate official relief measures. Private charity undoubtedly did save lives. The distribution of this relief was only made possible due to the selfless sacrifices of numerous, now largely forgotten, individuals. Strzelecki was one of the most remarkable members of this group. Until recently, his role was largely forgotten in Ireland, except in the work of a small number of historians.[103] Strzelecki is now recognized as a famine hero whose generous interventions and personal sacrifices on behalf of the Irish poor, especially the children, demonstrated the importance of humanity at a time of despair.

NOTES

1. Geoffrey Rawson, *The Count. A Life of Sir Paul Edmund Strzelecki, Explorer and Scientist* (London: William Heinemann, 1953), p. 3.

2. Marian Kaluski, *Sir Paul E. Strzelecki, A Polish Count's explorations of nineteenth century Australia* (Melbourne: A.E. Press, 1985), p. 12.

3. "Arrivals at the Royal Hotel," *Inverness Courier*, 8 August 1832. He was staying at the hotel, "on his way north."

4. Kaluski, *Strzelecki*, p. 14.

5. Ibid., p. 16.

6. "Obituary of Count Strzelecki," *South Australian Advertiser*, 26 December 1873.

7. "Strzelecki's New South Wales this day is published," *Sun* (London), 23 May 1845.

8. "Di Strzelecki on New South Wales," *Evening Mail*, 8 October 1845. The book continued to be the classic reference book for over 40 years, Kaluski, *Strzelecki*, p. 85.

9. "Climate of Australia," *Saunders's News-Letter*, 13 April 1846.

10. Quoted in "De Strzelecki on New South Wales," *Evening Mail*, 8 October 1845.

11. "The Count P. E. Strzelecki," *Morning Post*, 18 June 1846.

12. Rawson, *The Count*, p. 171.

13. *Gardeners' Chronicle and Gazette*, 13 September 1845.

14. *Mayo Constitution*, 4 November 1845.

15. During intermittent food shortages, the poor would pawn fishing tackle, wedding rings, or sell their pigs, eggs etc. For more on other periods of shortages see, Christine Kinealy and Gerard Moran (eds), *Irish Famines before and after the Great Hunger* (Cork University Press, 2020).

16. *Mayo Constitution*, 28 July 1846.

17. Minutes of the British Relief Association (BRA), National Library of Ireland (NLI), MS 2022, 1 January 1847, pp 2-3.

18. Ibid.

19. Christine Kinealy, *Charity and the Great Hunger: The kindness of Strangers* (London: Bloomsbury, 2013), chapter nine.

20. Minutes of BRA, 13 January 1847, p. 45.

21. Ibid., 20 January 1847, p. 72.
22. Ibid., 21 January 1847, p. 75.
23. Ibid., 22 January 1847, p. 80.
24. Strzelecki, Belmullet, 10 February 1847, *Report of the British Association for the relief of the extreme Distress in Ireland & Scotland* (London: Richard Clay, 1849), p. 93.
25. Minutes of BRA, 1 February 1847, p. 111.
26. Strzelecki, Westport, 25 March 1847, *Report of BRA,* p. 97.
27. Ibid., Strzelecki, Westport, 29 January 1847, p. 92.
28. Ibid., p. 20.
29. The problem of distances was pointed out by Lord Monteagle during a debate in the House of Lords in 1849, when he referred to the case of one pauper who walked 150 miles before receiving relief, Poor Relief (Ireland) Bill, *Hansard*, House of Lords, 13 July 1849.
30. Strzelecki, Belmullet, Minutes of BRA,10 February 1847, p. 92.
31. Daphne Wolf, "Nearly Naked. Clothing and the Great Hunger," in Christine Kinealy, Jason King and Ciarán Reilly (eds), *Women and the Great Hunger in Ireland* (Cork University Press, 2017).
32. Minutes of BRA, 16 March 1847, p. 231.
33. Strzelecki, Westport, 1 March 1847, *Report of BRA*, p. 94.
34. Ibid., Strzelecki, Westport, 5 April 1847, p. 99.
35. Ibid., Richard M. Lynch to Strzelecki, Westport, 24 April 1847, p. 104.
36. Ibid.
37. Minutes of BRA, various dates.
38. Ibid., 17 February 1847, p. 162.
39. Ibid., 1 March 1847, p. 95.
40. Ibid., 19 March 1847, p. 241.
41. Frederic Boase, *Modern English Biography: containing many thousand concise memoirs of persons who have died during the years 1851 to 1900* (Truro: Netherton and Worth, 1908, vol. 1), p. 1464.
42. Anthony Trollope*, An autobiography* (Edinburgh: William Blackwood and Sons, 1883, vol. 1), p.129.
43. BRA to M. J. Higgins, 31 March 1847, William Loney – Documents: http://home.wxs.nl/-pdavis/Famine5.htm.
44. Report of Higgins, Belmullet, 8 April 1847, *Report of BRA,* p. 108.
45. Ibid., p. 111.
46. Ibid., p. 109.
47. Ibid., Higgins, Belmullet, 14 April 1847, p. 113.
48. Chancellor of the Exchequer in House of Commons Debate on Destitute Persons (Ireland) bill, 8 July 1847, vol. 94, col. 72.
49. Report of Higgins, Belmullet, 8 April 1847, *Report of BRA*, 13 April 1847, p. 113.
50. *Times,* 22 April 1847.
51. Ibid.
52. *Report of BRA*, pp 21, 22.
53. Ibid., Higgins, Belmullet, 29 April 1847, p. 116.

54. Minutes of BRA, 23 March 1847, pp 247-8.

55. Strzelecki quoted by the Chancellor of the Exchequer in House of Commons Debate on Destitute Persons (Ireland) bill, 8 July 1847, vol. 94, cols 70-71.

56. *Report of BRA*, p. 29.

57. *Nation,* 27 October 1849.

58. Ibid.

59. Mr Bourke to Poor Law Commissioners, 11 May 1848, *Papers relating to proceedings for relief of distress, and state of unions and workhouses in Ireland*, BPP, 1848, p. 189.

60. Strzelecki, Dublin, 12 March 1848, *Report of BRA*, p. 135.

61. Strzelecki to Committee of BRA, 24 October 1847, *Papers relating ... unions and workhouses in Ireland*, BPP, seventh series, 1848, p. 4.

62. Regulations regarding relief through Schools, November 1847, Appendix D, *Report of BRA,* pp 186-87.

63. Ibid. Resolution of Westport union, 16 September 1847.

64. Ibid., 20 April 1847.

65. Ibid.

66. Report of BRA, p. 41.

67. Ibid., Treasury Minute, 27 June 1848, p. 46.

68. Memorandum by Lord John Russell, National Archives of England, T.64/367 B, 30 April 1848.

69. Commissioners to Strzelecki, 27 July 1848, *Papers relating to ... unions and workhouses in Ireland,* pp 3-4.

70. Rawson, *The Count*, p.171; When Strzelecki died, he left it to Thomson Hankey, "Will of Strzelecki," in Rawson, pp 191-3.

71. "The Count de Strzelecki," *Dublin Evening Post*, 9 September 1848.

72. Resolution of BRA, 20 July 1848, Papers relating to ... unions and workhouses in Ireland.

73. Ibid., Mr Jones-Loyd, Chairman of BRA to Count Strzelecki, 21 July 1848.

74. Rawson, *The Count*, p. 171. In his will, Strzelecki left the service to Lady Herbert of Lea Rawson, *The Count*, p. 187.

75. *Morning Chronicle*, 28 November 1848.

76. Ibid.

77. *London Gazette*, 21 November 1848.

78. *Morning Chronicle*, 28 November 1848.

79. Ibid.

80. George Nicholls, *History of the Irish Poor Law* (London: J. Murray, 1856), p. 137; subscription list in *Times*, 16 June 1849.

81. *Nation*, 27 October 1849.

82. Ibid.

83. *Times,* 19 October 1849.

84. Letter by O'Dowd to *Mayo Constitution*, 10 August 1849.

85. See chapter by Niamh Ann Kelly.

86. Evidence of Strzelecki, *Select Committee of House of Lords to Inquire into the operation of Irish Poor Law*, 4 May 1849, qu. 8637.

87. Ibid., qu. 8638.
88. Ibid., qu. 8639.
89. Ibid., qu. 8642.
90. "Female Emigration," *Sun* (London), 5 April 1850.
91. "Fund for Promoting Female Emigration," *Saint James's Chronicle,* 22 January 1850.
92. *Illustrated London News,* 24 August 1850.
93. "Destitution in County Clare," *Manchester Times,* 7 September 1850.
94. "The Nightingale Fund," *Caledonian Mercury*, 4 January 1856.
95. Kaluski, *Strzelecki,* p. 61.
96. William A Shaw, *The Knights of England. A Complete Record from the Earliest Time to the Present Day of the Knights of all the Orders of Chivalry in England, Scotland, and Ireland, and of Knights Bachelors* (London: Sherratt and Hughes, 1906).
97. The statue was installed in 1988, see: www.snowymonaro.nsw.gov.au/411/Strzelecki-Monument.
98. Strzelecki to Adyna, 5 June 1851, quoted in Rawson, *The Count*, p. 173.
99. *South Australian Advertiser*, 26 December 1873.
100. W. P. O'Brien, *The great famine in Ireland: and a retrospect of the fifty years 1845-95 with a sketch of the present condition and future prospects of the congested districts* (London: Downey and Co., 1896), p. 190.
101. *Sydney Morning Herald*, 8 October 1943.
102. "Pawel de Strzelecki," *Find a Grave*, at: www.findagrave.com/memorial/183164550/pawel-edmund-strzelecki.
103. In 2015, two small plaques were erected to him near to O'Connell Street: www.thejournal.ie/pawel-strzelecki-irish-famine-3788576-Jan2018/ and http://mtkosciuszko.org.au/english/dublin-plaque.htm. In 2018, a plague was erected by the Polish Ambassador to Ireland, Ryszard Sarkowicz, in Clifden, County Galway to the Count. Since then, supported by the Polish Embassy and the Polish community in Ireland, a more extensive recovery of Strzelecki's role has taken place.

CHAPTER THREE

CAPTAIN ROBERT BENNET FORBES (1804–1889)
And His Voyage of Mercy to Ireland

Catherine Shannon

"Black 47," considered by many historians as the worst year of the Irish Famine of the 1840s, also featured an unprecedented global response of generosity to alleviate the plight of the sick, starving and homeless in Ireland.[1] New England played a prominent and unique role in the nation-wide effort to assist Ireland in her hour of greatest need. Under the leadership of Boston mariner, Captain Robert Bennet Forbes, the U.S.S. *Jamestown* carried 800 tons of provisions worth $35,868 to the starving people of County Cork in a record-breaking Atlantic crossing of 15 days and three hours. The use of an American naval vessel for this humanitarian purpose was recognized then as a unique and inspiring event by the Rev. R. C. Waterston who wrote:

> I consider the mission of the *Jamestown* as one of the greatest events in the history of our country. A ship of war changed into an angel of mercy, departing on no errand of death, but with the bread of life to an unfortunate and perishing people.[2]

In launching the 2012 International Irish Famine Commemoration in Boston, President Michael D. Higgins stressed the importance of honoring men and women like Captain Forbes who responded generously and imaginatively to relieve Ireland's agony. This chapter will relate Captain Forbes' crucial role in the conception, organization and execution of the *Jamestown* mission in the spring of 1847, a role that marks him as one of the heroes of Irish Famine relief.[3] It will also demonstrate that in 1847, New England's Protestants and Irish Catholics put aside their hostilities, tensions and suspicions of the previous decade and joined, if only temporarily, in an extraordinary communal and ecumenical effort to send food and aid when Ireland faced mass starvation.[4]

When the RMS *Britannia* arrived in Boston on 20 November 1845 with news of the first, partial failure of the 1845 potato crop, the city's Irish Catholics responded quickly. The Boston Irish Repeal Association collected $2,114 from its 1,246 members for Irish relief. On 2 December, Father Thomas J. O'Flaherty established the Irish Charitable Fund, raising $1,000 in just nine days from people earning only 50 cents per day. A native of Kerry and a medical doctor, O'Flaherty was fully aware of the dire consequences that a crop failure held for hundreds of thousands of Irish people, especially children. A meeting at the Odeon Theatre, addressed by Father O'Flaherty, netted an immediate collection of $750, while an additional $264 was contributed by St. Nicholas Parish in East Boston. Daniel Crowley, a successful local contractor, raised $1,100 from his employees and associates. By the end of 1845, Boston's Irish Catholic community had sent at least $19,000 to Ireland.[5]

There was no organized relief effort in Boston for much of 1846 as no one anticipated a second potato crop failure. It was assumed that the public works program and British government's purchase of a large supply of American Indian corn, initiated by the Prime Minister Robert Peel, would enable the potato-dependent cottier class to survive. The Boston Irish Repeal Association returned its focus to the repeal of the Act of Union, arguing that private charity could never solve the fundamental problems of Ireland's economic ills and human misery.[6] Similar to the major British papers, on 6 January 1846 the *Boston Daily Atlas* asserted that famine fears were exaggerated. Upon the death of Father O'Flaherty on 27 March 1846, the Irish Charitable Fund ceased activity, and money from Boston to Ireland for the remainder of the year consisted primarily of individual donations by immigrants to their relatives at home.

These complacent assumptions that Ireland's crisis was contained were eroded when news reports of a second and complete potato crop failure and the distress filled the columns of the Boston *Pilot* during the autumn of 1846.[7] On 5 December, the *Pilot* reported that $10,000 in individual contributions had been sent to Ireland on the *Arcadia* and urged its readers to send whatever they could to their friends and relations in Ireland. The arrival of the RMS *Hibernia* in Boston on 20 January 1847, carrying the first British and Irish newspapers in a month, confirmed the earlier reports of escalating starvation, deaths and despair in Ireland as a result of the total failure of the 1846 potato crop. Over the next three weeks the *Pilot* published extracts from the Irish press detailing the horrific conditions in the Skibbereen area.[8] More ominous and disturbing was the news that the newly elected Whig government of Lord John Russell intended to close the public works in March, in keeping with their laissez-faire ideology. This program had provided limited wages to over 300,000 impoverished families to purchase alternative food, so its cancellation virtually guaranteed starvation in the absence of substantial private charity or alternative government intervention. The impact of these reports was so great that when the *Hibernia* left Boston for Ireland in early February, it carried $72,000 in relief money collected over the previous two weeks.[9] Ireland's friends in Boston realized quickly the absolute necessity of establishing a more organized approach to raising funds for Irish relief.

Boston's newly installed Catholic Bishop, John Fitzpatrick, the son of Irish immigrants, launched a diocesan-wide appeal in a powerful and emotive sermon at Holy Cross Cathedral on 7 February. Cavan-born Andrew Carney, the richest Irishman in Boston, chaired Fitzpatrick's relief fund and established an efficient network of local collectors with the result that, within six weeks, $20,000 was sent to Archbishop William Crolly in Armagh to distribute to the needy, irrespective of religion. The bishop sent another $4,000 only two months later. With the exception of Carney's personal donation of $1,000, most donations were small but represented great personal sacrifice by the Catholic poor who, as Fitzpatrick noted, were "… unwilling to think about tomorrow for themselves because they wish to do something for the relief of Ireland today."[10] Boston's Brahmin elite, who had considered the autumn reports of impending starvation as Irish exaggeration, responded to the shocking news brought by the *Hibernia* and the inspiring example of the charity of the city's Irish poor and quickly rallied to the cause of Irish relief. John Murray Forbes, Captain Forbes' brother, noted the great sacrifice of "… the Irish around us, who themselves contributed all they could to relieve their relations in the old country."[11]

Within a week of Fitzpatrick's pastoral and in response to the early January appeal of New York Quaker, Jacob Harvey, for a nationwide Irish relief effort, Boston's famous poet, humanitarian and abolitionist, John Greenleaf Whittier, and other New England literati called for all area citizens to assist the starving Irish.[12] Two influential Boston Protestant clergymen, Rev. Ephraim Peabody of King's Chapel, and Rev. Henry Giles of the Tremont Temple and a native of Craanford, Co. Wexford, urged their congregations to join in a broad public relief effort.[13] The *Boston Daily Atlas*, which had doubted the severity of the Irish situation in the fall, now joined the *Pilot*, the *Boston Vindicator* and the *New England Puritan* in calling for a public meeting to coordinate immediate relief efforts. On 9 February in Washington, D. C., Vice President George Dallas presided over a large public meeting to urge coordinated efforts in every major city to raise funds for the starving Irish. Massachusetts Senator

Daniel Webster immediately contacted Boston Mayor Josiah Quincy, and former Congressman Abbott Lawrence, asking them to coordinate a Boston relief effort.[14]

It was in this context that Mayor Quincy hosted, on 18 February, a public meeting in Faneuil Hall that led to the formation of the New England Committee for the Relief of Ireland and Scotland and to the involvement of Captain Robert Bennet Forbes in the historic voyage of the *Jamestown* to Ireland in the spring of 1847. Along with other influential businessmen, bankers and civic leaders attending, Robert Bennet and John Murray Forbes heard graphic reports of the unfolding crisis in Ireland and were inspired by the oratory of Harvard President Edward Everett, who said that they had "a duty so high and sacred that, could we neglect it, I shall almost expect the walls of our massy warehouses filled almost to bursting with every article of food ... would fall and crush us as we passed."[15] Everett's speech provided the clarion call to the assembled civic leaders to form the New England Committee for the Relief of Ireland and Scotland. In addition to the Forbes brothers, the committee included prominent Brahmin businessmen and philanthropists such as Abbott Lawrence, Patrick Tracey Jackson, Thomas Lee and Samuel Howe.[16]

Two days after the Faneuil Hall meeting, the Forbes brothers decided to petition the United States Congress to transfer the naval warship the *Jamestown*, then lying idle in the Charlestown Navy Yard, to the control of the New England Relief Committee so that food and supplies could be shipped from Boston to Ireland.[17] Captain Forbes offered to command the ship without recompense and to recruit the officers and crew. He enlisted the aid of Massachusetts Congressman Robert C. Winthrop in Washington with the result that on 3 March, in a joint Congressional resolution, Captain Forbes was authorized to take command of the *Jamestown* for the use of the New England Relief Committee. The same resolution designated Captain George Coleman de Kay to take command of the U.S.S. *Macedonian* for the use of the New York Irish Relief Committee. Ireland's friends in Congress, having failed to secure any Congressional funds for Irish relief, considered this plan the most pragmatic alternative.

Captain Forbes was an ideal leader for the *Jamestown* mission given his energetic, courageous, resilient and generous personality. After more than two decades as a successful sea captain and businessman in the China trade, he had the experience and organizational skills to execute the mission. His empathy and sense of duty toward suffering Ireland were undoubtedly shaped by his own experiences of family bereavement and prior financial loss and hardship, as well as gratitude for the secure and happy home life he enjoyed with his wife, Rose, and their three young children since his retirement from sailing in 1841.[18] Forbes took command of the *Jamestown* on 11 March 1847. He worked tirelessly over the next three weeks supervising the ship's refitting and cargo loading. All but two of its cannons were removed to allow greater capacity for food and provisions. Forbes also wrote numerous letters to his business contacts in Britain to ensure that no government red-tape would delay the ship's unloading once it reached Cove in Cork. Forbes also enlisted the famous Liverpool humanitarian, William Rathbone, to meet him in Cove so that the latter could supervise the efficient distribution of the Boston food supplies.[19] Forbes' position as President of the Boston Marine Society enabled him to recruit experienced officers who also undertook the voyage without recompense.[20] Pay for the 31 crew members, carpenters and other essential ship workers came either from subscriptions from the sailors' hometowns, or from a collection taken up at Boston's Protestant churches which raised $3,076 to cover the crew's wages and the ship's provisioning. In the end, Forbes used only $2,457 of these funds, returning the balance as well as the revenue from four returning passengers and the sale of ballast amounting to $1,365 to the New England Relief Committee.[21]

Meanwhile, the generosity of Boston and New England citizens was reflected in the cash and food donations received by the New England Relief Committee. Abbott Lawrence, Thomas Perkins, Peter Brooks and Garret Smith contributed $2,000 each, while Welcome Farnum and John P. Cushing gave $1,000 and $500 respectively. Smaller cash donations were collected by ward committees in Boston and other New England cities, and tons of food donations came from rural villages and towns. Railway companies and owners of Boston's wharves and storage sheds waived their fees.[22] The Boston police force contributed two days' pay. Concerts and balls were held at the Boston Museum and the Howard Athenaeum while the choirs of Holy Cross Cathedral and the Institute for the Blind did a benefit performance of Mozart's Requiem. The Charitable Irish Society canceled its annual 17 March dinner, and at least 19 of its members acted as neighborhood collectors or supported fund-raising events to benefit the *Jamestown*.[23] The enthusiasm for the New England Relief Committee's mission was so great that $151,000 was eventually collected, more than double the initial fund-raising goal of $60,000.[24]

While Christian charity and humanitarian feeling undoubtedly explained such generosity, other factors that motivated Edward Everett and other Brahmins had to do with preserving good relations with the British government now that the Oregon question had been settled.[25] Moreover, with strong abolitionist feeling among Boston's wealthy citizens, the project to convert two ships of war into ships of mercy was a way to protest the on-going Mexican War which, they believed, was started primarily in order to extend slavery. George S. Hillard, a Forbes family friend, expressed this anti-war sentiment to the Captain's anxious wife, Rose, writing:

> You must not only consent to Bennet going away, but rejoice in it. We all love and value him more for his generous self-sacrifice ... Such an act enlarges the inheritance of your children, and will make them more proud of the name they bear. The whole thing is beautiful to think of; the sympathy, the quickness to give relief, the warm benevolence running like an electric shock through the whole land, in aid of a distressed foreign country are truly exhilarating, and a comforting relief ... to the disgrace and inhumanity of the Mexican War. If he were my father, I should feel more filial pride and pleasure in such a voyage as this than if he made half a million of dollars by a voyage to Canton.[26]

Amos Lawrence wrote "We are in deep disgrace on account of this wicked Mexican business," seeing great merit that the *Jamestown* was carrying "bread to the hungry instead of powder and ball to inflict more suffering on mankind."[27] In his 22 February letter to the *Daily Advertiser* seeking ship crew applicants, Forbes subtly injected his own anti-war sentiment when he wrote: "Many a hearty web-footed citizen, who would fly from the drum and fife of the recruiting sergeant, would enroll himself under the flag of suffering humanity."[28]

Beginning on St. Patrick's Day, the mostly Irish Boston Laborers' Aid Society began loading the *Jamestown* with food and provisions sent from New England farms or purchased by the New England Relief Committee. Eleven days later, the *Jamestown* left the Charlestown Navy Yard at 8:30 am, towed out of Boston Harbor by the steam-powered tug the *R.B. Forbes*. The *Jamestown* flew a specially designed burgee flag depicting a circle of shamrocks surrounding a thistle and anchor.[29] It carried 800 tons of provisions worth $35,868. The cargo comprised various grains, but also 400 barrels of pork, 100 tierces of ham and some mutton as well as some dried local apples. There were also 28 barrels of clothing and 800 empty sacks to be used for distributing the barreled grain in smaller units. Despite storms and cold weather, the *Jamestown* made the Atlantic crossing in record time, reaching the Cork coast in 15 days and three hours.[30]

The *Jamestown* entered outer Cove Harbour, anchoring at White Bay on 12 April, but the currents and wind conditions as well as the absence of a British government steamer delayed her landing at the storage facilities at Haulbowline until the following day when the Bristol packet *Sabrina* towed her to the government quay. Forbes lost no time in contacting Rathbone to advise him of the ship's arrival, ten days early. He also told the local Cork relief officials that he hoped the food could be distributed within 15 days, the same time as the voyage. Forbes was obviously aware of the many complaints about how long it was taking the British government and various local relief committees to get food to hungry people. Such was the joy and relief of the local populace that aid had come from across the water that the Cove Temperance Band played *Yankee Doodle* repeatedly when they greeted the ship, and that evening the hills surrounding the harbor were illuminated by bonfires and the house windows by candles.[31]

In 1847, County Cork comprised one-tenth of the Irish population, or about 850,000 people, almost half of whom lived in abject poverty, only 27 percent of whom were literate, all factors that made Cork the third poorest county in the country. Forbes observed these conditions first-hand when Father Theobald Mathew, the great temperance leader, took him on a tour of Cork city. The scenes Forbes saw shocked him, prompting him to describe one lane as:

> [A] valley of death and pestilence ... I saw enough in five minutes to horrify me – hovels crowded with the sick and dying, without floors, without furniture and with patches of dirty straw covered with still dirtier shreds and patches of humanity: some called for water to Father Mathew, and others for a dying blessing.[32]

Letters of appeal came to Forbes from clergy and gentry in west Cork, the Kenmare area of County Kerry and from north Cork landlord, Lord Mount Cashell, all seeking to have some of the *Jamestown* provisions sent to their localities and making it clear that conditions in the rural areas were even worse than what Forbes had observed on his tour with Father Mathew.[33] Even before leaving Boston, Forbes had written to Bishop John Murphy of Cork and the Cork Lord Mayor, Edward Hackett, Esq., asking them to organize a distribution committee. But the bishop died a week before the *Jamestown* arrived, and the Lord Mayor was on his deathbed and died just after the ship's arrival.[34] Since the *Jamestown* arrived almost ten days ahead of schedule, Rathbone was not in Cove, but travelled immediately from Liverpool upon learning of the *Jamestown's* arrival. For these reasons, it was not until 17 April that a distribution committee was organized.

Meanwhile, the leading citizens of Cove insisted that Forbes and his officers be entertained at a lavish banquet at the Kilmurray Hotel on 15 April. The festivities were chaired by Maurice Power, J. P., who later filled Daniel O'Connell's Westminster seat upon the death of the Liberator. The event and all the speechifying of the local officials were fully reported in the contemporary newspapers, revealing how local officials dined sumptuously and drank heartily even while there was such misery, starvation and death surrounding them.[35] Forbes was gracious in accepting the many encomiums and hurrahs that came his way but insisted that he accepted them on behalf of the New England Relief Committee and all its donors. In his remarks, Forbes explained how "a sloop of war" had become "a sloop of peace." He saw great beauty in "disarming a national vessel in time of war to carry the aid and comfort of Massachusetts and New England to the suffering in "our fatherland." Realizing that conditions in Ireland would probably get worse, Forbes concluded by saying:

> Let us not in our conviviality today or hereafter, forget the poor without: Let us feel that every morsel of the crumbs which fall from your abundance must be treasured up for them; and let us pray to the Great Ruler for hearts and hands to meet the dreadful crisis which I fear is yet to come. [36]

With the ship unloaded, on 17 April, Forbes, Rathbone, Father Mathew, various clergy and local officials gathered at the Cork Institute to determine how the *Jamestown* provisions would be distributed. Captain William E. D. Broughton, a Poor Law government inspector, developed a plan which ultimately covered the entire county. He mapped out 160 localities and suggested that each should receive five tons of provisions to be distributed by local clergy and local relief officials. Cork City, given its high population and the steady influx of starving rural people, would receive 20 tons of provisions. Government steamers would ship between 60 and 100 tons each to Bantry, Glandore, Clonakilty, Kinsale and Youghal from which the food would be distributed inland. The larger inland towns of Mallow, Fermoy, Macroom, Millstreet and Kanturk would each receive similar amounts for their populations and their rural hinterland. It was estimated that Captain Broughton's plan covered 1,700,000 acres and would bring crucial food supplies to tens of thousands of people. At a meeting one week later, the plan was further refined so that the estimated 600 tons remaining would be sent to 18 districts where clergy, leading gentry and political officials were charged with their distribution. The amounts for these districts varied between four and 13 tons, depending upon the population and needs of each area.[37] Food supplies at this particular time were especially crucial as the public works program had begun to close down in late March and the soup kitchens authorized under the temporary relief legislation would not be fully functioning until July.[38]

Captain Forbes responded to various personal appeals, making donations to the Cove Sick Relief Fund, the Cork Female Employment Institute and the Ursuline Convent in Cork, which he had visited with Father Mathew and Rathbone. He donated some stores of the ship's officers and crew in response to urgent appeals from clergy at Kinsale and Skibbereen. Forbes also arranged that the majority of the $20,752 worth of supplies that were soon expected on the *Tartar*, a private ship coming from Boston, should be sent to Kerry, Limerick and Clare.[39] With the distribution plan formulated, Forbes attended another testimonial event on 19 April, held at the Cork Temperance Institute. Unlike the Cove banquet, this event of 300 was attended by ladies, a number of whom presented Forbes with tokens of appreciation, giving him embroidery and copies of verse that they had written in honor of the *Jamestown* voyage.[40] The captain was impressed by the Cork ladies, commenting that they "shake hands like men. It was no formal touching of the tip ends of the fingers, chilling the heart, but a regular grip of feeling."[41] Forbes' admiration for the ladies was well placed for many of those attending had taken part in important charity work both within Cork City and in the rural hinterlands. Forbes made a special grant to the Ladies' Association of Ballydehob after hearing of their good work there.[42] At this soiree, Forbes was presented with a lithograph of the *Jamestown* leaving Boston by the Irish artist, G.W. Atkinson, which was mounted in a gilded frame. In accepting this gift, he said he would hand it down to his "great, great, great, great grandchildren."[43]

Local Cork VIPs, anxious that Captain Forbes see some of the local sights, took him to Blarney Castle where he kissed the famous stone. He also climbed the recently erected Father Mathew Tower at Mount Patrick on the outskirts of Cork, but he commented that the experience was marred by his knowledge of the dreadful conditions in the vicinity. The leading citizens of Cork took up a public subscription that raised £140 sterling for an engraved silver salver for eventual presentation to Forbes. This remarkable item and its beautifully crafted wooden shipping case are at the Forbes House Museum in Milton, Massachusetts.[44] It is not surprising that Forbes received so much public and private hospitality, as well as a plethora of testimonials from Limerick, Galway, the City of Dublin and many other smaller locations. He declined invitations to receive the thanks of government officials in Dublin and London as he was determined to return to Boston as quickly as possible so that he could organize additional shipments of food for Ireland. By this time, he knew that the provisioning and sailing of the *Macedonian* had been delayed and he wanted to do all he could to expedite its departure. According to Forbes, every day spent on receptions in Ireland would mean more delays in getting food shipped from America (and ultimately more deaths), so he insisted on leaving as soon as possible.[45]

On 21 April, a day prior to the ship's departure from Cove, Forbes and the officers entertained 200 guests on the *Jamestown*. Having witnessed the epic scale of hunger, disease and deaths gripping the land, Forbes consciously served very light refreshments to his guests. In the evening, he hosted a dinner on board for about 20 local officials, including Admiral Hugh Pigot, who permitted admiralty funds to be used for the *Jamestown's* refitting, repairing and painting prior to its departure. Before departing, on 22 April, Forbes wrote to Charles Trevelyan, the doctrinaire British

Treasury official who was an ideological prisoner of laissez-faire economic theory and providential religious thinking regarding the Irish crisis. He strongly urged Trevelyan to arrange for more British government action to meet the crisis in Ireland and suggested that additional government steamers immediately be made available at Cove so that the anticipated supplies coming on the *Macedonian* and other expected vessels could be distributed quickly and efficiently.[46] Although Forbes did not agree with the frequent assertions that Britain was indifferent to Ireland's cry for help, he clearly thought that the current crisis demanded that the usual rules of political economy should be suspended. In responding publicly to one Bostonian who objected to the use of a naval vessel for Irish relief, he wrote: "it was not an everyday matter to see a nation starving," and he hoped that the Boston example would be emulated by others in Great Britain, Europe and the wider world.[47]

Forbes was unwilling to provide accommodation for Irish people wishing to emigrate to Boston, which he had made clear even before departing America in a letter to William Rathbone and again in a letter to the Cork press just before departing Ireland.[48] Responding to an address of thanks from the Roman Catholic clergy of Ballinrobe, County Mayo, two weeks after returning to Boston, Forbes wrote:

> I cannot but pray you to permit none to embark for this country unprovided (for) and destitute: this course tends to close the avenues of our sympathy, and sometimes to make us wish, that the gratitude of Ireland should be shown by keeping her poor at home. We have abundant room for those who can get to the Western States: they will be welcome there and will soon find independence.[49]

Echoing the widespread anxiety among Boston's leading officials over the huge numbers of poor Irish immigrants who had arrived in the city, Forbes told William Rathbone in November: "Our seaports have been so overrun with paupers and fever patients, coming directly through the provinces, that there is little chance of further relief."[50] In fact, these two letters were an accurate reflection of how the arrival of over 37,000 Irish in these months had diluted much of the sympathy shown in February and March.[51] As early as April, when the *Jamestown* was in Cork, the Massachusetts legislature was holding hearings regarding the growing costs of providing for these impoverished immigrants and the public health risks of "ship-fever" spreading widely. Deer Island in Boston Harbor became the receiving station for immigrants refused entry by the medical inspectors.[52] Ironically, only one day after the *Jamestown* returned to Boston, on 17 May 1847, the English brig *Mary*, carrying 46 immigrants from Cork, was refused entry by the port authorities because its captain refused to pay the per passenger bond that had recently been enacted by the authorities. It was diverted to Halifax, Nova Scotia, where it docked on 23 May.[53] By June, the hostility to the huge influx of Irish Famine refugees and their impact on Boston and its institutions was evident in the following editorial in the *Boston Evening Transcript*:

> ... the tide of immigration which is increasing daily to a most alarming extent, brings with it its necessary concomitant of poverty, sickness and crime, has excited as it ought the attention of the whole community, and the people in all parts of the country have at last become aroused, and are turning about to devise a means to check an evil which has reached such a height that the very vitality of our country has become endangered by it.[54]

Nonetheless, once he arrived back in Boston, Forbes threw himself into a campaign to raise funds for the full provisioning of the *Macedonian* and to cut the red tape that was delaying its departure from New York. He traveled to New York almost immediately upon his return with New England Relief Committee members David Henshaw and James K. Mills to assist Captain de Kay in meeting his quota of provisions. In response to a public plea from the famed Irish novelist Maria Edgeworth, on behalf of her tenants, Forbes arranged for 100 barrels of provisions and $280 in cash to be sent to her via the *Macedonian*.[55] A large portion of the $29,752 worth of supplies that arrived in Cove aboard the *Macedonian* on 16 July actually came from the New England Relief Committee. The total value of the supplies that went to County Cork from Boston aboard the *Jamestown*, the *Tartar*, the *Reliance* and the *Macedonian* from New York in 1847 was $121,547. The total amount sent by the committee to all ports in 1847 was $151,000, or half of the estimated $300,000 that was sent by all sources from Boston in that bleak year.

The *Jamestown* was only one of eight ships that sent aid from the New England Relief Committee to Ireland and Scotland in 1847. The Society of Friends sent nine ships of provisions to Cork that same year; yet the example of using a ship of war on an errand of mercy ensured that the *Jamestown* voyage would be remembered by the people of Cork for decades to come.[56] The food sent from New England could only make a small dent in the effort to prevent widespread starvation, disease and death in Cork and the southwest. The impact of these years on Cork was horrendous as by 1851 it had lost over 25 percent of its 1841 population through death and emigration.[57] The memories of these years would haunt survivors in Ireland as well as those who made it across the Atlantic, thereby nurturing strong anti-British and anti-landlord feelings that would be acted upon in the late nineteenth and early twentieth centuries.

During the worst of the 1847 Irish crisis, Forbes and the New England Relief Committee, together with thousands of citizens of all classes and religious beliefs who contributed to Irish relief, represented the highest standard of humanitarianism and generosity. Forbes considered his role in this effort as a great privilege and described the voyage as the "happiest event of my life."[58] The *Jamestown* voyage is a unique episode as it is the only time that a U.S. naval ship was transferred to civilian control to embark on a humanitarian mission of charity.[59] The story of the *Jamestown* and Captain Forbes' leadership provide an inspiration and example that contemporary society could emulate as the world continues to grapple with hunger, disease and economic and political structural inequalities that dehumanize far too many humans in ways similar to what the Irish people experienced in the dreadful Famine era.

NOTES

1. See Christine Kinealy, *The Kindness of Strangers: Charity and the Great Hunger in Ireland* (London: Bloomsbury, 2013) for a comprehensive account of global aid to Ireland; and Stephen Puleo, *Voyage of Mercy* (New York: St. Martin's Press, 2020) for additional details on American assistance in 1847.

2. Robert B. Forbes, *The Voyage of the Jamestown on her Errand of Mercy* (Boston: Eastburn Press, 1847), p. 8.

3. Ibid., Waterson to R. B. Forbes, March 1847, pp iv-v. President Michael D. Higgins, "Reflecting on the *Gorta Mor*," 5 May 2012. http://president.ie/en/media-library/speeches/reflecting-on-the-gorta mor-the great famine

4. For an account of conflict between Protestants and Irish Catholics in this era, see Robert H. Lord, *History of the Archdiocese of Boston* (New York: Sheed and Ward, 1944), vol. 2, pp 205-265.

5. Boston *Pilot,* 29 November, 6, 13, 20 December 1845; Oscar Handlin, *Boston's Immigrants* (Cambridge, Harvard University Press, 1991) p. 247; H. A. Crosby Forbes and Henry Lee, *Massachusetts Help to Ireland During the Great Famine* (Milton: Forbes Museum, 1967), pp 1-2.

6. Forbes and Lee, *Massachusetts Help to Ireland,* pp 3-4. Thomas D'Arcy McGee wrote to the Boston *Pilot* presenting this argument as the view of the Dublin leadership with the result that it soured the relationship between McGee and *Pilot* editor and his former mentor, Patrick Donohoe, when it was discovered that McGee had written without their approval. *The Pilot,* 30 January 1846. David A. Wilson, *Thomas D'Arcy McGee* (Montreal: McGill Queen's University Press, 2008), pp 118-121.

7. *Pilot,* 5, 12, 19, 26 September 1846.

8. Ibid., 23, 30 January, 6 February 1847.

9. Ibid., 6 February 1847.

10. Fitzpatrick to Crolly, 27 February 1847, Fitzpatrick papers, Boston Archdioceses Archives.

11. Sarah Forbes Hughes, *Letters and Recollections of John Murray Forbes* (Boston: Houghton Mifflin, 1899), vol. 1, p. 121.

12. *Boston Daily Courier,* 11 February 1847. Puleo, *Voyage of Mercy,* p. 63. For Jacob Harvey's efforts to mobilize the American Quaker community for Irish relief, see *Transactions of the Central Relief Committee of the Society of Friends During the Famine in Ireland,* (Dublin: Hodges and Smith, 1852), pp 216-219, 248. New England contributions to the Society of Friends fund were considerable, consisting of £753 from New Bedford, MA, £440 from Salem, MA, £1,181 from Lynn, MA, £278 from a group of Boston abolitionists. Woonsocket, R.I. sent $3,429 in cash and later 700 barrels of meal. *Transactions,* pp 232, 235, 477, 478.

13. *Daily Advertiser,* 16 February 1847; George Potter, *To the Golden Door: The Story of the Irish in Ireland and America* (Westport, CT: Greenwood Press, 1964), p. 252. Giles gave a lecture in Brooklyn, New York that raised $600 for famine relief, *Pilot,* 6 March 1847.

14. Daniel Webster to Josiah Quincy and Abbot Lawrence, *Boston Daily Atlas,* 10 February 1847, Forbes and Lee, *Massachusetts Help to Ireland,* pp 18-19.

15. For speeches see, *Boston Daily Advertiser,* 22 February 1847.

16. William Lloyd Garrison and John Greenleaf Whittier noted the strong impact of Everett's speech. Garrison to Central Relief Committee, 26 February 1847, *Transactions of the Central Relief Committee,* p. 234. Whittier to Anne E. Wendell, 21 February 1847, *Life and Letters of John Greenleaf Whittier,* ed. Samuel T. Pickard (Boston: Riverside Press, 1894), vol. I. p. 318.

17. Forbes and Lee, *Massachusetts Help to Ireland,* p. 27.

18. Forbes' older brother, Thomas, was lost at sea in 1829 in Asia, leaving Robert financially responsible for his mother and younger siblings when he was only 25. He and his wife Rose lost three babies in the first seven years of their marriage. His first fortune disappeared from a combination of the Depression of 1837 as well a risky investment he made in a cousin's business. He sailed to China again in 1838 and returned home two years later with a fortune of $200,000. See Puleo for details of Forbes early life at sea as well as his financial gains and losses.

19. Forbes to Rathbone, 18 March 1847, *Voyage,* Appendix 49, xxiv.

20. Captain William McCondray, James D. Farwell, James H. Foote and John B. White signed on as ship officers while Dr. Luther Parks joined the voyage as the ship surgeon. Forbes and Lee, *Massachusetts Help to Ireland,* p. 34.

21. Forbes and Lee, *Massachusetts Help to Ireland,* p. 34; *Voyage,* Appendix 107, cxxxvi.

22. Forbes and Lee, *Massachusetts Help to Ireland,* pp 21, 23, 68. n. 51; *Boston Evening Transcript,* 20 February 1847, *Boston Daily Atlas,* 22 February, 27 March, *Liberator,* 5 March, 9 April 1847.

23. This information is based on a list of volunteers in *Boston Daily Atlas,* 19 February 1847, and the 1917 master list of Charitable Irish Society members.

24. *Voyage,* Appendix 3, iii.

25. Josiah Quincy alluded to this reason in his Faneuil Hall speech.

26. Hillard to Rose Forbes, l7 March 1847, in Robert B. Forbes, *Personal Reminiscences* (Boston: Little Brown, 1878), pp 193-194.

27. William R. Lawrence, ed. *Extracts from the Diary and Correspondence of the Late Amos Lawrence* (Boston: John Wilson, 1855), pp 237-238, 241. Lawrence's appeal to students at the Mather School netted $160 for the *Jamestown* mission.

28. Letter from Forbes, *Daily Advertiser,* 22 February 1847.

29. The thistle represented the intention of the relief committee to send a portion of the cargo to Scotland, which was also suffering crop failures, although not as severely as Ireland. Contemporary images show this burgee flying from the second mast of the ship.

30. For a full list of the cargo, see *Voyage,* Appendix 106, cxxxii. Boston's donations were worth $30,106, while Charlestown's totaled $1,419. Donations from the rest of Massachusetts and New England amounted to $4,342. The speed of the crossing was almost as fast as the steam-powered Royal Mail packets' trans-Atlantic sailings. See *Voyage,* Appendix l7, pp xi-xv for Forbes' account of the stormy crossing.

31. *Voyage,* p. 10.

32. Ibid., p. 22. It is possible that Forbes heard accounts of horrific conditions in Skibbereen from dispatches of Elihu Burritt that were published in the *Boston Daily Atlas* on 25 February and 6 March 1847. Forbes offered Burritt free passage back to America, but the latter declined. When writing to Burritt on 20 April, Forbes described the Cork area as "a charnel house." Ibid., Appendix 83, cxii.

33. See Rev. John O'Sullivan to Forbes, 21 April 1847, *Voyage,* Appendix 80, cvii; Mount Cashell to Forbes, 20 April 1847. Mount Cashell enclosed a return naming 118 men, women and children who had died in the Kilworth area and reported that 5,000 of its 9,000 inhabitants were totally without food. See Lawrence M. Geary, "A Famine Document," *Dublin Review of Books* 32 (8 April 2013) for this return. Because of Mount Cashell's personal lavish life-style, Captain Broughton did not authorize any special grant to this landlord, and Forbes did not personally send him any funds.

34. *Cork Examiner,* 16 April 1847. The Lord Mayor's funeral took place when Forbes was in Cork. The bishop died on 7 April 1847. *Boston Pilot,* 8 May 1847.

35. The menu included "everything in season that could be desired by the most fastidious epicurean, from Turtle soup to Iced Champagne, both of which were most amply supplied and highly approved." Apples and American mutton were featured along with "other choice fruits ... for dessert." *Voyage,* Appendix 58 contains a full account of the proceedings including numerous speeches by Irish officials and Forbes.

36. *Voyage,* Appendix 58, lviii.

37. *The Southern Reporter,* 27 April 1847.

38. On the serious gap in food sources, see James Donnelly, *The Great Irish Potato Famine* (London: Sutton, 2001), pp 85-88.

39. For these personal distributions authorized by Forbes, see, *Voyage, p. 11;* Appendix 22, p. xvii; Appendix 21, xvii, Appendix 61, lxxx.

40. One poem was dedicated to Forbes' young son, James, who had contributed $5 to the cause.

41. *Voyage,* p. 12.

42. Ibid., Appendix 90, cxxi-cxxii.

43. Ibid., Appendix 63, lxxxvi.

44. Major Beamish proposed this gift which was enthusiastically backed by J. F. Maguire, the owner of *The Cork Examiner.* See *Voyage,* Appendix 59, lxx.

45. *Personal Reminiscences*, p. 190; Voyage, Appendix 95, cxxiv.

46. Forbes to Trevelyan, 22 April 1847, *Voyage,* Appendix 36, xxv.

47. Forbes letter to the Boston press, 22 April 1847, *Voyage,* Appendix, 36, xxv. See Kinealy, *The Kindness of Strangers,* for an account of the unprecedented global response to the Irish crisis, including donations from the Sultan of Turkey and the Vatican.

48. *Voyage,* p. ix, and Appendix 42, xxx.

49. Forbes to Michael Waldron, PP, 31 May 1847, *Voyage,* Appendix 93, cxxiii-cxxiv.

50. Forbes to Rathbone, 14 November 1847, Forbes Papers, Massachusetts Historical Society, MS N-49-70, Box 2, Folder 13. Forbes wrote this letter the same day that there was a public meeting chaired by Mayor Quincy in Faneuil Hall that addressed the financial and public health concerns that the large influx of impoverished Irish immigrants was causing. Potter, *The Story of the Irish in Ireland and America,* p. 466.

51. On 10 April 1847, approximately one thousand Irish immigrants arrived in Boston and over the summer nativist gangs marched through the Irish Fort Hill area intimidating the area's residents. Potter, *The Story of the Irish in Ireland and America,* p. 466.

52. Lord, *History,* vol. 2, pp 448-452. Between May 1847 and January 1848, 2,230 immigrants were sent to Deer Island, of whom at least 347 died and were buried there. A Celtic Cross in their memory was erected on the island in spring 2018.

53. "The ships' list. Emigration to America in 1847," at: www.theshipslist.com/1847/

54. *Boston Evening Transcript,* 26 June 1847.

55. *Pilot,* 25 April 1847.

56. *The Cork Examiner* reported on 30 April 1847 that 22 vessels carrying about 60,000 barrels of food supplies had arrived in Cobh in the past two days, and that in the previous week a total of 59 vessels had arrived with provisions.

57. Some Poor Law unions in west Cork, such as Skibbereen, Bandon, Dunmanway and Mallow lost between 34 percent to 36 percent of their population. James S. Donnelly, *The Land and People of Nineteenth-Century Cork* (London: Routledge, Keegan and Paul, 1975), p. 129.

58. Puleo, *Voyage of Mercy,* p. 198.

59. In 1880, when the west of Ireland was again threatened with starvation from a potato failure, the USS *Constellation* under U.S. Navy command sailed from New York to Cork carrying a cargo of potatoes and flour arriving in Cobh on 20 April 1880. For details see Harvey Strum, "America's Errand of Mercy to Ireland" in Christine Kinealy and Gerard Moran (eds), *Irish Famines before and after the Great Hunger* (Cork University Press, 2020).

Women's Agency

CHAPTER FOUR

LADY SLIGO OF WESTPORT HOUSE (1800–1878)

She Rolled up her Linen Sleeves and Did the Right Thing

Sandy Letourneau O'Hare

In 2011, Quinnipiac University acquired approximately 200 letters, many written by a woman in Ireland in the middle of the nineteenth century. Her name was Hester Catherine de Burgh Browne, second Marchioness of Sligo. Beyond that, no-one knew anything about her except, "that she was one of the wives," as one of her descendants, three times great-granddaughter Sheelyn Browne, said.[1] Moreover, nothing was known about her role during the Great Famine. Her letters provide a unique insight into her response, prompting Browne to respond:

> For years as a family, we were all deeply conscious that the Great Famine was never covered properly in the house and often visitors would be suspicious of what really happened in these big houses during the period... we know they were a very privileged generation, but the letters show that they followed the family motto, *Suivez Raison* [follow reason], and rolled up their beautifully ironed linen sleeves to do the right thing for their tenants during the Great Famine.[2]

Who was this forgotten wife? Her letters hold the key and add a unique new dimension to understanding the mid-nineteenth century tragedy of the Great Hunger. People assume the letters were about family, fashion and domestic matters because they were written by a woman. These topics were discussed but, when you look closer, they provide an insight into the role and influence of women, into the unusual and humanitarian response to tenants on the estate, and the difficulties faced by landlords, both socially and politically, during the Great Hunger. Christine Kinealy, founding director of Ireland's Great Hunger Institute at Quinnipiac University, remarking that Lady Sligo's letters demonstrated a keen awareness of contemporary politics and a concern for the poor, especially as the Famine unfolded in County Mayo.[3] The letters shed light on the life and struggles of an upper-class Protestant landlord who ran the day-to-day affairs of her estate, tended to her ailing husband and successfully raised 13 children to adulthood. They challenge the simplistic portrayal of good Catholic tenants versus evil and uncaring Protestant landlords. Most importantly, through these letters we hear of these things through a woman's voice, something that is rare.

As Anne Anderson, Ambassador of Ireland to the United States, remarked at the opening of the Lady Sligo letters exhibition at Quinnipiac University in 2014: "Women generally had walk-on parts, appearing in crowd scenes or cameo roles as sweethearts or muses."[4] She explained:

> Lady Sligo's voice interests us, not just as a woman's voice. It is very much a voice of her time imbued with the attitudes and, I would even say, some of the prejudices of her time … It is an Anglo-Irish voice, a landlord's voice, but it is also a humane voice in an inhumane time.[5]

Hester Catherine de Burgh was born on 16 January 1800 in County Galway into the privileged Protestant Ascendancy. She was the daughter of the 13th Earl of Clanricarde, General John Thomas de Burgh and Elizabeth Bourke. Hester Catherine was the couple's first daughter and the eldest child of three.[6] Her father was a progressive, forward-thinking man and in the year of her birth, he "obtained letters patent to permit his eldest daughter to become his successor, with the title of 'countess', in the event of a lack of male heirs."[7] This was not the only time a father in this family would change the rules of inheritance for his daughters. The 11th Marquess and Sheelyn Browne's father, Jeremy Ulick Browne, introduced a private bill into the Irish Parliament that allowed for the dissolution of a family trust so that his five daughters could inherit Westport House upon his death.[8]

On 4 March 1816, Hester Catherine married Howe Peter Browne (the second Marquess of Sligo) in Dublin before they celebrated their nuptials in Finnigan's Hotel. The first Lady Sligo and Howe Peter's mother, Louisa Catherine, hailed from London: this made Hester Catherine the first woman to marry into the Browne family who was a native of the west of Ireland.[9] Hester Catherine was a strong, dominant presence in her own right and, when she married Howe Peter, she joined a long line of formidable women in his family, the most notable being the "Pirate Queen of Connaught," Grace O'Malley.[10] Grace, also known as Granuaile in Irish, was the daughter of an Irish chieftain who defied Gaelic customs that barred women from clan leadership roles. Defying accepted rules is a trait that has carried down through the generations of the Browne family. At the beginning of her marriage, Lady Sligo travelled all over the world with her colorful husband, who was associated with Lord Byron, Napoleon Bonaparte, and many more famous contemporaries.[11] She entertained monarchs, moved in the highest circles, and even developed a fan-base after a gallery in Dublin commissioned a portrait of her to be sold to curious members of the public in 1836.[12] However, there was more substance to this celebrity couple than headlines and balls. They were both enlightened thinkers and while he was indisputably the head of his household legally, Howe Peter shared and consulted with his wife about political and business undertakings from the beginning of their marriage, making theirs a true partnership.[13]

Howe Peter, Lady Sligo and their children spent two years living in Jamaica beginning in 1834 when Howe Peter was appointed governor general of the island. In 1831, he had been asked to serve on a committee, together with fellow Irish man, Daniel O'Connell, to advise on measures to safely end slavery within the British Empire.[14] He was shocked by the evidence presented, leading him to explain: "I entered the room a colonial advocate. I left it an abolitionist."[15] Although slavery had been abolished in 1834, there was a period known as Apprenticeship, which was to last for 12 years, before enslaved people were finally free. This condition appalled abolitionists who had campaigned for immediate emancipation.[16] Howe Peter was asked to travel to Jamaica to oversee this transition. Through the marriage of his grandfather Peter Browne, second Earl of Altamont, to Elizabeth Kelly, Howe Peter had inherited two plantations on the island. Appalled by the atrocities he witnessed in Jamaica, Howe Peter and his wife worked for an early ending to the system of Apprenticeship, thereby invoking the wrath of other plantation owners. They were the first owners to free the slaves on their plantations. Back in Ireland, Howe Peter continued to speak out against Apprenticeship, now from first-hand experience. His words were a major influence in encouraging Irish anti-slavery societies in 1837 to draw up "a solemn protest against it."[17] In 1838, the Apprenticeship system was ended. The first post-emancipation free slave village in the world, Sligoville, was subsequently named in the family's honor and marks their legacy in Jamaica to this day.[18]

Generally, the nineteenth century in Irish history is not remembered as a time when landlords were interested in improving conditions for their tenants, but Howe Peter was an exception. He was one of the few Irish peers who supported Catholic Emancipation and believed in education for all. While in Jamaica, the couple paid the cost of a schoolmaster for the servants' children.[19] They also did their best to improve conditions for their tenants in Ireland so they would not be so dependent on the life of farming for their survival:

> He established a cotton factory in Westport in order, as he wrote, 'to benefit this Country by introducing such manufactures into it as will give employment to the People ... unless I do it to show the way nobody will follow.' He encouraged the development of kelp-harvesting and fishing and revitalised mining development in the area. He promoted trade and manufacturing in the town and port of Westport and influenced the establishment of the first bank there in 1825. As famine-like conditions engulfed the west of Ireland in 1831, at his own expense he imported cargos of grain and potatoes, built a hospital and dispensary to care for the sick and, through his contacts in the government, helped raise money for famine relief and to establish additional public works.[20]

There are numerous records of Lord and Lady Sligo's trips from Westport to London to attend society and charity events before Howe Peter became ill with gout in 1837. Lady Sligo was actively involved as a patroness in many charity functions such as the Society of St. Vincent De Paul's Bazaar for the Poor in Dublin, and the Annual Fancy and Full Dress Ball, held for the Sick and Indigent Roomkeepers Charity.[21] After Howe Peter became sick, he stayed in England to recuperate while Lady Sligo assumed the daily duties of running the estate from their homes in Tunbridge Wells and London and, following his death, from a rented house in Clontarf near Dublin.[22]

The Sligo estate was the largest in County Mayo, comprising over 114,000 acres. Lady Sligo's letters from this period show her discussing the influenza epidemic, patterns of linen, and the salary account for the estate.[23] In one letter to her estate agent, George Hildebrand, she included a sum of money with the instruction, "£20 is for the Dorcas Society, & £20 to lay out warm cloaks for poor women."[24] Lady Sligo relied heavily on Hildebrand, instructing him on mundane events such as what dress to send her or how much to tip the delivery boy. She went beyond being just the lady of the manor, questioning Hildebrand on matters such as weather conditions and their impact on crops and, in 1845, commented on the strange blight seen on potatoes in Dublin and wondered if it had appeared at Westport. She was concerned for the poor on the estate and instructed Hildebrand to purchase good quality blankets for them, whatever the price. It is through these letters, and Hildebrand's responses, that we learn firsthand what conditions were like at the time and how involved she was in the running of the estate. Her interest extended to what was grown on the estate, "In one dispatch, she sent a high-yielding strawberry plant to Westport in the hope that a similar crop could be grown there."[25]

Lady Sligo's letter to George Hildebrand, from Mansfield Street in London, dated 20 February 1845, was embossed in black, indicating that her husband had died. She informed Hildebrand that she had received a letter from Lord Altamont (her eldest son), from Madrid, sent on 13 February, saying that he had just heard of his father's death and that he was returning to England. Meanwhile, Lady Sligo intended to return to Ireland. Throughout this period, Lady Sligo displayed firm control over the running of Westport House as she continuously went beyond the traditionally accepted role of a woman, seeking information on topics such as the weather, crop conditions, and the state of the poor. As well as dealing with major estate issues, her letters provide insight into her persona as a fashion icon. She clearly enjoying her position in society. Her letters on these matters show that she directed what she wanted with a velvet-lined iron will, informing Hildebrand on one occasion, "I think you are mistaking the kind of fur I want. I want white ermine fur with long black tails ... I want all the white fur, but I do not want any dark fur."[26] In a letter dated 19 July 1845, she asked that a selection of silk and satin gowns and three or four of her "largest and showiest" fans be sent by coach to Dublin.[27]

From her homes in England and in Dublin, Lady Sligo showed her awareness of events in Mayo. In May 1845, then renting a house at Clontarf on the outskirts of Dublin, she corresponded freely with Hildebrand. Her letter of 21 May indicated that there were already economic problems in Westport:

> I fear there must be a great deal of distress and poverty about Westport now that there is so little money spent in the Town, and I do not at all grudge the money you gave away in charity for me.[28]

A letter from March 1846 demonstrated her awareness of local politics and their possible impact on Westport House and her family:

> I received your letter with the receipts for my subscriptions for Dorcas Repository & the Infant School enclosed ... Do you think that the tenants at Louisburgh who ran away, did so of their own inclination, or that they were afraid of their Priest's displeasure if they voted for Mr. Moore? ... I fear the expense to Lord Altamont caused by all this disturbance will be a great deal, but it cannot be helped. Some of the Dublin newspapers say that the woman was not shot until after the soldiers had passed. I wonder whether that was true.[29]

The person referred to was George Henry Moore, a neighboring landowner and relative, who had been defeated in a recent election. During a clash between the opposing factions, the military had inadvertently killed a local woman.[30]

When her 25-year-old son, and third-born child, George John Browne, inherited the estate in 1845 and succeeded his father in the House of Lords, Lady Sligo, now the Dowager Marchioness of Sligo, supported and advised him through the difficult years of the Great Hunger. She continued to take an active part in running the estate for many years to come.

Lady Sligo was concerned about the poor having the necessities needed to survive. Her letters provided documentation that she and the Browne family frequently made it a point to eschew cost in favor of the best aid that they could provide for tenants suffering from the effects of the potato blight.

> Which do you think best - that I should send you £25 to buy blankets for some of the very poor people at Westport or in the neighborhood of Westport, or that I should buy the blankets here & send them to you - I can get blankets here from 6 to 8 shillings a pair - at 8 shillings they are very good & thick -- I saw some as low as 5/ a pair—but they are thin & small.[31]

It is through these letters that we learn firsthand what conditions were like and how intrinsically involved she was in the running of the estate.[32] As early as October 1845, it was apparent that poverty was increasing. Lady Sligo wrote to Hildebrand: "I am very sorry to say that I hear every day more applications for charity than I have, or can ever have, the means of giving. I am obliged to refuse cases of <u>real want</u>."[33] By early December 1845, she was concerned about the availability of food supplies for the poor. Her general custom was to have blankets distributed, but at this point, she defers to what Hildebrand thinks best as he is in closer proximity to the tenants than she:

> As you do not think that there is at this moment a great want of blankets among the poor of Westport, I will, as you advise, keep what I can afford to give until it is more wanted – of course food must be even more required, if there is to be a scarcity of their own produce, which I fear is almost certain in Ireland generally, if not near Westport.[34]

Her private letters show her sympathy towards the local poor, a concern which was also evident in her 25-year-old son, George.

By early January 1846 George, then travelling in the Middle East, had been made aware of the increasing severity of the Famine and had instructed Hildebrand to help the poor on the estate. His mother wanted to go further and have a range of work programs in place to provide employment for the poor. While sympathetic to the poor, like many of her class, she did not believe it was good for people to give them money without receiving an appropriate return for it in the form of their labor:

> I think it would be a very wise thing in about six weeks' time, when the weather gets finer, to look over the property, & see in what way labour could be made use of in the most advantageous & profitable way to the estate.[35]

The following morning, she added:

> I see a report of the meeting in the *Telegraph* which arrived this morning. I am
> sure you have acted rightly so that nothing can be more foolish than giving the
> people ideas that they are to be supported without great exertions on their own.
> Nevertheless, I fear that although the potato disease may be little or nothing near
> Westport it is a serious matter in other places.[36]

In keeping with the orthodoxy of the time, Lady Sligo clearly disapproved of too
much government relief. She contended:

> It would certainly be ruin to the people if they were persuaded they were not to
> work hard and will be supported in idleness ... it must be admitted that the lower
> class are always fond of trusting to anything rather than their own exertions.[37]
>
> Nevertheless, Lady Sligo's views did not prevent her again from providing
> frequent acts of kindness to both the poor and the sick. In January 1847, Dudley
> Durkin, the Medical Attendant in the impoverished Louisburgh district in County
> Mayo, wrote to the editor of the *Mayo Constitution*, describing a recent donation he
> received. It appeared under the headline, "BENEVOLENT ACT OF MARCHIONESS
> OF SLIGO," and stated:
>
> Mr Hildebrand, under the directions of that benevolent and charitable lady, the
> marchioness of Sligo, forwarded to my charge nine hundred weight of rice for the
> suffering poor of this district. In the kind favour which I received from the excellent
> gentleman, he stated that it was the wish and desire of the generous and noble lady
> to make no distinction in its distribution. Many and very many times has the noble
> family of Westport House been distinguished for their generous spirit of benevo-
> lence and practical charity in relieving the wants of the distressed. Sickness, I regret
> to state, is raging to an enormous extent in this parish.[38]

The Dowager Marchioness assisted in other ways, including paying a visit to the
local Sisters of Mercy, who were feeding the children in their schools. On behalf of
the Marquess of Sligo, she bestowed a large portion of land, rent free, in addition to
a substantial financial donation.[39]

With her guidance, the new Lord Sligo aided his tenants by providing them
with corn and potatoes, his mother observing with satisfaction that he "has so good
a feeling towards the poor on his estate."[40] The town of Westport had been built
by John Browne in the 1780s, as a place for workers on the estate and tenants to
live.[41] After the potato crop failed for a second time in 1846, conditions in the town
rapidly deteriorated, with Paul Strzelecki of the British Relief Association reporting
in March 1847, "No pen can describe the distress by which I am surrounded ... what
I actually see surpasses what I ever read of past and present calamities."[42] Families
from nearby villages came flooding into the town in search of food, medical care or

workhouse relief, meaning that the local population increased by 15 percent between 1845 to 1851, which was in stark contrast to the decline throughout the rest of the county.[43] Unfortunately, this led to the spread of diseases such as typhus and bacillary dysentery. There were more deaths recorded in 1846 and 1847 from disease than from starvation the previous year. Throughout, Lady Sligo, alongside her son George, attempted to alleviate the suffering of the local inhabitants, just as she had done with her husband in 1831 during that period of famine.[44]

Despite his youth, the new Marquess had a great deal of sympathy for his tenants during the Famine. Initially, he did not charge them rent although he did have to pay taxes on his lands. The rental income from the estate was £7,500 but, for three years, none had been received. Things were so dire that he kept the workhouse, which held 800 paupers, open for weeks at his own expense. In 1846, along with his cousin, George Moore, and his neighbor, Sir Robert Blosse, George imported large quantities of meal from New Orleans on the *Martha Washington*, costing him £3,012, for distribution in Mayo."[45] Every workhouse in the west of Ireland was full by the end of 1846 and in 1847 Westport workhouse was in danger of shuttering its doors on several occasions. It was saved only by the Marquess intervening twice to keep it afloat with his own money.[46] By August 1847, it owed £800 and £1,000 was outstanding to builders.[47]

In the second year of the Famine, demonstrations had begun throughout the country. As John O'Rourke noted in his classic study *The History of the Great Irish Famine of 1847*:

> The earliest famine demonstration seems to have taken place in Westport on 22 August 1846. On that day, thousands marched, and in a very orderly manner, to Lord Sligo's residence, beside the town. They made their intention known beforehand to the inspector of police and asked him to be present to show they had no illegal designs. They were chiefly from Islandeady and Aughagower. Lord Sligo, as was the custom of his father, received them at his hall door.[48]

George Browne assured his tenants of his support. He told them he had already applied to Parliament for relief measures and would do so again if his appeal was denied. George Brown made an initial donation of £100 and promised a subscription of £5 per week to keep the workhouse open.[49]

Both mother and son were increasingly critical of the policies being pursued in London, in particular the interventions by Charles Trevelyan of the Treasury.[50] In a letter to the London *Times*, the Marquess accused the government of being responsible for the situation in Ireland. He stated that 26,000 people had been fed in the Westport union in 1847, and there was now no provision for them in the future. The Poor Law did not have the funds to care for them.[51] Despite his public criticisms of the actions of the Treasury, Lord Sligo enjoyed good relations with the British Prime Minister, with Lord and Lady Russell visiting Westport House in September 1848.[52]

A workhouse had been opened in Westport in 1842 as part of the 1838 Poor Law. The Westport union covered 533 square miles and included a number of islands, including Achill. It also included some of the most impoverished areas in the country which attracted a number of benefactors, including James Hack Tuke and Pawel Strzelecki, who made the county a base for their private relief operations. The Poor Law system was originally designed to accommodate one percent of the population or 80,000 people country wide but, as late as March 1851, famine had driven almost four percent of the population into the workhouses.[53] The Westport workhouse could accommodate 1,000 inmates, but by the end of 1846, like many workhouses in the west, it was struggling to meet the demands being placed on it.[54] In January 1847, a store in Westport was broken into. The thieves took seven barrels of flour, which they divided while still on the premises, leaving the empty barrels behind. The Westport guardians decided to close the workhouse in retaliation but, "Lord Sligo most humanely interfered and guaranteed to supply the house for three weeks, till the intention of government was known."[55] In August 1847, Hildebrand was instructed to pay for food supplied to the workhouse.[56] At this point, the third Marquess wrote that: "we have near 8,000 on outdoor relief & 1,000 in the Workhouse."[57] Its insolvent position resulted in the Poor Law Commissioners dissolving the board and replacing it with paid vice-guardians in late August 1847.[58]

Out of a deep frustration with the authorities' inability to either understand or act upon the dire situation in Ireland, the third Marquess compiled and had printed a 36-page booklet entitled, *A Few Remarks and Suggestions on the Present State of Ireland*. In this pamphlet, he criticized the government's woeful inadequacy in the handling of the disaster.

> With the insight and knowledge of someone who was living daily with the awful consequences, he sought Ireland's "just demands upon the Empire". His article covered the spectrum of what he saw as the main reasons for the disaster: The Poor Law, Tenant Right and the Rival Claims of the English and Roman Churches.[59]

The Irish Poor Law Extension Act of 1847 transferred the full burden of famine relief to only Irish tax-payers instead of those in the United Kingdom as a whole. Although he had not received any rent since the first appearance of blight, Lord Sligo had not evicted any tenants. In 1848, though, he was forced to borrow £1,500 to pay his poor rates, and he evicted some tenants, explaining that the additional fiscal burden meant he was now "under the necessity of ejecting or being ejected."[60] In 1852, Lord Sligo justified the evictions stating he had reinstated many of the evicted as caretakers and only those who were beyond help were let go.[61] He also published a letter requesting that the government adjust grain prices. The British government denied the request, on the grounds that it could not interfere with the free market.[62]

At a Famine Relief Committee meeting in Westport, Lord Sligo was challenged by the Church of Ireland's Archbishop of Tuam, who wanted to know what he intended to do. He responded by instantly writing a check for £1,500:

> This munificent donation called forth the loudest plaudits and the warmest bene-dictions from all present... Lord Sligo has by his conduct this day secured the affec-tionate esteem of the inhabitants of this town. It is but justice to say that no other landed proprietor in the distressed portions of this Country has exerted himself to the extent his Lordship has done, and it is considered rather unfair that any annoy-ance should be offered to a Nobleman who has devoted so much of his time and health and property to the alleviation of the miseries which now afflict this part of the country.[63]

The complex relationship that Protestant landowners, even benign ones, shared with both their tenants and members of the Catholic Church hierarchy was evident in 1850 following an election in County Mayo. A number of Irish newspapers reported that Lord Sligo "was most grossly insulted by a mob of ungrateful savages in Westport on Sunday afternoon, and followed up to the gate of Westport House."[64] The Marquess responded by closing his demesne to local people. One report pointed out: "This is not to be wondered at when it is to be remembered what both he and the marchio-ness have done for the poor of the town and surrounding counties during the late years of distress."[65]

Through the Famine and beyond, Lady Sligo continued to be a patron of the Sisters of Mercy charity. She was among those in attendance at "A Bazaar in aid of the starving poor of Westport" which was held on 28 November 1849. In December 1849, the family helped run a charity bazaar in what is now the Rotunda Hospital in Dublin to raise money for the people affected by the Famine.[66] The Dowager Marchioness also offered clothes to a great number of girls who were too poor to afford their own and forced to live in a state of partial undress: people of both sexes were nearly in a state of nudity according to the *Connaught Telegraph* in 1851.[67] Lady Sligo answered the call with her usual large supply of blankets, in addition to shawls and other clothing for those in need. She also provided many poor people with meals.[68] Not all accounts of the activities of the Sligo family were favorable. In 1851, a Dublin newspaper reported that in a workhouse "in the west," children had been taught to chant "God bless Lord Sligo; God bless Lady Sligo." They likened it to the submission expected of slaves in America, the *Nation* bluntly stating: "We have heard of such a psalm, 'God bless Massa,' out in Carolina, but nowhere else in the Christian world ... Pauperism, we verily believe, is manufacturing a slave caste in this country."[69]

After the Famine, the Dowager Marchioness moved to her primary residence in London on the fashionable Mansfield Street, although she continued to visit her home in Westport. One notable visit took place on 26 October 1857.[70] A number of newspapers reported on "rejoicings at Westport—with bonfires, gay and brilliant illuminations—when Lady Sligo returned from England in late October. Her ladyship's former acts of benevolence and Christian charity in this locality has endeared her name to a grateful people."[71] Despite her residency in England, Lady Sligo remained loyal to her roots and spent the last years of her life participating in fund raising for charity events in the west of Ireland. She continued to be a patroness for the Annual Bazaar & Drawing of Prizes in Aid of the Charities of the Sisters of Mercy, Castlebar and the Annual Bazaar & Drawing of Prizes for the Relief of the Poor under the Sisters of Mercy, Westport, Committee for the Erection of an Orphanage at the Railway Hotel, Westport and for the Sisters of Charity.[72] The Sisters of Mercy acknowledged her contribution to the events by thanking her, the most noble Marchioness of Sligo, for the exquisitely inlaid casket and valuable inkstand that she donated as prizes to be won.[73] Nor was she alone in supporting the activities of Catholic charities, as her son continued to donate thus carrying on a family tradition.[74] Unfortunately, by the 1870s, it appears that no members of the Sligo family were living in Westport House. Following the receipt of a number of threatening letters and a gun being stolen from the estate, the Marquis decided to leave Ireland, a decision lamented in the local press "on account of his high and noble qualities."[75]

Hester Catherine de Burgh Browne, Dowager Marchioness of Sligo, died on 17 February 1878, at the age of 78, at her home at 16 Mansfield Street, London. Her health had been in decline prior to her demise but little is known about the exact cause of death.[76] She was buried in the family vault at Kensal-Green cemetery in London, following a funeral service "of the simplest character."[77] The discovery of Lady Sligo's letters, which had been separated from the rest of the family papers, provide an insight into how one family dealt with the crisis of the Great Hunger. They also show the agency of women, the role of the big house during a famine, the complex choices facing a landlord who wanted to assist his tenants, and the relationship of Irish elites with the government in Westminster. It is also clear that George took his duties as an Irish representative in the British Parliament seriously.[78] The recently discovered collection of Sligo Letters held at Quinnipiac University has allowed a more nuanced view of the family's involvement in famine relief to emerge.

Lady Sligo's enduring legacy was the survival of an untold number of tenants, which was made possible through her multiple generous acts of kindness and the sense of duty that she instilled in her son.[79] The family and the estate survived the Great Hunger largely intact, but fractious relations between tenants and landlords in the decades that followed led them to leave their Mayo home. Lady Sligo's name and benevolence were lost for over a century. Through her letters, she now has been rediscovered as the matriarch who rolled up her finely pressed linen sleeves and ensured the Browne family would help alleviate the suffering of those most afflicted by the Great Hunger.

NOTES

1. *Westport House and the Launch of the Great Famine Exhibition*. Mayo Matters. Irish TV. Westport, Co. Mayo, Ireland, 23 November 2020.
2. Aine Ryan, "Westport House puts famine letters on show," *Mayo News*, 21 April 2015.
3. Christine Kinealy, "The Lady Sligo Letters." 2015: https://youtu.be/vc2lCub5M0Y
4. Anne Anderson was the first woman to occupy this position.
5. Simon Carswell, "Famine exhibit sheds new light on women's role; Letters by Lady Sligo contradict 'simple narrative' regarding landlords," *Irish Times*, 3 May 2014.
6. Caroline Gannon, "The Women of Westport House," BA dissertation (Galway-Mayo Institute of Technology, 2015), p. 19.
7. Anne Chambers, *The Great Leviathan: The Life of Howe Peter Browne, 2nd Marquess of Sligo, 1788-1845* (Dublin, New Island, 2017), p. 126.
8. Private Business—The Altamont (Amendment of Deed of Trust) Bill, 1990, Second Stage, *Seanad Éireann debate*, 21 November 1990, at: www.oireachtas.ie/en/debates/debate/seanad/1990-11-21/7/
9. Gannon, "The Women of Westport House," p. 19.
10. See Sandy Letourneau O'Hare and Robert A. Young Jr., "Lady Sligo and her letters: the mounting of an inaugural exhibition," in Christine Kinealy, Jason King, and Ciaran Reilly (eds), *Women and the Great Hunger* (Hamden, CT: Quinnipiac University Press and Cork University Press, 2017), pp 193-199.
11. Ryan, "Westport House puts famine letters on show."
12. Gannon, "The Women of Westport House," p. 18.
13. Chambers, *The Great Leviathan*, p. 127.
14. Christine Kinealy, *Daniel O'Connell and the Anti-Slavery Movement* (London: Pickering and Chatto, 2011), pp 32-33.
15. Quoted in A. Peckover, *Life of Joseph Sturge* (London: Swan Sonnenschein and Co., 1890), p. 19.
16. Kinealy, *Daniel O'Connell*, pp 53-56.
17. Hibernian Anti-Slavery Society, *Address of the Hibernian Anti-Slavery Society to the People of Ireland*, 18 September 1837 (Dublin, 1837), pp 1-2.

18. Anne Chambers, Mike Bunn, and Noel Kissane, "The Westport House Document Collection," *Irish Arts Review* 19, no. 1 (2002), pp 106-113.

19. "Westport Estate Papers," *National Library of Ireland,* 14 December 2020, p. 478.

20. Anne Chambers, "Champion of the Slaves—: Howe Peter Browne, 2nd Marquess of Sligo (1788–1845)," *History Ireland*, 26, no. 1 (2018), pp 22-24.

21. Gannon, "The Women of Westport House," p. 23.

22. Lady Sligo Letters, Arnold Bernhard Library (ABL), Quinnipiac University.

23. Ibid., H. Catherine Sligo to George Hildebrand, 4 January [1845] (Folder 20).

24. Ibid., H. Catherine Sligo to George Hildebrand, n.d. (Folder 2).

25. Clodagh Finn, "An Irishwoman s Diary," *Irish Times*, 29 September 2014.

26. O'Hare and Young, "Lady Sligo and her letters," pp 193-199.

27. H. Catherine Sligo to George Hildebrand, n.d. (ABL, Lady Sligo Letters, Folder 29).

28. H. Catherine Sligo to George Hildebrand, 21 May 1845 (ABL, Lady Sligo Letters, Folder 44)

29. H. Catherine Sligo to George Hildebrand, 15 March 1846 (ABL, Lady Sligo Letters, Folder 17).

30. "The Late Homicide near Westport," *Kerry Evening Post*, 25 March 1826.

31. H. Catherine Sligo to George Hildebrand, 4 December (ABL, Lady Sligo Letters, Folder 24).

32. O'Hare and Young, "Lady Sligo and her letters," pp 193-199.

33. H. Catherine Sligo to George Hildebrand, 22 October 1845 (ABL, Lady Sligo Letters, Folder 3)

34. Conor Kenny, *The Famine in Mayo: A View from the Big House* (Galway, n.d., n.p.).

35. H. Catherine Sligo to George Hildebrand, 14 January [1846] (ABL, Lady Sligo Letters, Folder 34).

36. Ibid.

37. Christine Kinealy, *Charity and the Great Hunger in Ireland: The Kindness of Strangers* (London: Bloomsbury, 2013), p. 161.

38. "Benevolent Act of Marchioness of Sligo," *Mayo Constitution*, 19 January 1847.

39. Gannon, "The Women of Westport House," p. 28.

40. Kinealy, *Charity and the Great Hunger*, p. 160.

41. Peadar Ó Flanágain, "An outline history of the town of Westport, part iv: The famine years and its aftermath, 1845-55" in *Cathair na Mart* (Journal of the Westport Historical Society), vol. iv (1986), p. 75.

42. Count Strzelecki, Westport, 15 March 1847, *Report of the British Relief Association for the Relief of Extreme Distress in Ireland and Scotland* (London: Richard Clay, 1849).

43. For details of populations changes see, "All-Island Research Observatory," Maynooth University at: http://airo.maynoothuniversity.ie/external-content/table-1-population-county-1841-2011.

44. Gannon, "The Women of Westport House," p. 27.

45. Kenny, *A View from the Big House*.

46. Kinealy, "The Lady Sligo Letters," 2015: https://youtu.be/vc2lCub5M0Y

47. Ó Flanágain, "Outline history of the town of Westport", p. 76.

48. John O'Rourke, *The History of the Great Irish Famine of 1847: With Notices of Earlier Irish Famines* (Dublin: J. Duffy and Sons, third ed., 1902), p. 228.

49. Christine Kinealy, "'The Widow's Mite:' Private Relief during the Great Famine." *History Ireland*, 16, no. 2 (2008): pp 40-45.

50. Christine Kinealy, "Why the forgotten Irish women who suffered and shaped events during the Famine have been ignored," *Irish Post*, 14 April 2017.

51. London *Times*, 17 December 1847.

52. "Lord and Lady Russell," *Limerick Chronicle*, 2 September 1848.

53. "Guide to the archives of the Poor Law," The National Archives of Ireland, at: www.nationalarchives.ie/article/guide-archives-poor-law/

54. James Hack Tuke, *A visit to Connaught in the autumn of 1847: a letter addressed to the Central Relief Committee of the Society of Friends, Dublin* (London: Charles Gilpin, 1848). Tuke, along with a number of fellow Quakers, had first travelled to Mayo in late 1846.

55. Ivor Hamrock (ed.), *The Famine in Mayo: A Portrait from Contemporary Sources 1845-1850* (Castlebar: Mayo County Council, 2004), p. 96.

56. "Westport Estate Papers," *National Library of Ireland*, 14 December 2020, p. 327.

57. Ibid., p. 512.

58. *Annual Report of Poor Law Commissioners for Ireland with Appendices* (Dublin: HMSO, 1848), p. 12.

59. Chambers, Bunn and Kissane, "The Westport House Document Collection," pp 106-13.

60. Kinealy, *Charity and the Great Hunger,* p. 53; Lord Sligo to Monteagle, 8 October 1848 (NLI, Monteagle papers, Ms. 13,400 (2)).

61. See letter in Joseph Hone, *The Moores of Moore Hall* (London: Jonathan Cape, 1939), pp 158-60.

62. *Correspondence from July 1846 to January 1847 relating to the measures adopted for the relief of the distress in Ireland (Commissariat Series),* BPP, 1847 [159-161], LI.

63. Kenny, *A View from the Big House.*

64. "Election Unrest," *Galway Mercury, and Connaught Weekly Advertiser*, 13 February 1847.

65. Ibid.

66. Finn, "An Irishwoman's Diary," *Irish Times*, 29 September 2014.

67. Gannon, "The Women of Westport House," p. 29.

68. Ibid., p. 29.

69. "The Wrongs of Pauperty," *Dublin Weekly Nation*, 12 April 1851.

70. "An Irish Cead Mille Failthe [sic]," *Connaught Telegraph*, 28 October 1857; "Rejoicings at Westport House," *Tuam Herald,* 31 October 1857.

71. Ibid.

72. "Bazaar for the house of refuge," *Freeman's Journal*, 30 May 1857.

73. Gannon, "The Women of Westport House," p. 29.

74. "Acknowledgement," *Freeman's Journal*, 30 August 1869.

75. "Editorial," *Mayo Constitution*, 1 May 1871.

76. "Deaths," *Yorkshire Post and Leeds Intelligencer,*" 20 February 1878; *Belfast News-Letter,* 21 February 1878; *Weekly Irish Times,* 23 February 1878; "Obituary of Eminent Persons," *Illustrated London News,* 23 February 1878. The papers gave her age as 76 and a number said she was Howe Peter's second wife.

77. "Obituary of Eminent Persons," *Illustrated London News*, 23 February 1878.

78. In addition to attending to his duties in the House of Lords, George was an active participant in meetings of Irish members in London, see, *Galway Mercury, and Connaught Weekly Advertiser,* 13 February 1847.

79. Clodagh Finn, "Battle to save Westport House," *Irish Independent,* 20 October 2015.

CHAPTER FIVE

MARY ANN McCRACKEN OF BELFAST (1770–1866)

"Better to wear out than to rust out."[1]

Peter Murphy

What characteristics or qualities make someone a hero? Throughout history there have been untold numbers of heroic people, such as Achilles in Homer's *Iliad* or the comic-book hero, Superman, but many were real-life persons who performed single heroic acts, or lived lives of quiet heroism, devoted to helping those less fortunate. Mary Ann McCracken of Belfast falls into the latter category. In a life span that, by any standard, was long—she dying aged 96—McCracken was engaged in a variety of important political and social causes, namely, supporting the United Irishmen during the 1798 and 1803 Rebellions; championing women's and children's rights; promoting education; preserving Ireland's musical heritage; ending the use of young boys as chimney sweeps; working to abolish slavery; and feeding and clothing the hungry and destitute during the Great Famine. From an early age, McCracken learned the lessons of equality, compassion, and empathy and the importance of helping others who were less fortunate. "Mary Ann was making clothes for the children of the Poor House when she was little more than a child herself."[2] She spent her life applying what she was taught in school and what she learned from the examples her middle-class Presbyterian family put forth. Always unconventional, in her early 20s McCracken persuaded her older sister Margaret to join her in a muslin business—an unusual venture for women.[3] Sadly, McCracken's life is frequently overshadowed by her beloved brother Henry's martyrdom, yet an objective analysis of her lifetime of heroic sacrifices and commitments place her among some of the most remarkable and enduring figures in Ireland's long history.

Mary Ann McCracken was born in Belfast in 1770 to John and Ann Joy McCracken, the second youngest of seven children. John was a ship captain who was described as "a man of polished manners, whose sincerity of disposition and integrity of principles caused him to be generally respected and esteemed."[4] In a day when ship captains and sailors augmented their income by engaging in smuggling, John McCracken would have none of that. He regarded a "custom-house oath as binding on conscience as any other."[5] One of the McCracken's sons, Henry Joy, played a leading role in the rebellion of 1798 as a founding member of the United Irishmen. Mary Ann McCracken was particularly close to Henry, whom she referred to as Harry.

Besides the influence of her extended family, McCracken's education was unusual. While boys were learning the three "Rs" and the classics, girls were given "elementary academic instruction provided by one or two impecunious ladies ... augmented by classes in sewing, knitting and embroidery."[6] This traditional approach did not suffice for families such as the McCrackens, who believed in a more enlightened approach to education. They sent Mary Ann McCracken to be taught by David Manson, a highly respected teacher in Belfast, who believed that young ladies should receive the same extensive education as the young gentlemen.[7] He was the author of a dictionary, known as "Manson's Spelling Book" and his advertisements for his school stated that he "teacheth by way of amusement, English Grammar, Reading and Spelling at moderate expense."[8] As her biographer, Mary McNeill, wrote, "such was the person from whom Mary Ann received her formal schooling, and the place where her subsequently advanced views on education were no doubt nurtured."[9]

Another important influence for McCracken was the eighteenth-century writer, philosopher and early feminist, Mary Wollstonecraft (1759-1797).[10] In 1792, Wollstonecraft wrote her controversial book *A Vindication of the Rights of Women*, in which she proposed that women and men be granted equal opportunities in education, business and politics. By her early twenties, McCracken was practicing what Wollstonecraft had encouraged: an "emphasis on sturdiness and energy as opposed to insipid feminine charms."[11] Further, McCracken was an educated woman who was running a business, followed politics closely and caring for those less fortunate, again adhering to Wollstonecraft's words:

> Women might certainly study the art of healing ... they might also study politics, and settle the benevolence on the broadest basis ... business of various kinds, they might likewise pursue, if they are educated in a more orderly manner.[12]

McCracken and her sister Margaret's motivation for starting a business was not financial, as they were from an affluent family, but instead "drew on a tradition of radical

Protestant dissent that identified industry with virtue, and as a religious, moral, and civic obligation."[13] McCracken's views on the women of Dublin society were somewhat cynical and condescending. In a letter to her brother Harry in Kilmainham Gaol in March 1797, she explained:

> I have a great curiosity to visit some female societies in this Town ... I wish to know if they have any rational ideas of liberty and equality for themselves or whether they are contented with their present abject and dependent situation, degraded by custom and education and beneath the rank in society in which they were originally placed.[14]

Wollstonecraft's treatise has been described as a "major attack on the eighteenth-century cult of femininity."[15] Mary Ann McCracken, as described by her niece, was the antithesis of this constructed view of femininity: "in personal habits she was scrupulously clean, but indifferent about her dress, unwilling to spend money on it, and gave it little thought."[16]

By the late 1700s, Belfast, indeed much of Ulster, had become the "undisputed thinking center of Ireland. Thomas Paine's *The Rights of Man* had created a new philosophy and the radical ideas set in motion created a political ferment that has yet to cease."[17] A nineteenth-century historian later noted that Belfast inhabitants "were most energetic in endeavoring to secure ... representatives pledged to do their utmost to obtain their desires" and that "reared amid such influences, McCracken was from her early years intensely interested in politics."[18] The French Revolution, following less than a generation after the American Revolution, inspired many on the island. Many felt that the persecution and oppression of Catholics was morally wrong. There was also a widespread interest in the writings of philosophers such as Locke and Rousseau. There is little doubt that McCracken shared many of her brother's egalitarian ideals.[19]

In July 1798, the Battle of Antrim was fought between British troops and Irish insurgents led by Henry Joy McCracken. The Irish rebels were defeated and many, including McCracken, fled to the hills. Mary Ann McCracken searched for her brother for days in order to supply him with money and clothes so he could attempt an escape to America. He was recognized before he could make it to the coast to board a ship. In the weeks following the defeat at Antrim, Henry was captured, tried and executed. Mary Ann McCracken, devoted to her brother to the very end, walked him to the gallows, before she was ushered away by the authorities. After she was given his lifeless body, she asked a doctor to see if her brother could be revived, but the effort was to no avail. Before his execution, Harry told his sister that he had an illegitimate daughter, Maria, who Mary Ann McCracken agreed to raise as her own

(McCracken never married and she never bore children). Maria remained with her for the rest of her life, and cared for her in her dotage. Mary Ann would later recall of raising Maria that "Good indeed to us came out of evil. That child became to us a treasure. My brother Frank and I would now be a desolate old couple without her."[20]

In the following decades, McCracken became involved in several charitable endeavors. In 1808, she was one of the founding members of the Belfast Harp Society, which had been established "primarily, to provide blind boys and girls with the means of earning a living by teaching them the harp; secondarily, to promote the study of the Irish language, history, and antiquities."[21] It was also part of a cultural revival of Irish traditional music. Among the other 190 subscribers who raised 284 guineas were Henry Joy, Dr. William Drennan, John Templeton, and the music collector, Edward Bunting. McCracken helped Edward Bunting assemble a treasure trove of traditional songs and lyrics and she contributed anonymously to the second volume of his work *The Ancient Music of Ireland* in 1809. Bunting, who resided with the McCrackens for more than three decades before moving to Dublin in 1809, was named the first Director of the Harp Society.[22] This first iteration of the Harp Society lasted only six years, as financial difficulties forced it to close.

In 1815, with Ireland mired in a financial difficulties, Mary Ann McCracken and Margaret made the difficult decision to close their muslin business. Mary Ann McCracken's concern, as always, was for others, she fretting over the welfare of her employees. She would write later that, "I could not think of dismissing our workers, because nobody would give them employment, and then we could not tell when a revival should take place, what would be most required."[23] Her concern for factory hygiene and conditions had been expressed in an anonymous letter written in 1803 to the *Belfast News-Letter*:

> The passages, stairs, floors and inner doors should be constantly kept clean...As much air as is convenient should be allowed into the rooms both day and night ... workers ought to be provided with warm coats and cloaks so as to be protected against the evil effects of wet and cold ... A very serious responsibility attaches to those who employ children; for if the morals of children become depraved, from what sources are we to procure virtuous men and virtuous women?[24]

In a letter to an anonymous recipient, she wrote: "I trust that the little which we got by my dear mother will enable us to pay all we owe, which is a great comfort, even if we should have nothing left."[25]

In the years following the closing of her business, McCracken's life shifted in direction and she devoted more time to charitable work: "She saw a road opening up before her where political weapons would be of little account, but along which she could work effectively for the ideals she never ceased to cherish; she was, in fact, on the threshold of her career as a pioneer social reformer."[26] The Belfast Charitable Society was originally set up to house an infirmary and a poorhouse. The poorhouse mission included training adults for occupations such as spinning and knitting for the women and oakum picking for the men. McCracken and the others found ways to occasionally circumvent the more formal process of asking for approval, including finding suitable employment for the girls. They formed a committee to oversee the female portion of the poorhouse, including training the resident girls in a skill, such as straw plaiting or tambouring, whereby they could obtain a livelihood. McCracken was given 30 shillings to purchase various items for the girls. She soon became treasurer for the committee, further adding to her responsibilities. They also arranged for the girls to apprentice in private homes for a few hours a day to learn housework. Throughout her years at the society, and serving on the Ladies' Committee, McCracken's "sympathetic understanding of the needs of little children…was not merely a question of having the children taught, or even 'minded', it was their training, their education in the widest sense, and their happiness that was at stake."[27]

First and foremost, McCracken's primary devotion was to the poor and destitute children in Belfast and the surrounding towns. One of her ideas was to establish an infant (nursery) school, which was initially met with a denial from the Men's Committee, who told her that there were no funds or time. McCracken bided her time and then, a few months later, made a second request. Again, she was turned down. Instead of asking a third time, she and her committee simply opened a school. With the school a *fait accompli*, she asked the men to "aid them in completing what they have commenced."[28] A school for children was established, as the children of the poor received little or no formal education. She insisted on hiring teachers of the highest quality and providing fair pay. With all that McCracken had been through in her life, there was "something unusually touching in the sincerity and success with which she championed the needs of the very young child."[29]

The Ladies' Committee advocated for cleaner facilities and sleeping conditions, including clean bedding and two sheets on each bed. Bugs and infectious diseases were commonplace and according to the minutes, "it is impossible otherwise to eradicate any infectious disease, as the infection remains in the Blankets, which cannot be so easily or so frequently washed as Sheets."[30] McCracken was direct in her approach to solving problems and rarely minced her words. The committee meetings' minutes were all written by her and she knew what the children or the facility needed, such as the time she noted that "the Ladies … recommend that sunblinds should be put up without delay in the children's hospitals. Some of them have very sore eyes & many are ill in measles whose eyes are consequently weak."[31] Another innovation in education that McCracken promulgated was that the children should have some sort of physical activity during the day, an idea that she learned from David Manson, her childhood teacher. She requested that poles be put in the yard for the children to play on.

In 1845, a blight (*Phytophthora infestans*) struck the potato crop in Ireland and in other regions of Europe. On 9 September 1845, the *Dublin Evening Post* reported that "within the last ten days, we have again had communications...stating that the disease had made its appearance, and the whole of the crops in the neighborhoods were rapidly perishing from the "rot."[32] The effect in 1845 was somewhat minimized by the blight's late arrival but the impact in 1846 was an almost complete destruction of the potato crop.[33] The Great Famine lasted from 1845 to 1852 and decimated the island's population.[34] As one historian has noted, the Famine has become an integral part of folk legend and "in the popular imagination, the Famine is associated with nationwide suffering, initially triggered by the potato blight, compounded by years of misrule and consolidated by the inadequate response of the British government and Irish landlords alike."[35] It seems more likely that the response from Westminster was a result of a policy based on *laissez-faire* capitalism. While the official response was lacking, the initiatives taken by individuals, associations, charitable organizations, churches, and even Native Americans, raised millions of dollars and resulted in tons of clothing being donated from around the world.[36] A considerable amount of money was sent from people who had no direct connection with Ireland. The British Relief Association for the Relief of Distress in Ireland received over £400,000, while Her Majesty, Queen Victoria, donated £2,000, making her the single largest donor.[37]

While many accounts of the Great Hunger focus on its deadly impact on the west of the country, no part of Ireland escaped from its ravages, including the town of Belfast.[38] By the mid-1840s, Belfast was under-going rapid industrialization, mostly associated with linen, but increasingly with shipbuilding. In the districts surrounding Belfast, there was an extensive domestic textile industry. All these industries depended on the availability of cheap and nutritious food in the form of potatoes.[39] The repeated failures of this crop exposed the delicate balance between town and countryside in Ireland, even in areas considered to be affluent. Unfortunately, the potato failures coincided with a trade depression and credit crisis throughout the United Kingdom, which resulted in the loss of employment and a reduction in wages for many employed in manufacture. By early October 1845, blight was appearing in areas adjoining Belfast, such as Holywood, causing some alarm in the local press.[40] The *Vindicator*, a supporter of Daniel O'Connell, suggested that the wealthy in the town should prepare for the coming shortages by purchasing food and selling it at reduced prices to the poor. More radical was the proposition that the government should intervene in the market-place and close local distilleries and that "the sliding scale and every other impediment to the free ingress of food should be at once removed for, if famine be added to the inflictions of bad laws, the result may be dangerous indeed."[41] The more conservative *Northern Whig*, however, urged against "needless alarm," on the grounds that it would "operate injuriously upon the commercial interest of the country."[42]

While districts in the west of Ireland grabbed the international headlines in 1846 and 1847, the poor in the north east of Ireland were also suffering. As early as March 1846, in the Ballymacarrett townland in Belfast, which was one of the most industrialized areas in the north of the country and one that was almost exclusively Protestant, 1,000 people were unemployed and "experiencing the most severe privation."[43] The *Banner of Ulster* warned: "The people are in absolute want, in absolute danger of starvation, perhaps before another week, unless effective relief be procured."[44] Shortly after this report, relief committees were formed in Belfast, to purchase food for resale.[45] Despite the existence of widespread hunger in the town, a number of local newspapers and elites continued to downplay it. As the *Vindicator* explained:

> The distress in Ballymacarrett was the first cry of want that unhinged the fine philosophy that would starve the poor for the honour of the rich ... to disturb the composure of those who hate distress because it is a disgrace to the province and wonder that persons will not be content to linger, sigh and die in silence, rather that sully the credit of Ulster.[46]

The reappearance of the blight in 1846—with its associated crop failure, trade depression, and influx of people from the surrounding countryside seeking employment, relief, or a means to emigrate—again impacted severely on Belfast. As early as October, the town's streets were "crowded with a greater number of paupers than at any time within our recollection."[47] In response, private soup kitchens were opened, which either sold food at a reduced rate or provided it for free—an option disliked by both the government and local elites.[48] At this stage, several private relief committees were formed throughout Ireland, the largest one being formed by the Society of Friends in Dublin in November. The work of these charitable bodies was supported and underpinned by the involvement of women throughout the country.

In Belfast, a number of charitable bodies were founded, including at least three by women, namely the Belfast Ladies' Association for the Relief of Irish Destitution, the Belfast Ladies' Society for the Relief of Local Distress and the Belfast Ladies'

Association for the Relief of Destitution in Connaught. Although each proclaimed that they were non-sectarian, the Connaught Association was increasingly regarded as being involved in covert attempts at proselytism in the west of Ireland.[49] McCracken was a founder of the Belfast Ladies' Association for the Relief of Irish Destitution. Their first meeting was on 1 January 1847, in the Commercial Buildings and consisted of women of all religious denominations; their aim was "to sink all doctrinal distinctions for one benevolent purpose of alleviating distress and preventing starvation without considering the religious denomination of those to be relieved."[50] Several committees were formed, including one for clothing, which McCracken served on, as well as the Collecting Committee.[51] She became one of the most "ardent" collector of funds and, at the age of 77, "threw herself with her accustomed energy into this practical expression of sorrow."[52] One of the methods that she employed to raise money was through publicly-attended lectures. A talk on Shakespeare held in the public library, given by a Mr. Vandenhoff, raised £76.[53] Because conditions in the west of Ireland appeared worse, the Association's efforts were initially directed there, but it became increasingly "clear that there was famine elsewhere, even in industrial towns such as Belfast, and so their involvement became nationwide."[54]

The funds that McCracken helped procure were distributed both within Belfast, as well as to places as far away as Roscommon, Cork and Dingle. The *Belfast News-Letter* reported that £10 were distributed to Mr. John Minnows, the secretary of the relief committee, Tempe, Roscommon; to Thos. Kelly, relief committee in County Galway; and to relief committees in Dingle, Connemara, County Cork, and many other corners of famine-torn Ireland.[55] A considerable amount of clothing was also sent to numerous relief committees. McCracken would go and collect and distribute donations, but she once told her niece the "ladies would not let her visit, for she would give too much, and would tell of cases in which she had been imposed upon. It was a hard trial for her to refuse any who seemed in distress."[56] Asenath Nicholson, an American visitor to Ireland, admired how hard the women in Belfast worked at helping the poor. She described McCracken as "indefatigable."[57]

Another fund-raising event that the committee utilized was a bazaar in Belfast at Easter in the Spring of 1847. An advertisement in the *Belfast News-Letter*, as well as the *Northern Whig*, featured:

> A proposal to hold a Bazaar of Ladies' work ... in aid of the funds of the association... all who take interest in the cause of the suffering poor of our land will, it is hoped, contribute, to the utmost of their ability ... but all will encourage the Committee in their attempt to relieve, as far as possible those who are bowed by the heavy hand of famine.[58]

The local newspapers took notice of their efforts and praised their hard work. The *Northern Whig* editorialized that "it is altogether unnecessary for us to claim, for the ladies engaged in this work, the respect and homage of every man and woman who has a heart to feel for our suffering fellow-creatures ... we cannot adequately express the feelings of grateful respect which we entertain to those ladies of Belfast ... who have laboured to relieve human suffering."[59] When Nicholson arrived in Belfast in July 1847, she noted that "women were at work; and no one could justly say that they were dilatory or inefficient. Never in Ireland, since the famine, was such a happy combination of all parties, operating so harmoniously together, as was here manifested."[60]

One of McCracken's greatest contributions to the welfare of the poor was in education. She told her niece that:

> I have been visiting the Lancasterian School for the last twenty-five years, generally once a-week, and I find the children taught there for the last two or three years much better acquainted with the Scriptures than the scholars of any former period.[61]

McCracken had been intimately involved in establishing an infant (nursery) school years previously through her tenacity in dealing with a reluctant Men's Committee. At the urging of John Edgar, moderator of the Presbyterian Church of Ireland, industrial schools were established to teach poor and destitute females how to earn their income. After extensive travel throughout Connaught and witnessing the overwhelming poverty from the Famine, Edgar returned to Belfast to raise awareness and money. Upon his return, he gave a speech at the May Street Presbyterian Church where he decried the idea that the poor were lazy, a common misconception at the time:

> It is a libel, therefore, on the poor Irishman to say that he is too lazy or too savage to seek for better food than potatoes; his only nourishment is potatoes, because the other products of his farm go to his landlord.[62]

By the end of 1846, Edgar and his followers had established 144 schools, mostly in the western counties of Mayo and Sligo.[63]

The Ladies' Industrial School was established in 1847, with the then 77-year-old McCracken very much involved. In every annual report published by the school, her name was mentioned and she was given the position of president, a title she held until her death.[64] Nicholson described the women and how they found the students. She wrote: "the highways and hedges were faithfully visited, the poor sought out, their condition cared for, and the children of the most degraded class were taken and placed in a school."[65] Another paper noted that the "formation of schools of industry marked such another change in moral means...it infused hope into what seemed previously to be hopelessness, and actively wrought well everywhere to rear an intelligent, a moral, and an industrious generation from the residium of society—from its depth of poverty."[66] In a lengthy article entitled, "Reproductive Pauperism—The Industrial Schools of Belfast," the *Belfast News-Letter* gave an in-depth overview of the Industrial School. In referring to McCracken and the others, it noted the "warm and expanding benevolence of a few individuals looked out upon this wide field of nascent tares and poisons and resolved to reclaim it." The paper went on to point out the benefits to the local community:

> For two years past, there has been in existence, in this town, an industrial asylum for the children paupers who used to infest our streets by day and night—the annoyance and even terror of our shopkeepers—the employees of the abandoned and vile—the apt learners of every species of vice and profligacy which could render them future denizens of our jails. The industrial schools, under the management of a committee of ladies, were established, and have since continued in active operation. [67]

Some of the approximately 160 children, who were divided roughly equally by gender, were taught sewing, weaving, knitting, and how to tease hair, while others learned to read, write and to "cast accounts." They receive two meals a day, generally consisting of Indian meal stirabout and buttermilk. The benefit was that "many of the youths who, in this institution, learned a profitable and respectable trade, are now supporting themselves in various establishments in town." The results are "clean, healthy, active, intelligent, quiet (young adults); most of them about to become valuable members of society." The article pointed out that the students, upon finishing, were expected to "labour, assist in their own support, and cease to be paupers."[68] Nicholson observed that:

> This school has the benefit of being taught the elementary branches of an education, and the most useful needlework and knitting; and the squalid looks of the children were soon exchanged for health, and that indifference to appearance which the hungry, neglected poor soon wear, was, like magic almost, transformed into a becoming tidiness and self-respect.[69]

In March 1850, a meeting of the patrons and subscribers of the school held a meeting. The scene, as described in the *Belfast News-Letter*, consisted of the schoolchildren at one end of the room, seated on benches, "all clean and well-looking, and in the body was assembled a large concourse of ladies, to whose generous efforts owes its organization."[70] The Lord Bishop of Down, Connor and Dromore was invited to make some remarks. He expressed his support for "this valuable institution." He spoke for a time directly to the children when he urged them to "show their thankfulness for this institution by their careful attention and diligence" and that they should "listen with respect and attention to the mistresses set over them." He went on to say that the students "owed a deep debt of gratitude to those ladies who spend some portion of their time every day in inspecting that school." Dr. Malcolm, another subscriber, said the school "was one of those good things that came out of the famine and pestilence of 1847 – a year that will be remembered for a long time in this country."[71]

McCracken advocated for other causes as she approached her 80th birthday. She was part of a committee set up in Belfast to abolish the use of so-called "chimney boys" in chimney sweeping. There were several health risks attached to this dangerous occupation, including cancer caused by the soot and creosote in the chimney. The boys were often in the chimney when fires were lit, causing them to burn or suffocate. Because the difficult and arduous task required someone of a small size to fit in the narrow flutes, boys as young as five or six were often sent up the chimneys. McCracken was a lifelong opponent of slavery, dating back to her younger days. She refused to use sugar as it was produced with slave labor. Frederick Douglass's visit to Belfast in 1845 and 1846 led to the formation of a Ladies' Anti-Slavery Committee, of which McCracken was an active member. They worked closely with the women abolitionists in Boston.[72] In a letter to Dr. Richard Madden in 1859, she wrote that she was "both ashamed and sorry to think that Belfast has so far degenerated in regard to the Anti-Slavery cause."[73] In another letter to Madden she said of America: "the land of the great, the brave, may more properly be styled the land of the tyrant and the Slave."[74] Even in her late 80s, she could be seen on the docks of Belfast, "the little frail, bent figure, standing by the gangway with her leaflets as the jostling crowds made their way on board: it was the only service she could still render to the cause of liberty, that dominating passion of her life."[75] Until her age caught up with her and she was limited physically, she could be found visiting schools and communicating extensively with Madden as he wrote his history of the United Irishmen.

Mary Ann McCracken's life should be remembered for the self-sacrifice, courage, selflessness, determination and strength that she displayed continuously for nearly a century. In a letter to Madden in her late 80s, she wrote that "this world affords no enjoyment equal to that of promoting the happiness of others, it so far surpasses mere selfish gratification from its not only being pleasant at the time but from affording agreeable recollections afterwards."[76] At her passing, the Industrial School noted in its annual report that:

> We must record this year the death of a beloved friend and associate in our work, Miss M'Cracken, who was connected with the school from its foundation, and

whose place was never vacant at our weekly meetings as long as she was able to attend. We know not how to speak of the worth that no words can express, and the loss too little felt, perhaps because it came so gradually. But though the loss may never be repaired, we trust she has left a precious legacy that will never perish from this place of her habituation, in the memory of a life so rich in all good works, and a spirit so full of love. When we would think of 'those things that are pure, and lovely, and of good report', let us remember her who was so long among us, her ardent charity, her large and tender sympathy, her sweet humility and self-forgetfulness.[77]

Today, she lies in the shadow of the poorhouse and has bequeathed to her birthplace a legacy of unusual nobility and courage.[78] Belatedly, her life of altruism is receiving the recognition that it deserves. In January 2021, a Mary Ann McCracken Foundation was launched by the Belfast Charitable Society, with her role as an abolitionist and as Henry's favorite sister being especially highlighted.[79] For many reasons, Mary Ann is a hero, not least of which was for her commitment to saving lives during the Great Hunger.

NOTES

1. This phrase was used on both sides of the Atlantic, but was attributed to Mary Ann McCracken in the archives of the Belfast Charitable Society: https://cliftonbelfast.com/mary-ann-mccracken-faithful-until-death-2/

2. The Belfast Charitable Society is the city's oldest charitable foundation and Clifton House is her oldest building still standing. See, Belfastcharitablesociety.com.

3. Mary McNeill, *The Life and Times of Mary Ann McCracken* (Newbridge, Co. Kildare: Irish Academic Press, 2019), p. 44.

4. Helena Walsh Concannon, *Women of Ninety-Eight* (Dublin: M.H. Gill & Son, 1919), pp 217-18. See also Anna McCleery, "Life of Mary Ann McCracken, Sister of Henry Joy McCracken," in R.M. Young (ed.), *Historical Notes of Old Belfast and Its Vicinity* (Belfast: Marcus Ward & Co., 1896), p. 178.

5. Ibid.

6. McNeill, *Mary Ann McCracken,* pp 31-32.

7. "The Life of David Manson," *The Belfast Monthly Magazine*, 28 February 1811, vol. 6, no. 31, pp 126-32.

8. Mary Lowry, *The Story of Belfast and Its Surroundings*, www.libraryireland.com.

9. McNeill, *Mary Ann McCracken,* p. 36.

10. The use of the word "feminist" does not appear until the late nineteenth-century. It began to be used more widely in France in the 1890s, and then principally as a synonym for women's emancipation. Karen Offen, "Defining Feminism: A Comparative Historical Approach," *Signs* 14, no. 1 (1988), pp 119-157. Wollstonecraft had two daughters, one of whom committed suicide in her twenties, and the other, the noted author Mary

Wollstonecraft Shelley, who was the author of *Frankenstein*. Wollstonecraft died, aged 38, ten days after giving birth to her daughter, Mary.

11. McNeill, *Mary Ann McCracken,* p. 94.

12. Mary Wollstonecraft, *A Vindication of the Rights of Woman* (London: Walter Scott, 1897) pp 208-09.

13. Nancy Curtin, "Women and Eighteenth-Century Irish Republicanism," in Margaret MacCurtin and Mary O'Dowd (eds), *Women in Early Modern Ireland* (Edinburgh: Edinburgh University Press, 1991), p. 141.

14. Mary Ann McCracken to Henry Joy McCracken c/o Kilmainham Gaol (Public Record Office of Northern Ireland, T.1210/1-46/7), quoted in Priscilla Metscher, "Mary Ann McCracken: A Critical Ulsterwoman within the Context of Her Times," *Etudes irlandaises*, no. 2, 1989, p. 148.

15. Margaret Walters, "The Rights and Wrongs of Women: Mary Wollstonecraft, Harriet Martineau, Simone de Beauvoir," in Anne Oakley and Juliet Mitchell (eds), *The Rights and Wrongs of Women* (London: Harmondsworth, 1976), pp 304-305.

16. McCleery, "Life of Mary Ann McCracken," p. 196.

17. Teresa Brogan, Review of "The Life and Times of Mary Ann McCracken," *Books Ireland*, no. 128, December 1988, pp 213-214.

18. McCleery "Life of Mary Ann McCracken," p. 180.

19. Christine Kinealy, *Charity and the Great Hunger in Ireland The Kindness of Strangers* (London: Bloomsbury, 2014), p. 146.

20. Richard R. Madden M.D., *The United Irishmen Their Lives and Times* (London: J. Madden Co., 1848, vol. II), p. 497. Mary Ann McCracken and Madden communicated extensively during the 1840s and 1850s when he was writing his history of the United Irishmen.

21. "Notes and Queries," *Ulster Journal of Archaeology*, 1, no. 4 (1895), pp 301-03.

22. Janet Harbison, "Bunting and the Belfast Harpers' Festival of 1792," *The Linen Hall Review,* vol. 3, no. 3 (Autumn, 1986), 23-25, p. 24.

23. Mary Ann McCracken to R.R. Madden, 22 February 1859, McCracken Letters, Trinity College, Dublin, Ms. 873/156; McNeill, *Mary Ann McCracken,* p. 233.

24. Anonymous letter to the *Belfast News-Letter*, 17 May 1803. Her biographer, Mary McNeill, attributed the letter to McCracken. McNeill, *Mary Ann McCracken,* pp 195-96.

25. McCracken letter, 1815, No recipient named, Young, p. 193.

26. McNeill, *Mary Ann McCracken,* p. 237.

27. Ibid., p. 259.

28. Belfast Charitable Society Archival Notes, at: https://cliftonbelfast.com/mary-ann-mccracken-her-first-battle-with-the-mens-committee-the-infant-school/.

29. McNeill, *Mary Ann McCracken,* p. 260.

30. Belfast Charitable Society, *Ladies' Committee Minutes*; McNeill, *Mary Ann McCracken*, p. 243.

31. *Minutes of the Ladies' Committee*, quoted in R.W.M Strain's "Address to The Ulster Medical Society," 13 November 1952, p. 51.

32. *Dublin Evening Post*, 9 September 1845.

33. Ciara Boylan, *"Famine,"* in Richard Bourke & Ian McBride, eds. *The Princeton History of Modern Ireland* (Princeton University Press, 2016), pp 407-08.

34. Benjamin Disraeli, *Lord George Bentinck. A Political Biography* (London: Archibald Constable, 1905), p. 258.

35. Christine Kinealy, *This Great Calamity. The Irish Famine 1845-52* (Boulder: Roberts Rinehart Publishers, 1995), p. 342.

36. The Choctaw Indians, who had been forced to resettle in Oklahoma in 1831 in a journey that became known as "The Trail of Tears", donated $170 to the cause of famine relief. See: Christine Kinealy, *A Death-Dealing Famine* (London: Pluto Press, 1997), p. 111.

37. Christine Kinealy, *Charity and the Great Hunger in Ireland The Kindness of Strangers*, p. 95.

38. See, for example, Christine Kinealy and Gerard MacAtasney, *The Hidden Famine. Poverty, Hunger and Sectarianism in Belfast, 1840-50* (London: Pluto Press, 2000).

39. Brenda Collins, "The Linen Industry and Emigration to Great Britain during the mid-Nineteenth Century," in E. Margaret Crawford (ed.) *The Hungry Stream. Essays on Emigration and Famine* (Belfast: Institute of Irish Studies, 1997), pp 156-157.

40. *Northern Whig*, 27 September 1845, 14 October 1845.

41. *Vindicator*, 15 October 1845, 1 October 1845.

42. *Northern Whig*, 21 October 1845, 1 October 1845.

43. *Banner of Ulster*, 27 March 1846.

44. Ibid.

45. Ibid., 3 April 1846, 10 April 1846.

46. *Vindicator*, 22 April 1846.

47. *News-Letter*, 27 October 1847.

48. *Banner of Ulster*, 20 November 1846, 11 December 1846.

49. For Belfast philanthropy. see Kinealy and MacAtasney, *Hidden Famine*, pp 109-38.

50. "Belfast Ladies' Association," *Belfast News-Letter*, 1 January 1847.

51. Asenath Nicholson, *Annals of the Famine in Ireland in 1847, 1848 and 1849* (New York: E. French, 1851), p. 73.

52. McNeill, *Mary Ann McCracken*, p. 281.

53. *Belfast News-Letter*, 5 March 1847; *Northern Whig*, 6 February 1847.

54. Christine Kinealy, "The Widow's Mite: Private Relief during the Great Famine," *History Ireland*, March-April, 2008, vol. 16, no. 2, pp 40-45.

55. *Belfast News-Letter*, 12 March 1847.

56. McCleery, *Life of Mary Ann McCracken*, p. 195.

57. Nicholson, *Annals of the Famine*, p. 76. See also chapter by Maureen Murphy.

58. *Belfast News-Letter*, 29 January 1847; *Northern Whig*, 26 January 1847.

59. *Northern Whig*, 9 March 1847.

60. Nicholson, *Annals of the Famine*, p. 72.

61. McCleery, *Life of Mary Ann McCracken*, p. 195.

62. W.D. Killen, *Memoir of John Edgar, DD, LL.D.* (Belfast: William Mullan, 1869), p. 211.

63. Rev. John Edgar (1798-1866) was an indefatigable reformer whose work in the west of Ireland was increasingly associated with "souperism" or proselytism, see, *Dictionary of Ulster Biography* at: www.newulsterbiography.co.uk/index.php/home/viewPerson/2007

64. Belfast Charitable Society Archival Notes, "Mary Ann McCracken: Faithful Until Death," July 2020.

65. Nicholson, *Annals of the Famine,* p. 73.
66. *Banner of Ulster*, 11 January 1848.
67. *Belfast News-Letter*, 5 December 1848.
68. Ibid.
69. Nicholson, *Annals of the Famine,* p. 73.
70. *Belfast News-Letter*, 29 March 1850.
71. *Belfast News-Letter*, 29 March 1850.
72. "Communications. Boston Female Anti-Slavery Society," *National Anti-Slavery Standard,* 16 April 1846.
73. Mary Ann McCracken to R.R. Madden, 2 August 1859, McCracken Letters, TCD, Ms. 873/83, quoted in McNeill, *Mary Ann McCracken,* p. 283.
74. Ibid., Mary Ann McCracken to R.R. Madden, 21 June 1859.
75. Ibid.
76. Ibid., Mary Ann McCracken to R.R. Madden, 13 November 1857, McCracken Letters, TCD, MS 873/70, p. 295.
77. McCleery, *Life of Mary Ann McCracken*, p. 195.
78. McNeill, *Mary Ann McCracken,* p. 295.
79. "Mary Ann McCracken: Belfast woman who fought slavery remembered," BBC News Northern Ireland, 23 January 2021, at: www.bbc.com/news/uk-northern-ireland-55752571

CHAPTER SIX

ASENATH NICHOLSON (1792–1855)

Heroine of Ireland's Great Hunger

Maureen Murphy

If you had lived in Ireland in 1847—possibly the most lethal year of the Great Famine—you might have encountered a middle-aged, middle-class American woman, traveling alone and mostly on foot throughout the country. As she walked, she often sang hymns. You may even have previously encountered this woman in 1844 or 1845, when she first visited. On that occasion, she came to Ireland to distribute Protestant religious tracts from the depths of her large, black bearskin muff. Her appearance and demeanor were unusual in other ways. She wore Indian rubber boots, a polka coat, a bonnet and, when they were not mislaid, silver-rimmed spectacles. On her face was a large wart, which she chose not to have removed. Her return to Ireland was prompted by her compassion for the Irish poor and her desire to provide them with relief. By doing so, she was putting her own health at risk. But this famine heroine was intrepid.[1]

The woman was Asenath Hatch Nicholson: teacher, reformer, abolitionist, writer and traveler who was born in Chelsea, a village in the White River Valley of eastern Vermont on 24 February 1782, to pioneering settlers Michael (c. 1747-1803) and Martha (Rice) Hatch (c.1748-1837). Her name, a popular Hatch name, was prophetic. It appeared in the Book of Genesis as the name of the daughter of an Egyptian high priest, Potiphera, who was from the city of On. Asenath was given by the pharaoh as a wife to Joseph.[2] She shared Joseph's life while he managed the food supply so that the Egyptians did not starve when famine came. Prophetically also, Joseph had predicted there would be seven years of famine.[3] Asenath Nicholson would face the Great Irish Famine and would devise her own plan to manage her resources to provide relief to the Irish poor. Nicholson's mother "remembered the poor and entertained strangers, hated oppression, scorned a mean act and dealt justly with all,"[4] and Asenath had come to Ireland to investigate the condition of the poor.[5] Nicholson's sympathy for the Irish was probably informed by the admonition, "Remember, my children, that the Irish are a suffering people and when they come to your doors never send them empty away."[6]

Nicholson's account of her travels, *Ireland's Welcome to the Stranger* (1847), is one of the most valuable records we have about Ireland on the eve of the Famine. She spent six months investigating conditions in rural Ireland before beginning her self-appointed mission: to bring the Bible to the Irish poor. She filled two bags with bibles supplied by the Hibernian Bible Society, attached the bags to a stout cord twisted under her polka coat and set off in her Indian rubber boots to distribute them to those who could read, and to read them herself to those who could not. Her mission was not as straight forward as it might appear. In fact, she moved in a kind of vacuum between the predominantly Catholic Irish poor, the Protestant Anglo-Irish gentry and the Protestant missionaries who were proselytizing in the countryside. Her position was not enviable: Catholics were suspicious of any Bible-reading stranger, while Protestant missionaries suspected Nicholson's broad tolerance towards the poor and her democratic ideas.

While her account of her travels is not a jeremiad, it outlines the conditions that would lead to periodic famines: the want of employment, the land system, the dependence on a single food source and poor housing. She left Ireland in the fall of 1845, just before the first reported failure of the potato crop. She returned in 1846 determined to do what she could to relieve famine suffering. When she returned, it was not as a Bible reader but as a relief worker. She was unique in that she was the only woman who travelled to the afflicted areas of the west and who left an account of her work among the poor. As she had described the character of the Irish poor in *Ireland's Welcome to the Stranger*, Nicholson depicted their suffering in *Annals of the Famine* (1851). Hers was the lone voice that spoke to women's work and lives. Many of her views about famine relief programs, employment and proselytism have been validated by the work of later historians and social scientists.

Nicholson landed in Dublin on 7 December 1846. Her return during these difficult circumstances was informed by her sense that she was on a divinely appointed mission. She paraphrased the words of St. Luke (22:42), "Father, if you are willing, remove this cup from me, nevertheless, not my will but Yours be done." Nicholson's previous experience in Ireland gave her a singular understanding of the poor as they coped with the catastrophe of the Famine. Her sense of mission involved bearing witness to their suffering and explaining to her readers not only how the Irish suffered, but why they suffered. She challenged absentee landlords and the land system, the British government and the Church of Ireland's stewardship of the resources entrusted to them for the starving; she rebuked them for their attitudes towards the poor. Her own famine relief efforts were matched equally by practical and sensible practices and by a spirit of Christian charity.

Arriving in Kingstown, Nicholson went to work immediately dispensing food from the house where she lodged, probably De Vesci Lodge, the Monkstown home of James Webb, brother of her good friend, Richard Davis Webb, as Richard was out of town.[7] Her first famine experience was a special horror for her. She heard the story of a woman cooking a half-starved dog with potatoes that she had gleaned from a harvested field.[8] When she left Monkstown to establish her own relief operation in Dublin, she despaired that she could do so little:

> I would not say that I actually murmured but the question did arise, "Why was I brought to see a famine and be the humble instrument of saving some few alive, and then see these few die because I had no more to give them?"[9]

Providentially, a parcel arrived from New York with money for her work and, with it, the promise of further help. The letter was not only a means of providing practical relief, it was a sign.

> I adored that watchful Hand that had so strangely led and upheld me in Ireland, and now, above all and over all, when my heart was sinking in the deepest despondency, when no way of escape appeared, this heavenly boon was sent.[10]

When Nicholson moved into Dublin, the Central Relief Committee of the Society of Friends established a soup kitchen in Charles Street, Upper Ormond Quay. Between January and July, when the public works were closed and the Temporary Relief Act became operative (establishing government soup kitchens), the Quakers provided soup, on average 1,000 quarts each day, for a penny a quart. They also sold soup tickets that could be distributed to the poor.

The Central Relief Committee established by the Quakers almost single-handedly provided relief to the poor in the spring of 1847. The government had decided to abandon its public works relief scheme in favor of the direct distribution of food, but the program did not exist in the spring of 1847.[11] Nicholson described the Quaker women at work in their soup shops: "Quaker matrons and their daughters with their white sleeves drawn over their tidy-clad arms, their white aprons and caps, all moving in that quiet harmony so peculiar to that people."[12] The official Quaker

89

famine report, *Transactions of the Central Relief Committee of the Society of Friends*, refers to women forming associations in towns for making, collecting and distributing clothes; however, it lists only the names of the men of the Central Relief Committee who were the sub-committee officers. In her account, Nicholson included vignettes of women in Belmullet and Ballina, both in County Mayo, who were working to provide clothes for the poor.

Although Nicholson admired the Quaker women working together in their soup shops, she went her own way establishing her own *modus operandi* in the spring of 1847. From her lodging in a house overlooking the Liffey, she walked through Dublin each morning with a large basket, distributing slices of bread *en route* from her house to her own soup kitchen on Cook Street, a street with ten tenement houses and nine vacant houses in 1847.[13] As was her custom, Nicholson located herself in a place selected for its poverty. In the spring of 1847, she was also busy correcting the proofs for her first Irish book, *Ireland's Welcome to the Stranger*, which she had written to raise money for famine relief.

Officially, the Quakers ran their soup kitchens on a purchase system. Nicholson gave her food away *gratis*; however, a system of triage prevailed. She decided that £10 divided among 100 people helped no one, so she committed herself to a limited number of families in the Liberties for whom she cooked daily. During the six months that the Quakers ran their Charles Street soup shop, Nicholson cared for her own small group of Dublin poor. The English Quaker, William Bennett, wrote about meeting Nicholson during the first week of April 1847, in the home of his "earliest friend in Ireland."[14] While Bennett did not mention his friend by name, it was probably Richard Webb, the Dublin Quaker printer who shared Nicholson's commitments to abolitionism and temperance. Bennett's description of Nicholson speaks to her character. He described her mission and his impression of Nicholson struggling with her meager resources as, at once, heroic and hopeful:

> I found her with limited and precarious means, still persevering from morning to night in visiting the most desolate abodes of the poor, and making food—especially of Indian meal—for those who did not know how to do it properly, with her own hands. She was under much painful discouragement, but a better hope still held her up. Having considerable quantity of arrowroot with me, at my own disposal, I left some of it with her, and five pounds for general purposes.[15]

Nicholson also received aid from supporters in New York. The records of the New York Quaker Meeting for Suffering held on 22 May 1847, note that a committee collected the sum of $4,013 to purchase food for the Irish, sent aboard the U.S.

frigate the *Macedonian*, which arrived at Haulbowline on 16 July 1847.[16] In the shipment consigned to the Quakers were 50 barrels of Indian corn for the writer Maria Edgeworth, and along with the food for Edgeworth were five barrels of Indian meal, flour and biscuit designated for Asenath Nicholson.[17] There is no record that the two remarkable women ever met; however, they shared similar views about the Irish poor: their criticism of absentee landlords, their concern that poverty did not take away the dignity of the poor and, more than anything, the need for employment.

Nicholson was told that she would have to pay the costs to have the food that arrived in barrels be shifted into sacks. She refused to comply on two grounds: that meal stored in sacks was liable to become damp and moldy and that the sacks cost money that could be spent on food for the poor. The Central Relief Committee did not charge her. Before the five barrels actually arrived in Cork, Nicholson left for Belfast. She left a "few barrels" sent from Ward School #3, a New York pauper school to "a school in the poorest convent in Dublin [that] was in a state of the greatest suffering."[18] The school was probably the Presentation Convent School at George's Hill. Nicholson would have had an entrée with the Presentation Nuns through her friendship with the Irish temperance crusader Father Theobald Mathew, who was related to the late foundress of the order, Mother Nano Nangle.

With the last of her Dublin stores distributed and the Central Relief Committee closing their soup shop when the British government established soup kitchens under the Temporary Relief Act, Nicholson left Dublin on 6 July 1847 and traveled by steamer to Belfast. She was interested in meeting members of the Belfast Ladies' Association for the Relief of Irish Destitution that had been founded in January 1847. There she found an organization of about 150 ladies of all denominations working at different aspects of famine relief.[19] Nicholson contrasted the work of the Belfast women with their Dublin counterparts, saying, "Never in Ireland, since the famine, was such a happy condition of all parties, operating so harmoniously together as was here manifested."[20] Nicholson's analysis of the group's success turned on their energy and on their spirit of cooperation. It was just the characteristic that contemporary feminist historians identify with the women's organizations that put cooperation before competition. Moreover, philanthropy was one of the few areas in the mid-19th century where it was acceptable for women to engage in the public sphere.[21]

Nicholson's trip north which took her to the coast of Antrim, to Donegal, as well as to Belfast was the prelude to an extended journey to County Mayo, an area of extensive suffering. She returned to Dublin briefly to collect some money and a box of clothing and to arrange that the grant she expected to arrive go to Mrs. Susan Hewitson, a Donegal friend who could make the best use of the funds. Then

Nicholson set off by coach for Tuam, and from there by an open car to Newport in Mayo, a location that she had visited in 1845. Finding western Mayo a place of "... misery without a mask," she stayed until April 1848.[22] While she knew Mayo from Westport to Achill, she was unfamiliar with the area of greatest destitution—from Ballina west to the Erris Peninsula. She followed the route of the Quakers: William Forster, James Hack Tuke, William Bennett and Richard Davis Webb. She mentioned Forster's tour that lasted from 30 November 1846 to 14 April 1847, which sounded the Famine alarm and mobilized the Quakers to begin their program of relief to the area. It was also an opportunity to locate people in the afflicted areas who could be counted on to administer local relief to those in need. Having met William Bennett, she would have had the benefit of his advice for travelling in west Mayo; and she wrote praising Bennett's scheme to distribute seeds for green crops in the west, noting the scheme's success on Arranmore. Distrustful of institutions, even ones as praiseworthy as the Central Relief Committee, she observed with approval that Bennett acted as an individual and not as a member of a committee.

Nicholson's friend, Richard Davis Webb, would have been helpful to Nicholson as she planned her visit to Mayo. She does not mention Webb's tour in the *Annals,* but he visited Mayo and Galway in May 1847, stopping in the places and meeting the people who Nicholson describes in her *Annals.* When Webb returned to Mayo in February 1848, it is likely that he met Nicholson in Ballina as she was in the town until 28 February, when she left, relocating to Castlebar. In Newport, Nicholson set about bearing witness to famine suffering. Her *Annals* differ from the account of her male Quaker contemporaries. She combined documentary evidence with other forms of discourse including parables, dramatic scenes and dialogues written in the cadences of the Old Testament. While the men focused on the logistical demands of providing relief, Nicholson looked at the human face of suffering. On 28 November 1847, she described a scene that anticipated John Millington Synge's "Riders to the Sea." A fisherman's widow traveled 20 miles to "prove" that her husband has been washed ashore and buried without a coffin. She brought the coffin to the spot where he was buried and with her own hands, she dug him from his grave and "proved" it was him by the leather button she had sewn on his clothes. Synge's biographer, W. J. McCormack, has concluded that Synge must have read Nicholson's *Annals* for those details.[23]

In recording such scenes, Nicholson made it clear that she believed that the Famine was not a divine judgement, a common explanation for the Irish tragedy, but the failure of man to use God's gifts responsibly. She considered herself as "acting entirely as a passive instrument; moving because moved upon,"[24] but there is nothing passive about her indictment of the British government and the Established Church for failing in their stewardship of the relief resources entrusted to them and in their attitude toward the Irish poor for whom they were responsible. She distinguished between hired relief officers whom she dismissed as bureaucratic, hierarchical and self-serving and local volunteer relief workers whom she praised for their compassion, egalitarianism and selflessness. Scrupulous herself about her own expenses, she reported that she allowed herself 23 pence a day for food: a diet of cocoa and bread and that she dispensed with her seven pence worth of cocoa, milk and sugar when she was running short of stores for her poor. She continued to ask herself whether she was doing enough to economize; therefore, she was critical of official relief officers who lived well while those they were charged to care for went hungry. Nicholson was particularly disparaging of government relief officers for putting record keeping before the needs of the hungry and she described the dying poor turned away and told to return another day to be first entered on to the roster. This story would become the incident upon which the contemporary Irish composer Donnacha Dennehy based his opera *The Hunger*. Nicholson also described two orphans aged 5 and 7 who were sent by relief officers from Newport to the poorhouse in Castlebar. They walked ten miles through the rain and arrived late at night. The girl was accepted but the boy was turned away and walked ten miles back to the door of Nicholson's friend, Mrs. Margaret Arthur, the widowed postmistress of Newport. Nicholson intervened and brought the boy to school where he was fed and clothed for the winter.

It was often stated that the government allowed food to be exported while Ireland starved. Nicholson looked at the matter of diverting food from another point of view. She suggested that the grain used for distilling alcohol could have been used to feed the Irish poor. The 60,000,000 pounds of grain or 30,000 tons of grain used to distill six million gallons of 80 proof spirits in 1847 could have provided more than 300 thousand of servings of grain-based cereal.[25] Even with alcohol consumption reduced, Father Mathew complained to Charles Edward Trevelyan, assistant secretary to the Treasury, about the make-shift drink shops erected at some relief work sites. In at least one case, a publican member of the local relief committee recommended men for work only if they spent part of their wages on drink.[26]

Concerned as she was about stewardship, Nicholson was far more interested in the attitude of the relief worker toward the poor. Over and over, she contrasted the lack of charity on the part of officials with the compassion of the volunteer workers. The lack of charity on the part of officials appears to have been based on the view that the Irish brought their troubles on themselves. Christopher Morash observed in his study of the literature of the Great Irish Famine that contemporary works often cites Thomas Malthus in trying to explain the tragedy. He also argues that Malthusian doctrine informs the fictional representation of nineteenth-century Ireland in novels such as Anthony Trollope's *Castle Richmond* and in William Carleton's *The Black Prophet*.[27]

Critical as she was of government relief officers, Nicholson was quick to praise the Coast Guard's generosity and that of their families toward their poor neighbors. Many guardsmen were recruited by the Quakers to administer relief to the local suffering. The Coast Guard Inspector, General Sir James Dombrain, supported the work of his men. Having experienced the 1839 Famine, Sir James prevailed on the relief officer at Westport to issue free meal and he directed the captain of the government steamship *Rhadamanthus* to take 100 tons of meal to the Killeries where, on 22 June 1846, the cutter *Eliza* was overtaken by a boatload of starving men begging for food. Sir Randolph Routh, who had the responsibility for distributing the Indian corn, complained about Sir James to Charles Trevelyan.[28] Seamus Heaney based his poem "For the Commander of the *Eliza*" on the episode; his closing lines speak to the Malthusian bias of the speaker:

> Sir James, I understand, urged free relief for famine victims in the Westport sector
> And earned tart reprimand from good Whitehall. Let natives prosper by their own
> exertions; Who could not swim might go ahead and sink.[29]

As far as Nicholson was concerned, the problem was not that the Irish avoided work, but that they had no employment. On 30 October 1847, she wrote to her English friend William Bennett from Belmullet, a letter he passed along to his neighbors, William and Mary Howitt, who published *Howitt's Journal*. Her letter appeared on 27 November 1847. "Every effort of the friends of Ireland is battled by the demoralizing efforts that feeding a starving peasantry without labor produce," she wrote. Nicolson went on to observe that the conditions of the resident landlords in the west had an adverse effect on local relief efforts:

> You sir, who know Erris, tell, if you can, how the landlords can support the poor by
> taxation, to give them food, when the few resident landlords are nothing and worse
> than nothing, for they are paupers in the full sense of the word.[30]

Nicholson contended that relief work, subject as it was to the variables of local lobbying efforts, meant that the number and power of local resident landlords accounted for the great differences in expenditure on public works.[31] The amount spent between April 1846 and January 1847 in Erris was £4 to £4.99 per family, while in north Clare the amount was ten pounds per family.

Nicholson made her own case for local employment and, as always, she took a special interest in work for women and in work women were doing:

I must and will plead, though I plead in vain, that something must be done to give them work. I have just received a letter from the curate of Bingham's Town saying that he could set all his poor parish, both the women and the children, to work, and find a market for their knitting and cloth, if he could command a few pounds to purchase the materials. He is young and indefatigable, kind-hearted, and poor and no proselyte. Mrs. Stock has done well in her industrial department. The Hon. William Butler has purchased cloth of her, for a coat to wear himself, which the poor women spin, and he gave a good price for it.[32]

While Nicholson's witness to suffering and her challenges to the authorities on behalf of the Irish poor are, in themselves, of interest, it is her own active efforts to offer aid and comfort that command our attention. She distributed her supplies of food and clothes; she visited the distressed and brought their stories to the world; she helped the relief workers she admired, and she left a record of their names and their service. The Quakers left invaluable accounts of their relief workers, but it is Nicholson who tells the reader about remarkable women like Mrs. Stock who ran a soup kitchen from the Belmullet rectory and who organized a women's clothing industry, the charitable Mrs. Margaret Arthur, the postmistress of Newport and Mrs. Garvey of north Mayo, who forgave her suffering tenants their rent. Above all, Nicholson was moved by the generosity of the Irish to one another. Irish oral tradition, down to our own time, includes the charitable woman who gives her last measure of meal to a beggar at her door and who is rewarded with an inexhaustible supply of food. It is a legend that complements the Irish proverb, *Ar scáth a chéile a mhaireas na daoine* (We live in one another's shadow). Throughout, Nicholson read the Bible. She read the Bible to the Irish to save them from the superstitions of Rome, so she was, in principle, supportive of the efforts of Protestant missionaries; however, she wanted conversions to be the result of reason, not coercion. It is not surprising, then, that she condemned proselytizers:

It requires the Irish language to provide suitable words for a suitable description of the spirit which is manifested in some parts to proselyte, by bribery, obstinate Romans to the Church which had been her instrument of oppression for centuries.[33]

Nicholson predicted accurately that the proselytizers' gains would be short-lived and quoted children who told her that they would be going back to their own chapels when the stirabout time was over. What was more common in Nicholson's experience was cooperation among many of the clergy of different denominations who worked together to help the poor.[34]

Nicholson left Mayo in the spring of 1848 and went to Cork to see her old friend Father Mathew once more. En route from the west, she stopped at the Presentation

Convent School in Tuam in County Galway, where she found, for the first time in her famine travels, a school where the 400 children had normal behavior and appearances. When she arrived in Cork in June, she visited the Presentation Convent School in the city and again recorded the work that the "indefatigable" nuns did to feed some 1300 children in their care.[35] She may have found their religious life as incomprehensible as Catholic theology, but she responded to the charitable works of religious women. Nicholson left Ireland in the fall of 1848 when she felt her work was over and that she could not live through another winter of such palpable suffering. There is some suggestion that she was planning to return to America; however, she went to London where she wrote the first edition of *The Annals of the Famine* which appeared in a volume called *Lights and Shades of Ireland* (1850).

Nicholson's relationship with Ireland was complex. Initially, she came to proselytize, so it is not surprising that her second visit should have been viewed by some through a similar lens. When Nicholson was in Ireland on her mission of mercy in 1847, her first publication, *Ireland's Welcome to the Stranger*, was reaching the public. In May, it received a favorable review in *Tait's Edinburgh Magazine*, which drew a comparison with Johann Georg Kohl's 1841 *Travels in Ireland*: "We have derived much pleasure from Miss Nicholson's book—it is worth a cart-load of such absurd books as Kohl's, which, brimful of blunders, was nevertheless much praised and widely circulated."[36] Not all reviews were so positive. In a long and scathing review that appeared in the *Freeman's Journal* in September 1847, the writer pondered, "whether we ought to be amused by its whimsicalities or indignant at its many exaggerations."[37] The writer was dismissive of her attempts to proselytize the Irish poor and the "evangelical wrath" with which she viewed them. It concluded by stating that "We regret that we cannot congratulate Miss Nicholson on the likelihood of any real good resulting from her peregrinations."[38] Such criticisms should not detract from the real good that Nicholson did during her second visit, when she visited Ireland simply to save lives.

Even when no longer in Ireland, Nicholson continued to follow what was happening in the country. In September 1848, her letter praising the installation of the "Mathew Tower," honoring the "apostle" of Irish temperance, was published in a number of newspapers, "though I return to my people with a sorrowing heart, that the tear is still on the long wasted cheek of Ireland, she rejoiced in this tribute to temperance. Her postscript to the letter stated, "Ireland. 'I love thee still.'"[39] It was a reminder of Nicholson's complex relationship with Ireland: her desire to save lives, to save souls and to save the people from the evils of alcohol.

One could argue that Asenath Nicholson was a woman who was ahead of her time—a vegetarian, a teetotaler, a pacifist and an outdoor exercise enthusiast. Critical of the superstitions associated with the Roman Catholic Church, her *Annals of the Famine* speaks of her sense that she was on some divinely appointed mission. She challenged the system, marshalled resources to accomplish her ends, and her straightforward questions, impromptu sermons, impassioned letters and candid accounts of impressions in journals and in her books marked her, by some, like the Rev. Edward Nangle of the Achill Island Mission, as a maverick whose "principal object" was "to create a spirit of discontent among the lower orders."[40] In the longer term, however, Nicholson shared the fate of other worthy, outspoken women; she was ignored. Her name appeared on one or two relief lists; she was praised in an article in the *Cork Examiner* on 30 August 1848, and the decent William Bennett paid tribute to her famine work in his *Narrative of a Recent Journey of Six Weeks in Ireland* (1847); but, in the end, she spoke for herself in books that were not reprinted until 1998 and 2002.

When Nicholson died in Jersey City, New Jersey on 15 May 1855, she was buried in the J.T. Sanger family plot (Lot 2247. Section 111) in Brooklyn's Green-Wood Cemetery. On 3 June 1862, her remains were removed to an unmarked grave (#645) in Lot 8999, one of the cemetery's public lots. More recently, in 2015, Kathleen McDonough has added Asenath Nicholson to her annual fall tour of historic Irish graves in Green-Wood cemetery.[41] In the same year, Nicholson's biography *Compassionate Stranger* was published. Green-Wood president, Richard Moylan, and historian Jeff Richman proposed a memorial headstone for the Nicholson grave. When the stone was unveiled, it carried the inscription: "Asenath Nicholson. Heroine of Ireland's Great Hunger."

NOTES

1. Parts of this chapter appeared in Maureen Murphy, "Asenath Nicholson and the Great Famine," *La Clé des Langues [en ligne], Lyon*) ,March 2015 at: http://cle.ens-lyon.fr/anglais /civilisation/domaine-britannique/irlande-et-ecosse/asenath-nicholson-and-the-great-famine , and Maureen O'Rourke Murphy, *Compassionate Stranger: Asenath Nicholson and the Great Irish Famine* (Syracuse University Press, 2015).
2. *Book of Genesis*, 41: 45. See also, "Asenath: Bible," *The Encyclopedia of Jewish Women* at: https://jwa.org/encyclopedia/article/asenath-bible
3. *Book of Genesis*, 47:13-27.
4. Maureen Murphy (ed.), *Ireland's Welcome to the Stranger* (Dublin: Lilliput Press, 2002), p. 4.
5. Ibid., p. 2.
6. Ibid., p. 4.
7. The Quaker Webb brothers were involved in famine relief. They were also prominent abolitionists who hosted Frederick Douglass in 1845, see Christine Kinealy, *Black Abolitionists in Ireland* (London: Routledge, 2020).

8. Maureen Murphy (ed.), Asenath Nicholson, *Annals of the Famine in Ireland in 1847, 1848 and 1849* (Dublin: Lilliput Press, 2002), pp 36-37.

9. Ibid., p. 40.

10. Ibid., p. 41.

11. Christine Kinealy, *The Great Irish Famine. Impact, Ideology and Rebellion* (London: Palgrave, 2002), pp 40-43.

12. Nicholson, *Annals,* p. 43.

13. Thom's, *Dublin Directory for 1847* (Dublin: Pettigrew and Oultron, 1848), p. 672.

14. William Bennett, *Narrative of a Recent Journey of Six Weeks in Ireland: In Connection with the Subject of Supplying Small Seed in Some of the Remote Districts* (London: Charles Gilpin, 1847), p. 96.

15. Ibid., p. 98.

16. James Tertius DeKay, *Chronicles of the Frigate Macedonia, 1809-1922* (New York: W.W. Norton, 1995), p. 237.

17. Christine Kinealy, *The Kindness of Strangers. Charity and the Great Hunger* (London: Bloomsbury, 2013), pp 156-8.

18. Nicholson, *Annals*, p. 69.

19. Kinealy, *Kindness*, pp 146-7.

20. Ibid, p. 72.

21. Maria Luddy, *Women and Philanthropy in Nineteenth-Century Ireland* (Cambridge University Press, 1995).

22. Nicholson, *Annals*, p. 83.

23. W.J. McCormack, *Fool of the Family: A Life of J. M. Synge* (New York: New York University Press, 2006), pp 246-247, p. 24.

24. Nicholson, *Annals*, p. 42.

25. Elizabeth Malcolm, *Ireland Sober, Ireland Free: Drink and Temperance in Nineteenth-century Ireland* (Dublin: Gill and Macmillan, 1986), p. 144.

26. Cecil Woodham-Smith, *The Great Hunger. Ireland 1845-1849* (New York: Harper and Row, 1962), p. 145.

27. Christopher Morash, *Writing the Irish Famine* (Oxford: Clarendon Press, 1995), pp 31-32, 93, 95, 163.

28. Woodham-Smith, *The Great Hunger,* p. 85.

29. Seamus Heaney, "For the Commander of the *Eliza,*" *Death of a Naturalist* (London: Faber and Faber, 1969), p. 25.

30. Nicholson, *Annals*, p. 156.

31. Similar criticism of absentee landlords was also made by the young, English Quaker, James Hack Tuke, in *Transactions of the Central Relief Committee of the Society of Friends During the Famine in Ireland in 1846 and 1847* (Dublin: Hodges, 1852), p. 212.

32. Ibid., p. 156.

33. Ibid., pp 300-301.

34. Desmond Bowen, *Souperism: Myth or Reality: A Study of Catholics and Protestants during the Great Famine* (Cork University Press, 1970), pp 124-5.

35. Nicholson, *Annals*, p. 244.

36. "Review," *Tait's Edinburgh Magazine*, 14 May 1847.

37. Review, *Freeman's Journal*, 4 September 1847. The paper was a supporter of Daniel O'Connell and Nicholson had written critically of her visit to Derrynane.

38. Nicholson, *Annals*, p. 244.

39. "The Mathew Tower. Mrs Nicholson," *Cork Examiner*, 6 September 1848. When introducing the letter, the paper described her as "this amiable lady."

40. Asenath Nicolson, *Ireland's Welcome to the Stranger: or, Excursions Through Ireland in 1844 & 1845 for the purpose of personally investigating the condition of the poor* (London: Charles Gilpin, 1847), p. 437.

41. See, https://brooklyneagle.com/articles/2015/09/22/commodore-barry-club-participates-in-irish-heritage-event-at-green-wood/. This article appeared online on 22 September 2015.

Medical Heroes

CHAPTER SEVEN

DR. RICHARD GRATTAN (1790–1886)

And the Great Famine in County Kildare: A Teacher of the People

Ciarán Reilly

The ignorance of the individuals may be pardoned when the consequences affect themselves only—the errors of the minister who voluntarily undertakes the management of the concerns of an entire people are of a more serious nature, and becomes sins against society, when the safety of the people is trifled with and compromised, or sacrificed to political or party purposes.[1]

In a stinging address to Lord John Russell in the winter of 1847, the members of the Edenderry Board of Guardians in King's County (now County Offaly), but covering large parts of Counties Kildare and Meath, openly criticized the failure of the public works schemes in Ireland and the mismanagement of the crisis by the British government. According to the board, the failure of the government to continue outdoor relief would have a detrimental effect on the program of Famine relief across the country. It was not their first, or last, public admonishment of the government and, in the weeks following the first signs of potato blight in 1845, they claimed, that "we all knew famine was fast approaching and this board warned you of it." Presented to Queen Victoria in November, the address averred that the British government had mismanaged the country in the past and wondered what was to be done in Ireland if there was not a single potato fit for consumption.[2] Later, again addressing the Queen, the Edenderry guardians noted that "we have had enough, more than enough of that vaguely directed and restless agitation."[3] These and other letters were signed on behalf of the board of the guardians by the union's clerk, Thomas Byrne, but the composition and style was undoubtedly the work of Dr. Richard Grattan, a medical doctor by profession and chairman of the Edenderry Board of Guardians during the Famine. Grattan was also a prolific writer and played a prominent role in the leading nationalist organizations, both locally and nationally, for much of the 19th century. He also experienced two personal tragedies during the Famine. This chapter explores his resilience and compassion towards the suffering of the poor and the efforts to which he went to alleviate their sufferings. Described as "a gentleman of great talent and industry, and of undoubted patriotism," Richard Grattan was born at Drummin, near Carbury in County Kildare, the son of Richard Grattan Senior and Elizabeth Biddulph.[4] His grandfather, Rev. William Grattan, was remembered as a "zealous cleric and a benevolent doctor" and was a prominent member of the local community. Having attended Trinity College, Dublin at the age of 15, Richard Grattan later graduated from Edinburgh as a medical doctor and commenced working in Dublin almost at once. In his professional career, Grattan worked at French Street from where he was attached to the Cork Street Fever Hospital at York Street and later the Coombe Hospital. Working with the poor of Dublin during the cholera epidemics of 1816 and 1817, Grattan saw first-hand the prevalence of fever amongst them and recommended ways of overcoming this. His treatise published in 1826 on the topic, *Observations on the Causes and Prevention of Fever and Pauperism in Ireland,* was widely read and Grattan was praised for his contributions to medical discussion.[5] His contribution to medical matters resulted in his appointment as Censor of the King's and Queen's College of Physicians, as an inspector of apothecaries' shops, appointed by an Act of Parliament and, in 1865, as senior fellow of the Royal College of Physicians of Ireland. His role within the Royal College prior to the Famine also included examining estates belonging to the college, which provided further evidence to him of the plight of the lower orders.[6]

Throughout his long life, Grattan was a prolific writer and a frequent contributor to the national newspapers including *The Nation* and *The Freeman's Journal.* He regularly petitioned Parliament on a range of social issues, including 11 separate petitions between the 1830s and 1870s. He also corresponded with the leading figures of the day including Valentine Lawless, or Lord Cloncurry, who came to his defense on a number of occasions.[7] His publications included *Considerations on the Human Mind* (1861); *The Right to Think: Addressed to the Young Men of Great Britain & Ireland* (1865); *Vox Hiberniae e Deserto Clamantis: or, Ireland, her Grievances and their Remedies* (Dublin, 1870) and an influential broadside, published in April 1875, in which he called on England to repeal the Act of Union.

In politics, Grattan played a prominent role in a number of organizations including the Irish Land Improvement Society, where he proposed a number of ways in which agriculture, and thereby productivity, could be improved but little was made of these suggestions.[8] He was present at the first meeting of the Repeal Party in 1831. Grattan also played a prominent role in the Anti-Tithe movement of the 1830s at Carbury, preaching that peaceful protest would be more effective than agitation and riot. Indeed, Grattan addressed a large crowd at Carbury on the subject in the weeks after the death of his wife, Rosetta in 1834.[9] The burden of the tithe tax meant that many in Carbury were living in great distress and, to overcome this, Grattan proposed the formation of a cooperative society made up of the local elite.[10] Elsewhere, Grattan's signature was affixed to many of the most important political documents of the period, including the Morpeth Testimonial Roll in 1841, and the William Smith O'Brien petition in 1848.[11] After the Famine, Grattan was prominent in the Tenant League, formed in 1850, and was a founding member of the Home Government Association in 1870. Vocal on most topics, his outspoken approach was said to have been molded by the fact that he shared the same ancestry as the celebrated parliamentarian, Henry Grattan.[12] A member of the Church of Ireland by persuasion, Grattan described himself as a "Dissenter" and claimed that he had been twice offered the role of churchwarden in Carbury but had declined the offer. It was probably for this reason that he lent no support to the Anti-Maynooth fervor of 1845, which demonstrated religious animosity against the Catholic seminary.[13]

On the eve of the Famine, Grattan continued to be vocal about the problems which beset the country. In evidence before the Devon Commission, which reported on the occupation of land in Ireland, he put forward his own ideas about the condition of the people and how land could be improved, some of which he had proposed as early as the 1820s. In particular, Grattan advocated for the drainage of land, and he had done so quite profitably on the portion of his estate which was covered in bog.[14] However, like many others who gave evidence, his suggestions fell on deaf ears, or at least there were not the capabilities to introduce them. Elsewhere, at the weekly meeting of the Edenderry Board of Guardians, Grattan initiated a practice ending their discussions by examining ways of improving the plight of the poor.[15]

Examining his crops in late October 1845, Grattan noticed a change in the potatoes planted at his own 400-acre estate near Carbury. After he had planted 23 acres of potatoes earlier in the year, a heavy frost in early October had stunted their growth.[16] However, acting cautiously, but conscious of the growing number of reports across the country of the demise of the crop, Grattan did not advise that the potatoes should be taken up, a decision he would come to regret. Having walked over several potato fields he learned that the crop was "to a great extent infected and destroyed." According to Grattan, not a field in that part of Kildare or in the adjoining King's

County was unaffected. He lamented that "my apple potatoes are not worth digging ... the lumper is totally gone," and only a variety known as the "crow cup" had escaped the mysterious disease that he believed was caused by changes in the atmosphere. At neighboring Newberry Hall, Edward Wolstenholme, the chairman of the Edenderry Board of Guardians and a member of the Repeal party, reported to Grattan that turnips were as badly affected by this mysterious disease. Alarm was starting to spread in the local community, further compounded by the fact that there would be no seed potatoes to plant for the coming season. Unless measures were put in place by the government, wrote Grattan, "I anticipate nothing short of the most widespread and destructive famines that history has yet placed on record." One of the measures that Grattan proposed in those early months was to halt the brewing and distilling industries in Ireland as a means of providing grain for the poor. At the Edenderry Board of Guardian meetings Grattan argued that it was better to communicate with the Queen than to lose time "with the castle people"—a reference to the British administration in Dublin Castle.[17]

Grattan's report on the condition of the potato crop in west Kildare was at odds with the projected figures of the third Duke of Leinster at Carton House, near Maynooth. Leinster was absent from the country when the blight first appeared in September and upon his return to Carton was quickly informed about conditions by his agriculturalist, Mr. McLennan. Distressed to learn that one third of the crop would be lost, although this projection was soon revised, Leinster also claimed that there was little need for relief committees in the county.[18] However, in the same month as Grattan noticed the blight at Carbury, one of Leinster's tenants at Athy wrote:

> There is a curse on Paddy's Land. The people here are finding out to their sorrow the failure of the potato crop ... I hope the calamity will not be found to be so great as is represented.[19]

Amid the confusion in these reports as to the extent of the potato blight in County Kildare, Grattan tried to remain optimistic and oversaw the last of the harvest work on his farm at Drummin. However, in late November disaster struck and Grattan was lucky to survive after his hand was caught in a threshing machine. From Carbury he was rushed to Dublin, but as he approached the village of Clane, the cart in which he was travelling crashed after the horse became distressed. The parish priest of Clane, Father Conroy, came to his aid and arranged for him to continue to Dublin where an amputation on his crushed hand was performed shortly afterwards.[20] The incident would have a profound effect on Grattan. He no longer practiced medicine and instead retired permanently to County Kildare. Surviving photographs of

Grattan show him covering the amputation site and facing away from the camera lens. Following the accident, Grattan threw himself further into political matters, and, in particular, to Famine relief in Kildare and King's County.[21]

The deepening crisis in the early months of 1846 necessitated action locally and Grattan, still recovering from the amputation, was involved in efforts with other local landowners, including Richard More O'Farrall of Balyna House near Moyvalley, to put people to work on drainage projects in the barony of Carbury.[22] These works alone were not enough to stem the tide of hunger with the failure of the second successive potato crop. In the summer of 1846, Grattan and others turned their attention to securing further relief for the poor. Despite his best efforts, there was little progress made with forming a relief committee at Carbury, although he was actively involved in Edenderry where he attended the Board of Guardians. At Edenderry, the guardians, with the help of a number of local shopkeepers, established a soup kitchen which provided soup and bread for over 150 people in the winter of 1847.[23] Witnessing the continued poverty at Carbury, Grattan decided to acquire Indian corn at his own expense. As the crisis worsened, he also began to employ local people in his demesne; draining and clearing land in an effort to provide support for the poor. He kept over 20 families alive by these means. Perhaps his greatest contribution during this time was to provide medical assistance to the sick and elderly.

However, Grattan's benevolence was tested in August 1846 when his efforts to stem the growing pangs of hunger at Carbury were thwarted by his staff and members of the local community. There was considerable distrust in the community that Indian corn was not suitable for consumption and should be avoided, a claim that Garrett Lynam, Grattan's steward, supported. Lynam, who had been born on the estate and employed since his youth on the farm before being made steward, was adamant that he would have nothing to do with the imported corn. Discussing the matter with Lynam, but unaware of his aversion to the corn, Grattan believed that his plan to relieve the poor would be beneficial if a good quality supply could be guaranteed. What followed said much about the public perceptions of relief, especially amongst the lower orders who both feared and misunderstood what was being provided for them.

On 16 August 1846, Grattan secured at his own expense the delivery of half a ton of Indian corn from Dublin and began making plans to distribute it to the poor of Carbury. However, the food, described as "yellow meal," was rejected by the staff at Drummin House who refused to handle it. It was later claimed that Jane Maher, the cook, declared to other employees that "the master is going to stall feed us in the morning with Indian Meal" and suggested that the food was unwholesome. She also claimed that she did not know how to cook the corn, contending that it was alien to their diet. Maher and others refused to have anything to do with the corn and a standoff with her employer ensued. Realizing that the poor of Carbury would likely reject his offer of assistance, Grattan decided that his own family should eat the corn in an effort to do away with any prejudice toward the food. To do so, Grattan ordered that "stirabout," or porridge, be made on the following morning for the family breakfast. Maher reluctantly followed orders and made the porridge, but Garrett Lynam refused to eat it and went home to his own house. That evening, Grattan, outraged at the conduct of his servants, instructed that anyone who did not eat the Indian meal on the following morning would be dismissed.[24]

On the morning of 18 August, Maher again prepared breakfast for the family. After serving it to Mrs. Grace Grattan (who Dr. Grattan had married in 1836) and her children, they immediately fell violently sick, their stomachs went into spasms and their retching was occasionally accompanied by short, hysteric outbursts of laughing. When Grattan came in, he found his wife and five children in a terrible condition and immediately tried to offer medicine to them. He accused Maher of having put something in the stirabout, which she denied, claiming that it could only have been the Indian corn which made them sick. Soon afterwards, two female servants lay sick after eating the stirabout. The leftovers were given to the calves, one of whom died almost instantly, while two more died the next day. Despite the best efforts of his father, Richard Grattan Jr., aged 15, died from poisoning. According to several witnesses, Maher showed no compassion as the family and staff lay sick. In the kitchen, Maher could clearly hear the moans of the family as they became violently ill, but she made little attempt to help or offer assistance. Realizing this, she was instantly dismissed by Grattan.[25]

Brought before the Kildare assizes in late March 1847, Jane Maher and Garrett Lynam were charged with the murder of Richard Grattan Jr. In the early stages of the trial, it became clear that the cause of their grievance towards the Grattans was the fact that a man named Moran, with whom Maher had struck up an "improper relationship,"[26] had been dismissed from employment at Drummin. In Maher's case it was alleged that she had "feloniously and wilfully put, mix, and mingle certain quantity of white arsenic with flummery, of which one Richard Grattan did eat and die."[27] Garret Lynam was indicted for "hiring and counselling" Maher to commit the act.[28] The pair pleaded not guilty from the outset. According to Mr. Corballis, Queen's Counsel, the act of poisoning Grattan was of "a most heinous and abominable nature."[29] Giving evidence at the trial, Jane Mulligan, the children's maid who had not taken part in the crime, claimed that Maher had confided in her and others about her contempt for the Indian corn. When the family had been poisoned, she alleged that Maher took the pot in which the stirabout was made and disposed of it, possibly in an effort to conceal her crime.

In preparing for the trial, Grattan went to great lengths to prove that his son had been poisoned, obtaining expert witnesses and information which he hoped to present. His actions in removing part of his son's stomach for autopsy was seen amongst the medical fraternity and others as being particularly proactive and should have been enough to secure the conviction before the court.[30] Dr. Geoghegan, a Professor of Medical Jurisprudence of the Royal College of Surgeons, gave evidence of examining five vessels which had been sent to him, including part of Richard Jr.'s stomach, the stirabout itself and the stomach of one of the dead calves. Both Geoghegan and a Dr. William Barker, professor of chemistry at Trinity College, discovered traces of arsenic in the vessels they examined. Dr. Michael Gilligan of Edenderry who carried out the post-mortem examination on the body was of the same opinion. Examining the dead calves, Grattan himself found arsenic in their stomachs. The poison, it was claimed, had been purchased about a month before the incident and given to Lynam to kill sick cattle on the farm. This, the defense argued, was the substance which had been given to Maher to poison the family. Despite the community's esteem for Grattan, a number of people came forward as character witnesses for the prisoners. After nearly four hours of deliberation, the jury returned a verdict of acquittal for both prisoners.[31]

As he had done following the amputation of his hand, Grattan once more threw himself into alleviating the suffering of the poor and it appears that he bore no malice towards members of the local community who denounced his efforts to distribute Indian corn. Less than a month after the poisoning, Grattan was writing publicly about ways in which the poor could be profitably employed, both for their own advantage and that of their employer. He also reported to have once more lost 20 acres of potatoes from blight, but there was some delight in the fact that the harvest of wheat was "splendid."[32]

Periodicals such as *The Farmers' Gazette and Journal of Practical Horticulture* praised Grattan's insights into these matters, claiming that they had long been an admirer of what he had to say on Irish affairs.[33] Indeed, in October, Grattan even supplied *The Farmers' Gazette* with specimens of wheat and barley which had been grown on reclaimed bog land at Carbury.[34] His attentions were also directed toward a long running dispute with the Lord Chancellor regarding the law which prevented medical doctors from becoming magistrates.[35] Later, in what became a landmark case, Grattan was dismissed from the magistracy owing to his involvement in the Irish

Alliance, a body which came together in 1849 and was deemed to be "radical" by the government.[36] Grattan presided over what was known as the "Aggregate Meeting" held in the Music Hall, Lower Abbey Street, on the 20 November 1849, the meeting called for the Irish Alliance to "take the most prompt and effective measures for the protection of the lives and interests of the Irish people, and the attainment of their natural rights." The requisition was supported by:

> 80 dignitaries and 110 curates of the Catholic Church; 22 members of the regular clergy; 120 magistrates; landed proprietors, corporators, and poor law guardians; 200 members of the learned professions; 700 land-owners and farmers, and 900 merchants, traders and artisans.[37]

Grattan's activities during the Famine also concerned the dissemination of knowledge regarding infectious diseases, much of which he had learned from his time as a doctor in Dublin during the 1816-1817 cholera epidemic. In the mid-1820s, Grattan had published ways in which to prevent the spread of disease and fever in his book *Observations on the Causes and Prevention of Fever and Pauperism in Ireland*.[38] The spread of cholera throughout the country in 1848 and 1849 revived memories of this, and Grattan presented papers on various aspects of controlling the disease.[39] In the summer of 1848, Grattan cautiously observed the potato crop in the Carbury area once more, hoping that it would be free of blight at harvest time. However, following heavy rains, the "distemper" had reappeared by early August.[40] According to Grattan the cause of the disease in the crops was "altogether atmospheric" and would cause ruin in the country: "The landlord, the farmer, the labourer are all like men embarked in the same ship, which lies a wreck upon the waters, and is fast sinking," he wrote.[41] Three years of Famine had also had an effect on the workhouse in Edenderry where over 1,800 people were residing in a building that was only meant to accommodate 600. As chairman, Grattan was keen to make the house self-sufficient and proposed that inmates of the workhouse be put to work making their own clothes. Always anxious to promote local industries, he proposed to the Edenderry Poor Law Union in February 1849 that "in future this board will, as far as possible, give a decided preference to arti-cles of Irish manufacture."[42] He also established a working farm near the workhouse for inmates. His motto was simple—promote and help the poor by providing mean-ingful work within the workhouse system rather than idle labor. Interestingly, Grattan was opposed to the emigration of female paupers from workhouses, complaining about a plan to send over 100 girls from Edenderry Union in the early 1850s.[43]

Grattan's attitude toward the poor from other areas, or "strangers" as he referred to them, was at odds with his previously benevolent disposition.[44] Grattan and the

Edenderry guardians were determined that no alms would be afforded to these "strangers" and people from other districts, blaming the poor law and its failings for the havoc which was being wreaked upon agricultural districts. Grattan was particularly displeased with the *modus operandi* of the poor law in shunting people into slums in towns and cities. He wrote: "With you it plasters the sore, and you are satisfied—with us, the sore remains exposed and putrefying under our eyes, spreading disease and tainting society in every direction."[45] In particular, the guardians had decided that they would no longer cater to those who flooded the town from the "famine-stricken counties" on their way to Dublin. "The people of Edenderry," Grattan declared, "are determined not to have the frightful scenes of other places enacted there, of hundreds of corpses lying unburied on the roads and ditches and devoured by dogs."[46] Furthermore, the guardians proposed that "all wandering and unlocated persons" would be removed' and a "fund be raised, by voluntary contribution to supply these strangers the means of migrating elsewhere."[47]

As the Famine drew to a close, Grattan appeared to have had boundless energy throwing himself into a host of projects. In 1852, he brought a petition to Parliament hoping to have it put on record the Duke of Wellington was an Irishman and a kinsman.[48] His involvement in the local community at Carbury and Edenderry in providing relief was not forgotten. In 1853, the people of Carbury petitioned Parliament looking for answers as to why Grattan had been dismissed from the magistracy of Kildare. However, on the subject of poverty and alleviating the plight of the poor which still existed after the Famine, Grattan had grown somewhat weary of his efforts, writing: "For more than thirty years, I put myself prominently forward as a teacher of the people." For him, improving the plight of the laborer was the only means of improving the country. "The stability of society, and of the entire community, depends on the regular and profitable employment of the industrious classes," he wrote.[49] Long after the Famine, Grattan continued to write about the calamity and, in particular, the mismanagement of affairs by the British government. In his book *Considerations on the Human Mind* (1861), Grattan blamed the British government once again for the Famine. He contended that:

> The Famine, aggravated by the gross mismanagement of Lord John Russell, and the betrayal of the freeholders, by their leaders, and by their Bishops, who forced them into collision with their landlords, have compelled the labouring classes to fly to America, in countless numbers. I never approved of this depopulation of the country. It is due to myself to say, that I never unroofed a house, or coerced a single individual to leave my land. None of my people were compelled by me, to encounter the dangers of the sea; or to perish on Grose Island [Grosse Île] or to wander, through the streets of New York, as mendicants, or outcasts.[50]

These opinions had not altered since the 1840s when he openly criticized the government as the "Famine did its work." In one missive, he lambasted government officials for the fact that:

> No remedial measure was introduced. The people died of starvation, in the very ports from whence cargoes of oats were, at the moment, exported to feed the carriage and dray horses of London.[51]

Grattan continued in public service after the Famine and played an influential role in a number of nationalist movements.[52] Moreover, he produced a number of political pamphlets which caused considerable debate including "The Right to Think," addressed to the Young Men of Ireland in 1865, and which was published "to correct the evils of social and sectarian intolerance."[53] Active in the Home Rule movement from its beginning, Grattan was once more troubled by local affairs when the Land War commenced. In 1880, at the age of 90, he believed he could "render service" to the people of County Kildare and offered to stand at the forthcoming elections if required.[54] Grattan remained an influential member of the Edenderry Board of Guardians into the 1880s and was instrumental in the shift in power from unionists on the board.[55] He continued to express opinions on social, economic and political matters until his death. Shortly before he died in May 1886, in correspondence with Alfred Webb, a Quaker nationalist MP, Grattan recalled:

> During my long life I have neither observed nor experienced any intolerance from my Catholic fellow-countrymen, and I never had the slightest apprehension that, should Repeal be granted, my co-religionists would be treated with injustice or intolerance. I would rather be governed by a Parliament of Roman Catholics than a Parliament of Orangemen.[56]

Although he faced considerable setbacks and tragedies during the early years of the Famine, Dr. Richard Grattan continued to exert his influence both locally and nationally in bringing about legislative change for the benefit of the poor and laboring classes. At Edenderry Workhouse, he actively tried to improve the lot of the inmates, who he hoped could become self-reliant and thus allow them to leave and recover from the setback which the Famine wrought. His devotion to public affairs was, he believed, part of his duty. Responding to a perceived slight on his name and character in 1852, Grattan reminded a former member of the Edenderry Board of Guardians that, "in the days of Swift, the Grattans possessed influence, and they have not lost that influence yet."[57]

NOTES

1. *The Nation*, 18 December 1847.
2. *The Dublin Weekly Register*, 22 November 1845.
3. *The Nation*, 1 January 1848.
4. *The Freeman's Journal*, 8 October 1852.
5. Richard Grattan, *Observations on the Causes and Prevention of Fever and Pauperism in Ireland* (Dublin, 1826). He also published a number of other important medical pamphlets including "A case of gangrene, occasioned by the use of Mercury" published in the *Journal of Medical Science* (1822).
6. Dr. Grattan and Dr. Farran, *The report of Doctors Grattan and Farran, to the King and Queen's College of Physicians in Ireland, relative to the estates of Sir Patrick Dun, in the county of Waterford* (Dublin, 1827).
7. William John Fitzpatrick, *The Life, Times, and Contemporaries of Lord Cloncurry* (Dublin, 1855), p. 523.
8. Ibid., p. 558.
9. *The Pilot*, 29 October 1834.
10. *The Dublin Morning Register*, 2 July 1834.
11. "Lord Viscount Morpeth's Testimonial Roll, 1841," see, Christopher Ridgway (ed.), *The Morpeth Roll. Ireland Identified in 1841* (Dublin: Four Courts Press, 2013); there are over 80,000 signatures on the petition appealing for clemency for William Smith O'Brien in 1848/1849. It has been digitized and is available at: https://search.findmypast.com/search-world-records/the-william-smith-obrien-petition-1848-49
12. See *The Clare Journal, and Ennis Advertiser*, 7 October 1839.
13. *The Cork Examiner*, 31 October 1845.
14. House of Commons, "Land Occupation, Ireland: Minutes of evidence taken before Her Majesty's Commissioners of Inquiry into the State of the Law and Practice in respect to the occupation of land in Ireland" (London, 1844), part iii, p 624.
15. *The Catholic Telegraph*, 6 November 1852.
16. *The Freeman's Journal*, 29 October 1845.
17. Ibid.
18. Duke of Leinster to Relief Commissioners, Dublin Castle, 7 December 1845 (N.A.I., Relief Commission papers, 2/Z17412).
19. Journal of Michael Carey, Athy, Co. Kildare (N.L.I., MS 25,299). See also Duke of Leinster to Relief Commissioners, 22 March 1846 (R.L.F.C., 3/1/ 881).
20. *The Kerry Evening Post*, 3 December 1845.
21. *The Dublin Weekly Register*, 29 November 1849.
22. *The Farmers' Gazette and Journal of Practical Horticulture*, 26 December 1846. See also *Dublin Evening Mail*, 10 February 1847.
23. *The Freeman's Journal*, 25 January 1847.
24. *London Medical Gazette: Or, Journal of Practical Medicine*, vol. 4 (London, 1847), pp. 734-735.
25. Ibid.

26. Ibid.

27. Ibid.

28. Ibid.

29. Ibid.

30. For example, *London Medical Gazette, or Journal or Practical Medicine and the Collateral Science (1847)*, pp 733-8.

31. Ibid.

32. *Farmer's Gazette and Journal of Practical Horticulture*, 19 September 1846.

33. Ibid.

34. Ibid., 24 October 1846.

35. Richard Grattan, *Considerations on the Human Mind: its Present State, and Future Destination* (London, 1861), pp 308-309.

36. *Cork Examiner*, 3 December 1849.

37. See for example, *The Freeman's Journal*, 17 December 1849.

38. Richard Grattan, *Observations on the Causes and Prevention of Fever and Pauperism in Ireland* (Dublin, 1826).

39. *The Cork Examiner*, 1 May 1848.

40. *The Kilkenny Journal, and Leinster Commercial and Literary Advertiser*, 12 August 1848.

41. Ibid.

42. *The Nenagh Guardian*, 23 June 1849.

43. *The Freeman's Journal*, 5 April 1853.

44. *The Nenagh Guardian*, 23 June 1849.

45. Ibid.

46. *The Freeman's Journal*, 28 May 1849.

47. Ibid.

48. *The Kerry Evening Post*, 24 November 1852.

49. *The Catholic Telegraph*, 6 November 1852.

50. Grattan, *Considerations on the Human Mind*, p. 273.

51. Ibid., p. 328.

52. *The Nation,* 31 December 1864.

53. Ibid., 9 December 1865.

54. *The Freeman's Journal*, 20 March 1880.

55. For more on this see, Ciarán Reilly, *Edenderry 1916 and the Revolutionary Era* (NP: Naas, 2016).

56. J. J. Clancy, *Short Lessons on the Irish Question; or, The leaflets of the Irish Press Agency* (London: Irish Press Agency, 1890), pp 1-2.

57. *The Catholic Telegraph*, 6 November 1852.

CHAPTER EIGHT

DR. DANIEL DONOVAN (1808–1877)
A Famine Doctor in Skibbereen

Marita Conlon-McKenna

> Starvation is stamped on every countenance; men that were once athletic thrust out their fleshless hands to implore assistance and the cry of "I'm starving ... I am hungry" is dinned into your ears by hosts of famishing women and dying children.[1]

In December 1846, during the darkest days of Ireland's Great Famine, Dr. Daniel Donovan, the dispensary doctor and medical officer for the Skibbereen Union Workhouse, took out his pen and began to write in his diary describing the daily tragedy and calamity he faced. His diary gave a harrowing picture of a desperate people fighting to survive and created a valuable record of those terrible times:

> Legions of half-naked starving people parade the streets of this town, from morning until night, whose importunities are unceasing, and in every direction nothing but misery, the most extreme is to be witnessed.[2]

It was published as *"Distress in West Carberry—Diary of a Dispensary Doctor"* by *The Southern Reporter and Cork Commercial Courier* newspaper over December 1846 and January, February and March 1847. His was a first-hand account written by a professional medical man determined to accurately record conditions faced by those caught up in a humanitarian disaster. Extracts appeared in other newspapers both at home and abroad, including *The Illustrated London News*. His diary not only attracted a flood of charitable donations, but it also drew attention to the town of Skibbereen which was at the very heart of the Great Famine.

Dr. Daniel Donovan, or Dr. Dan as he was known locally, was born in 1808. A son of Daniel Donovan and Frances Galwey, he grew up in a well-to-do family in

Roscarberry, about 12 miles from Skibbereen. He received a fine classical education there at a college run by Mr. George Armstrong. He then studied in Dublin before moving to study medicine at the renowned University of Edinburgh, taking the licence of both the Royal College of Surgeons of Ireland and Edinburgh.[3] A skillful surgeon with a keen interest in diseases of the eye, he then returned to Skibbereen.[4] In 1830, Donovan was appointed medical officer to the nearby Union Hall and Glandore Dispensaries where the young doctor proved himself by working valiantly to save his patients and contain the spread of cholera during the epidemic of 1832-1834. Similar to Dr. William Henry Duncan in Liverpool, his detailed observations on treating cholera were published in a number of medical journals.[5] A tribute by the people of Glandore to Dr. Donovan for his unceasing efforts was published in *The Cork Constitution* in March 1834, to which he responded by expressing:

> [T]he high sense of gratitude that I entertain towards them for the manner in which they have been pleased to express their approval of my conduct since my appointment Medical Officer to that Institution. That I should be instrumental in relieving the suffering of the poor, would be to me at all times a source of the greatest pleasure.[6]

In 1835, Donovan married Henrietta Flynn and they had a large family of five sons and six daughters. Three of his sons would follow in their father's footsteps and study medicine. Donovan was appointed as the first medical officer for the new Skibbereen Union Workhouse and the Skibbereen Dispensary around 1839, which was considered a prestigious position.[7] The Skibbereen Union Workhouse had opened in 1842 with Donovan ensuring that those in need of good medical care received it.[8] Donovan was an active member of the Temperance Society, an advocate for tenants' rights and a regular contributor to medical journals including *The Lancet, The Dublin Medical Times* and *The British Medical Journal*. He was considered an expert on eye diseases and "numbers flocked to him for treatment from all parts of Ireland, England and Scotland."[9] A talented surgeon, he could easily have found position and fortune practicing in Dublin, London or Edinburgh, but instead chose to work in his native area taking care of the local people.[10] He operated on a woman in the workhouse who had lost her sight and suffered from fits: "Dr Dan trepanned her skull and she recovered both her health and her sight. As a surgeon he was bold and skilful and usually successful."[11] At the time, Skibbereen was a large and prosperous provincial town with a brewery and mills. In June 1843, the Great Liberator and MP, Daniel O'Connell, held one of his Monster Repeal meetings in Skibbereen, which attracted a crowd of almost 70,000 people.[12] Most of the land in the district was owned by a handful of landlords with many of their tenants eking out a subsistence living on small, subdivided holdings, totally dependent on their food crop of potatoes.

September 1845 saw the arrival of a strange potato blight which had spread across different parts of Europe. It wreaked havoc on Ireland and its large population of 8.5 million, as more than half of them were dependant on potatoes to feed and sustain them over the long months ahead. Donovan reported at the Carbery Agricultural Society Dinner on 28 October 1845 that, "the wail all around him was that the potatoes were rotting everywhere ... one-third of the entire crop was lost."[13] Families began to suffer, animals were sold and clothes and possessions pawned to buy meal and seed potatoes for the spring. Donovan, a landowner himself, refused to take any rent from his own tenants in Poundlick, one explaining, "It is our family's good fortune that such a sympathetic man as Dr. Donovan leased his land to Timothy. Many other leasees had hard-hearted, absentee landlords, more interested in cash charges than the welfare of their contracted charges."[14]

Numbers entering the workhouse began to rise as the hungry and weak were admitted. The growing amount of people in distress prompted a large and influential meeting to be held in Skibbereen in December 1845. Participants pressed for a public employment scheme to be set up and a fund to provide grain and corn for the needy of the district who endured great hardship. As stored potatoes rotted many were left with little to eat over the long months ahead. Hopes of a plentiful potato crop in 1846 were dashed with the return of the deadly potato blight—the murrain. By 1 August 1846, the certainty of a total failure of the Irish potato crop became known and Lord John Russell, the British prime minister, informed Parliament "that due to the ravages of the potato disease the house would have to take extraordinary measures of relief."[15] Public works would be undertaken with the cost to be borne by local ratepayers. However, the consequences for an already weakened people were disastrous. Alarmed by such a crisis, nearly 1,000 people packed into the courthouse, in what was perhaps the most important meeting ever held in Skibbereen. Gentry, land proprietors, local clergy, solicitors and business people all united in a desperate effort to avert catastrophe. Donovan, a fine orator, gave a landmark speech, urging that they act quickly and petition the Queen to beseech her not to discharge Parliament, which was due to be prorogued on 27 August. He declared that suffering was likely to increase:

> [U]ntil such measures be adopted in reference to Ireland as will tend to relieve the frightful distress that at present pertains and over the universal famine with which the people are threatened ... I have been for eighteen years in close connection with the poor of this county, my professional pursuits bring me into daily

intercourse with them, and I can solemnly assent that within the whole period of my life I never saw such misery and distress as prevails at this moment and I can also assert gentlemen, though I have attended people in disease and distress that my heart never before quailed at human misery, that I have never seen one tenth of the present destitution. ... The whole length and breadth of the union there is not a single potato garden that has escaped; the crop is entirely gone and the people are living on food which is producing unequivocal symptoms of cholera ... all their bed clothes and bedding are in pawn, their articles of dress, almost to their inner garments, are in pledge, and the wretched rags that clothe them by day constitutes their clothing by night.[16]

The Skibbereen Committee of Gratuitous Relief was set up to help alleviate the terrible distress in the district. Donovan would become an important member of this committee and a central figure in relief provision over the next few years as Skibbereen grappled with a tragedy of epic proportions.[17] The committee purchased meal and Indian corn to distribute as there was no food to purchase in the town except on such terms as placed it out of the reach of people: "At the market day in Skibbereen on 12 September 1846 there was not a loaf of bread or an ounce of meal to be had in the town."[18]

By 14 September, 600 people had been admitted to the workhouse, and patients in the fever hospital were sleeping three to a bed. Donovan warned that unless there was intervention, the numbers would grow. Moreover, "great numbers of famished creatures were following members of the relief committee about begging for food."[19] Public works schemes were quickly over-subscribed as undernourished men worked digging roads and breaking stones to earn eight pence a day, barely enough to buy a loaf of bread. Many would collapse or fall ill.[20] Due to an inept bureaucracy, payments to workers were often delayed for weeks. On 30 September 1846, Donovan noticed a group of between 800 and 1,000 tattered skeletal men from the Caheragh works making their way towards the town. He rode ahead to warn them: "those once stalwart men but now emaciated spectres ... marched along bearing upon their shoulders their spades, shovels etc. ... in the glitter of a blazing sun."[21] Shops were closed and 75 soldiers armed with rifles gathered in North Street to stop them. Local magistrate, Michael Galwey, ordered the men to disperse, promising they would be paid in a few days. Donovan sent for the grain depot manager Mr. Hughes, who was ordered by the magistrate to issue them with food. Within a week, Donovan would carry out autopsies on the bodies of two men from the relief works: Jeremiah Hegarty and, a few days later, Denis McKennedy from Caheragh. Shocked by the absence of any sign of food in their bodies, he noted that Hegarty had not been paid for eight days, while McKennedy had not been paid in two weeks. His forthright testimony at both inquests was damning with the headline "Death by Starvation" appearing in *The Cork Examiner* on 16 October:

> Daniel Donovan, Esq. MD sworn: stated that he had examined the body of the deceased ... the stomach and the upper part of the intestines were totally devoid of food ... His opinion as to cause of death is, want of sufficient nourishment was the remote, and exposure due to the cold, the direct cause of death.[22]

On 6 November, McKennedy's inquest was held in the Skibbereen Courthouse:

> Doctor Donovan swore the body was one of the most attenuated he ever saw; there was no appearance of fat either on the surface of the body or within the abdomen; there was scarcely a vestige of omentum. So complete was the absorption of the adipose matter and from the appearance of the body, from the flaccid, empty and blanched condition of the intestines and the fact of having a small quantity of cabbage in the bowels, he was clearly of the opinion that he had died of starvation.

The verdict of the jury, which included Donovan, was that McKennedy had died of starvation owing to the gross negligence of the Board of Works.[23] Unfortunately, many more would die on the public relief works.

On 9 October 1846, *The Cork Examiner* reported the arrival of more troops for the starving inhabitants of Skibbereen and its vicinity: "Instead of bread they received a troop of mounted horsemen."[24] With no official assistance forthcoming, the Skibbereen Committee of Gratuitous Relief took matters into its own hands. It agreed, on 31 October, that relief was urgently needed that did not involve hard labor or admittance to the already crowded workhouse and that the relief would be given at no cost. The committee decided to open a soup kitchen capable of feeding large numbers of people. Thomas Marmion offered the use of the new steam mill overlooking the River Ilen to hold the Charity Soup House, which would be funded by subscriptions. Donovan insisted that the soup served must provide adequate nutrition for the hungry. It was also decided to send a delegation comprising of Rev. Richard Boyle Townsend and Rev. Caulfield to London to appeal directly to the government for urgent assistance for the district.

On 7 November 1846, the Relief Committee proudly opened the doors of Skibbereen's soup kitchen, one of the first large-scale soup kitchens in Ireland.[25] Hundreds of starving men, women and children lined up in the bitter cold to receive a cup of soup and a piece of bread at the mill. Tickets for the soup kitchen were issued at the dispensary. Numbers grew as word spread across the district and thousands flocked there to be fed day after day. Many lives were saved by the foresight and quick and generous action of the committee. It was an enormous achievement that pre-dated many Quaker-financed soup kitchens. Moreover, the British government did not open official soup kitchens across Ireland until the spring of 1847. The Skibbereen committee fed up to 8,600 people every day from the Steam Mill building in Ilen Street.[26] Donovan also set up an emigration scheme with James Swanton, a miller, assisting those with a prospect of work to sail in the empty holds of Swanton's ships to Liverpool and Newport. He ensured passengers were fit to travel, redeemed their pawn tickets for clothing, and gave them two shillings for food. Due to demands on his time, he later handed over the running of the scheme to Thomas Marmion.[27]

The winter of 1846-1847 was one of the coldest on record in Ireland with ice, snow and freezing temperatures lasting long into the spring. Even with the opening of the soup kitchen, the situation in Skibbereen continued to deteriorate and by late November there were more than 890 people in the workhouse with crowds outside begging to be admitted. Donovan noted that many had pawned their clothing and were left only with rags to wear. He noted:

> to what extent they must suffer privations from want of clothing may be judged from the fact that in this town, with a population considerably under five thousand persons, forty thousand pawn tickets, some representing eight or ten articles have been issued within three months.[28]

Such was the suffering in the town that Donovan agreed to let a reporter from the *Cork Examiner* (likely Jeremiah O'Callaghan) accompany him on his medical rounds. The reporter observed that:

> In Bridge Street I visited upwards of 35 houses accompanied by the respected and most indefatigable medical gentleman ... in every instance did I find no less than two members of each family extended on the bed of sickness, labouring under either severe fevers or confirmed dropsical complaints. In one or two instances I saw nine in family disabled by disease without a single individual to procure them nourishment of any description ... anxiously awaiting death to terminate their earthly sufferings.[29]

Three hundred unpaid men from the works in Lisheen, weak from hunger, marched into Skibbereen. Donovan ordered that they be fed immediately at the soup kitchen, warning "that before the close of spring, half the population of this portion of Carbery would have been swept off the earth by starvation."[30] He continued to carry out autopsies, meticulously recording in great detail the terrible effects of starvation on the human body. There had already been seven inquests in the town, where death by starvation had been clearly proven, but there were deaths occurring every day from a similar course of which no cognizance was taken.[31]

Committee members, Rev. Townsend and Rev. Caulfield, had met with Charles Trevelyan, assistant secretary to the British Treasury, on 2 December 1846 in London, and while he appeared impervious to their pleas, on 5 December, he ordered that a portion of funds meant for Ceylon be diverted to Skibbereen.[32] Richard Inglis, a commissariat officer, was also ordered to Skibbereen on 17 December. He saw three dead bodies lying in the street and he buried them with the help of the constabulary. Shocked, he gave an official donation of £85 to the committee towards the soup kitchen and the establishment of another.[33] Donovan suggested that given the huge numbers to be fed that they use rice. He noted:

> [T]he cheapest food that could be got was rice; and if that diet were introduced into the workhouse, and disposed of amongst the people generally, it would save hundreds and hundreds from distress.[34]

Nicholas Cummins, a well-known magistrate from Cork, visited Skibbereen on 15 December, going to the village of Reen first, before meeting with Donovan, who showed him the terrible conditions in the town. Appalled by what he witnessed, Cummins wrote to a number of influential people with no result. He then wrote to the Duke of Wellington, an Irish man. "to save the land of your birth." The letter, which first appeared in the Cork press, was reprinted in the *Times* of London on Christmas Eve:

> My Lord Duke ... The scenes that presented themselves were such no tongue or pen can convey ... six famished and ghastly skeletons, to all appearance dead were huddled in a corner on some filthy straw ... I approached in horror, and found by a low moaning they were alive ... In a few minutes I was surrounded by at least 200 of such phantoms ... Their demonic yells are still ringing in my ears and their horrible images are fixed upon my brain ... my clothes were nearly torn off in my endeavour to escape from the throng of pestilence around.
>
> A mother, herself in fever, was seen the same day to drag out the corpse of her child, a girl about twelve, perfectly naked, and leave it half covered with stones. In another house, within 500 yards of the cavalry station at Skibbereen, the dispensary doctor found seven wretches lying, unable to move under the same cloak, one had been dead for many hours, but the others were unable to move themselves or the corpse ... Lord Duke, in the name of starving thousands, I implore you, break the frigid and flimsy chain of official etiquette, and save the land of your birth.[35]

His pivotal letter caused a huge public outcry and resulted in a flood of donations and the founding of the British Relief Association to help Ireland. A few days later, on 28 December, Donovan wrote with a heavy heart of the worsening crisis in his diary:

[I]n this town [with] the triumph of pestilence and the feast of death … I was told this day by the police that a man had been unburied in a house set on the Windmill: there, one of the most revolting scenes I ever witnessed before me. In a nook in this miserable cabin lay upon a wad of straw a green and ghastly corpse that had been for five days dead and that was already emitting the intolerable exhalations of putrefaction. At the feet of this decomposing body lay a girl groaning with pain; and by its side was a boy frantic with fever.

The wife of the deceased sat upon the filthy floor stupefied from want and affliction. I asked her in the name of Heaven why she did not get her husband buried, her answer was that "she had no coffin." I enquired why she did not go out and look for one, decency would not allow her, for she was naked; the few rags that she had after the fever had rotted off her, and she hoped that a coffin would be her next dress –the children have been removed to the fever Hospital and are now improving… I solemnly declare that no words can exaggerate and no pen can describe the misery that the people of this neighbourhood are enduring.[36]

Donovan agreed to the publication of his own diary, *Distress in West Carbery—Diary of a Dispensary Doctor*. It appeared over a number of months in 1847 in the *Cork Southern Reporter*, with extracts published in Ireland, England and overseas. As a doctor, he was in a unique position to document the terrible suffering endured by the people he attended to. He became known as "The Famine Doctor" and was instrumental in not only raising awareness and much-needed relief for Skibbereen, but also in in attracting other reporters to the town.

By January 1847, people were collapsing and dying on the freezing streets and roads. Typhus and dysentery had begun to spread like wildfire throughout the entire town. The workhouse was "full to suffocation," with 1,169 inmates, for whom staff could not even provide food, as they could no longer get credit from local merchants. They had run out of pallets and blankets for the 332 who were sick in the fever hospital. Donovan called an urgent meeting of the Board of Guardians. The workhouse master, Mr. Falvey, informed them that:

Seven members of the resident staff have been attacked by inmates this past week. One of the nurses has demanded her discharge; the apothecary signified his intention to tender his resignation yesterday and Dr Donovan is nearly broken down in his bodily powers by his persevering exertions.

The shocked board agreed to close the workhouse to further admissions with a few members offering to provide temporary credit.[37]

Donovan continued his heroic duties tending to the sick as a fever epidemic swept through the town, resulting in a high death rate amongst its population. As he recorded in his diary:

Distress is in every hovel and in every hamlet. Corpses in many instances remain uninterred until they become black and bloated, and are then consigned to the grave without the adjunct of a coffin.[38]

He added that his peace had been disturbed on a gale-soaked night by a woman at his door who "appeared as if the grave at that moment had vomited her forth." He gave her a shilling, but she asked him instead to help her to bury her son's body so that the dogs would not eat it. He and his assistant, Mr. Crowley, went that evening to a scene of misery. Dr. Donovan recorded:

The mud floor was one mass of filth-the rain pouring down through the rotten thatch. On the ground ... lay two children, upon whose bodies the anatomy of the bones could be studied as perfectly as on a dried skeleton; and in a ditch in front of the door was a coffin, containing the putrid body of a dead boy seven years old . On my inquiring where she had procured the coffin, her answer to me was that with the shilling I had given her to buy food she had purchased it, and that neither "she nor her children cared about victuals now as they forgot the taste of them."[39]

With no neighbour to help, the two men dug a grave and buried the boy. Dr. Donovan also wrote of seeing Mrs. Keating again, bearing the body of her dead daughter in her arms. "As no Christian will come near me, I carried her into town myself to lay her alongside her father," he lamented. He took the girl's body for burial in the graveyard in Chapel Lane, and at her request sent two men to fetch her son's coffin, which was being disturbed by pigs. The men refused to move it. However, Mrs. Keating carried it into town so that her son could be buried with his father. A week later, the sick woman pleaded with him for money to buy a coffin for her last child. Unable to refuse, he watched in dismay as she set off home carrying it. There, she was found dead at her cabin door, with the empty coffin beside her. He arranged for mother and son to be buried with the rest of her family, vowing in the future to raise a headstone "to this martyr to maternal duty ... this humble heroine."[40] His reports of such human tragedies touched readers deeply.

Skibbereen had become infamous as a place of disease and death, with concerned observers drawn to write about this epicenter of the Famine. One such visitor was the artist James Mahony.[41] He was sent by *The Illustrated London News*, who had published extracts of Donovan's diary. Donovan agreed to let the artist accompany him and Mr. Crowley while they visited patients in the lanes and hovels of the town. Mahony captured these scenes of great suffering and hardship in his sketchbook. He wrote:

I can now, with perfect confidence, say that neither pen nor pencil ever could portray the misery and horror, at this moment, to be witnessed in Skibbereen ...

> We first proceeded to Bridgetown ... There I saw the dying, the living, and the dead, lying indiscriminately upon the same floor, without anything between them and the cold earth, save a few miserable rags upon them. Not a single house out of 500 could boast of being free from death and fever.[42]

Mahony's iconic engraved images and report, *Sketches in the West of Ireland*, appeared in *The Illustrated London News* over three weeks, provoking huge public reaction and donations to Ireland's famine relief. Two students from Oxford, Lord Dufferin and George F. Boyle, also came to Skibbereen. In their *Narrative of a Journey from Oxford to Skibbereen during the Year of the Irish Famine*, they noted that they had "called on Dr. Donovan, the zealous and indefatigable Physician of the place; he is night and day employed in ministering to the poor."[43] Deeply shocked by what they witnessed, the young men published an account of their visit, giving the proceeds to the town.

By February 1847, fever was widespread and with the local bank manager, solicitor and his own family sick, Donovan recorded: "The great amount of professional labour that I have to go through and the serious illness of four of my children, who have caught the prevailing epidemic."[44] Despite this, the doctor was concerned for a young boy who usually called to him for food and when he went to his home, he found the boy trying to bury his father's body. In his diary, Donovan wrote:

> I took the spade from his hands and tried to affect the internment myself; the ground was too hard and we ultimately threw down a portion of an old fence on the body and then laid on some large stones and left it to be, perhaps to some future generation, a monument of the horrible famine era of 1847 ... I had occasion to visit a family of the name of Collins, living about two miles from Skibbereen; in the house there were four children and their mother recovering from fever, they had no nutrient of any kind, and although now convalescent from disease will no doubt perish from want.[45]

Elihu Burritt, an American humanitarian who came to Skibbereen in February, described it as a "Potter's Field of destitution and death." He accompanied Donovan on some of his medical visits. In *A Journal of a Visit of Three Days to Skibbereen, and Its Neighbourhood*, Burritt recounted:

> As soon as Dr. D—— appeared at the head of the lane, it was filled with miserable beings, haggard, famine-stricken men, women, and children, some far gone in the consumption of the famine fever ... In every hovel we entered, we found the dying or the dead.[46]

However, it was the children with staring eyes, stick-like limbs and extended swollen bodies which Burritt admitted "haunted me during the past night, like Banquo's ghost."[47] Having witnessed "as much as my heart can bear," and fearful of contagion, Burritt left the area, but his moving account reached a wide readership in America, which helped relief efforts.

As the death rate climbed, Donovan oversaw the opening of large burial pits in Abbeystrowry graveyard, and the town employed men with a cart to collect the bodies and bring them for swift interment. Despite some opposition, he instigated a cull of all dogs in the district: "I see the domestic animals converted into beasts of prey that feed upon the bodies of their previous owners," Donovan lamented.[48] He also arranged for soup to be delivered to the homes of those too weak or ill to walk to the workhouse along with clean straw for bedding and the floor. The committee also delivered large pots of soup on carts to outlying areas. Donovan, a compassionate man, showed enormous fortitude in the face of such human disaster, using his diary and writings to express his fears for a people on the brink of death. He declared that:

> I cannot remain silent; I cannot refuse to proclaim the miseries of the working classes when I see them reduced to a hoard of shivering wretches ... I cannot relinquish my efforts to arouse the benevolence of the wealthy when my fellow creatures are drooping around me like windlestraw in the snow.[49]

Working in such atrocious conditions, Donovan fell ill with typhus but, upon his recovery, returned to his medical duties. However, he later admitted that "almost every person actively engaged in the administration of relief to the poor was attacked with fever."[50] Two physicians calculated that, in 1847 alone, 131 medical men succumbed to epidemic and contagious disease—an extraordinary toll out of 2,600 doctors in Ireland.[51]

Skibbereen was fortunate to have so many good men, prepared to not only put pen to paper, but also to act in a practical way to help the starving and the sick. Donovan paid tribute to them:

> The Skibbereen Committee will pass unscathed through any ordeal, and the members may without flattery claim to themselves to have done some good for the country at large. They were the first who called a public meeting as early as the month of August, at which the perilous state of the country was made known; they were the first who sent a deputation to England and aroused the sympathies of that benevolent people; they were the first who, in conjunction with some estimable members of society now stricken with pestilence, the consequences of their meritorious exertions for the poor, established a soup kitchen, and they (a service never to be forgotten) were the first who instituted inquests on those that died of starvation on the public works.[52]

By summer 1847, temporary fever hospitals were opened across the union, most still in operation up until later in 1848. The Soup Kitchen Act which had fed up to three million people across the country since April, ended in September 1847, and was replaced by an amended Poor Law that permitted "outdoor relief."[53] This provided that those unable to work or destitute widows with children would either be admitted to the workhouse if there was space, or receive food from it. However, the addition of the Gregory Clause meant that those who held a small quarter acre of land were not entitled to any form of relief unless they were prepared to give up their holding. They were "starved into the workhouse and out of their own homes."[54] Landlords took advantage of this provision, and evictions soon followed with people faced with choosing between the workhouse, the roads, or assisted passage on ships to Canada and America.

More than 5,300 people were on the list of Skibbereen Union for outdoor relief in November 1848 with at least 3,100 in the workhouse. By April 1849, the number in the workhouse had risen to 3,784, with 15,748 on the list for outdoor relief.[55] A number of auxiliary workhouses had opened, including one for women in Swanton's Store on Levis Quay.[56] Between 1848 and 1850, Donovan helped to select 110 orphan girls from the workhouse, aged 14 to 18, to take part in the Earl Grey Irish Orphan Assisted Emigration Scheme to Australia. Most were employed as domestic servants on their arrival.[57]

Donovan continued over the years to work tirelessly on behalf of the people of Skibbereen. His meticulous reports about the effects of starvation on the human body and famine fever based on his extensive medical experience were published in numerous medical journals and textbooks. His work was quoted in almost every medical text as an authority on famine, fever and cholera.[58] In 1863, he was presented by the surrounding gentry with a service of plate and a purse of 150 guineas in recognition for his services to the poor.[59] Due to poor health, Donovan retired from his duties in the Union Dispensary and Workhouse in 1868. His son, Daniel, returned from serving as a doctor in the navy to take over his father's position.[60] Donovan's later years were filled with failing health and the loss of his sight. Confined to his home, he also suffered financial difficulties as the company that managed his pension failed and he had only his meager Union pension to live on. An appeal was published in the *Times* of London and *The British Medical Journal* seeking an increase in his pension: "This much esteemed physician is still alive, utterly broken down in health ... and in poor circumstance," it entreated.[61] He and his wife, Henrietta, also endured the sad loss of their son, Henry, in 1873, followed by Jerrie, a surgeon in the navy, who died after contracting malaria in West Africa.[62]

Dr. Donovan died on 30 September 1877, at age 69, and was buried in Roscarbery. His funeral was one of the largest held in the district. Hundreds of people flocked to Skibbereen from the neighboring country and towns. The people insisted on carrying the remains on their shoulders for a long distance from the town. Carriages of the surrounding gentry followed, forming a procession of nearly a mile and a half in length. A noticeable feature of the sad cortege was a procession composed of the children from Skibbereen Workhouse, the institution which had for so many years been the scene of Donovan's unceasing labors.[63]

The heroic doctor was remembered in glowing tributes as one of the finest medical men of his time. According to the *Freeman's Journal*:

> We know of no other case in which a man who never left a small provincial town is regarded in the world of medical science as a great original authority. His exertions day and night succouring the poor and afflicted were almost superhuman.[64]

The Skibbereen Eagle also paid tribute:

> When we consider what he must have endured in visiting the sick, in this then extensive Union on those cold and dreary nights—entering sooty cabins, dens of pestilence ... we ... are astounded how human nature was capable of such endurance. But his elastic frame and constitution of steel were equal to the occasion.[65]

Tributes were paid to the doctor by his peers in the medical world:

> Seldom outside of some large city or metropolis has a medical man gained for himself so wide a reputation as Dr Donovan ... During those memorable famine years, when so many were paralysed with fear and doubt, Dr Donovan's energy rescued hundreds from starvation and death.[66]

Following his death, Donovan's widow received a Royal Bounty of £200 in consideration of the humane and successful efforts of her late husband during the Famine of 1846-1847.[67] Henrietta Donovan died in 1883.

On 4 June 2002, the Skibbereen Famine Commemoration Committee erected a plaque at the entrance of Abbeystrowry graveyard to Dr Daniel Donovan "in memory of his care and compassion to the people of Skibbereen during the Famine."[68] Nine to ten thousand famine victims lie buried there, and it is considered a National Famine monument. Donovan also features prominently in the Great Irish Famine Exhibition in the nearby Skibbereen Heritage Centre. It honours him as a hero of the Famine— just as he was described in 1877, upon his death:

> Dr. Daniel Donovan, one of the heroes of the most melancholy chapter of our melancholy history—the great Irish famine. We need scarcely remind anyone who

has ever heard or read of that awful catastrophe that the place where the misery culminated, where the most fearful want was felt, was the town of Skibbereen ... His exertions day and night in succouring the poor and afflicted were almost super-human. He was the soul, the centre, and the organiser of all the plans of relief by which aid was brought to the agonised people.[69]

NOTES

1. Doctor Daniel Donovan, "Distress in West Carbury, Diary of a Dispensary Doctor," *The Southern Reporter*, 23 January 1847.

2. Ibid.

3. Rev. Richard J. Hodges, *Cork and County Cork in the Twentieth Century* (Brighton: Pikes New Century Series, 1911), p. 141.

4. Edel Kavanagh, "A Short Biography of a Dispensary Doctor," *Skibbereen and District Historical Society Journal 2010-2012*, vol. 8 (Cork Local Studies, 2012), p. 9.

5. See chapter nine by Christine Kinealy.

6. "Address to Dr. Daniel Donovan," *The Cork Constitution*, 4 March 1834. Philip O'Regan, "Dr Daniel Donovan –Heroic Figure of the Famine in Skibbereen," *The Southern Star*, 25 May 1929.

7. Hodges, *Cork and County*, p. 141.

8. Kavanagh, "A Short Biography of a Dispensary Doctor," p. 9.

9. Ibid.

10. Ibid., p. 10.

11. Ibid., p. 9.

12. Patrick Hickey, *Famine in West Cork: The Mizen Peninsula, Land and People 1800-1852* (Cork: Mercier Press, 2002), pp 110-111.

13. *The Cork Constitution or Cork Advertiser*, 1 November 1845.

14. Thomas Philip O'Driscoll, "The Irish Origins of the O'Driscoll Family of Grass Valley, Western Australia—Natives from Skibbereen, County Cork."

15. Cecil Woodham-Smith, '*The Great Hunger. Ireland 1845-49* (London: Hamish Hamilton, 1962), p. 106.

16. *The Cork Examiner,* 21 August 1846.

17. The Skibbereen Famine Commemoration Committee, *Sources for the History of the Great Famine in Skibbereen and Surrounding Areas*, vol. ii (Skibbereen: Skibbereen Heritage Centre, 2000), p. 8.

18. Woodham-Smith, *The Great Hunger*, p. 124.

19. Skibbereen Famine Commemoration Committee, vol. ii, p. 38.

20. Woodham-Smith, *The Great Hunger*, p. 124.

21. Canon John O' Rourke *The Great Irish Famine* (Dublin: Veritas, 1989), pp 130-131.

22. *The Cork Examiner*, 16 October 1846.

23. O' Rourke, *The Great Irish Famine*, pp 130-131.

24. Skibbereen Famine Commemoration Committee, vol. ii, pp 43, 49-51, 56-59; *The Cork Examiner*, 9 October 1846.

25. Pat Cleary and Philip O'Regan, *Dear Old Skibbereen* (Skibbereen: Skibbereen Printers Ltd., 1995) pp 52-57.

26. Ibid.

27. Terri Kearney and Philip O'Regan, *Skibbereen: The Famine Story* (Dublin: Macalla Publishing, 2015), p. 55.

28. Donovan, *Diary,* 23 January 1847.

29. *Cork Examiner,* 18 December 1846.

30. Peter Foynes, *The Great Famine in Skibbereen* (Skibbereen: Irish Famine Commemoration, 2004), p. 51.

31. Donovan, *Diary*, 23 January 1847.

32. Foynes, *The Great Famine in Skibbereen,* p. 55.

33. Woodham-Smith, *The Great Hunger,* p. 163.

34. *The Cork Southern Reporter*, 18 December 1846.

35. N.M. Cummins, JP, To His Grace, the Duke of Wellington, 17 December 1846, *The Cork Examiner*, 21 December 1846.

36. Donovan, *Diary*, 18 December 1846.

37. "The Close of the Workhouse," *The Cork Examiner*, 25 January 1847; Foynes, *The Great Famine in Skibbereen,* p. 62.

38. Donovan, *Diary*, *The Cork Southern Reporter*, 26 January 1847.

39. Ibid.

40. Ibid.

41. Also see chapter sixteen by Niamh Ann Kelly.

42. James Mahony, "Sketches in the West of Ireland," *The Illustrated London News*, 30 January 1847.

43. Lord Dufferin and the Hon. G.F Boyle, *Narrative of a Journey from Oxford to Skibbereen during the Year of the Irish Famine* (Oxford: John Henry Parker, 1847), p. 20.

44. Donovan, *Diary*; *The Southern Reporter*, 15 February 1847.

45. Ibid.

46. Elihu Burritt, *A Journal of a Visit of Three Days to Skibbereen, and Its Neighbourhood* (London: Charles Gilpin, 1847), p. 2.

47. Ibid., p. 11.

48. Donovan, *Diary*, *The Cork Southern Reporter*, 20-March 1847.

49. Ibid.

50. Breandán Mac Suibhne, "Disturbing Remains; A story of Black '47," *The Irish Times*, 27 January 2018.

51. Ibid.

52. Donovan, *The Cork Examiner*, May 1847.

53. Kearney and O' Regan, *Skibbereen: The Famine Story,* pp 39-42.

54. Ibid., p. 52.

55. Ibid., p. 39.

56. Ibid., p. 55.
57. Ibid., p. 59.
58. Hodges, *Cork and County*, p. 141.
59. *British Medical Journal,* 27 October 1877, p. 610.
60. Hodges, *Cork and County*, p. 141.
61. *The British Medical Journal,* 8 September 1877, p. 364.
62. Hodges, *Cork and County*, p. 141.
63. *The Cork Examiner,* 5 October 1877.
64. *Freeman's Journal*, 2 October 1877.
65. *The Skibbereen Eagle,* 6 October 1877.
66. *The British Medical Journal,* 27 October 1877.
67. Ibid., 2 September 1878.
68. Emily Mark-Fitzgerald, *Commemorating the Irish Famine: Memory and the Monument* (Liverpool University Press, 2015), p. 145.
69. "Death of Dr. Donovan of Skibbereen," *Dublin Weekly Nation*, 6 October 1877.

CHAPTER NINE

DR. WILLIAM DUNCAN OF LIVERPOOL (1805–1863)

"A City of Plague"

Christine Kinealy

As is evident from a number of chapters in this volume, the deadly impact of the Great Hunger was not confined to the island of Ireland. By the end of 1846, the Famine was being transported overseas as thousands of Irish poor, often diseased and desperate, sought a new life outside Ireland. For many, the Port of Liverpool in the north west of England was the first stage in the journey; for others, it proved to be a final resting place. The response of the city to the unfolding crisis was diverse as the authorities sought to satisfy unprecedented demands on their resources. Moreover, even before the Famine influx, Liverpool had been labeled the unhealthiest city in the United Kingdom. This chapter explores the contributions of those people who helped the Irish in their quest to survive, in particular, the contributions of a local doctor, William Duncan, who was also a pioneer in public health reform.

William Henry Duncan was born on Seel Street in the center of Liverpool on 27 January 1805, to a wealthy merchant family of Scottish origin. After studying medicine in Edinburgh, he returned to his home city and by 1830 was practicing medicine in his lucrative private practice in Rodney Street, but he was also serving in a voluntary capacity in the Liverpool Infirmary and two local dispensaries.[1] The cholera pandemic, which swept through Europe in 1832, brought Duncan into the limelight as a believer in the link between the spread of epidemics and the environment.[2] The work of Duncan and a handful of other medical practitioners during the epidemic was an important step in the advent of what became known as a "public health agitation."[3] Duncan emerged as a leader of this movement based on his considerable and painstaking empirical research gathered in the back-alleys of Liverpool, home to the poorest of the poor, many of whom were Irish. With the support of the prominent social reformer, Edwin Chadwick, the young Duncan became a champion of public health reform throughout the United Kingdom.[4]

In 1840, Duncan showed himself to be an expert on public health when he gave evidence before a Select Committee to examine circumstances affecting health in "large towns and populous districts."[5] The committee included Irish MP, William Smith O'Brien, although little time was given to Ireland. Duncan was described in the minutes as "an intelligent physician resident at Liverpool."[6] His insights into the living conditions of his home city were disturbing. He estimated that over 20 percent of the working population, approximately 38,000 people, were living in cellars which were "dark, dank, confined, ill-ventilated and dirty." Moreover, sometimes three or more families resided in one cellar.[7] A further 86,000 people were living in courts, which were also high density and low quality housing.[8] At this stage, almost one-quarter of the population of Liverpool (approximately 60,000 people) were Irish and Duncan confirmed that "spirity [sic] drinking" was prevalent amongst them—English men preferring ale.[9] Based on his research, the poor Irish disproportionately accounted for people seeking medical relief, comprising 50 percent of all patients. When asked about the discontent of the lower classes, he responded:

> I hardly ever see a discontented Irishman; he seems quite contented in whatever condition he may be ... nearly one-half of the patients who come to the dispensary are Irish. They seem to be satisfied and contented in whatever state they are, and have no desire to improve their condition ... A greater number of cases of fever occur among the Irish, comparing the portion of Irish to the great working population in general ... and they pay less attention to cleanliness and congregate together in great numbers.[10]

Duncan's suggestions for improved health amongst the lower classes were progressive, including better dwellings, sanitation, sewerage, ventilation, and parks for adults and playgrounds for children.[11] Side by side with this abject poverty, Duncan explained that sections of the city of Liverpool and its population were thriving economically. The dock area was expanding, a new custom house was opening, property prices were rising and the wealthy inhabitants lived in villas surrounded by pleasure grounds. As Duncan told the committee, "the external appearance of the place, whether from its docks, from its warehouses, or the general aspect of the buildings in its surrounding districts, is that of the most prosperous description."[12] Duncan's testimony was an unequivocal reminder of the great social and economic disparities that had accompanied industrialization and urbanization.[13]

Over the next few years, Duncan consolidated his position as an expert on public health through many publications and lectures.[14] A pamphlet published in 1843 was frequently quoted in the national press, contributing to a growing momentum for public health reform. Duncan had identified poor housing as a key factor in the spread of disease, especially the existence of cellar dwellings in cities such as Liverpool and Manchester. Duncan's description was frequently quoted:

> The cellars are ten or twelve feet square, generally flagged, but frequently having only the bare earth for floor, and sometimes they are less than six feet high. There frequently is no window, so that the light and air can gain access to the cellar only by the door, the top of which is often not higher than the level of the street. In such cellars, ventilation is out of the question. They are, of course, dark; and, from the defective drainage, they are also very generally damp. There is sometimes a back cellar used as sleeping apartment, having no direct communication with the external atmosphere, and deriving its scanty supply of light and air solely from the first apartment.[15]

However, largely due to Duncan, the city was also in the forefront of taking measures to address public health issues. In 1846, the Liverpool Sanitary Act had provided for the appointment of three men, including Duncan, to tackle this problem.[16] This made Duncan the first medical officer of health in the country. A series of meetings on public health was held in the city, including a large one on 8 December 1846. Duncan was keynote speaker and the audience included, "a numerous attendance of the working-classes." The message was dismal in regard to the health of the city, which had deteriorated rapidly over the previous 30 years:

> The mortality amongst the children in Liverpool was frightful to contemplate, for, out of every one-hundred children born, forty-nine died before they were five years old, and in Vauxhall Ward, the average was sixty-four out of every hundred: in addition to that, the average age at which the working-classes died in Liverpool was fifteen years.[17]

Regardless of these grim statistics, the meeting concluded on a positive note, with Duncan outlining the measures that were being put in place and calling on the working classes to play their part to assist, promising if they did so, "there could be little doubt of ultimate success ... If they only persevered, a complete revolution would be made in this respect in a very short time."[18] However, events unfolding across the Irish Sea made this a hollow promise. Nobody at the meeting predicted that a famine in Ireland would bring new and more deadly dangers to Liverpool, leading Duncan to describe it as "the city of plague."[19]

The year 1847, often remembered as "Black '47" in Irish lore, proved to be a dark year for Liverpool too. As early as February, Duncan warned that "should the destitute Irish continue to flock into Liverpool as they are still doing, there can be little doubt that what we now see is only the commencement of the most severe and desolating epidemic which has visited Liverpool for the last ten years."[20] The "new" Poor Law of 1834 had created the Liverpool Poor Law Union, which was coterminous with the parish, with the workhouse located in Brownlow Hill. The workhouse had been expanded in 1842-1843, with accommodation for 3,000 inmates, making it the largest in the country.[21] Rather than being governed by the more usual Board of Guardians, a Select Vestry, consisting of 25 men, controlled matters relating to the relief of the poor in the parish.[22] In his new capacity as medical officer, Duncan reported to them.

By early March, the arrival of the Irish poor was having a detrimental effect on mortality in the town. Already, a number of parish officers had died of fever or smallpox, thought to be caught while they were assessing claims for assistance. One local newspaper urged that "prompt and severe remedies be taken" to stop the influx of the Irish to Liverpool. In addition to the risks to the health of the city, their presence was placing a heavy burden on the parochial rates. The paper warned that unless the influx was stopped, "we shall be shunned by the healthy and opulent, and by those who now frequent the port for purposes of business or pleasure."[23] Disease was also taking its toll on the front-line workers. Duncan's report to the Select Vestry on 27 April recorded:

> Three of the relieving officers have already died of typhus fever, and one now lies dangerously ill. One of the medical officers is dead; another is dangerously ill. One of the nurses of the Lying-in Hospital is dead; another ill. 654 paupers have been buried in the Workhouse Cemetery during the last month, the average number of interments during the last twelve years being only 1,367 annually; so that in one month the interments have nearly equaled half the number which they usually amount to in one whole year.[24]

To meet the emergency, it was proposed four additional surgeons be employed to support the two already in place. To cope with the rapid spread of fever, erecting temporary fever sheds near the workhouse was also proposed.[25]

As the mass of Irish poor flocking to the city showed no signs of abating, local newspapers started to provide statistics on the number reaching Liverpool each day. In the final two weeks of April, an average of 12,000 paupers were arriving daily in the city, climbing to over 13,000 on 24 April.[26] Lieutenant Hodder, the emigration agent, stated that 40,662 persons from Ireland had emigrated from Liverpool to America since December last.[27] The impact was quickly felt by the local poor law authorities. A report by the governor of the workhouse revealed the depth of the crisis he was facing, with applications for admission being made hourly. Virtually all of the applicants were suffering from fever or dysentery, but the fever wards were full, leaving him with a dilemma: "To send them away was perhaps to send them to perish in the streets, whilst to admit them was to incommode the other inmates, and, perhaps, risk their lives." He feared the workhouse was turning into a "lazar-house."[28] The Select Vestry responded by directing the governor to admit no more when the workhouse became full and creating a sub-committee to consider what additional accommodation could be utilized.[29] This response mirrored what was happening in many poor law unions within Ireland.

As the situation continued to deteriorate, with fever in the city becoming out of control, appeals were made to the government for assistance, including financial support. Similar to their response to Irish pleas for aid, the government was insistent that local ratepayers in Liverpool should bear the burden of local poverty, even if that poverty was imported. Nonetheless, in recognition of Liverpool's problems, two experienced medical officers were sent to the city to work with the local doctors in early May.[30] Additionally, responding to repeated demands by the Select Vestry for lazarettos to be situated in the River Mersey, they were informed:

> The lords of her Majesty's Privy Council have given instructions to the superintendent of quarantine, at Liverpool, to place, without delay, at the disposal of the parochial authorities, two of the lazarettos now in the river, to be used as hospitals for the sick.[31]

The Privy Council further decreed:

> All passenger vessels arriving from Ireland shall be boarded by the tide surveyors, who shall cause the yellow flag to be hoisted and kept flying at the mast head, until such vessel shall have been examined by the medical staff appointed for the purpose, and until the sick, there be any such on board, shall have been removed direct to the lazaretto. [32]

To ensure that these measures were stringently observed, "notification will be given to the commanders of all passenger vessels from Ireland, that should any of their vessels arrive here a second time with sick on board, they will be subjected to quarantine for a certain length of time."[33] These measures were an admission of a city overwhelmed by the demands being placed on its already strained medical services.

A proposal to locate fever sheds between Brownlow Hill and Mount Pleasant alarmed the population of the nearby affluent Abercromby Square and Rodney Street areas—the latter including the home and practice of Duncan. Throughout April, a number of concerned inhabitants convened meetings to protest against this location. They met with the Health Committee of the Select Vestry, who were "courteous" but not helpful.[34] A deputation attended the weekly meeting of the Select Vestry and "complained that the establishment of fever sheds at Brownlow Hill had filled the respectable portion of the inhabitants of that neighborhood with alarm, and they stated that it was the decided opinion of the medical profession that the fever cases should be removed out of Liverpool."[35] They argued that the sheds were damaging the local economy as neither visitors nor merchants would travel to the city. The delegation suggested that all fever patients should be relocated to the floating lazarettos. The chairman of the Select Vestry defended the location of the sheds, pointing out that with 3,000 fever victims in the city, the lazarettos were inadequate.[36] Other members of the Select Vestry were more forthcoming, one informing the delegation that:

> The parish authorities were beset with difficulties; they wished not to do anything which might tend to raise apprehension in the minds of the inhabitants; but the emergency was great, and the sheds, which were ready for the reception of fever patients now, were erected upon the emergency of the moment.[37]

It was pointed out to the delegation that some years earlier, a cholera shed had been erected in Haymarket and they had not objected. To allay their concerns, the Select Vestry promised to convert the privies into water-closets, raise the walls and extend the ventilation.[38] The delegation remained dissatisfied and held a further meeting, creating a subcommittee of seven men, and "memorials were ordered to be drawn up and presented to the Poor Law Commissioners and to Sir George Grey against the occupation of the obnoxious sheds."[39] At the end of April, a "numerous meeting of the burgesses of the ward" was held to again ask for the sheds to be removed, with a memorial signed by over 200 inhabitants.[40] They had hoped to include support from Duncan, but he was away in London.[41] One of the arguments used against the erection of the sheds was the question of whether the fever was contagious, a topic that split medical opinion. However, as the Select Vestry informed the various delegations, they had sought the advice of Duncan before erecting the sheds and he was firmly of the opinion that the fever was not contagious.[42]

In May, as the inflow to Liverpool continued from Ireland and the warmer weather exacerbated the spread of disease, the alarmed inhabitants of the Abercromby Ward continued to demand the Select Vestry remove the sheds from the union altogether. Two separate delegations, one from the Abercromby Ward and one of local ratepayers, attended the Select Vestry meeting of 11 May with the same common purpose. On their behalf, Dr. Sutherland spoke in his capacity as a medical man. Sutherland, who had been educated in Edinburgh, was a senior physician to the Liverpool dispensaries. Like Duncan, he was a campaigner for better sanitation and in 1844 had been a founding member of the Health of Towns Association.[43] Unlike Duncan, Sutherland believed that the fever epidemic did present a danger to local inhabitants and could spread among them.[44] He informed the meeting: "If he had his will, he would not only not use these sheds, but remove all fever cases out of the boundary of Liverpool."[45] Again, the Select Vestry stood firm. To Sutherland's suggestion that more use be made of the lazarettos, the chair pointed out that while the government had promised to supply three vessels, only one had been made available and the lower parts of the ship were not appropriate for fever victims. He reaffirmed that the land adjoining the workhouse (which they owned) was the best place for the fever sheds, pointing out, "if no place had been found, they should have had the town about their ears, and wherever they were placed there would be an outcry."[46] When the deputation withdrew, the issue was revisited and a motion put that the fever sheds should be located in the poorer north end of the city, an area known as Sandhills. It was rejected on the grounds that the two men who proposed it rarely attended the Select Vestry meetings and that sick people needed immediate attention. At the end of a long and quarrelsome meeting, it was decided that the fitting of the fever sheds and lazarettos should proceed as had been originally planned. Also, the worsening situation led the Select Vestry to meet weekly rather than fortnightly. Each alternative meeting would be devoted to matters connected with the Irish inflow by the newly convened Irish Relief Committee.[47]

In early June, Duncan informed the Select Vestry that all privies in the sheds had been converted to water closets, adding, "the inhabitants of Abercromby Ward ought to be satisfied.[48] They were, however, far from happy. Arguing that their incomes had been damaged, the inhabitants sent a memorial to the town council demanding financial compensation for the lodgers and tenants who had left their houses.[49] At this stage, mortality had risen to 20,000 deaths a year, far higher than the previous average of 8,000 annually. Mortality was highest in the impoverished (and largely Irish) Exchange, Vauxhall, and St. Anne's Wards, although mortality had not risen in the Abercromby Ward. In response to the mounting crisis, Duncan recommended additional fever sheds be made available. Consequently, more fever sheds were opened in Great Howard Street, close to the dock area, notably the Clarence Dock where immigrants from Ireland landed. The inhabitants of the area also objected, sending a memorial to the Select Vestry. Duncan responded to them directly:

Sir,—With reference to the memorial from the householders of Great Howard-street, Chadwick-street, and the neighbourhood, complaining of the fever sheds which have been opened in that locality, and which was referred to me by the Health Committee at their last meeting, I beg to report that I have made the necessary examination, and that I am of opinion that no danger is to be apprehended to the health of the inhabitants of the neighbourhood, from the existence of the sheds in question. Theory and experience alike justify me in giving this opinion in the most decided terms. No instance is recorded, so far as I am aware, of the contagion of typhus fever having been propagated under such circumstances. —I have the honour to be, your most obedient servant.[50]

The residents in both the Abercromby Ward and Great Howard Street were supported by some of the local press who were similarly critical of the doctor's suggestions that the sheds were safe and that fever was not contagious. They challenged his assertions by sarcastically pointing out:

> It is pleasant and conducive to the comfort of the people who are so happy as to live in the locality of fever hospitals, to see cart loads of coffins brought in daily, of course to be freighted back with the bodies of human beings. It is pleasant too to see fever-stricken wretches staggering by your door, in search of the means of dying under proper medical superintendence, and being buried at the cost of the parish.

They added that Mount Pleasant was no longer pleasant and suggesting that Great Howard Street be renamed "Great Fever-street."[51]

While the death of doctors or priests and vicars was usually noted in the local press, the deaths of those who supported them was often ignored, rendering them invisible in the historical record. One article in a local newspaper provided an unusual insight into the risks faced by nurses:

> Their daily contact with the disease so rife amongst the immigrants from Ireland, it is pleasant to find that we have amongst us a class of persons who, from the remuneration offered them, must be presumed to be unsusceptible of contagion. We saw, a week ago, an advertisement from the Select Vestry for nurses for the patients at the fever sheds, the salary offered being eight pounds per annum. Of course, any poor woman, whose necessities may induce her to risk her life for such a pittance, will be allowed to hope for a legacy from some of her Irish patients some of these odd days; or the chance of a matron dying off, and a nurse stepping into her shoes, may be held out as a prospect of benefit of survivorship.[52]

Despite the opposition to the fever sheds, by mid-June, upon the recommendation of Duncan and his medical officers, the Select Vestry decided to open more. Space was now required for 5,000 patients. The expansion would cost the ratepayers an estimated £35,000. For some members of the Select Vestry even these measures were inadequate, leading to a proposal to erect additional sheds on the shore in nearby

Crosby, for as many as 6,000 patients. An argument was made that they should undertake this expansion whatever the cost, on the grounds that "unless they rooted out the evil now from the cellars, they never could get clear of it."[53] One of the proposed locations was Athol Street, close to Great Howard Street and to the docks. Here though, the plan was to take over a vacant building. Again, the local people objected on the grounds that the building had almost no ventilation and no yard, and there was no sewerage in that or the adjoining street. They pointed out that it would lead to a deterioration in property prices and small owners "would be brought to disgrace and ruin."[54] Throughout the summer, complaints against the fever sheds continued to be made, with Duncan being called on repeatedly to assure those living in adjoining properties that they were safe, based on his personal inspections.[55] The state of the city led the authorities to again appeal to the government for more assistance, even sending a delegation to London to meet the Home Secretary, George Grey. Duncan was part of the group.[56]

By mid-July it was estimated that over 300,000 paupers had arrived from Ireland and many were living in the cellar dwellings. Over the summer months, in an attempt to limit the spread of fever, the Liverpool authorities, under Duncan's guidance, undertook to "purify" the cellars inhabited by Irish paupers as they were regarded as a major source of disease. In the longer term, the solution was to fill the cellars with sand so they could not be lived in, but it would mean that the poorest would have nowhere to go.[57] Despite all Dr. Duncan's efforts, fever continued to spread. In the space of four months, mortality from fever had risen by 2000 percent, an increase that not even Duncan had foreseen.[58] He reported that since the beginning of June, it had appeared in the wealthier parts of the city and 100 "English" residents had died, most of whom, in Duncan's opinion, would have been alive if "the grievous Irish influx had not occurred."[59] Duncan estimated that 5,000 people in the city had fever and a new threat had appeared in terms of a small pox epidemic. Again, the latter was attributed to the Irish influx, it being stated that vaccinations were rare amongst the Irish poor. Duncan recommended that more hospital accommodation be found and more medical staff be employed.[60] His labors were being hampered in another way, however, with the parish registrar demanding his usual fee of one shilling for each extract the doctor took from the death records. The Select Vestry felt they had no recourse but to ask the government to intervene and make the records more readily available.[61] In late July, the government offered the city an additional hospital ship, the *Lancaster*, but, following a lively debate, the Select Vestry turned it down on the grounds that the expense of making her ready for patients was prohibitive. The combined fever sheds could now accommodate 900 people, although there were only 600 patients, meaning that one shed in Brownlow Hill was empty.[62]

For some people in Liverpool, a solution to the problems they were facing was to return the Irish poor to Ireland. "Settlement" had been part of the English and Welsh Poor Law since the time of Elizabeth 1, which meant that the Irish poor had no legal right to poor law relief in either country. A law passed in 1846 introduced the concept of "irremovability," but only following five years' residence.[63] The Famine Irish clearly had no such entitlement. Removal, however, was a complex and costly process that involved a magistrate. Towards the end of April 1847, the Select Vestry of Liverpool sent a long petition to the House of Commons appealing for the regulation of the pauper influx from Ireland to ports like Liverpool and Glasgow, pointing out that not only were the poor dying, but many medical personnel who tended to them had died.[64] Over the summer, an act was passed that meant it was no longer necessary to involve a magistrate in the process.[65] As a consequence, removals from Liverpool immediately increased and by August, between 400 and 500 Irish were being shipped home each week.[66] The Liverpool authorities hoped that the new policy would deter other new arrivals from seeking relief.

In mid-September, Duncan reported that fever was abating in the city. Since early August, mortality had been decreasing and fallen to 354 a week compared with the figures in excess of 400. While fever remained the main cause of death, diarrhoea, smallpox and measles had proved fatal to sections of the population over the summer. Included amongst those who had died were several medical practitioners. Displaying his love of statistics, Duncan had prepared a chart for the Select Vestry, showing "in a very clear and compendious manner the progressive rate of mortality, both from fever and from ordinary causes, since the commencement of the year."[67] The respite proved to be brief. In October, a Liverpool newspaper reported with alarm that Irish pauper immigration was again increasing at a "fearful rate." Describing many of them as "clamorous beggars," it warned: "We have borne our heavy affliction thus far with tolerable patience; but even the most patient will be forced to kick at last."[68] An adjoining column in the paper reported that Dr Duncan had been elected treasurer of the Liverpool Literary and Philosophical Society.[69] It was a reminder that life went on even as the Famine continued its deadly work.

For Duncan, despite his best efforts, Liverpool in 1847 had become a city of plague, but even as he wrestled with the immediate need to save lives, he implemented measures to improve the longer-term health of the city's poor. In March 1848, Duncan reported a reduction in mortality, with deaths from fever at the lowest in 12 months.[70] Since the beginning of the year, Duncan had closed 7,840 cellars and enforced a rigorous cleaning of filthy houses and streets under the newly passed Sanitary Act. Despite the challenges that the city had faced, Duncan remained optimistic that Liverpool could lead the way in public health reform.[71] In the summer, Duncan reported that mortality had returned to its usual pre-1846 rate. Moreover, fever, which had accounted for 30 percent of all mortality in the previous year, had largely disappeared.[72] In June 1848, there had been 26 deaths from fever, whereas in June the previous year, there had been not fewer than 769.[73] It was a positive development but, just as Liverpool was showing signs of recovery, another pandemic appeared—cholera. It was a disease that Duncan had some familiarity with, as it had last appeared in the city in 1832. Cholera had a devastating, if short-term, impact on Liverpool and other ports in the United Kingdom where it was most virulent.

Duncan responded to the new public health crisis with a rigorous program of cleaning measures, which included emptying cesspools, removing "nuisances" (debris) from the streets, repairing middens, court flagging and water channels.[74] Duncan's work was hampered by the reluctance of the Select Vestry—largely for financial reasons—to implement sanitary measures required by the Public Health Act of 1848.[75] Duncan's direct appeal to the General Board of Health in London led to them directing the Select Vestry to initiate the immediate appointment of 20 additional medical men to undertake house to house visits, as required by the legislation. This outside intervention was regarded as intolerable by many members of the Select Vestry who believed they were doing everything to arrest the spread of disease. For some, Duncan's actions were regarded as an act of betrayal.[76] The tensions between the medical officer and the Select Vestry intensified further when the Board of Health in London sent its own medical officer, Dr. Grainger, to the city. His report was scathing, accusing the Select Vestry of having "done nothing" and insisting that they had "violated the law." Furthermore, they had ignored Duncan's advice to move the hospital from Queen Anne-Street, which was at the center of the cholera outbreak, to another district.[77] An angry Select Vestry responded to these criticisms by laying the blame on their medical officer, stating, "had Dr. Duncan been more frank and communicative to the Vestry, much more might have been done." More moderate members of the Vestry, however, prevailed and all references to Duncan were removed from the final response.[78] The incident provided an insight into the differences between the medical board and the Select Vestry and how divisive a figure the city's foremost medical officer had unintentionally become.

It was not until mid-September 1849, that Duncan was able to announce that "the scourge of cholera" was materially abating in the city.[79] His report to the Select Vestry in December 1849 revealed that the mortality from cholera in the parish during the year had reached 4,167. The total number of deaths for the first nine months of the year had been 11,119 and during the same period in 1847 it had been 14,547.[80] The discussion that followed this report revealed deep divisions regarding Duncan's role during the various health crises. Whereas Archdeacon Brooks suggested that a vote of thanks be made to Duncan for giving his services "readily and willingly," a Mr. Mellor objected, stating: "It might as well be left out for what good he has done us." The latter was supported by Mr. Churchwarden Dover, who condemned the "health-mongery" in the country. Criticism was made of Duncan's insisting on having so many fever sheds in the preceding years, which had imposed great expense to the parish. These criticisms were supported by Mr. Hodson who opined that the public health movement was "a great humbug."[81] Again, the moderates prevailed and a unanimous vote of thanks was passed to Duncan.[82] The discussion was a telling revelation of the deep divisions that existed regarding public health, with the cost being measured in pounds rather than in lives saved. Clearly, for some members of the Select Vestry, Duncan was the villain.

Duncan died in May 1863, at age 58. He had spent his final few months in Scotland in an unsuccessful attempt to restore his "shattered health."[83] He was celebrated in the local Liverpool press as the man who had done more than any other to reduce mortality in Liverpool, thus making it one of the healthiest cities in Britain.[84] The greatest challenge to Duncan's vision had undoubtedly occurred as a result of the Famine influx. When reflecting on the response of the various authorities to this crisis, he defended the local Select Vestry for their actions in 1847, believing they had acted promptly and efficiently given their resources. However, he lamented the fact that the government had not intervened sooner and introduced the 1848 Public Health Act a year earlier.[85] In keeping with his views on public health, Duncan was adamant that the mortality experienced in Liverpool and other cities had not been inevitable, but was largely attributable to the overcrowded conditions in which the poor were forced to live:

> It was not simply over-crowding, but the huddling together of a host of half-starved vagrants, in miserable dwellings, in the worst-conditioned districts of the town— over-crowding in filthy, ill-ventilated houses; confined, abominable courts; and dark, damp, underground habitations, affording, in many instances, not more than 30 or 40 cubic feet of air to each inmate.[86]

More radically, he challenged those who doubted the link between poverty and the propagation of disease, especially regarding the deaths of the Irish in Liverpool:

> I would simply ask such objectors whether they really believe that if these destitute Irish had been lodged in clean, well-ventilated, wholesome habitations, such

as could be commanded by proper sanitary regulations, with 300 or 400 cubic feet of air to each inmate, fever would have prevailed among them to the extent it did? Or, do they suppose that, crowded together in the dwellings I have described, the dietetic regimen of a London alderman would have materially diminished the register of deaths?[87]

Duncan's comments were a reminder that government intervention in the late 1840s could have alleviated much of the suffering of the Irish poor. Instead, famine, disease and death were transported to cities overseas, including Liverpool, Glasgow, Boston, Toronto and Montreal.

Was Duncan a famine hero? Probably not in the typical sense of somebody who championed the cause of Irish Famine refugees unreservedly.[88] Yet, as a frontline worker in a city that faced overlapping fever, smallpox and cholera epidemics, he repeatedly risked his health and his life amongst the sick and dying of Liverpool and Ireland. Perhaps Duncan's heroism lies in his dogged insistence that mass mortality through disease was preventable, and that the poor, whatever their origin, had a right to live in a clean and healthy environment and to public health care.

NOTES

1. S.P.W. Chave, "Duncan of Liverpool— and some lessons for today," *Community Medicine* (1984), 61-71, p. 63.
2. Dr William Henry Duncan, *Medical Memories* at: https://medicalmemories.wixsite.com/medicalmemories/dr-william-henry-duncan
3. W.M. Frazer, *Duncan of Liverpool* (London: Hamilton, 1947), p. 49.
4. Edwin Chadwick (1800-1890) was an English social reformer who was associated with Poor Law reform and public health reform.
5. *Report from the Select Committee on the Health of Towns; Together with the Minutes of Evidence Taken before them, and an Appendix, and Index*, BPP (London: House of Commons, 17 June 1840), p. xi.
6. Ibid., p. viii.
7. Ibid., Minutes of Evidence, qu., 2373 and 2374, p. 141.
8. Ibid., qu., 2522, p. 150.
9. Ibid., qus, 2465 and 2466, p. 146.
10. Ibid., qus, 2536, 2539 and 2540, pp 150-151.
11. Ibid., p. xx.
12. Ibid., qus, 2529, 2530, 2531 and 2532, p. 150.
13. Ian Morley, "City Chaos, Contagion, Chadwick, and Social Justice, *Yale Journal of Biology and Medicine* (June 2007), 80 (2), 61–72, at: www.ncbi.nlm.nih.gov/pmc/articles/PMC2140185/

14. W.H. Duncan, "On the physical causes of the high rate of mortality in Liverpool: read before the Literary and Philosophical Society, in February and March 1843" (Liverpool: Joshua Walmsley, 1843).

15. "Important Document on the Health of Towns," *Montrose, Arbroath and Brechin Review; and Forfar and Kincardineshire Advertiser*, 16 October 1846; "Health of Towns," *Liverpool Mercury*, 21 November 1845.

16. Sanitary Act (Liverpool), 9 & 10 Vic. cap. 127.

17. "The Health of Towns Association," *Liverpool Mail*, 12 December 1846.

18. Ibid.

19. W.H. Duncan, *Report to the Health Committee of the Borough of Liverpool, on the Health of the Town during the Years 1847-50* (Medical Officer of Health Reports, 1851), Lancashire Record Office, H352.4/HEA, p. 7.

20. "On the Epidemic Fever lately Prevalent in Liverpool, by Dr. Duncan," *Liverpool Standard and General Commercial Advertiser*, 6 June 1848.

21. "The Workhouse. The story of an Institution," at: www.workhouses.org.uk/Liverpool/

22. Ibid.

23. "The Reports of Dr. Duncan," *Liverpool Mail,* 13 March 1847.

24. "Select Vestry—Tuesday," *Liverpool Standard and General Commercial Advertiser*, 4 May 1847.

25. Ibid.

26. "Irish Paupers," *Liverpool Mercury*, 30 April 1847.

27. Ibid.

28. "State of the workhouse," *Liverpool Mercury*, 30 April 1847.

29. Ibid.

30. "Liverpool and the Irish. The Health of the Public," *Manchester Courier and Lancashire General Advertiser*, 12 May 1847.

31. Ibid.

32. Ibid.

33. Ibid.

34. "The Fever Sheds in Mount Pleasant," *Gore's Liverpool General Advertiser*, 29 April 1847.

35. "Spread of Fever, Liverpool," *Manchester Courier and Lancashire General Advertiser,* 12 May 1847.

36. Ibid.

37. "Meeting of the Select Vestry," *Liverpool Mercury*, 30 April 1847.

38. Ibid.

39. "The fever sheds in Mount Pleasant," *Gore's Liverpool General Advertiser*, 29 April 1847.

40. Memorials were a commonplace way of solicitation in Britain and Ireland, they being "a written statement of facts submitted to a government, authority, etc., in conjunction with a petition."

41. "The Fever Sheds in Mount Pleasant," *Gore's Liverpool General Advertiser*, 29 April 1847.

42. "Select Vestry—Tuesday," *Liverpool Standard and General Commercial* Advertiser, 4 May 1847.

43. John Sutherland (ed.), *The Liverpool Health of Towns' Advocate* (Liverpool: J. Walmsley, 1846).

44. "Select Vestry," *Liverpool Mail*, 15 May 1847.

45. "Meeting of the Select Vestry, Tuesday, MAY 11, 1847," *Liverpool Mercury*, 14 May 1847.

46. Ibid.

47. Ibid.

48. "Health Committee," *Liverpool Mail*, 5 June 1847.

49. "Monthly meeting of Town Council," *Liverpool Standard and General Commercial Advertiser*, 8 June 1847.

50. Letter from Duncan, 27 May 1847, from Rodney Street, Liverpool, reprinted in "Health Committee," *Liverpool Mail*, 5 June 1847.

51. "The Fever Sheds," *Liverpool Standard and General Commercial Advertiser*, 8 June 1847.

52. "Value of a Hospital Nurse's Life," *Liverpool Standard and General Commercial Advertiser*, 8 June 1847.

53. Ibid., "Meeting of Select Vestry," 22 June 1847.

54. Ibid.

55. "The Health Committee," *Liverpool Mail*, 17 July 1847.

56. No title, *Liverpool Standard and General Commercial Advertiser*, 22 June 1847.

57. "The Health Committee," *Liverpool Mail*, 17 July 1847.

58. "On the Epidemic Fever lately Prevalent in Liverpool, by Dr. Duncan," *Liverpool Standard and General Commercial Advertiser*, 6 June 1848.

59. "The Health Committee," *Liverpool Mail*, 17 July 1847.

60. Ibid.

61. Ibid.

62. "Select Vestry," *Liverpool Mail*, 7 August 1847.

63. "The Poor Removal Bill," House of Commons, *Hansard Debates,* 23 July 1846, vol. 87, c. 1383.

64. "To the Honorable the Commons of Great Britain and Ireland," *Liverpool Mercury*, 30 April 1847.

65. "Poor Removal (England and Scotland) Bill," House of Commons, *Hansard Debates*, 7 May 1847, vol. 92. c. 546.

66. "Select Vestry," *Liverpool Mail*, 7 August 1847.

67. "Health of the Town," *Liverpool Standard and General Commercial Advertiser*, 21 September 1847.

68. Ibid., "Irish Pauper Immigration," 19 October 1847.

69. Ibid., "The Liverpool Literary and Philosophical Society."

70. "Health of Liverpool," *Liverpool Mail,* 11 March 1848.

71. "On the Epidemic Fever lately prevalent in Liverpool, by Dr. Duncan," *Liverpool Standard and General Commercial Advertiser*, 6 June 1848. The Sanitary Act was part of the 1848 Public Health Act.

72. Ibid.

73. Ibid., "Health of the Town," 25 July 1848.

74. Ibid., "The Health Committee," 5 December 1848.

75. R.J. Morris, *Cholera 1832—The Social Response to An Epidemic* (New York: Holmes & Meier, 1976), p. 197.

76. "Dr. Duncan—the Board of Health and the Vestry," *Liverpool Mail,* 11 August 1849.

77. Ibid., "Special Vestry Meeting," 29 September 1849.
78. Ibid.
79. *Saint James's Chronicle*, 22 September 1849.
80. "The Medical Officer," *Liverpool Mail*, 1 December 1849.
81. Ibid., "The Select Vestry."
82. Ibid.
83. "Death of Medical Officer of Health," *Gore's Liverpool General Advertiser*, 28 May 1863.
84. "Death of Mr Lloyd and Dr Duncan," *Liverpool Mail,* 6 June 1863.
85. "On the Epidemic Fever lately prevalent in Liverpool, by Dr. Duncan," *Liverpool Standard and General Commercial Advertiser*, 6 June 1848.
86. Ibid.
87. Ibid.
88. In Liverpool, Duncan is commemorated with a number of public buildings, and even a Public House, being named in his honor.

CHAPTER TEN

DR. CHARLES EDWARD STRUTT (1814–1897)

A Modest Famine Hero

Rebecca Abbott

In late August 2013, Jude Collins McBride stood in St. Francis Xavier's Roman Catholic Church in Arncliffe, south of Sydney in New South Wales, Australia. As her husband, Terry McBride, and a grandchild played in the background, she pointed to a stained glass window with the inscription: "In loving memory of Thomas Collins, died October 28, 1930." Jude and Terry had only learned about the window in the 1990s, when a parish priest contacted the family to explain it was a memorial to an ancestor. Jude's nephew, Peter Coll, remembered his elderly grandmother telling a fantastical story (which the family thought she might have imagined, in her dotage) about a girl and her cousin traveling all the way to Australia from Ireland in the mid-nineteenth century. The news of the memorial window inspired the family to research into Thomas Collins. To their delight, they discovered he was the son of Mary Ann Roughan, who had traveled to Australia from Ireland at the tender age of 16. Mary Ann left a workhouse in County Clare in 1849 with her 18-year-old cousin, Eliza Roughan. They boarded a ship, the *Thomas Arbuthnot*, bound for Australia as part of the Earl Grey Irish Orphan Assisted Emigration Scheme. The Great Hunger had killed both girls' parents, leading them to choose perhaps their only option for survival. Still, it seems impossible that Mary Ann could imagine, as she and Eliza experienced the frightening unfamiliarity of their 99-day voyage to Sydney, that within ten years she would marry John Harvey Collins and give birth to six children, including Thomas, only to die a month after bearing her last child.[1] Equally unimaginable was that her children—like those of so many other assisted emigrants—would create ever-widening circles of descendants. It is one of the wonders of endurance in the lasting wake of *An Gorta Mór*, the Great Famine—an endurance that was amelio-rated by the work of Dr. Charles Edward Strutt.

Mary Ann Roughan's story echoes that of many of the 4,114 young women who took part in the Earl Grey Assisted Emigration Scheme of 1848-1850. The scheme was initiated by Henry George Grey, the third Earl Grey, who was the British secretary of state for the colonies in Lord John Russell's administration. Grey's responsibilities included emigration and convict transportation to the colony of Australia. His eponymous scheme offered orphan girls in disease-ridden, over-crowded Irish work-houses the opportunity to travel to Australia to begin new lives working in domestic service, as farm hands, or in other occupations during a year-long indenture. The cost of their passage and the full kit of clothes and travel necessities provided for them was underwritten through assisted emigration. The scheme was motivated both by the alarming number of "inmates" in Ireland's famine-stressed workhouses, and the need—in the predominantly male-populated Australia—for more young women of employable and marriageable age.

Within that context, Mary Ann Roughan is part of a smaller and especially fortu-nate group, the 200 girls who sailed on the *Thomas Arbuthnot* under the compas-sionate and caring watch of the surgeon superintendent, Dr. Charles Edward Strutt. The story of Strutt and his voyages on the *St Vincent* and the *Thomas Arbuthnot* are detailed in his personal journal held in the La Trobe Library, Melbourne, Australia.[2] Much of the journal from the *Thomas Arbuthnot* has also been reproduced—with extensive details about Strutt and the young women in his care—in *A Decent Set of Girls: The Irish Famine Orphans of the Thomas Arbuthnot 1849-1850* by Richard Reid and Cheryl Mongan, which provided the fullest existing account of Strutt's life, but is sadly out of print.[3]

Charles Strutt was born in 1814 in Colchester in England. Little is known about his early life, except that he qualified in medicine in Edinburgh and London. His voyages to Australia during the height of the Great Famine marked him as a pioneering medical practitioner, willing to be part of a new project to take orphaned teenage girls from Ireland half-way across the world. The voyage on the *Thomas Arbuthnot* was not Dr. Strutt's first as a surgeon superintendent. He supervised four voyages to Australia between 1848 and 1851, and possibly a total of 20 in his life-time.[4] Strutt was rare among his colleagues for his professionalism and humanity and because, in addition to the travel logs newly required by the Colonial Office for government-assisted ships, Strutt kept his own private journals for the voyages on both the *St Vincent* and the *Thomas Arbuthnot*. The journals are among the few remaining documents of life onboard emigrant ships during that period. As surgeon superintendent, Strutt took full responsibility for the health and welfare of emigrants traveling in 1848-1849 on the *St Vincent*, which carried 251 assisted emigrants (individuals and families including 83 children), plus additional paying passengers. During the voyage he wrote:

> The grand reason of the good state of health is the great attention I pay to cleanliness in all parts of the ship. Then we have fiddling and dancing every evening from seven till half past eight, which is good for the spirits, and excellent exercise.[5]

Francis L. S. Merewether, an agent for immigration in Sydney, was impressed that the vessel was "in an unusually cleanly state on arrival."[6] Once the ship had docked, young women who had no one to meet them were sent to the female immigrant depot at Hyde Park Barracks. There, Strutt was distressed to observe their poor treatment in comparison with other passengers. He visited them the next day when they were presented for hire. Strutt played an active role as their advocate, making sure they were well-placed and well paid.[7] Shortly afterwards, he was enlisted by local immigration authorities to care for passengers of the newly arrived *Steadfast*, a ship that made port in a state of filth and disarray and on which disease had cost the lives of 11 of its 218 passengers. Strutt arranged a thorough cleaning of the ship and successful care for the sick passengers, which included the ship's own doctor.[8]

Strutt traveled during a time of greatly increased migration, the dangers of which caused demands for a closer oversight from the Colonial Land and Emigration Commission.[9] These dangers predated the Famine exodus of the late 1840s. As Haines noted:

> In the 1830s—the first decade of systematic emigration—a number of ships suffered high mortality as the Colonial Office agency responsible for mobilizing assisted emigrants (the Colonial Land and Emigration Commission) fine-tuned its regulations, especially those concerning the surgeon superintendent's authority to enforce health-promoting routines on board.[10]

Still, "little could the Emigration Commission have envisaged, as colonial demands for labour grew shrill in the late 1840s, that the proportion of emigrants dying would soar on a number of ships only a few years later."[11]

Part of the difficulty in securing dedicated surgeon superintendents for emigrant transport was their remuneration. They were paid "10*s*. a head on all emigrants landed alive in the colony,"[12] an amount that increased when families were transported but not when orphan girls were the sole passengers. Strutt returned to London after his voyage on the *St. Vincent* just as the Colonial Land and Emigration Commission was discussing the need to increase pay for the doctors accompanying orphan ships.

Strutt's appointment to supervise the *Thomas Arbuthnot* proved to be a case in point. As noted in Colonial Office records:

> We have further to state, that in the case of the "Thomas Arbuthnot" which we are about to dispatch on the 22nd instant with Irish orphans to Sydney, and to which we have appointed ... a gentleman named Strutt, who has once been employed in our service with much credit to himself, is one to which we think that the increased scale of remuneration might very properly be expended.[13]

Upon accepting his new appointment, Strutt arrived in Plymouth in the south of England on 10 October 1849. There, he met 208 young and unsophisticated orphan girls who had just arrived from Irish workhouses on an open-deck steamer journey from Dublin. Finding them cold, wet, exhausted and most likely apprehensive—if not terrified—about the long voyage ahead, Strutt arranged for them to have warm baths and haircuts, after which he "examined them all again, they now appear a decent set of girls."[14]

Strutt would have been familiar with the news reports of prejudice and anger that the Earl Grey scheme had generated in a colony already beleaguered by its early history as a penal colony, during which time, British and Irish courts had sentencing convicted criminals to a punishment of transportation to Australia. The *Sydney Morning Herald* protested:

> [T]he thing has turned out altogether different from what we were given to expect. Instead of a few hundreds, the girls are coming out by thousands ... For Irish emigrants we read Irish paupers misnamed female orphans.[15]

The paper later observed that "there is shown by the public a decided preference for other bounty immigrants, on account of the inexperience and incapacity for household work of the orphan girls."[16] The *Goulburn Herald and County of Argyle Advertiser* similarly complained that:

> [W]e do not in anywise compromise our expressed opinion, that orphan girls, union paupers and ragged schoolboys are not fit to form the parents of a future colonial population ... We are not quite certain but that prisoners would be preferable to this kind of emigration for it is utterly impossible to guard against the impositions of new arrivals who land with a "clean bill of health," from the emigration officers.[17]

Regrettably, these authors could not imagine the hundreds of thousands of descendants of the original 4,114 orphan girls now living and flourishing in Australia.

Strutt was accompanied on the *Thomas Arbuthnot* by several matrons who, with Strutt, gave instruction in arithmetic, reading, writing and needlework. He persuaded the girls, who were both Protestant and Catholic, to be tolerant and kind to one another.[18] Strutt's manner combined parental discipline with benevolence, and tutorial instruction with encouragement and understanding—quite distinct from many, if not most, surgeon superintendents on other orphan ships. Trevor McLaughlin has highlighted this difference in attitudes:

> [H]ow the attitudes and reports of Surgeons from orphan ships coloured the way the orphans were viewed and received in Australia. There's a very marked difference between Surgeon Strutt (*Thomas Arbuthnot*) and Surgeons Douglass (*Earl Grey*), Eades (*Roman Emperor*), Ramsay (*Inchinnan*) and Hewer (*Elgin*). Surgeon Hewer was to write "I was so disgusted by the behaviour of the orphans per "Elgin,"—so worried by their tricks, simulating fits day after day to procure porter and spirits—so disheartened by their misrepresentation and utter disregard for truth, that I would not come out in another Irish orphan vessel if the Government would pay me £10 per orphan."[19]

Strutt, in comparison, demonstrated a warm understanding of adolescent psychology and an innovative practicality as he focused on the welfare of his charges. His daily journal entries reveal his solicitude. On 1 November, during a rough night, Strutt "went below to console and encourage my people." Several days later things had improved: "A fine day, with gentle fair breeze ... Washing day and had some difficulty in getting it fairly to work. The girls, however, begin to find that some cleanliness and order are necessary, in which laudable idea I shall encourage them as much as I can."[20]

Strutt applied a kind, guiding hand throughout the voyage, combining structure with playful diversion. For example, he wrote in his journal on 8 November, "Began preparations for the schools. Had lanterns on deck, and let the girls remain till eight o'clock, singing and dancing." On 7 December he noted, "My girls have become much more orderly and tidy under the constant steady pressure." By 10 January, he was proud that they "keep their place very clean and neat" and "are at last full of emulation to excel." Strutt also found inventive ways to improve conditions on board ship:

> November – Friday 9. Therm. 76 and a half. Had a wire grating made for the main hatch; it is to be kept open all day, and locked at night, whereby two doors and four windows can be kept open between decks. A great improvement for the ventilation although it had been pronounced impossible in London; and I have had no small difficulty in overcoming the objections to the expense, which it was said would amount to several pounds. It was made in one day and cost half a crown.[21]

Strutt and "his girls" spent Christmas in rolling seas just off the Cape of Good Hope, but they made the best of it. Strutt noted that: "The Captain gave them a supply of plum pudding and I made them five bucketfuls of punch, by way of cheering their spirits ... I gave the girls leave to make a moderate noise till 10 o'clock so altogether the day passed off well enough."[22] When they finally arrived in Sydney Cove on 4 February, they were met by several officials including immigration agent, Francis Merewhether, who, Strutt observed, "were greatly pleased with the order and regularity of the ship, the fatness of my girls and the cleanliness of their berths, tables, decks, etc."[23] He felt the girls deserved high praise for their hard work.[24]

Despite the great success of their journey, Strutt and Merewhether experienced lingering distrust in Sydney over the introduction of additional Irish orphans into the area. An alternative was proposed to find opportunities for the girls further afield. On 11 February, Strutt wrote, "Mr. Merewether [sic] talks of sending some of the girls to Yass; so, I volunteered to go with them, and beat up for recruits. 130 at once expressed their wish to go any place that I might be going to."[25] Mary Ann Roughan was once again fortunate to be among them. The group traveled with matron, Mary Collins, on horse-drawn drays (wagons) over rough and mountainous dirt roads to the Yass/Gundagai region near Canberra, a trip of over 230 miles (376 km) that took two and a half months. Strutt traveled with them as their champion, and to find them work placements that he considered to be wholesome, suitable and safe.

On 18 February, they departed Sydney by steamer to Paramatta where they joined their horse-drawn transports. That evening, Strutt wrote that he had "housed them comfortably ... and saw that they got their dinners. A grand thing to keep them well fed."[26] Strutt continued making daily entries in his journal, many of which reflect the often-perilous challenges facing a wagon train of 14 large, horse-drawn wagons. Sleeping on the ground meant being "tormented by ants, fleas, or some creature that bit like fury," and on a rainy night Strutt would gather "as many as I could under my tarpauling [tarpaulin]." Other localities had no rain. As Strutt recorded: "everything dried up and parched...Saw several dead bullocks...they perish from fatigue, thirst, starvation ... we had to go nearly a mile down a sort of gully, for water."[27] Misfortune occurred just two days into the journey. On 20 February, Strutt wrote:

> Got to Camden early in the afternoon, but very unluckily, not without accident – One man, Willis, was passing another dray driven by Connor, when a link in the harness of the latter's horse broke, and the two drays came into collision, and two girls, Mary Brandon and Mary Conway, were thrown off, or jumped off, and the wheel went over their legs. They were obliged to be left at Camden under the care of the Surgeon Magistrate, Mr. Bransby, a rough, uncouth, uncourageous personage. I consoled them as much as I could, and fortunately a priest, an Italian, was there, and undertook to see them well cared for.[28]

Illness was also a challenge. As Strutt recounted on 19 February:

Williams was knocked up, with sore throat, headache, etc., and I had all the work to do: cooking and everything ... Three girls also were taken ill with headache, sickness and purging—Got them to bed as soon as we could, and gave them some hot tea which set them to rights. On lighting the fire, a vast tarantula walked out not liking the flame -- I instantly killed him. Today we have made 15 miles.[29]

As they approached the settlement of Yass—the first opportunity to find employment—on 1 March, Strutt noted that "the girls got at their boxes to make themselves smart for entering Yass tomorrow, 3 miles off."[30] He spent the next days at the Yass depot arranging placements for the young women.

As Strutt secured employment opportunities, he also ensured that placements were worthy. For example, he wrote in his journal: "Thursday 7. Having heard that two of our girls had been engaged by improper persons, I consulted the Magistrates."[31] Strutt learned they were "improper persons to have the care of female orphans—whereupon I took them away. The one mistress was anxious to have another girl instead so I took away the one she had at once, leaving her to discover that she would not get one."[32] Strutt's travels with the girls continued past Gundagai to Wagga Wagga and Tumut, and Mary Ann Roughan—one of the last to find employment—was hired by John Jenkins on 15 April from Gundagai Depot.[33] She worked as a house servant for Jenkins in Fish River (near Jerrawa) where she met John Collins, a laborer in Yass. Mary Ann and John were married in November of that year and lived at his farm at Fairy Hole Creek.[34]

Strutt's journal reflected his friendly and sociable contact with each community as he sought work for his charges and, where needed, helped with illness or injuries. On 7 April 1850, he noted in his journal: "Went to see one of Mr. Whitty's men who had fallen and hurt his shoulder about five weeks ago. I found the humerus was dislocated forwards ... I succeeded in reducing it, to the old fellow's great satisfaction."[35] On his return trip from Gundagai, Strutt visited as many as he could of the newly settled girls. In most cases, he was satisfied they were in good hands, but when not, he found them new situations.[36] After passing Yass on 28 April, he wrote: "At Camden I saw Mary Brandon who had been hurt on our passage up the country—she was better and at service though her leg was not quite well."[37]

Newspapers that had disparaged the Irish orphans' arrival in Australia took a different tone after witnessing Strutt's efforts. The *Goulburn Herald and County of Argyle Advertiser* declared on 30 March:

[W]e [of Yass] feel great pleasure in recording the fact that, although the women are Irish and Roman Catholic, and their Surgeon Superintendent an Englishman and Protestant—there is not one of them who hears his name mentioned without blessings and expressions of gratitude—which speaks volumes for the kindness liberality and Christian-like feeling of all ... In conclusion, we have to express our regret that any reflections should have been made upon the capabilities and conduct of these young women—for howsoever much they may have given room for censure elsewhere—in this township and district they are highly appreciated and respected.[38]

Several weeks later, the Yass community published a one-paragraph encomium to Strutt:

Sir, We the undersigned inhabitants of the town and district of Yass, beg to convey to you on the occasion of your departure from our district, the expression of our thanks for the admirable manner in which you have discharged your duties as Surgeon Superintendent of the Female Irish Orphan Immigrants, during your stay amongst us; and we feel that it will be as satisfactory to you to learn, as it is pleasing to us to mention, the general good conduct of the fifty girls who have obtained situations amongst us.[39]

The letter concluded: "We are, Sir, Your very obedient servants," followed by 48 signatures. Strutt published his appreciative reply a week later:

[W]hile returning you my best thanks for the flattering opinion you have been pleased to express, it is but right to add that my duties have been comparatively light, as not a single girl occasioned any trouble by misconduct during the whole voyage from England, nor on the journey from Sydney to Yass and Gundagai.[40]

Strutt returned to London on the *Thomas Arbuthnot* a few weeks later.

The thoughtful words of Charles Edward Strutt in his *St Vincent* and *Thomas Arbuthnot* travel journals convey such a strong sense of the often-delightful warmth and care he felt for his charges, that the reader is inclined to feel a personal familiarity with the doctor himself.

Yet, despite the record of his birth in 1814 to doctor/painter Jacob George Strutt and writer Elizabeth Strutt,[41] there is little else known about his life before his work as a surgeon superintendent other than confirmation from the Royal College of Surgeons of Edinburgh that Strutt received the college licentiateship in 1840 (although he was not a Fellow there).[42] It is possible that, during some of the intervening yearsm Strutt accompanied his father, mother, and younger brother, Arthur, on their travels to France, Switzerland and Italy to work as artists and writers. Their names appear in an article from the *Victorian Periodicals Review* about the creation of an English-language publication in Rome titled *The Roman Advertiser*, whose first editor was "replaced by the painter and travel writer Arthur John Strutt (1819-88), who arrived in Rome as a child with his parents: the landscape painter Jacob George Strutt and the travel writer Elizabeth Strutt."[43] Jacob Strutt's work has been termed both Italianate and in the style of the well-known painter—and Strutt's acquaintance—John Constable.[44] As a novelist and travel-writer, Elizabeth Strutt was described as having "various literary ability, and competent to almost all sorts of work."[45]

Charles Strutt made his return trip to London on the *Thomas Arbuthnot* on 8 April 1850. The ship must have passed in transit the *Maria,* the last of the 20 ships that had conveyed Irish orphan emigrants to Australia between 1848 and 1850, which arrived in Sydney on 1 August of that year. Had there been less of the controversy that led to the abrupt end of the Earl Grey Scheme, Strutt would probably have continued to accompany more ships carrying Irish orphans to Australia. As it was, he immediately signed up as Surgeon Superintendent to assist emigrants on the *Harry Lorrequer* in 1850 followed by the *Elgin* in 1851.[46] New opportunities then beckoned and Strutt settled in Geelong in the state of Victoria, Australia with two appointments in June 1852: the first to the permanent staff of the Victorian civil service, and the second as assistant immigration agent in Geelong.[47] The next year he was made assistant health officer there.[48] Then in 1854, on 24 May, Charles Edward Strutt married Margaret Bridget Ryan in Christ Church, Geelong. Strutt was 39, Margaret—an Irish immigrant—was 22 and originally from Ennis, County Clare.[49] Their first child, a daughter named Elizabeth Sarah Strutt, was born in Geelong the next year.[50] In 1856, Strutt was named acting immigration agent for the Colony of Victoria.[51]

Strutt's career in Australian civil service progressed rapidly. 1856 saw Strutt become the first police magistrate of Echuca, 200 km north of Melbourne in Victoria.[52] Echuca was a frontier border town established only a few years earlier by the operator of a pontoon bridge and dock allowing passage across the Murray River into New South Wales, a location that eventually became a major inland port. Strutt and his growing family began their life there in rough circumstances. When they left Echuca ten years later, to the great sadness of a community that had grown to love them, a newspaper tribute described the family's early life: "For over twelve months his family had to live in tents on the banks of the Murray and many inconveniences and privations were suffered by them during that time. Ultimately, however, he built for himself a brick house on the banks of the Campaspe. Four of his children were born there, one of which died in its infancy."[53] In addition to being police magistrate and physician, Strutt accepted a wide variety of additional appointments, including Assistant Commissioner of Public Lands,[54] Guardian of Minors,[55] work as a commissioner appointed to improve the condition of the Murray River[56] and to create the Echuca School,[57] and quite a few other responsibilities. For three years, he "commuted" to Rushworth and Murchison, a 170 km round trip, in order to perform the duties of police magistrate there.[58] Strutt was praised, upon his departure, for his "kindly, considerate, and charitable disposition," his "impartial and consistent conduct on the Bench," and for "ever being found ready as a private gentleman to act the Good Samaritan."[59] In addition to the many contributions he made to these communities, another role that Charles Strutt undertook—as honorary guardian of Aborigines—would situate him at least at the fringes of the struggle for Aboriginal autonomy and identity.

Arriving in Australia as they did during the mid-nineteenth century, Dr. Strutt and the Irish orphans were unaware, at least initially, that they were part of a vast upheaval transforming life on the continent. Since its establishment as a penal colony in 1788 by the British government, the eastern and southern areas of Australia under-went increasingly rapid settlement through emigration, convict relocation, agri-cultural development, and, ultimately, the discovery of gold in 1851, which brought hundreds of thousands of immigrants from around the world into Victoria and New South Wales.[60] But this surge in European influence was also a time of profound and devastating change for those who had called the continent home for 40,000 years or more. "At least 1,600 generations of Aboriginal people have made a continuous life in Victoria," notes Richard Broome. [61] Some Australian settlers became alarmed by the impact their own increasing presence was having. An early "Protector of the Aborigines"[62] observed: "nowhere else in the empire did 'there exist a people so help-lessly situated so degraded, so neglected, so oppressed.'"[63] By 1860, the population of Aboriginals had fallen from 60,000 to around 1,800.[64] The oppression and demise of the original peoples of Australia had been movingly written about by the Polish explorer, Paul de Strzelecki, in 1845.[65]

The beginnings of colonial settlement of south-eastern Australia coincided with forms of religious evangelism that, for some, inspired a sense of responsibility towards Indigenous peoples, as seen through groups that earlier had worked to abolish the slave trade and slavery in Great Britain.[66] Such humanism often clashed with the relentless demand, from settlers, ranchers, squatters, miners and entrepreneurs, for access to the vast areas of rich land that were the traditional homes of Australia's Indigenous peoples. These tensions produced conflicting policies from the colonial government, which eventually created a system of land reserves or stations where Aboriginal groups were moved. Government overseers who managed these reserves often struggled with a conflict between their sense of moral and religious duty to protect Indigenous peoples as children of God and equal subjects of the crown, and the vying impulse to convert and assimilate Aboriginal peoples into a structure of European religious and cultural conventions.[67]

Strutt found himself on the periphery of this. In 1861 and 1862, he was quoted in annual reports as an honorary correspondent of the newly created Central Board Appointed to Watch Over the Interests of the Aborigines in the Colony of Victoria. Strutt, in his testimony, spoke mainly as a medical professional from his location in Echuca, lamenting the difficulty of providing Aboriginal groups there with good medical care.[68] In 1868 Strutt and his family left Echuca on short notice for Geelong, where Strutt had been appointed acting police magistrate. Echuca mourned the loss of their "most painstaking astute, and impartial magistrate," who was "in his private capacity a man of very superior parts, a public spirited and valuable citizen."[69] A year later, Strutt became police magistrate of Heidelberg, north-east of Melbourne, where he also served as Local Guardian of Aborigines starting in 1871.[70] Strutt's work on behalf of Aboriginal groups in both Echuca and Heidelberg coincided with the early development of Coranderrk reserve, where its residents—with the help and support of Scottish missionary, John Green—transformed it into a mostly self-supporting and "successful farming community for themselves and their children, and for other displaced clans who came to live there."[71] Controversy followed, ultimately reaching London, where a Royal Commission on the Aborigines was formed in 1877.

Strutt was called to testify before the Royal Commission, which sought advice on creating a new station for Aborigines on the Murray River. He exhibited the same paternalism that he did in accompanying emigrant orphans to Australia. Stutt asserted that:

> [T]he main thing that appears to me necessary in the conduct of any station for the blacks is to gain their affections; that is not done by harshness or knocking about nor, on the other hand does it do to give way to all the whims that they may have, but with a mixture of kindness and firmness they generally get on very well.[72]

He also advocated for Aborigines to receive "wages in proportion to their work."[73] As to independence, Strutt said: "If they are capable of looking after themselves, I would not make any difference between black and white," and when "he can be permanently employed on the stations round about, the native would be in the same position as a white man" while those "not capable of looking after themselves I should treat as children."[74] Although paternalistic, Strutt was well intentioned.

It was perhaps a similar impulse that made Strutt a father-figure, in the best way, to the female orphans in the Earl Grey Scheme. In 1850, the matron of the Ennis Workhouse, Mrs. O'Brien, received a letter from Strutt written after the *Thomas Arbuthnot* had arrived in Sydney, noting that "the two hundred orphan girls on board acquired a high character for their general good conduct. Amongst these some of the best girls were from the Ennis union. Several of them are in good service in the country."[75] Strutt further complimented her by saying the young women "behaved exceedingly well on board...some of our best scholars were from their number, and they have much reason to be indebted to those under whose care they have been brought up." Mrs. O'Brien had sent the largest, single group from one workhouse as 40 of the young women on board the *Thomas Arbuthnot* had come from Ennis in County Clare. Also, 23 girls came from Ennistymon, and 20 from Scarriff. Two dozen or more came from County Galway, specifically from Gort, Loughrea, and Tuam; ten from Dingle in County Kerry; seven from Dublin, two from Wicklow, and one each from Limerick and Cork.[76] Once settled, many of the Earl Grey orphans thrived. Nearly one-third of them were married within a few years, and they tended to live long lives with large families. On average, the "number of births per woman still married in her 40s exceeded nine."[77] Thus, from the *Thomas Arbuthnot* alone, the 200 young women likely brought into the world 1,500 or more offspring in just the first generation. It was a most promising start to a new life in their new home.

In 1878, Dr. Charles Edward Strutt retired from Victorian Public Service, returned to England, registered as a medical practitioner with the Royal College of Surgeons in London, and was a witness at the marriage of his daughter, Elizabeth.[78] He built a home in Surrey, England that he called "Wyuna," an Aboriginal word meaning "clear water" that was also the name of a station for Aborigines near the Murray River, not far from Echuca. During the next 20 years, he saw the marriages of two more of his daughters, Alice and Bertha. Released, finally, from his many years of uninterrupted civil service, Strutt returned to the work that had started his career by resuming duties as surgeon superintendent on voyages between Plymouth and Sydney, which he did for at least five more years. He made his twelfth roundtrip on the *North* in 1883.[79]

Charles Edward Strutt died at Wyuna on 6 January 1897 at the age of 83. He was a man who dedicated himself fully and compassionately to the health, safety, and wellbeing of the many people he encountered, most especially, the 200 young Irish orphan girls whose lives he so positively transformed. He was a humanitarian who was always prepared to assist those who were put in his care. While the experiences of the vast majority of the workhouse girls sent to Australia under the Earl Grey scheme were not always positive, this was not the case with those sent out on the *Thomas Arbuthnot* under Strutt. Not only did he ensure that they were properly cared for on the voyage, he also went above his remit in making certain that the girls had a positive experience as they started new lives in the colony. Similar to the experiences of Dr. Duncan in Liverpool and Dr. Grasett in Toronto, Strutt's story is a reminder that the devastating impact of the Famine extended thousands of miles beyond Ireland, and that without the dedications of these, and many more, medical workers, thousands more Irish poor would have perished.

NOTES

1. Irish Famine Memorial Sydney, orphan database https://irishfaminememorial.org/details-page/?pdb=5827

2. Charles Edward Strutt, "Journal of Voyage on the *St Vincent* and the *Thomas Arbuthnot*, 1848-50." Typescript of original, MS 8345, Box 913/5, La Trobe Library, Melbourne.

3. Richard Reid and Cheryl Mongan, *A Decent Set of Girls: The Irish Famine Orphans of the Thomas Arbuthnot 1849-1850* (Yass: Yass Heritage Project, 1996).

4. Robin Haines, *Doctors at Sea: Emigrant Voyages to Colonial Australia* (New York: Palgrave MacMillan, 2005), p. 133.

5. Strutt, *Voyage*, entry headed "Thursday 4 [January 1849]."

6. Papers Relative to Emigration to the Australian Colonies, Accounts and Papers of the House of Commons, BPP, 1850, vol. 8, p. 54.

7. Haines, *Doctors at Sea*, pp 138-139.

8. Ibid., pp 139-140.

9. *Colonial Office: Land and Emigration Commission, etc.* Reference CO 386, The National Archives of the Government of the United Kingdom: https://discovery.nationalarchives.gov.uk/details/r/C4577

10. Haines, *Doctors at Sea*, p. 17.

11. Ibid., p. 18.

12. Papers Relative to Emigration to the Australian Colonies, p. 125.

13. Ibid., p. 12.

14. Strutt, *Voyage*, entry headed "Wednesday 24th" (October 1849).

15. *Sydney Morning Herald*, 13 March 1850.

16. Ibid., 4 November 1850.

17. *Goulburn Herald and County of Argyle Advertiser,* 20 April 1850.

18. Haines, *Doctors at Sea*, p. 141.

19. Trevor McLaughlin, *Earl Grey's Famine Orphans,* at https://earlgreysfamineorphans.wordpress.com/category/earl-greys-irish-female-orphans/page/7/

20. Strutt, *Voyage,* entry for Tuesday 6 (November 1850).

21. Ibid., entry for Friday 9 (November 1850).

22. Ibid, entry for Tuesday 25 – Christmas Day (December 1850).

23. Ibid., entry for Monday 4 (February 1850).

24. Ibid.

25. Ibid., entry for Monday 11 (February 1850).

26. Ibid., entry for Monday 18 (February).

27. Ibid., entry for Friday 22 (February).

28. Ibid., entry for Wednesday 20 (February).

29. Ibid., entry for Tuesday 19 (February).

30. Ibid., entry for Friday 1 (March).

31. Ibid., entry for Thursday 7 (March).

32. Ibid.

33. Reid and Mongan, *A Decent Set of Girls*, p. 104.

34. Irish Famine Memorial, Sydney.

35. Strutt, *Voyage*, entry for Sunday 7 (April 1850).

36. Ibid., entry for Tuesday 16 (April 1850).

37. Ibid., entry for Sunday 28 (April 1850).

38. *Goulburn Herald and County of Argyle Advertiser*, 30 March 1850.

39. Ibid., 20 April 1850.

40. Ibid., 27 April 1850.

41. Reid and Mongan, *A Decent Set of Girls*, p. 168.

42. Electronic correspondence with library and archive assistant, Aaron Fleming, The Royal College of Surgeons of Edinburgh, 8 December 2020.

43. Isabelle Richet, "Publishing beyond Borders: *The Roman Advertiser,* the *Tuscan Athenaeum,* and the Creation of a Transnational Liberal Space," *Victorian Periodicals Review,* vol. 51, no. 3 (Fall 2018), p. 445.

44. *Suffolk Artists,* at: https://suffolkartists.co.uk/index.cgi?choice=painter&pid=2971

45. *Orlando,* Cambridge University Press website, http://orlando.cambridge.org/public/svPeople?person_id=struel

46. Haines, *Doctors at Sea*, p. 146.

47. Reid and Mongan, *A Decent Set of* Girls, p. 170.

48. Editors. "Local Intelligence," *The Banner* (Melbourne), 16 September 1853.

49. Marriage certificate # 823243-2020 Geelong, Victoria, Australia.

50. Reid and Mongan, *A Decent Set of Girls*, p. 170.

51. Editors. "Domestic Intelligence," *The Argus* (Melbourne) 6 February 1856.

52. Reid and Mongan, *A Decent Set of Girls*, p. 170.

53. Editorial, "The Late Police Magistrate of Echuca," *Riverine Herald*, 2 February 1868. Newspaper clipping in Strutt Family Papers, State Library of Victoria, Box 3694/5.

54. Editorial, *The Age* (Melbourne), 21 April 1858.

55. Editorial, *The Argus* (Melbourne), 18 May 1859.

56. Strutt, C. E., et al. "Victoria. Royal Commission Appointed to Examine into and Report upon the Best Means of Clearing the River Murray" (Melbourne: Government Printer, 1867).

57. Letter from Ros Shennan to Mr. A. E. Joynt, 9 July 1986. Family Papers, State Library of Victoria, Box 3694/5.

58. Editorial, "The Late Police Magistrate of Echuca," *Riverine Herald*, 2 February 1868. Newspaper clipping in Strutt Family Papers, State Library of Victoria, Box 3694/5.

59. Editorial, "Dinner to Dr. Strutt, P.M," *Riverine Herald* February 1868.

60. Editors. "Defining Moments: Gold Rushes 1851: Gold rushes in New South Wales and Victoria begin," *National Museum of Australia,* at: www.nma.gov.au/defining-moments/resources/gold-rushes

61. Richard Broome, *Aboriginal Victorians: A history since 1800* (Crows' Nest, NSW: Allen & Unwin, 2005) eBook locations 151 and 203 of 9848.

62. An office established by the British government in 1838. In some cases, Protector proved to be a misnomer, as in the case of Mathew Moorhouse, the first Protector, who slaughtered 30 to 40 Aboriginal people in the Rufus River Massacre in 1841.

63. Leigh Boucher and Lynette Russell, "Introduction: Colonial History, Postcolonial Theory and the 'Aboriginal problem' in colonial Victoria," in *Settler Colonial Governance in Nineteenth-Century Victoria,* ed. Leigh Boucher and Lynette Russell (Acton, Australia: ANU Press and Aboriginal History, 2015), pp 2-3.

64. Broome, *Aboriginal Victorians,* location 2051 of 9848.

65. See chapter two by Christine Kinealy on Count Strzelecki.

66. Boucher and Russell, "Introduction," pp 2-3.

67. Broome, *Aboriginal Victorians*, location 3712 of 9848.

68. Central Board, *Second Report of the Central Board Appointed to Watch Over the Interests of the Aborigines in the Colony of Victoria* (Melbourne: John Ferres, 1862), p. 20.

69. Editors. "The Late Police Magistrate of Echuca," *Riverine Herald*, 2 February 1868.

70. Reid and Mongan, *A Decent Set of Girls*, p. 173.

71. Giordano Nanni and Andrea James, *Coranderrk: We Will Show the Country* (Canberra: Aboriginal Studies Press, 2014), p. 12.

72. Royal Commissioners, *Royal Commission on the Aborigines Report of the Commissioners* (Melbourne: John Ferres, Government Printer, 1877) p. 20.

73. Ibid.

74. Ibid., pp 20-22.

75. "Female Pauper Emigrants," *The Freeman's Journal and Daily Commercial Advertiser* (Dublin), 14 October 1850.

76. Reid and Mongan, *A Decent Set of Girls*, pp 7-8.

77. Cormac Ó Gráda, "The Next World and the New World: Relief, Migration and the Great Irish Famine," in *The Journal of Economic History,* vol. 79, no. 2 (June 2019), pp 345-346.

78. Reid and Mongan, *A Decent Set of Girls*, p. 173.

79. Ibid., p. 175.

CHAPTER ELEVEN

DR. GEORGE GRASETT (1811–1847)

Toronto's Response to the Typhus Outbreak of 1847

Laura J. Smith and Robert G. Kearns

As medical superintendent of the city's temporary Emigrant Hospital, surgeon Dr. George Grasett faced firsthand the medical emergency wrought by an unprecedented influx of Irish emigrants to Toronto in the summer of 1847. Regrettably, Grasett did not survive that summer, contracting typhus and succumbing to the very disease he had volunteered to treat amidst chaos and difficult conditions. Grasett's story is not unique to Toronto or to North America for that matter. Medical practitioners and other medical workers tasked with receiving and treating Irish typhus patients that year frequently contracted the illness. All too often they died, in many cases side-by-side with the emigrants they treated.

By virtue of his socio-economic status, we know more about Grasett's life and character than about any of the other eight medical personnel from Toronto's Emigrant Hospital who did not survive that unprecedented summer. By all accounts, Grasett had made serving the poor an integral part of his medical practice. His choice to take on a role at the Emigrant Hospital made complete sense to those who knew him. That said, his story is no more heroic nor significant, but rather emblematic, of the remarkable sacrifice made by Head Nurse Susan Bailey, nurses Sarah Duggan, Anne Slocomb, Catherine Doherty, orderlies Richard Jones, John McNabb and physician Dr. Joseph Hamilton, all personnel from the Emigrant Hospital who succumbed to fever in 1847. Other Torontonians who were at the forefront of the city's response to the Famine migration, like Emigrant Agent Edward McElderry and Bishop Michael Power, discussed elsewhere in this volume, also paid the ultimate price. These men and women, and many others, of Irish, English, and Canadian extraction, Protestant and Catholic, overcame sectarian and class divisions and the rudimentary medical infrastructure of the colonial city to respond to the needs of newcomers amidst the chaos of an unprecedented migration season.

Dr. George Robert Grasett was born in Lisbon in 1811, the second of six sons to a British military surgeon Dr. Henry Grasett and his wife Ann Bligh Stevenson.[1] Dr. Henry Grasett had been educated in Ireland where his father practiced medicine. His military travels took him throughout Europe. Upon retirement in 1814, he moved his family to Quebec City. It was at Quebec City that George Robert apprenticed with his father as a surgeon and was licensed to practice medicine in 1837.[2] That Grasett passed the notoriously difficult (particularly for apprentices) Lower Canadian licensing examination and that of Upper Canada two years later, speaks to his abilities and to the quality of his father's mentorship.[3] Grasett referred to himself as a physician *and* a surgeon, which was probably an indication of his varied and exceptional abilities and training, but also of the degree to which the medical hierarchy was not so rigid in that province as it was elsewhere in the British Empire.[4]

Dr. Grasett began his practice in Amherstburg in the extreme southwest of the province of Upper Canada.[5] There, he quickly ingratiated himself with the community, joining local organizations,[6] mentoring young doctors,[7] and serving as assistant surgeon in the Essex Light Infantry which saw action during the Upper Canadian Rebellion.[8] Aspiring to emulate his father's career, he sought military service and consequently never intended to make Amherstburg a permanent home. He actively pursued a position as a surgeon in the British army during the period, but with no medical degree or formal British medical education, he was turned down for an immediate appointment.[9] With that window closed, Dr. Grasett's father urged the young doctor to give up the "limited circle" of the "country settlement" and relocate to Toronto where many more opportunities awaited a young respectable doctor with good references.[10] For their part, the residents of Amherstburg got up a petition to protest against Grasett's imminent departure. The petition praised Grasett's "valuable professional service," and his "zeal" for the "improvement" and "advancement of the best interests of all classes."[11]

His father's entreaties eventually worked, and Dr. George Grasett relocated to Toronto by the fall of 1844.[12] His eldest brother, Henry James Grasett, probably helped Dr. Grasett's entree to Toronto society. Henry was a prominent Church of England clergyman and curate to Bishop John Strachan at St. James' Cathedral, Toronto. The Rev. Grasett was active in the city's charitable institutions, serving on the board of the House of Industry, amongst other endeavors. It was noted in the summer of 1847 that he was one of the few Protestant ministers to visit the Emigrant Hospital regularly.[13]

It did not take Dr. Grasett long to establish himself within the "respectable" medical community of the city.[14] He was secretary and librarian of the Toronto Medico-Chirurgical Society, corresponded with Dr. Christopher Widmer, the most prominent medical practitioner in the city and province,[15] and was called to attend Dr. William Rees, the superintendent of the Toronto Lunatic Asylum, when he was attacked by a patient.[16] In addition to his own medical practice, Grasett also served the Toronto General Dispensary, which gave "medical and surgical advice and medicines to the indigent sick."[17] Within a few short years, he had established himself as a competent and compassionate medical professional with a clear interest in the welfare of the lower classes. With this reputation and perhaps a few words from his brother and the other connections he had fostered in the city, Dr. George Grasett was appointed by the city's Board of Health as medical superintendent and chief attending surgeon of the newly created Toronto Emigrant Hospital on the 22 June 1847.[18] Regrettably, Grasett's time at the Emigrant Hospital was short. He would hold the position for less than a month. Grasett succumbed to the very illness he had dedicated himself to treating and was buried at the cemetery at St. James' Cathedral on 17 July.[19]

Obituaries in the aftermath of his death testified to Grasett's dedication to the poor and spoke to his potential cut short. On Grasett's service, *The British Colonist* newspaper wrote that his:

> exertions in life were unceasingly devoted to the amelioration of the sufferings of his fellow men, irrespective of hire or reward. Whenever his aid was required, however trying —we had almost said however frightful— the circumstances, there was the lamented gentleman found giving his professional knowledge and physical exertions, that the affliction which had fallen on any around him might be some wise softened, and they reconciled to the dispensations of an all-wise Providence. Since his appointment as hospital superintendent, he knew no other duty than that of staying disease and alleviating the sufferings of those who, driven from their own land by famine and pestilence, sought a refuge among us, their brethren in Canada.[20]

The *British American Journal of Medical and Physical Science*, called Grasett "a young man of great promise" and "one of those men whose places in society it is very difficult adequately to fill." On the impact of his death on those who frequented the dispensary, the *Journal* wrote: "in the humble abodes of the suffering poor of this large town, in the reception room of the Dispensary where his benevolent smile was wont to greet them, his virtues are the theme of daily praise, and his death the subject of deep and lasting sorrow."[21] Condolences to the Rev. Grasett and the Grasett family came from Dr. Grasett's friends throughout Toronto and they illustrated the extent to which the doctor had made a deep impact during his very short stay in the city. Bishop John Strachan wrote immediately to express his distress at "this great and unexpected calamity."[22] A deputation from the House of Industry conveyed its "deepest regret" at Dr. Grasett's passing and noted that all, "particularly the poor, were so deeply indebted by his uniform kindness."[23] The Upper Canada Bible Society, of which Dr. Grasett was secretary, expressed similar sentiments of "melancholy and regret at the loss we have all experienced" and resolved to use his example to inject "renewed diligence" into its charitable activities.[24]

What had Dr. Grasett experienced? Under what conditions did he and his fellow medical workers labor only to pay the ultimate sacrifice? In all, approximately 38,000 migrants arrived in Toronto between May and December 1847.[25] The majority were Irish, Catholic and destitute traveling under government support. The logistics of receiving, triaging, housing, treating, burying and transporting a group of newcomers that was nearly double the population of the city itself, fell to a consortium of municipal and provincial officials. In what has been called a "herculean operation," these bodies worked in parallel and occasionally at odds, to make do with a rudimentary medical and settlement infrastructure and limited resources.[26]

Management of migration to the province was the purview of the provincial Emigrant Agency, represented locally by Emigrant Agent Edward McElderry. Toronto was a central port in the provincial government's system of emigrant reception agencies strung along the north shore of Lake Ontario.[27] It is not difficult to imagine the chaos of a landing at Rees' Wharf where migrants were received, triaged, and if necessary, housed temporarily in sheds. The number of individuals, an average of 300 a day, needing to be processed on a typical day proved overwhelming for McElderry and his staff.[28] Emigrants disembarking at Toronto had traveled not only across the Atlantic and passed quarantine at Grosse Île, but had also survived the weeks-long process of being transported to Montreal and further along the St. Lawrence River by a steamer-towed open-top barge to Kingston.[29] That trip could take upwards of a week during which emigrants frequently ran out of rations, and were exposed to the elements.[30] From Kingston, those who were still healthy went further west by steamer to Toronto. The conditions on lake steamers were similarly difficult. The press condemned reports that steamboats arriving at Toronto were crammed with upwards of 1,000 suffocating passengers as "barbarous cruelty."[31] One observer reported witnessing Edward McElderry, "stagger back like one struck" upon encountering the smell emanating from a newly-arrived steamer.[32] McElderry's task was to send those appearing healthy out of the city whether to Niagara or Hamilton by boat, or inland to rural communities by cart. Those who were obviously ill were housed in sheds at the wharf, or by late June, sent to the Emigrant Hospital. Moving migrants out of the city as quickly as possible was the priority, and transportation records produced by McElderry and his staff attest to the volumes of migrants transported, supporting the government's contention that the majority of those 38,000 arrivals to Toronto were not allowed to sojourn in the city.[33]

The Toronto Emigrant Hospital had not long been in operation when Dr. Grasett was appointed its medical superintendent on 22 June 1847. The city's Board of Health, itself a creation of that year, had repurposed the Toronto General Hospital in mid-June when its initial plan to house sick emigrants at sheds on the waterfront proved entirely inadequate.[34] The Board guided the civic response to the migration and, in addition to managing the Emigrant Hospital and, later, a Convalescent Establishment and a Widows and Orphans home, also kept records at the wharf and hospital, and issued policy guiding the transportation of the sick and the burial of the dead. One such example was the edict forbidding the transportation of migrants away from the wharf without the permission of the emigrant agent.[35] Such measures were intended to prevent the spread of disease to the city's residents, but the measures had the added benefit of preventing emigrants from loitering in the city and facilitated their eventual removal.

The Toronto General Hospital had been built in the aftermath of the war of 1812 on a 400-acre hospital reserve on what was then the periphery of the city.[36] The building was Georgian-style, two-story, red brick and oriented to ensure proper ventilation and a cooling breeze from the lake in summer months.[37] Inside, the wards were spacious and airy, with accommodations for about 100 patients. After acquiring the hospital building, the Board of Health worked quickly to procure furniture and medical supplies, issue contracts to food suppliers, and hire and appoint medical staff. An initial order to a local merchant for 50 beds with corresponding linens was quickly increased by another 75 when demand was made abundantly obvious.[38] The initial complement of staff was similarly increased. Within a few days of Dr. Grasett's appointment as medical superintendent and chief attending surgeon, it was determined that he needed assistance, and Dr. Francis Primrose was appointed as his co-medical officer. The same day, a resident Apothecary and an Assistant Steward were hired.[39]

The Emigrant Hospital reached capacity almost immediately upon opening and it is not difficult to imagine the strain on the staff and the facility. The steady stream of typhus patients into the city quickly necessitated the expansion of the hospital's facilities. Two sheds constructed on the hospital grounds, each 75 feet by 25 feet, filled rapidly and the process was repeated multiple times over the course of the summer.[40] Additional wages were offered to hasten the work of laborers tasked with building as many as 14 more sheds, which eventually covered much of the land around the hospital.[41] By August, the 125-bed hospital housed over 800 patients. With sheds and wards at capacity, the Board of Health ordered that the hospital's dining rooms be converted into wards.[42]

It has been estimated that approximately 10 percent of the new arrivals to the city that summer were ill, but incomplete and potentially inaccurate records for all municipal and provincial points of contact with migrants makes it difficult to determine exactly how many passed through the Emigrant Hospital. The official report indicated that 4,355 patients had been admitted to the Emigrant Hospital.[43] Of the 1,124 migrants who had died in the city, 863 had done so at the hospital.[44] Weekly Board of Health reports published in the newspapers, and transportation records generated by McElderry at the wharf, shed some light on the volume of patients who passed in and out of the hospital. In five days in August, for example, 164 patients were admitted to the hospital, 50 were buried, 63 discharged to the Convalescent Establishment, and 23 previously discharged to the Convalescent Establishment were readmitted to the hospital having relapsed.[45] The Convalescent Establishment had opened in July to alleviate pressure on the hospital. It housed 300 patients and was intended to separate the recovery of those who had been ill and to provide them with support until such time as they could subsist independently. It is clear from surviving records that cases of relapse were common however, and patients returned with some frequency to the Emigrant Hospital.[46]

With a patient to nurse ratio of seventy-to-one, a typical shift at the Emigrant Hospital was undoubtedly difficult and exhausting for Head Nurse Susan Bailey and her peers.[47] So-called night nurses who lived on site were particularly overworked with very little time to sleep between 16-hour shifts. Nursing wages were low at approximately £1-15s a month, far less than the orderlies and the hospital washerwoman; shifts were long, often 16 hours minimum; and there was no job security as nursing positions and wages were often the first cut or eliminated when costs needed to be trimmed. While medical training for nurses was beginning in Britain, it was non-existent in Upper Canada, and the majority of nurses in this period would have been uneducated working-class women. Their work was closer to that of a domestic servant than to the highly trained medical professional of the twenty-first century. With continual employment, a nurse might make between £20 and £30 annually, a sum insufficient to live on without additional family income.[48]

Scenes at the hospital were undoubtedly chaotic. Recovered patients awaiting discharge, or perhaps with nowhere else to go, continued to occupy space and mingled with infected patients.[49] Some migrants, who had been deemed healthy and transported out of the city, arrived back to the city on foot, now too ill to work.[50] Others, discovered to be sick by their neighbors, were brought to the hospital by force.[51] The number of children transported alone from the wharf to the hospital suggests the sounds of terrified children likely filled the air. Their anxious parents and siblings might have lingered, keeping watch and taking up space on the wards and in the sheds. In warm weather, emigrants slept outside, scattered about on the hospital field rather than in the sheds.[52] In such an environment disease control was undoubtedly problematic and accurate record keeping impossible. Patients not only returned after discharge, but others departed the hospital without permission.[53] City officials complained about sick emigrants who continued to "infest the streets of [the] city" making "Toronto a general Lazaretto."[54] A scandal resulted when inconsistencies in patient records and statistics were made public in late August, putting additional pressure on the hospital and its staff.[55] The errors were blamed on the chaos of the early months of the hospital's operation, but also on the disruption of persistent illness amongst the hospital's physicians and staff.[56]

By virtue of their sex and class, we know very little about Susan Bailey and her fellow nurses. Bailey's death was reported in the newspaper with one short sentence that identified her as "Mrs. Susan Bailey, Head Nurse." Her burial record at St. James' Cemetery added not only her religion, but her age, 32, and her birthplace— Ireland. Bailey was predeceased by Anne Slocomb, 26, born in England, and by Sarah Jane Sherwood, 23, from Ireland. Sarah Duggan, only 18, succumbed a week after Bailey. Duggan was presumably a Roman Catholic as she was not buried at St. James' Cemetery. Irishwoman Catherine Doherty, 55, was the last Emigrant Hospital nurse to die on 22 September 1847. All of these women died at the hospital, alongside their patients. So too did orderlies, William Harrison, John McNabb and Richard Jones, who all died within days of each other in late August.[57]

The hospital's physicians were also susceptible to the fever and there were frequent reports in the newspapers of doctors battling the illness and unfit for duty. Dr. Grasett's death on 17 July was the first death amongst the hospital's staff and appears to have magnified the difficulty of finding and keeping physicians and surgeons healthy and willing to work at the hospital. After a series of hires, resignations and illnesses amongst the hospital's physicians and surgeons, Dr. Joseph Hamilton was appointed to Grasett's former post as medical superintendent.[58] Hamilton, the scion of the prominent Niagara-based family, succumbed to typhus in November 1847. His headstone at St. James' Cemetery reads: "A man much revered." Edward McElderry, the emigrant agent at the wharf, succumbed to "fever" on 29 October 1847. He left behind a pregnant wife and a large family of seven young children. In a petition to secure a pension for McElderry's widow, his superior, Chief Emigrant Agent for Canada West, Anthony Hawke, wrote that McElderry was:

> A good man in every relation of life and has certainly fallen a victim of duty. Had he less zeal he would have given himself time to recover from the effects of fever, but he persisted in working beyond his strength and the dysentery set in fatally.[59]

Hawke's efforts were in vain, so too were petitions from others and from McElderry's widow herself.[60]

In late August, the conditions at the Emigrant Hospital prompted its nurses, orderlies and other staff to petition the Board of Health for an increase in wages. They argued that their remuneration should be on par with that of their contemporaries at the Montreal Emigrant Hospital. After some deliberation and a visit to the hospital to investigate conditions, the Board acquiesced.[61] The announcement of additional remuneration came the day John McNabb died from typhus and it was also too late for the four nurses and orderlies who had predeceased him. The newspapers the following week carried an advertisement looking for personnel in all facets of the hospital's operation. The management of the building and the formal transfer of care of the remaining patients from the Board of Health to the General Hospital were completed by May 1848. Similarly, the Convalescent Hospital and Widows and Orphans' Home ceased operations that same month. While questions remained about the immense sums of money spent to manage and contain the outbreak, it was clear the city had survived a monumental challenge. Over the course of the summer of 1847, the Emigrant Hospital had admitted 4,355 patients of whom 2,869 had been discharged and 863 had died.[62] This was a considerable onslaught for the facility, and the city's medical practitioners. The General Hospital had averaged about 500 admissions a year, with 100-1,800 outpatients treated at its dispensary.[63] The cost was also significant. The Emigrant Agency had spent over £3,000 in Toronto on salaries and expenses, including the transportation and food costs for indigent migrants. The medical costs to the city of Toronto for food, medicine, and other supplies topped £5,000 by the end of the season.[64]

The response to the influx of Irish immigrants to Toronto marshaled the resources and talents of medical, civic and religious leaders of all denominations. Overcoming sectarian, ethnic and class divisions, these men and women set a standard of care for emigrants in the city of Toronto which persists to this day. From the perspective of writing amidst an extraordinary global pandemic, the story of Dr. Grasett, Nurse Bailey and their fellows, rings uncomfortably familiar. We are struck by the rudimentary, but effective strategies employed by the city's Board of Health, the province's Emigrant Agency and the city's Emigrant Hospital, who triaged and quarantined new arrivals and restricted their movements within the city, but who also offered support by way of food, shelter, and medical assistance. We also see parallels in the selfless dedication of these front-line workers to their patients in the men and women who currently fight an extraordinary global pandemic in Toronto's hospitals, clinics and long-term care homes.

The Canada Ireland Foundation's "Dr. George Robert Grasett Park" in downtown Toronto is located on the site of the former Emigrant Hospital.[65] The park commemorates the heroism of Dr. Grasett, but also of the individuals who died while serving sick and dying Irish emigrants in Toronto in the summer of 1847. The park provides a vital link to the history of Irish immigration and settlement in Toronto and highlights the role these individuals played in the history of health and medicine in the city.

NOTES

1. A branch of the Grasett family were planters in Barbados from at least the eighteenth century. Dr. Henry Grasett's father, Dr. James Grasett, was born in Barbados, but educated in Britain and practiced medicine in Ireland until his death in 1822. Henry was educated in Ireland, but his military travels took him to Malta, Gibraltar and Portugal. St. James' Cathedral archives, Strathy papers, R. Grasett to Dr. G.R. Grasett, 24 June 1846; same to same, 24 September 1846; Walter Canniff, *The Medical Profession in Upper Canada, 1783-1850 : An Historical Narrative with Original Documents Relating to the Profession, Including Some Brief Biographies* (Toronto: William Briggs, 1894), pp 393-394; H.E. Turner, "Grasett, Henry James," in *Dictionary of Canadian Biography*, vol. 11, University of Toronto /Université Laval, 2003, at: www.biographi.ca/en/bio/grasett_henry_james_1808_82_11E .html

2. Though formal medical education was already established at medical schools in Montreal by this time, informal medical education, usually through an apprenticeship of at least seven years, was still a common and accepted option for prospective doctors. Canniff, pp 394-395; "Licentiates of the Medical Boards, CE," *British American Medical and Physical Journal*, vol. 3, 1 December 1847, p. 217, at: https://books.google.ca /books?id=M6BXAAAAMAAJ&lpg=PA216&dq=List%20of%20MD's%20and%20 licentiates%20from%20Dec%201%2C%201847%20issue%20The%20British%20 American.&pg=PA217#v=onepage&q&f=false

3. The Quebec or Montreal Medical Board examined prospective doctors on topics such as: Latin, anatomy, pharmacy, midwifery and chemistry. There was a high failure rate

particularly amongst apprentices. As his father's apprentice, George would have worked in his father's practice, assisting him with medical procedures, preparing medicines and compounds, and keeping the practice's books. Dr. Grasett would have ensured his apprentice had access to his medical library and that he attended medical lectures at a hospital or medical school. St. James' Cathedral archives, Grasett family scrapbook, License to practice medicine in Upper Canada for Dr. G.R. Grasett, 25 February 1839; Danielle Terbenche, "'A Soldier in the Service of His Country;" Dr. William Rees, "Professional Identity, and the Toronto Temporary Asylum, 1819-1874." *Histoire Sociale. Social History* 43 (2010), pp 97–129; Terrie M. Romano, "Professional Identity and the Nineteenth-Century Ontario Medical Profession." *Histoire Sociale - Social History* 28, no. 55 (1995), pp 7-98; J.T.H. Connor, *Doing Good: The Life of Toronto's General Hospital* (Toronto: University of Toronto Press, 2000).

4.   In Britain, a strict hierarchy ordered medical practitioners. Classically trained physicians (often with an MD) who served upper-class patients were at the top, next came apothecaries who were analogous to the general practitioners of today, followed by surgeons who had technical training and, according to historian J.H. Connor, "relied more on manual skills." Connor, *Doing Good*. p. 18; In Upper Canada (now Ontario) where Grasett began his practice in the late 1830s, physicians with a medical degree from a British university held prominence, followed by surgeons (including military surgeons such as Dr. Henry Grasett) also licensed in Britain. At the bottom were those with apprenticeship training or limited medical education, but who had passed the Medical Board of Upper Canada examinations. Terbenche, "A Soldier in the Service of His Country," p. 101. It is unlikely that Grasett had an MD. The degree was not required for medical practitioners, nor was it common, particularly in Quebec, before the 1850s. Some extant correspondence does append "MD" to Grasett's name, but the usage was not consistent, and may have indicated an assumption on the part of a sender rather than of fact. Barbara Tunis, "Medical Education and Medical Licensing in Lower Canada." *Histoire Sociale. Social History* 14, no. 27 (1981), pp 67–91.

5.   *Western Herald,* 4 September 1838.

6.   Ibid., 2 June 1841, 2 December 1841, 11 February 1842, 7 April 1842. Grasett was secretary of the Amherstburg Branch Bible Society, was a member of a committee attempting to build a monument to the memory of the War of 1812 hero Tecumseh in Amherstburg and was a founding member of the Western Medical Society for which he served as secretary.

7.   One Dr. Theophilus Mack trained with Dr. Grasett in Amherstburg and is credited with opening the first nursing school in Canada. Canniff, *The Medical Profession*, p. 489.

8.   Library and Archives Canada, MG 13 War Office 13, vol. 3678, "Pay List of Captain Henry Rudyerd, Company of Essex Volunteer Light Infantry from the 1 January to the 28 February 1838 inclusive." Grasett as assistant surgeon was paid £44-5-0 for 59 days. Grasett appears on the payroll until at least March 1840. He was present when the Patriot-commandeered schooner Ann, which had been shelling Amherstburg, was run aground and its crew captured. Grasett later recounted that some confusion during the battle meant that he did not provide immediate assistance to the wounded, but

in the aftermath his duties included recording the names and injuries of the captured men and providing medical assistance to those men for the duration of their stay in Amherstburg. *Western Herald*, 10 July 1839. His regiment saw action during the unrest of the Upper Canadian rebellion and particularly in early 1838, when the Detroit peninsula was attacked by self-styled "Patriot" militia groups bent on seizing the territory and instituting American-style government.

9. The Army had questions about his qualifications and he was invited to England to prove himself qualified by taking examinations. For unknown reasons he declined the offer in the fall of 1840. St. James' Cathedral archives, Grasett family scrapbook, unknown to Sgt. McGrape, 27 March 1840; J. Russell to Sir George Arthur, 9 May 1840; unknown to Dr. G.R. Grasett, 23 June 1840; unknown to Dr. G.R. Grasett, 5 October 1840.

10. St. James' Cathedral archives, Strathy papers, transcription of letter from Dr. H. Grasett to Dr. G.R. Grasett, 1838.

11. The signatories pledged sums of money to secure Grasett's medical services for themselves and their families when they were required. St. James Cathedral archives, Grasett family scrapbook, petition from the residents of Amherstburg, July 1840.

12. Toronto Public Library, *Toronto Directory and Street Guide for 1843-44*, http://static.torontopubliclibrary.ca/da/pdfs/1607301.pdf

13. *The British Colonist*, 13 August 1847.

14. City of Toronto Archives, City of Toronto assessment rolls, 1845 and 1846.

15. Canniff, *The Medical Profession*, pp 164-165.

16. *Appendix to the Journals of the Legislative Assembly of the Province of Canada*, 1851, Appendix O.O., p. 4 "Report of the Special Committee ... relating to the Petition of William Rees."

17. St. James" Cathedral Archives, Grasett family scrapbook, Toronto General Dispensary Referral Card, no date; Toronto General Dispensary Newsletter, 1846; Toronto Public Library, *Brown's Toronto City and Home District Directory, 1846-7*, http://static.torontopubliclibrary.ca/da/pdfs/541681.pdf

18. St. James' Cathedral Archives, Grasett family scrapbook, George Gurnett to Dr. G. Grasett, 22 June 1847; *The British Colonist*, 25 June 1847.

19. St. James' Cathedral archives, Grasett family scrapbook, Funeral Card.

20. *The British Colonist*, 20 July 1847.

21. *The British American Journal of Medical and Physical Science*, vol. 3, p. 110, at: http://books.google.ca/books?id=M6BXAAAAMAAJ&lpg=PA216&ots=sNiRbnEVIw&dq=List%20of%20MD's%20and%20licentiates%20from%20Dec%201%2C%201847%20issue%20The%20British%20American.&pg=PA110#v=onepage&q=Grasett&f=false.

22. St. James' Cathedral archives, Grasett family scrapbook, Bishop John Strachan to Rev. H. Grasett, 16 July 1847.

23. Ibid., House of Industry to Grasett family, 23 July 1847.

24. Ibid., K.L. Howard to Rev. H. Grasett, 1847; resolutions of the Upper Canadian Bible Society, 11 August 1847.

25. The details of the city of Toronto's experience in 1847 have been covered in detail in Mark G. McGowan, *Death or Canada: the Irish Famine Migration to Toronto, 1847* (Toronto: Novalis-Bayard, 2009).

26. Ibid., p. 49.

27. Lisa Chilton, "Managing Migrants: Toronto 1820-1880," *Canadian Historical Review* vol. 92, no. 2 (2011) pp 231-262, provides a good overview of this important government project.

28. McGowan, *Death or Canada,* p. 58.

29. Coleen Marie Towns, "Relief and Order: The Public response to the 1847 Famine Irish Migration to Upper Canada" Masters' thesis, Queen's University, 1990. This thesis has a good description of the journey emigrants took in 1847 from Grosse Ile to Canada West. The trip by steamer-towed open-top barge was notorious for its terrible conditions. Conditions on the St. Lawrence barges were also infamous and not just in 1847. See: "Caution to Emigrants and to the Public at Large;" *Chronicle and Gazette*, 16 June 1841; Library and Archives Canada, Provincial Secretary correspondence, Poole to Provincial Secretary, 6 July 1847. In his famous report on Irish migration to the Canadas in 1847, Stephen de Vere blamed the conditions on the St. Lawrence barges for the distribution of typhus throughout Canada West. Arthur Doughty (ed.) *The Elgin-Grey Papers, 1846-1852*, Stephen de Vere to T.F. Elliott, 30 November 1847, https://primarydocuments.ca/the-elgin-grey-papers-1846-1852-vol-1/.

30. Archives of Ontario, Records of the Department of Immigration, RG 11, Arthur Hawke letter books, (hereafter Hawke papers) A. Hawke to A.J. Buchanan, 3 July 1847; Hawke to Buchanan, 20 July 1847; Hawke to Buchanan, 3 July 1847; Chief Emigrant Agent for Canada West Arthur Hawke, then stationed at Kingston at the east end of the lake, complained "if they leave Montreal in a weak or sickly state the chances are that they will be dying or dead before they reach Kingston. Five or six days exposure on the river is more than they can bear." Towns (47) has an example of a boat that took 12 days to make the trip between Lachine and Kingston.

31. "Health of Toronto," *The Daily British Whig*, 17 July 1847. Steamboats contracted by the Emigrant Department moved upwards of 1,200 emigrants a week. Archives of Ontario, Hawke papers, A. Hawke to A.J. Buchanan, 20 July 1847.

32. Doughty ed., Stephen de Vere to Elliott, 30 November 1847. One observer's account of a landing in Toronto is particularly striking: "We got rid of most of our living cargo, whom they treated just like cattle driving them about...they were all turned out and kept back with sticks till their luggage would be tumbled out after them." Quoted in McGowan, *Death or Canada,* p. 53. The scale of daily arrivals was unpredictable. On 8 June, one steam ship deposited 700 adults and children at the wharf. Of the 400 adults on board, 250 were reported to be destitute and travelling under government assistance.

33. The transportation policy was not without its problems. Rural and peripheral communities protested the apparent transportation of disease and poverty to their communities and it is clear that many migrants found their way back to Toronto and other port cities particularly at the onset of winter. Laura J. Smith, "We Have Scattered Them Far and Wide:" Transporting Indigent Irish Emigrants in the Canadas, 1843-1847," in Christine Kinealy and Gerard Moran (eds), *Irish Famines before and after the Great Hunger* (Hamden: Quinnipiac University Press, 2020), pp 77-100.

34. The Board of Health had been created that year in anticipation of a remarkable migration season and the potentially grave implications for public health. The Board of Health had, as early as May, debated constructing an Emigrant Hospital, but put off the project, preferring to improve the government sheds at the wharf. McGowan, *Death or Canada*, pp 50-53.

35. Towns, "Relief and Order," p. 61.

36. The impetus behind the construction of Toronto's first General Hospital was the aftermath of the war of 1812 and the escalation of the city's population in the post-war period. The hospital reserve land was part of a 400-acre endowment provided by the Upper Canadian government in 1819 for medical purposes. The hospital's board of trustees attempted to raise revenue for the construction and operation of the hospital by selling and renting portions of the hospital reserve land. Neither scheme was particularly profitable and, in its first few decades of operation, the hospital suffered from perpetually limited financial resources. The General Hospital was constructed in 1820, but finances, infighting amongst Board members, disputes about the mandate of the institution, and a four-year stint replacing the fire-destroyed Upper Canadian Parliament, meant the building did not function as a hospital until 1829. See Connor, *Doing Good*, for a history of the hospital.

37. Situated on the southeast corner of the hospital reserve land, the hospital was constructed to align exactly with the north, east, south and west points of the compass. An observer remarked that the building consequently "had the appearance of having been jerked around bodily, the streets in the neighborhood not having been laid out with the same precise regard to the cardinal points."

38. *The British Colonist*, 22 June and 2 July 1847.

39. Ibid., 25 June 1847.

40. Ibid., 25 June 1847, 2 July 1847.

41. By August, there were 700 patients at the hospital and many more housed in sixteen sheds on the premises. *The British Colonist*, 31 August 1847. McGowan, *Death or Canada*, p. 65.

42. A 27 August report from the Board of Health noted that 807 patients were being treated at the Emigrant Hospital, *The British Colonist*, 31 August 1847.

43. McGowan, *Death or Canada*, p. 70.

44. A compiled list of the dead from newspaper and other religious sources can be found in McGowan's *Death or Canada*. Additionally, the Ireland Park Foundation has engraved the names of nearly 600 dead on the granite walls at Ireland Park on the downtown waterfront.

45. *The British Colonist* 27 August 1847.

46. Of those discharged from the Convalescent Establishment in August, for example, nearly 50 per cent were being returned to the hospital.

47. *The British Colonist*, 2 November 1847.

48. Connor, *Doing Good*, p. 50.

49. *The British Colonist*, 27 August 1847.

50. McGowan, *Death or Canada*, p. 73.

51. *The British Colonist*, 27 August 1847.

52. Ibid., 7 September 1847

53. Ibid., In one example, the Hadwin/Hedwin sisters, aged 11, 8 and 6 absconded from the Convalescent Establishment, 29 August 1847.

54. McGowan, *Death or Canada,* pp 72-73; AO, Hawke Papers, Davis to Mayor Boulton, 28 August 1847; Hawke to Boulton, 10 November 1847; *British Whig*, 22 September 1847.

55. *The British Colonist*, 27 August 1847, 7 September 1847; McGowan, *Death or Canada*, pp 71-72.

56. Ibid., 7 September 1847.

57. St. James' cemetery burial register.

58. *The British Colonist*, 3 August 1847.

59. Archives of Ontario, Hawke Letter book, Hawke to J.E. Sullivan, 4 November 1847.

60. Ibid., RG 22-305, York County Surrogate Court estate files, petitions related to Edward McElderry (Guardianship), 1847-1851.

61. *The British Colonist*, 27 August 1847.

62. McGowan, *Death or Canada,* p. 97.

63. Connor, *Doing Good*, p. 40.

64. McGowan, *Death or Canada*, p. 60.

65. The hospital site was excavated between 2006 and 2010.

Role of Religious Orders

CHAPTER TWELVE

EDWARD MAGINN OF DERRY AND DONEGAL (1802–1849)

Bishops, rebels and contagions

Turlough McConnell

Bishop Edward Maginn was one of the great humanitarians of his age. His relief efforts during the Great Hunger had one aim: to rescue the poor of Derry and Donegal from starvation. Maginn's origins were humble. He was born in Fintona, County Tyrone in December 1802, the son of a tenant farmer. He was brought up in Buncrana after the family relocated there and was educated locally. Following a family tradition of entering the church, Maginn attended the seminary at the Irish College in Paris in 1818 and was ordained in June 1825. He served as curate in Moville before being appointed parish priest of Fahn and Desertegny in 1829.[1] In August 1845, he was appointed to administer the diocese of Derry, becoming coadjutor to Bishop John McLaughlin in early 1846, as the health of the latter was failing.

The Catholic Church in Derry had a long and troubled history. Saint Columba, the sixth-century missionary monk from County Donegal, founded a prominent monastery in that area. In the twelfth century, the magnificent *An Teampall Mór* was built as Derry's diocesan cathedral. When English forces sacked the city in the 1560s, Commander Randolph used *Teampall Mór* as a gunpowder storehouse until an explosion seriously damaged it. The ruin was eventually razed after Sir Henry Docwra entered Derry in April 1600 with 4,000 soldiers. Its stones were used to build the walls and ramparts of Derry City.[2] The Penal Laws, introduced after 1695, restricted the civil rights of Catholics throughout Ireland. Though some of these restrictions were eased in the late eighteenth century, their very existence spurred Daniel O'Connell to form the Catholic Association in 1823 to spearhead his campaign for Catholic Emancipation. The Association gained immediate traction, and O'Connell drew crowds of over 100,000 to his rallies. His popularity carried him to a County Clare by-election victory in 1828. O'Connell became the first Catholic to win a seat in the British Parliament in more than 100 years.[3] A staunch advocate of O'Connell, Maginn had come out powerfully against the injustices of the local magistracy and for the repeal of Ireland's Union with Great Britain enacted in 1801. After Emancipation was granted in 1829, he was an important player in the restoration of the Catholic Church in Ulster. He also engaged in nationalist politics and was the inspiration behind the Monster Repeal meeting at Carndonagh on 7 August 1843.[4] Maginn's letters on land use and the Poor Law administration, together with his evidence before the Devon Commission, provide important insights into the social condition of Ireland in the first half of the nineteenth century. In 1844, he gave evidence before the commission and suggested land reform through the creation of an independent district estate evaluator and the provision of limited compensation for tenant improvements according to the duration of the lease held.[5]

No Catholic Bishop was permitted to serve or reside in Derry until 1720, and it was not until the 1829 Emancipation Act that the Catholic community could contemplate building a cathedral again. In 1838, a number of Derry Catholics advanced the idea of a new cathedral. They sanctioned the purchase of the King's Arms Hotel on Pump Street to be designated as a residence for the bishop and his clergy, a new diocesan seminary and the site of the new cathedral. These would take more years after Maginn's time to come to fruition, but founding St. Columb's College and planning St. Eugene's Cathedral were Maginn's first set of challenges as a young bishop.[6] From the outset, Maginn demonstrated his vision and ambition for his flock in Derry, transforming the diocese by planning to build six new churches, confirming 11,000 adults and children, and creating the groundwork for establishing a seminary at St. Columb's. When he was elevated to the episcopacy in May 1846, the Catholics of the city presented him with a carriage, a jaunting car and a purse containing one hundred guineas, "as a mark of their esteem and congratulation."[7] Maginn's successes alarmed some of the Protestant population of the town who protested against the "high-sounding pretensions of the address to Maginn" and pointed out that the gifts "are only calculated to generate feelings of pride and a love of worldly display."[8] Within a short space of time, Maginn had become a controversial figure, but as potato blight appeared in Ireland for the second consecutive year, his ambitions would turn to more practical matters.

The impact of the second potato failure was swift and severe. Three-fifths of the country's food supply disappeared, leaving three million people in desperate circumstances. The new bishop was confronted by urgent priorities across Derry and Donegal, with tenants facing eviction, the homeless dying in ditches, and famine-related diseases spreading. It was local priests and ministers who were often on the front line of tending to those who were the most vulnerable in the community. In a letter to the editor of the *Derry Journal*, dated 19 December 1846, a member of the Buncrana Relief Committee wrote:

> The clergymen here are not able to attend the dying, or bury the dead. Night and day they are being hurried from one place to another, to administer religious consolation to those whom food would save from speedy dissolution; and yet, still, there has not been a single person employed in this locality in public works, although the presentment Sessions, you know, were held in Buncrana, nine weeks ago. These victims of famine, who have been summoned before their God, from a heartless world, have one satisfaction, viz., that they cannot lie arraigned for injustice towards the proprietors of the soil, they paid their rents them, with what God had sent them for their own subsistence.[9]

On the western side of County Donegal, the suffering was equally acute, especially in the islands. Although the British government had imported a supply of food, it remained in storage as they had made the—seemingly heartless—decision not to make it available until spring 1847. The despairing local relief official, Commissary-General Thomas Gem, informed his superior in December 1846:

> [T]he distress of the wretched people is heart-rending. Something ought to be done for them; they can get nothing to purchase. The carters have stopped bringing supplies...the people in Arranmore Island are living on seaweed ... There is absolutely nothing in the place for food. It strikes me as very unfeeling on our part to keep corn in the store without issuing it ... I hope I may soon get the authority to issue.[10]

In early 1847, Bishop Maginn reported: "In the diocese of Derry we have a Catholic population of 230,000 souls. Of these, at the present time, there are at least 50,000 in actual starvation."[11] In the adjoining County Donegal, government relief measures were being supplemented by private charity. In early February 1847, the newly formed Belfast Ladies' Association for the Relief of Irish Destitution sent £60 and a package of clothing to the people on Arranmore Island; £30 and a package of clothing to the parish of Clondevadock on the Inishowen Peninsula, which was immediately followed by a second grant of £10; £10 to Leck Glebe in Letterkenny; £10 to the island of Inishkeel; and £10 to the parish of Neva.[12] The Quakers, William E. Forster and James Hack Tuke, confirmed the atrocious conditions in Donegal during their tour of the county in 1847. When they visited Dungloe, there was no meal available and Tuke wrote: "a more miserable town I never saw."[13] They witnessed corpses being taken to the graveyard without a sheet or a coffin on open carts and those who were alive had neither the seed nor the money to sow the land for the coming harvest.[14]

Not even Maginn's great hero O'Connell could help. O'Connell's health was failing. He informed a friend, Father John Miley, rector of the Irish College, in Paris, of his poor health:"I feel I am almost gone, my powers have almost departed me," he wrote. "My voice is almost mute. I am oppressed with grief."[15] Regardless, the 71-year-old O'Connell traveled to London to make one last desperate plea to save the people of Ireland. On 8 February 1847, O'Connell stood for the last time before the House of Commons in London. He informed his fellow parliamentarians: "Ireland is in your hands—in your power. If you do not save her, she cannot save herself. I predict ... one-quarter of her population will perish unless Parliament comes to their relief."[16] He pointed out that 15,000 people were dying each day from famine. In the debates that followed O'Connell's deadly prediction, his fellow repealer, Robert Dillon Browne, MP, informed the House: "The hard-worked priests could not relieve them—multitudes died on the road side—their corpses were mutilated by rats, or they dragged their weary limbs into the poorhouses, that their bodies might not be desecrated by uncoffined burial."[17] In the spring of 1847, the British government opened soup kitchens, which did alleviate starvation, but closed them a few months later, when, in August, the Poor Law became responsible for all relief.

Realizing that assistance from the British government would be inadequate, Maginn canvassed widely for assistance, with some success. By the summer, he could thank a group in Paris for donations totaling £360, the bishop of Hyderabad for £20, and organizations in Canada, Italy, England and the United States. One contributor was Bishop John Hughes of New York. Like Maginn, Hughes was born in Ulster and became a driving force behind the young Catholic Church in the United States.[18] Hughes was well aware of the suffering in Ireland. On 20 March 1847, Hughes spoke passionately about the Irish Famine at the Broadway Tabernacle in Manhattan. Unlike many men of the cloth, he did not offer a providentialist view of the Famine, but blamed British misrule. In contrast, he praised American generosity:

> The year 1847 will be rendered memorable in the future annals of civilization, by two events; the one immediately preceding and giving occasion to the other; namely, Irish famine, and American sympathy and succor. Sympathy has, in its own right, a singular power of soothing the moral sufferings of the forlorn and unfortu-nate. There is no heart so flinty, but that, if you approach it with kindness, touch it gently with the magic wand of true sympathy, it will be melted, like the rock

of the wilderness, and tears of gratitude on the cheeks of the sufferer will be the prompt and natural response to those of interest, of pity, of affection, which in imagination, he will have discovered on yours. Who will say that Ireland is not an unfortunate sufferer?[19]

The lecture was also a fund-raising event, with $529.11 donated, of which $4.50 was deducted for advertising.[20] The letter of thanks from Maginn to Hughes was edged in black which was customary to signify sympathy for the dead—in this case, for O'Connell. It was dated 2 July 1847:

> My Dear Good Lord,
>   I cannot find language to express how deeply I feel indebted to your Lordship, for your kind and considerate attention to the poor of this Diocese.
>   ... America has nobly done its duty and our gratitude to it will be as enduring as the foundations upon which our Island rests. Ireland will be henceforth to her (if not her ally) at least her friend with a friendship ever green as her own native shamrock and whether in war or peace the full spread Eagle's honor or disgrace we shall consider our own.
>   ... Receive my Lord, you and all our American benefactors, this faint expression of our gratitude and of our heartfelt wishes that a good God may repay you a hundredfold for your charity,
>   Your obliged and devoted Servant in J.C. Edward Maginn.[21]

Similar to Hughes in New York, Maginn blamed the British government for the death toll in Ireland. Assisted by his fellow Roman Catholic priests in Derry, Maginn compiled a list of all those who had died of starvation in the city between November 1846 and April 1847. It was then rolled in black crepe and placed in the diocesan archive with the inscription:

> The Records of the Murders of the Irish Peasantry, perpetuated in A.D. 1846-47, in the 9 and 10 Vic. in the name of political economy, during the administration of the professedly Liberal, Whig government, of which Lord John Russell was Premier.[22]

Maginn's outspokenness was praised in the Catholic newspaper, *The Vindicator*, which believed his actions gave hope to the whole country:

> Honour to the Catholic Bishop and clergy of Derry. The Right Rev. Mr. Maginn and his clergy utter what indignant Irishmen should feel and utter at the present momentous crisis. There still is a soul in Ireland ... What could be more alarming—O'Connell gone,—the land enveloped in the darkness of death,—a cowering, broken-hearted population flying before the destroying angels of famine and pestilence ... The resolutions of the Bishop and clergy of Derry, which now lie before us, prove that the chain of silence which has so long hung over the country, is no testimony

that its spirit has fled. While such burning language flow from patriot priests in torrents of indignation at the increasing accumulated wrongs of our country, we will hopingly struggle on.[23]

In September 1847, as the country entered its third year of food shortages, *The Ballyshannon Herald* outlined the devastation that had already been visited on Ireland:

> Social disorganization is nearly complete. The mass of the people are steeped to the lips in poverty ... Class is divided against class. The proprietors of the soil are generally regarded as oppressors of the cultivators of the soil. Dreadful hatred of England, of her institutions—is widely diffused among the humbler orders in Ireland.[24]

One of Maginn's responses to the ongoing distress in the city of Derry was to establish a nunnery for the Sisters of Charity, as an act of "humanity."[25] Realizing that longer-term, structural changes were required if such deadly famines were to be prevented from occuring again, Maginn threw his weight behind the tenant right movement, led by William Sharman Crawford MP. Its supporters were drawn from all denominations. As the bishop wrote, "should we not be united in all things conductive to the common weal?"[26]

Despite the awful condition of the poor, Maginn remained opposed to emigration as a solution to their plight, especially when the British government was involved. In 1846, John Robert Godley, son of a landowner in County Meath, issued a memorial which had the support of a number of Irish landlords, including Lords Sligo, Lucan and Ormonde and 21 MPs. They proposed a colonization scheme to British North America which would result in up to 300,000 people emigrating, with the majority of the funding coming from the government.[27] While many of the Catholic hierarchy opposed the proposal, Maginn was the most critical, stating that the Irish landlords were the cause of Ireland's problems and they now wanted to send the poor and their clergy to Canada. If the Irish had to emigrate, he would rather they left for "the land of the brave and home of the free" rather than Canada.[28] Most of Maginn's criticism was directed at Daniel O'Connell's son, Morgan John, for allowing his name to be associated with the project. Maginn accused him of being "devoid of patriotism." He added, "God gave us Ireland, to feed us, clothe us, and provide us with every means of substance ... but your committee, dissatisfied with God's gift to us, would exhibit their surpassing benevolence by transporting us to the woods of Canada."[29] Maginn was praised in the Irish press for again standing up for the rights of the poor Catholics in Ireland.[30]

Maginn was strongly nationalist in his political views and denounced the Young Irelanders when they split from the O'Connellite movement. This changed as the horrors of "Black '47" became apparent. He stated that he was ready to "grasp the cross and the green flag of Ireland and rescue my country or perish with its people."[31] At the same time, he repudiated the Earl of Derby's assertion that the Catholic clergy were inherently disloyal, but maintained that "it [was] incumbent on every follower of the Redeemer to stand by the oppressed against the oppressor—for the poor and needy against those who stripe them."[32] Maginn also publicly challenged Lord Stanley who, in the House of Lords on 23 November 1847, had accused the Irish Catholic clergy of using the confessional to encourage lawlessness and crime.[33] When praising his "splendid letters" to Stanley, the *Freeman's Journal* averred that Maginn was "to Ulster, what MacHale is to the West."[34] Maginn's political convictions were not revolutionary. His principal objective was to unite the O'Connellite and Young Ireland movement under peaceful, legitimate and Christian policies, despite allegations that he was party to the Young Ireland Rising of 1848.

The Famine accelerated the push toward revolution, even though its leaders knew that the outcome of a rising would be defeat and possibly their own deaths.[35] Thomas D'Arcy McGee was a participant in Ireland's brief rebellion of 1848, but he escaped arrest and fled to New York. While in the States, McGee became disgusted with Irish republicanism and American democracy, reversing his beliefs and becoming intensely conservative in his politics and his support for the Pope. He moved to Canada in 1857 and worked hard in the following decade to convince the Irish Catholics to cooperate with the Protestant British (members of the church) in forming a Confederation that would make a strong Canada from separate British North American colonies.[36] McGee turned his powerful gift for rhetoric to prose, and in 1857, among his many publications, he published *A Life of the Rt. Rev. Bishop Maginn*. McGee's flair for the pen does justice to the elevated spirit of Maginn:

> In this Province, in this state and period of society, about the commencement of the Catholic Restoration, the late Dr. Maginn's lot was cast. He was born of an orthodox stock; he grew up among a gallant and pious, but rash and much-abused peasantry; he retired from amongst them for a time, to reappear again with the highest authority upon their altars. We will see him planning and laboring in lake-bound Innishowen, and within the walls of "the maiden city," as a Priest and Leader, for a quarter of a century. All who have patience to peruse—"The short and simple annals of the poor," will witness how truly he approved himself the father of his flock. His public spirit, his moral courage, his thorough identity with the country, his fervid eloquence, his unwearied industry, his application to details, made him, in some sort, the judge and legislator of his people. His external influence was limited by his enjoyment of the Episcopal dignity to three short years. Yet in these three years he undoubtedly did arduous and honorable things, never sparing mind or body,

parse or person, where duty called or conscience pointed. In the prime and height of his life, he sank suddenly into the grave, lamented by his own nation, and regretted by all those throughout Christendom who take any interest in the Catholic affairs of Great Britain and Ireland. Of the works and days of this excellent person, I have told in the following pages all I could glean, from the very interesting papers committed to me for that purpose, by the surviving members of his family.[37]

In 1848, a decade before he penned the biography, Thomas D'Arcy McGee, then 23, was a fugitive on the run from his trial in Dublin when he met the bishop. McGee's biographer David Wilson writes: "Although it is unclear whether or not Maginn supported the rising, there is no doubt that he sympathized with the revolutionaries and wanted to keep them out of the clutches of the authorities."[38] Maginn may not have personally made the arrangements for the young revolutionary to escape, but, as McGee wrote, "some of his kind and courageous clergy were the chief promoters of it."[39] Local Donegal lore celebrates that McGee was taken to Tremone Bay, to the west of Inishowen Head, where he was rowed by one Robert McCann to a waiting ship, the *Shamrock*, bound for Philadelphia.[40]

Sadly, Maginn's service as bishop was cut short. On the eve of the third anniversary of his consecration, Maginn died in January 1849 of typhus, then called famine fever. News of Maginn's illness and his likely death was carried by newspapers throughout the country. The *Limerick Reporter* opined: "What a blow to our religion and our country ... but God moves in mysterious ways."[41] Catholics throughout Ireland mourned the passing of the "illustrious Bishop of Derry."[42] He was described as "the darling hope of his country and his church."[43] Maginn was buried in the family vault in Buncrana.

Death by fever was all too common among relief providers, including members of religious orders. In *The Great Hunger,* Cecil Woodham-Smith noted:

> The Irish people spoke of "famine fever," but in fact two separate diseases were present, typhus and relapsing fever, both conveyed by the common louse and both already familiar in Ireland ... a brush in passing was enough to transfer the fever-transmitting louse or its dust-like excrement to a new victim, and one fever-stricken person could pass on infection to a hundred others in the course of a day.[44]

Woodham-Smith further adds: "Thus, benevolent persons who gave aid to the resident victims of the great Irish epidemic of 1847—clergy, nuns, doctors, resident landlords and Government officials—contracted typhus and died, though they themselves never have harbored a louse."[45] More recently, scientists have recognizing the deadly impact of disease during the Famine years. Writing in 2020, as the world faced another deadly pandemic, British microbiologist Hugh Pennington stated:

The Irish Famine stands as the most lethal pandemic in the British islands since the Black Death. The four cholera pandemics that struck between 1831 and 1866 killed 113,000 in England and Wales. The 1918-19 influenza pandemic killed 179,624 in Britain and Ireland ... One million died in Ireland during the Famine.[46]

Priests, vicars and nuns, no less than medical workers, were on the front-line of trying to save lives during the Famine, both inside Ireland and overseas. Many religious gave their lives in the service of the Irish poor. Maginn was one such person, sharing the same fate of many of his poor parishioners. His actions and speeches, which brought repressed tensions to the surface, left no doubt that his thoughts and concerns were with the poor and oppressed of his flock. Moreover, during the decline and subsequent death of O'Connell, Maginn filled the vacuum, becoming an outspoken champion of "Catholic Ireland." He also proved himself fearless when it came to challenging the government about its inadequate and inappropriate response to the Famine. Maginn's premature death was not only a loss to his parishioners in Derry and in his adopted home of Donegal, but to the Catholic Church in Ireland as it sought to provide leadership in the wake of the devastation caused by the Famine.

NOTES

1. "Edward Maginn," *Catholic Encyclopedia* at: www.catholic.com/encyclopedia/edward-maginn
2. John McGurk, *Sir Henry Docwra 1564–1631: Derry's Second Founder* (Dublin: Four Courts Press, 2007), p.18.
3. Fergus O'Ferrall, *Catholic Emancipation: Daniel O'Connell and the Birth of Irish Democracy 1820-3* (Dublin: Gill & Macmillan, 1998), p. 41.
4. Thomas D'Arcy McGee, *A Life of the Rt. Rev. Edward Maginn: Coadjutor Bishop of Derry: With Selections from his Correspondence* (New York: P. O'Shea, 1857), p. 64.
5. Ibid., p. 87.
6. Ibid., p. 174.
7. "The Coadjutor Catholic Bishop," *Londonderry Sentinel*, 23 May 1846.
8. Ibid.
9. Letter to the Editor, *Derry Journal*, 19 December 1846.
10. Deputy-Assistant Commissary-General Gem to Deputy Commissary-General Dobree, 16 December 1846, p. 382. *Correspondence Explanatory for the Measures taken for the Relief of Distress in Ireland, July 1846 to January 1847. Commissariat Series*, BPP, 1847 [761]
11. Maginn to McGee, Acknowledging the Paris Committee, summer 1847, McGee, *A Life*, p. 94.
12. "Belfast Ladies' Association for the Relief of Irish Destitution," *The Belfast Protestant Journal*, 13 February 1847.

13. James Hack Tuke, *A Visit to Connaught in the Autumn of 1847. A Letter Addressed to the Central Relief Committee of the Society of Friends, Dublin* (London: Charles Gilpin, 1848), p. 55.

14. Helen Hatton, *The Largest Amount of Good: Quaker Relief in Ireland, 1654-1921* (Montreal & London, McGill-Queens University Press, 1993), pp 98-99. For an account of the Famine in Donegal see, Pat Conaghan, *The Great Famine in South-West Donegal, 1845-1850* (Killybegs: Bygones Enterprises, 1997).

15. Andrée Murphy, "Remembering Daniel O'Connell's final tragic plea to save Ireland from famine on his birthday," 6 August 2020.

16. "Ireland—Destitution," House of Commons, *Hansard Debates,* 19 February 1847, vol. 90, cc. 251-293.

17. Ibid.

18. John Loughrey, *Dagger John: Archbishop John Hughes and the Making of Irish America* (New York: Cornell University Press, 2018), p. 71.

19. *Complete Works of the Most Rev. John Hughes, D.D., Archbishop of New York. Comprising his Sermons, Letters, Lectures, Speeches, Etc.* (New York: Lawrence Kehoe, 1866), p. 544.

20. *Report of General Relief Committee of the City of New York* (New York: The Committee, 1848), p. 44.

21. Bishop Maginn to Archbishop John Hughes, 2 July 1847, Archives at Archdiocese of New York.

22. Monthly Report of Board of the Public Works for May, *Reports of the Board of Public Works in Ireland relating to the measures adopted for the relief of distress,* 1847, BPP [80], p. 10.

23. "Honour to the Bishop and Clergy of Derry," *The Weekly Vindicator*, 24 April 1847.

24. *Ballyshannon Herald*, 17 September 1847. Quoted by Breandán Mac Suibhne and David Dickson (eds) in Hugh Dorian, *The Outer Edge of Ulster* (Dublin: Lilliput Press, 2000), p. 23.

25. "The Sisters of Charity in the City of Derry," *Nation*, 30 October 1847.

26. Maginn to Sharman Crawford, Buncrana, 27 October 1847, reprinted in *Kerry Examiner*, 12 November 1847.

27. For the Godley colonization scheme, see Gerard Moran, *Sending Out Ireland's Poor: Assisted Emigration to North America in the Nineteenth Century* (Dublin: Four Courts Press, 2004), pp 70-80.

28. "Irish Colonization Scheme," *Freeman's Journal*, 14 April 1847.

29. *Nation,* 9 April 1847.

30. "Colonization," *Kerry Examiner*, 16 April 1847.

31. McGee, *A Life*, p. 101.

32. Donal Kerr's *'A Nations of Beggars.' Priests, People, and Politics in Famine Ireland, 1846-1852* (Oxford: Clarendon Press, 1994), p. 199.

33. McGee, *A Life*, Addenda to the Appendix, Letters to Lord Stanley, p. 307; *Tablet*, 15 January 1848.

34. "Third Letter to Lord Stanley," *Freeman's Journal*, 26 January 1848.

35. Christine Kinealy, *Repeal and Revolution: 1848 in Ireland* (Manchester University Press, 2009), p. 1.

36. David A. Wilson, *Thomas D'Arcy McGee: Passion, Reason, and Politics, 1825–1857* (Montreal: McGill-Queen's University Press, 2008), vol. 1.

37. McGee, *A Life*, p. ix.

38. Wilson, *Thomas D'Arcy McGee*, p. 220.

39. Ibid.

40. Ibid.

41. "Alarming illness of Right Rev. Dr. Maginn," *The Limerick Reporter*, 19 January 1849.

42. "Funeral Oration on the Late Most Rev. Dr Maginn, the illustrious Bishop of Derry," *Galway Vindicator, and Connaught Advertiser*, 3 February 1849.

43. "Death of the Right Rev. Dr Maginn," *The Newry Examiner and Louth Advertiser*, 20 January 1849.

44. Cecil Woodham-Smith, *The Great Hunger: Ireland 1845-1849* (New York: Harper and Row, 1962), pp. 188-189.

45. Ibid.

46. Hugh Pennington, "Like Typhus, but also Not," *London Review of Books*, 30 November 2020.

CHAPTER THIRTEEN

BISHOP MICHAEL POWER OF TORONTO (1804–1847)

A Reluctant Hero

Mark G. McGowan

Michael Power would never have considered himself a hero. He would have found such an identification both embarrassing and incompatible with his ideas of Christian humility. Yet, anyone observing his speeches to the people of Toronto in 1847, or witnessing his work among Famine refugees that year, would have disagreed. In Black '47, the 42-year-old Power was only in his sixth full year of service as Bishop of Toronto, a diocese that territorially spanned at least 1,400 kilometers north to south, and 420 kilometers east to west. The challenges of pastorally serving some 50,000 Catholics spread across a territory covering a land mass nearly the size of six Irelands combined was difficult enough, but the arrival of over 38,000 emigrants in a period of five months to Toronto, a city of nearly 20,000, was catastrophic.[1] Most emigrants were fleeing *An Gorta Mór* and had arrived in Canada's second largest city after six to eight harrowing weeks at sea, followed by surviving the quarantine station at Grosse Île, and then, finally, travelling 800 kilometers into the Canadian interior from Quebec City. In Toronto, city constables moved healthy Irish emigrants quickly into the interior of the province, to nearby cities, or to jumping off points to the United States.[2] Board of Health officials transported the sick and diseased Irish to the overcrowded Emigrant Hospital and to 16 hastily erected fever sheds to accommodate the overflow of sick patients. With all of his local priests stricken with typhus, Power worked alone. He crossed the muddy expanse of the frontier city several times each day in order to visit the sheds, offer the sacrament to the sick, pray over the dying and comfort the survivors. Throughout his entire career, Irish people had always been the object of his pastoral care. Now, unknown at that time to both himself and the Irish he cared for, it would be his last summer in Toronto.[3]

Power was neither a Canadian nor an immigrant from Ireland. He was born in Halifax, Nova Scotia, the first of eight children of Captain William Power of Waterford and Mary Roche of Youghal. Captain Power had chosen to live in Halifax, Britain's naval bastion in the North Atlantic, to engage more efficiently in maritime trade between the United Kingdom, Newfoundland, the United States and the British Caribbean. Michael Power rarely saw his father during his childhood since the captain was often at sea, and he was shipwrecked and given up for lost at least twice. His mother was the dominant influence in his life as was his parish priest, Father Edmund Burke. While Nova Scotia had been subject officially to the Test Acts and Penal Laws, in reality these restrictions were not strictly enforced and, as early as 1784, the Catholics of Halifax were permitted a chapel.[4] Here, Power caught the eye of Burke, who recognized the potential for the priesthood in the young boy. Power's formal education was undertaken at the Halifax Grammar School, and he learned his catechism from Burke in St. Peter's Church rectory. Without a Catholic seminary in Halifax, Burke made arrangements with Bishop Bernard-Claude Panet of Quebec for Power to be trained in French Canada. Thus, at the age of 11, Power and two companions set out in 1816 by sea to Quebec. Power would not return to Halifax for nearly 25 years, during which time his father, three brothers and Father Burke (Bishop Burke as of 1817) would pass away.[5]

The culture shock of studying at the Collège de Montréal did not appear to have an immediate effect on Power, although he was separated from his home and its Irish community by over 1,600 kilometers. While he may have struggled with his suitability for the priestly vocation as he neared the end of his studies, letters from his mother seemed to direct him back on course, in the way that only "Catholic guilt" from a mother could.[6] Culturally, in Montreal and later Quebec City, he was a quick study. He mastered French, Latin, Greek and while serving as a seminarian-assistant in the St.-Francois-du-Lac First Nation mission south of Quebec in 1826, he became fluent in Abenaki.[7] In 1827, after having studied less than three years at the Grand Seminary of Quebec, Bishop Panet assigned Power to the city of Montreal, and the jurisdiction of Jean-Jacques Lartigue, who was to become that city's bishop in 1836, when the Diocese of Quebec was divided. In August 1827, Bishop Jean DuBois of New York, who had been visiting Montreal, ordained Power. There was a chronic shortage of priests in Quebec, and Panet had been anxious to get more young men in the field. It was a great show of confidence in Power, whose superiors at St.-François-du-Lac had begged the bishop to assign Power permanently to the Abenaki mission. Bishop William Fraser of Halifax also had hoped that Power would return to his native Nova Scotia, but the young priest was granted an exeat from his home diocese to remain in the Diocese of Quebec.[8] By now, all of his colleagues were French-Canadian priests, and his former classmates from the Collège de Montréal provided him with a network of friendships among French Canada's rising class of liberal professionals.

Ironically, despite his complete immersion in French-Canadian society, Power's first pastoral charge at St. Frédéric Parish, Drummondville, in the upper St. François River valley, placed him in the heart of pre-Famine Irish emigration and settlement in Canada. Here, he dealt with all of the problems faced by new Irish settlers. He chased away itinerant "bogus" Irish priests without official "faculties" who were exploiting their newly arrived countrymen; he tried to regularize marriages among settlers who were cohabiting; and he covered hundreds of kilometers along the valley by horseback to say Mass, hear confessions and tend to the sick, both Irish and French Canadian.[9] His parishioners were not generous, as this frontier parish produced little revenue to sustain him.

Power was unflinching, and adept at this saddlebag Christianity, and Panet transferred him, in 1831, to an even wilder frontier in the Ottawa River Valley, northwest of Montreal, which was essentially the end of French-Canadian seigneurial settlement. His multilingualism and Irish heritage were clearly a factor in this appointment because the Ottawa Valley was quickly filling with Irish migrants keen on carving out new farms and felling the towering pine forests that grew majestically on either side of the great river. At Notre-Dame-de-Bon Secours Parish in Petit-Nation (now Montebello), Power challenged the seigneurs, the Papineau family[10] over church funds, the seigneur's harshness in collecting rents, and lax religious practice. When Power founded the parish's first school, Irish settlers were the first to send their children. Tenant farmers and working-class Catholics came to regard Power as a defender of their rights. At his next parish, Ste-Martine (1833-39), south of Montreal, Power would encounter the Papineaus again, this time in a rebellion led by Louis-Joseph Papineau against the Crown in 1837-1838. In the latter year, a handful of rebels from Ste-Martine placed Power under house arrest. When British troops vanquished "les patriotes," Power intervened with the government to ask for leniency for several parishioners he felt were innocent of any capital crime.[11]

It was at his fourth parish, La Nativité de Très Sainte-Vièrge in Laprairie, that Power came to the attention of the second bishop of Montreal, Ignace Bourget.[12] In his time on the frontier trying to steer parishioners to adherence to church practices, proper sacramental observance, and morality, Power had become an expert in Canon Law, and he began to build an impressive library of legal texts, theology books and Church histories. Moreover, government officers regarded Power as a safe non-political priest, who sympathized with the constitutional nationalism of Daniel O'Connell, and promoted loyalty to the Crown and its representatives in British North America. His training under the loyal Halifax priest, Edmund Burke, in the heart of the British naval garrison, helped him to cultivate an appreciation of his British citizenship and a rational constitutional approach to political reform. He was by no means a radical Irish nationalist. It was clear that British authorities trusted him.[13]

Bourget made him a close advisor, which was convenient for Power since his parish was just south of the city of Montreal, across the St. Lawrence River. Multilingual, intelligent and with a keen sense of Canon Law, he became Bourget's emissary on a number of projects. In 1841, the Bishop took Power with him on his *ad limina* visit to Rome, that is, a report to the Pope and Curia made by a bishop every five years, preferably in person. It was Power's first trip outside North America. During his deliberations with Pope Gregory XVI and the Curia, Bourget convinced them that the Upper Canadian Diocese needed to be divided in two, and that the new western portion required an able bishop—namely Power. Power was unaware of Bourget's maneuver and continued to help his superior argue for a new frontier diocese. Bourget sent Power to London where he was successful in convincing the Colonial Office that a new Catholic bishop would:

> in case of an emergency ... possess more authority over those committed to his care than an ordinary clergyman; his presence and his advice might also prove highly serviceable to Her Majesty's Government in quelling that spirit of insubordination and fierce democratic spirit which unhappily exist in a formidable degree on many parts of the Frontier line.[14]

With London's approval secured, Pope Gregory XVI created the Diocese of Western Upper Canada in December 1841. Bourget's plan of having the Pope appoint Power was also successful, both in Rome and in London. When Lord Stanley informed the governor general of Canada, Sir Charles Bagot, that Power had been appointed, he included praise for Power's "high character for piety, for moral conduct, and for loyalty to the British Crown."[15] Power was completely unaware of his appointment. The final leg of his journey included a trip to Ireland where he unsuccessfully attempted to recruit clergy and religious to the Diocese of Montreal.

Bourget informed Power of his appointment to Western Upper Canada, as its new bishop in April 1842.[16] Power was completely embarrassed by the situation and requested that he be passed over. He felt unworthy of the position and physically unable to work in the demanding frontier territory. Writing to Bourget, he conceded:

> The more I reflect, the more I am convinced that the choice that has been made of me, is poor and I will not make good in the new bishopric ... I am keenly aware that I am not strong enough to face the obstacles and difficulties that present themselves in the administration of such a vast and poorly organized diocese.[17]

Neither Bourget nor Bishop Ignazio Giovanni Cadolini of the Propaganda Fide would hear it. The Catholics of Upper Canada were a fragile minority but were increasing weekly because of Irish migration. The province needed a loyal, talented, English-speaking bishop who, in Bourget's blunt words, would "prevent the rape [of Catholics] by Protestant ministers."[18] Just as Irish immigrants had necessitated Power's transfer to frontier Canadian dioceses, as a young priest, so now Irish immigration to the western Canadian frontiers was a significant factor in placing him, once again, in a spotlight not of his choosing. He accepted his fate and, by June 1842, arrived in his new diocese, now renamed Toronto after its largest and most important city.

Power's new diocese was vast geographically, multicultural in terms of its settlers and populated mostly by Protestants. There would be no sense of the Catholic ethos that he had experienced in either Quebec or Montreal, and he would come to experience only pockets of Catholics settled along the frontier, in established rural areas, and in sections of major towns like Hamilton, London, Sandwich (Windsor), and Toronto. The latter city was the largest, containing just under 20,000 people of whom perhaps only a fifth were Catholics.[19] Of the general Catholic population of the diocese, most were of Irish birth or descent, with a strong French-Canadian presence in the southwest of the diocese at Sandwich, Germans in Wilmot and Waterloo, Indigenous Catholics in Coldwater, Manitoulin Island, and Fort William, and Highland Scots scattered across the entire region. Toronto itself was a muddy colonial backwater, with a strong Protestant character and the omnipresence of the Loyal Orange Lodge, to which many Protestant politicians belonged.[20] The city had been the capital of Upper Canada until 1841, when the Parliament at Westminster amalgamated Upper and Lower Canada into the United Province of Canada, with its new capital temporarily placed at Kingston. By his own admission, Power arrived at the "edge of civilization" with the tiny St. Paul's Church serving as his cathedral, one fledgling school and a temporary residence at the North American Hotel, because there was no rectory in the city.[21]

Much could be written about Power laboring to build a diocese out of a rag-tag collection of frontier parishes and mission stations in a region dominated in almost every facet of life by Protestantism. Let it suffice to say that Power came to know his diocese early by using the summer of 1842 to travel by boat, canoe, cart and on foot, covering close to 1,000 kilometers in his pastoral visits to Hamilton, Niagara, Sandwich, Sault Ste. Marie, Manitoulin Island, Penetanguishene, and the farmlands north of Toronto.[22] Armed with the knowledge of the territory and its peoples, he supervised the training of his small cadre of 20 priests, monitored the erection of new parish churches, established formal relations with several Indigenous Nations in the diocese, began the construction of St. Michael's Cathedral and developed numerous ways of delivering Catholic education to children. He also invited the Society of Jesus (Jesuits) to the diocese to oversee the Indigenous missions and secured the Loretto Sisters of the Institute of the Blessed Virgin Mary from Rathfarnham in Ireland to establish Catholic schools. His most notable ecclesiastical achievement, however, was creating the legal structure of an "Episcopal Corporation," which placed all church property in the possession of a corporation of one—the bishop.[23] This elimination of the control of parishes by lay trustees was made possible by the cooperation of Protestant politicians in the Legislative Assembly of Canada, one of whom introduced the bill in 1844.[24] In fact, he built strong, cooperative, and friendly relationships with Protestant clergy, including Egerton Ryerson, the leading Methodist cleric and superintendent of education in Canada West, and Bishop John Strachan, the leader of the Anglican Church. His soothing of Protestant-Catholic tensions in the region perhaps served as a foundation for his ability to mobilize a multi-denominational approach to emigrant relief when Irish refugees descended on the province, *en masse*, in 1847.

Power seemed to encounter the presence of the Irish everywhere he went in his pastoral ministry. His new assignment to the Diocese of Toronto was no different from his previous experience. The Irish migrations to Canada West (formerly Upper Canada) began after the cessation of the Napoleonic Wars in 1815. The period between 1815 and 1845 witnessed the arrival of nearly half a million Irish migrants to British North America, tens of thousands of whom arrived in the western province to farm, harvest the forests, build canals, or simply sojourn in Canada and move on to the United States.[25] In fact, the Irish settlement grid in Canada West was well established before the first Famine migrants arrived, and the general characteristic of Irish settlement, regardless of religion, was rural. This markedly contrasted with Irish settlement in the United States, which has been characterized by historian Kevin Kenny as urban.[26] Power would soon discover that most of his existing Irish parishes were rural small towns and villages. Another difference between Irish settlement in Canada West and the other British Colonies and the United States was that it was primarily Protestant. Perhaps two-thirds of Canada West's Irish residents were adherents to the Church of Ireland, Presbyterianism, or several other dissenting Protestant groups. When Power faced the religious configuration of his new diocese, he quickly became aware that the sectarian difficulties of the old world could quickly re-ignite in the new. Just after his arrival, he read with horror how Protestant farmers in Cavan Township, just across the eastern boundary of his diocese, burned all the Catholic farmers out of the district. The "Cavan Blazers" became emblematic of what might happen to Irish Catholics, should they not adhere to the old adage "croppies lie down."[27]

While there were periodic outbursts of sectarian tension, some violent, generally Power's time in Toronto was marked by peace between Christian groups. To this end, Power was a strong supporter of the St. Patrick's Benevolent Society (SPBS), which had both Catholic and Protestant members.[28] While the SPBS focused on local charitable works, its Irish Canadian members were acutely aware of events taking place in Ireland. The local weekly Catholic newspaper, *The Mirror*, edited by Irish expatriate Charles Donlevy, reported on Daniel O'Connell's movement for the repeal of the Act of Union, the exclusion of Catholic from Irish juries, and the general defense of Catholic rights in Ireland. There were numerous Repeal Associations in the urban centers of the diocese, although Power, himself, never made a public pronouncement. While he collected books on Irish history and subscribed to *The Mirror* and, in an earlier period, the more radical newspaper, *The Vindicator,* Power was always conscious of the balance he would have to maintain on political issues, lest the loyalty of his Catholic community be called into question.[29] Canadians of all backgrounds responded with monetary aid when they heard there were looming signs of an economic and social crisis in Ireland, coming because of the initial potato blight in 1845, and the subsequent distress during the winter. At his packed St. Patrick's Day Mass, in March 1846, Power made an impassioned plea for assistance to Ireland in her time of need. One reporter commented that it was one of the most eloquent and earnest appeals he had ever heard.[30] Canada received about 32,242 migrants, mostly Irish, from British ports in 1846,[31] but this would merely prove to be the calm before the proverbial storm.

The crisis facing Ireland became shockingly real to Power in 1847. In January, he set off to Rome via New York for his first *ad limina* visit. Having met Pope Pius IX, who evidently reported years later that he had been most impressed with Toronto's bishop,[32] Power ventured to Paris to solicit funds for his diocese, and then proceeded to London, to address some urgent issues at the Colonial Office. Pope Pius IX had written a Pastoral Letter calling for aid to Ireland, and he deputized Power to disseminate it as he travelled.[33] For his own part, Power wrote his own Circular Letter to his diocese while in London, acknowledging that while Canadians had already been generous in responding to Irish relief, more prayers and alms were needed. Power was deeply affected by the daily gruesome reports of starvation and disease in Ireland. He sent his Circular Letter ahead of him by steamer so that it could be promulgated in every parish by the time of his return to Toronto.[34]

Power's final leg of the European tour was Ireland. Here Power travelled to Rathfarnham, then outside of Dublin, where he met with Mother Teresa Ball, the head of the Institute of the Blessed Virgin Mary (Loreto Sisters).[35] His visit was a follow-up to his correspondence with Ball regarding her sending several sisters to Toronto to establish Catholic schools. After his failure to attract any religious or clergy in Ireland during his previous visit in 1841, Power could claim success when Mother Ball agreed to send five sisters to Canada in a few weeks time. His elation must have been deeply muted, however, by the scenes that he witnessed while travelling in the Irish countryside, and his observations of thousands of migrants waiting to depart from the Port of Dublin in the hope of finding a better life anywhere. His Irish experience seared into his mind the imperative to marshal aid for Ireland and to prepare his colleagues at home for what he thought would be a crush of Irish refugees. As such, he may have been one of the few Canadian leaders who witnessed the Irish tragedy on both sides of the Atlantic.

In early June, Power departed from Dublin on a steamer bound for Boston. On 13 June, the steamer stopped in Halifax, and he was able to visit his mother and sisters, before re-embarking and sailing to Boston. His haste to return to Toronto was so great that he sent an apology to his friend, Bishop William Walsh of Halifax, that he had not enough time in his brief stop to visit him.[36] Power knew that dozens of ships, filled with Irish migrants, had already departed on their transatlantic journeys that would normally take six to eight weeks. His steamer gave him the luxury of making the crossing in less than ten days, allowing him to reach Toronto, via rail from New York, just as the vanguard of Famine migrants arrived in Canada West. Power found Toronto in a frenzy of activity. In February, the city council had established a Toronto Board of Health to manage the expected intake of refugees. By 7 June, the Provincial Government had ordered the creation of boards of health, fever hospitals, and sheds, in all major municipalities. Toronto was already ahead in this respect having begun the search for a hospital site as early as May.[37] The Board of Health abandoned the idea of isolating migrants on the large, crescent-shaped peninsula that enclosed Toronto's massive harbor, and the Toronto General Hospital at King and John Streets, was designated as the Emigrant Hospital on 16 June. The property adjoining the stone building would house at least 16 fever sheds by the end of the season.[38] The migrants would be restricted to landing at only one quay, Dr. Rees's Wharf, where they would be triaged by city employee Edward McElderry, who would authorize transportation vouchers for the healthy, send the sick several blocks north to the hospital, and manage crowd control at the pier, which some days might receive 1,000 emigrants. Power had strongly endorsed the hiring of McElderry who, with his wife and eight children, was a faithful parishioner at St. Paul's Church.

There are conflicting reports suggesting that the Board of Health's plans sometimes did not play out in reality. Irish migrants arrived by the hundreds each day, having taken Durham boats and steamers from Kingston, and having already survived the typhus outbreaks in that city—and in Montreal and Quebec City prior to that. In June, during the early days of emigrant reception, Larratt Smith, a traveller from England, reported back home that:

> The city has passed some very stringent regulations with regards to immigrants and measures are adopted to keep them as much as possible from being a nuisance to us. They arrive here to the extent of 300 to 600 by any steamer. The sick are immediately sent to the hospital which has been given up to them entirely and the healthy are fed and allowed to occupy the Immigrant sheds for 24 hours, at the expiration of this time, they are obliged to keep moving, their rations are stopped and if they are found begging, are imprisoned at once. Means of conveyance are provided by the Corporation to take them at once to the country.[39]

As the season wore on, into July and August, however, the conditions on board the steamers bringing migrants to Toronto were likened to "slave ships" with "poor creatures ... crowded together like herrings in a barrel."[40] Stephen de Vere, a landlord from Limerick who actually made the voyage across the Atlantic with his tenants, described the steamer landing in Toronto as "incommodius" and "ill-ventillated" with some steamers towing extra barges crowded with exposed passengers who were often sick.[41] Constable J.B. Townsend, who was responsible for managing the hospital precinct, indicated in August, that the sheds were over capacity due to the many sick emigrants arriving in the city.[42] Toronto was overwhelmed, its hospital and sheds were full, McElderry was madly shipping off as many healthy migrants as he could each day to other parts of the province, and typhus was infecting and killing dozens of migrants and hospital staff each day.

Power deployed four priests to attend to the sick and dying in the sheds. Housed in the newly-erected episcopal residence, Power was joined by J.J. Hay (his secretary), Thaddeus Kirwan, and John O'Reilly. All of these priests were under 32 years of age, and Hay, at 29, was the veteran having been a priest for five years. Their task was to care for the spiritual needs of those emigrants committed to the hospital and sheds. Each morning they would leave their rectory in the east end of the city, and make their way through the streets of Toronto which, after rain, earned the nick name "Muddy York." The sheds were in the extreme west end of the city, far away from the locus of population. The remote location of the hospital helped to contain the spread of the typhus epidemic, protecting the more populous center and the eastern wards of Toronto. Now treatable by antibiotics, in the 1840s typhus had no known cure and spread quickly from hosts to new victims, killing over half of those infected. In 1847, Toronto witnessed the deaths of 1,124 people, including migrants, physicians, nurses, and hospital staff.[43] Despite their youth, Power's priests all fell ill, as did Fathers Jean-Baptist Proulx, Jeremiah Ryan, and John Carroll, who came in relief for those who had been incapacitated. They all survived and Kirwan spearheaded the placement of Irish orphans in Catholic homes.[44] Nevertheless, with all of his priests sick, Power alone made the daily trek to the sheds, in addition to his other duties.

During the epidemic Power received an additional surprise. On 20 September, he answered a call to his front door one afternoon and, to his astonishment, the five Loretto Sisters promised by Mother Teresa Ball were on his doorstep dressed in their "travelling clothes." He had expected their arrival in the autumn, and their presence in the midst of the typhus epidemic caused him additional anxiety. One of the women, Teresa Dease, would later comment that Power's "heart was evidently oppressed by the scenes of sorrow he had witnessed in the early part of the day, during his visits to the hospital, where the emigrant fever was raging."[45] Power was greatly agitated; he had sent Kirwan to recuperate in Niagara, from where John Carroll[46] had just arrived to assist the bishop. Fathers Ryan and Hay were still sick but in recovery, and there were now five women—whom he needed desperately for schools—seeking food and lodging in a town plagued with fever. Yet these sisters had no other lodgings and had to stay with him temporarily.

After they changed into their habits and were offered supper by their host, Dease reported that Power was subdued during the meal, as was Hay, although she and her colleagues appeared to be put at ease by Carroll's sense of humor.[47] Dease also commented that the new episcopal residence was as bleak as the bishop's demeanor; its dining room and parlor "looked bare and oppressively lonely."[48] Evidently, Power's personal austerity and preoccupation with the epidemic and the welfare of the Irish accounted for the spartan apartments in what normally might be called "the episcopal palace." During the supper, Power was a nervous wreck. Fearful that the sisters might contract the fever, he examined every piece of fruit before he invited them to eat. Dease reported that he ate little, if anything at all, and appeared flushed. When, in concern, he was asked by his guests about his daily labors and the mounting casualties of the pandemic, he responded wearily, "Don't speak of them, I anointed so many today and heard their confessions."[49] Clearly, the emigration season was taking its toll on him physically and mentally.

Power's fatigue did not cause him to retreat from pleading for the relief of the suffering Irish in the city. Two days before the arrival of the Loretto Sisters, Power and the city's leading clergy and civic officials called a public meeting to address the emigrant and public health crisis. One of the key resolutions of the meeting was to re-double efforts by the city to secure funding from the Legislative Assembly for emigrant relief.[50] Participants were concerned that there was inadequate housing or hospital facilities to accommodate the Irish sick during the coming winter, and there was also a sense that the city should find employment for those emigrants able to work.[51] When it came time for him to speak, Power rose to his feet and redirected questions, recasting them in the light of the immigrant experience itself. He detected an element of blame in the suggestions that immigrants themselves deftly hid their illnesses, so that they could move inland from Grosse Île, Montreal or Kingston. With his usual sense of timing and eloquence, Power placed the Irish migrant in proper context, by relating his own personal observations of what he had seen on his recent trip to Ireland. The Irish whom he witnessed, explained Power, had left Dublin showing all of the outward signs of health; symptoms of disease were revealed once they had reached Liverpool, but they appeared to shake off the illness and were permitted passage to America, "such was the nature of the disease." Once on the Atlantic, the symptoms reappeared. Power also related how similar lapses in symptoms were evident in those arriving at Grosse Île, as their symptoms would also reappear later. For Power, "the disease seemed to be of that insidious character, as to baffle all the skill that might be employed in treating for its cure and it did not seem to be affected by change of season." Power's principal point in this tour de force was that "the Irish themselves were not responsible for the sickness, they were victims of an erratic and uncontrolled malady through no fault of their own." The point was taken and the tone of the proposed resolutions amended accordingly.[52]

It was shortly after this meeting and the subsequent arrival of the Lorettos that Power's health seemed to falter. By 22 September, he showed visible signs of fatigue and fever. For five days he battled hard and his colleagues at the residence thought he might recover, just as Kirwan, and the others had. By 29 September, Power was unable to leave his bed or eat. He could not even lift a pen and, in what may have been his last dictated letter, he asked Hay to send a note to Bishop Walsh in Halifax to relay any news of his health to his mother, Mary Power. All attempts to save the young bishop proved futile. His fever did not break, he was in constant pain, and could not move. At 6:30 am on the morning of 1 October 1847, Michael Power died, just about two weeks shy of his 43rd birthday.[53] His was the largest funeral in Toronto to that date. Thousands of people, many of whom were the Irish emigrants he served, paid tribute as the massive funeral procession made its way along Queen Street, from St. Paul's Church in the eastern ward to the site of the new cathedral in the center of the city. Both Catholics and Protestants were involved in the procession and gathered as onlookers. All of the city councillors, local priests, the mayor, police, the president of King's College, physicians, school trustees, and prominent civic leaders marched behind the wagon that carried his remains.[54] His body was placed in the crypt of the yet unfinished cathedral. Everyone in attendance that day knew of Michael Power's selfless service to his city, his diocese, and to the Irish emigrants in that summer of sorrow. A French-Canadian Catholic periodical likened him to St. Charles Borromeo, calling him a true "martyr of charity."[55] In 2017, Cardinal Thomas Collins of Toronto began preparing a case for the founding bishop's canonization.

NOTES

1. The comparison between Ontario and Ireland is taken by dividing the total area of Ontario by two, based on the two dioceses at the time (Toronto and Kingston) and then dividing the land mass of Ireland into the result: 504,000 km² divided by 84,000 km².

2. Laura J Smith, "'We Have Scattered Them Far and Wide: Transporting Indigent Irish Emigrants in the Canadas, 1843-1847," in Christine Kinealy and Gerard Moran (eds), *Irish Famines Before and After the Great Hunger* (Hamden, CT: Quinnipiac University Press, 2020), pp 77-99; Mark G. McGowan, *Death or Canada: The Irish Famine Migration to Toronto, 1847* (Toronto: Novalis, 2009), p. 50.

3. The only full-length scholarly biography of Power is Mark G. McGowan, *Michael Power: The Struggle to Build the Catholic Church on the Canadian Frontier* (Montreal & Kingston: McGill-Queen's University Press, 2005).

4. Terrence Murphy and Cyril Byrne, eds. *Religion and Identity: The Experience of Irish and Scottish Catholics in Atlantic Canada* (St. John's: Jesperson Press, 1987).

5. McGowan, *Michael Power*, pp 35-36.

6. Archives of the Roman Catholic Archdiocese of Toronto (ARCAT), Power Papers (PP). AA04.06, Mary Power to Michael Power, 20 February 1824.

7. Archives of the Archdiocese of Quebec (AAQ), 210-A, Register 13, Bernard-Claude Panet to Laurent Amiot, 14 February 1827, pp 128-129.

8. McGowan, *Michael Power*, pp 54-55.

9. Archives of the Diocese of Nicolet, Paroisse Ste Frédéric, Box 1, Power to Panet, 19 January and 10 August 1828.

10. The seigneury was managed by Denis-Benjamin Papineau. His brother, Louis-Joseph, was a radical leader in the legislature of the Province of Lower Canada who, with several Anglophone radicals including Irishman Edmund Baily O'Callaghan, fomented a violent insurrection in 1837. Although the "patriotes" were defeated in several pitched battles with British troops, the rebellion erupted a second time in 1838.

11. Archives National de Quebec, *Evénements 1837-1838*, Michael Power to Military Authorities, 24 January 1839.

12. Bourget replaced Jean-Jacques Lartigue, the first bishop of Montreal (1832-1840) and to whom Power reported after the creation of the new diocese, which covered the western portion of Lower Canada (Quebec) including the frontier areas of the east bank of the Ottawa River, northwest of Montreal and the burgeoning eastern townships south of Montreal.

13. McGowan, *Michael Power*, pp 128-129 and 232-234.

14. Library and Archives Canada (LAC), Lord Stanley Papers, Summary of the Roman Catholic Archbishop for North American Colonies, Appendix 1, Power to Stanley, 27 September 1841.

15. Ibid., Appendix 9, letter 217, Stanley to Sir Charles Bagot, 3 August 1842.

16. ARCAT, Letterbook (LB) 01.013, Papal Bull, Gregory XVI, 17 December 1841 and 01.014 Appointment, 17 December 1841.

17. ARCAT, LB 01.012, Power to Bourget, 10 April 1842.

18. Archives of the Propaganda Fide—SOCG, vol. 920, doc. 193, Bourget to Ignazio Cadolini, 20 July 1841.

19. *Censuses of Canada, 1665-1871*, vol. 4, *Census of Canada 1870-1871* (Ottawa: I.B. Taylor, 1876), pp 165-166, Table II.

20. William J. Smyth, *Toronto, The Belfast of Canada* (University of Toronto Press, 2015).

21. ARCAT, PP, AD01.03, Bill, North American Hotel, 9 July 1842.

22. McGowan, *Michael Power*, p. 149.

23. He was influenced by the American precedent enacted at the Council of Baltimore.

24. Archives of the Archdiocese of Montreal, Toronto Correspondence, 255.104, file 845-7, Angus Macdonell to Power, 12 February 1845; Elizabeth Nash, ed., *Debates of the Legislative Assembly of the Province of Canada* (Montreal: Presses de l'Ecole des Hautes Etudes Commerciales, 1970), pp 300, 365-366, 1101, 1106.

25. Cecil J. Houston & William J. Smyth, *Irish Emigration and Canadian Settlement: Patterns, Links, and Letters* (University of Toronto Press, 1990), pp 20-25; Donald Harmon Akenson, *The Irish in Ontario: A Study in Rural History* (Montreal & Kingston: McGill-Queen's University Press, 1984), p. 32.

26. Kevin Kenny, *The American Irish: A History* (Harlow, UK: Pearson Educational Ltd., 2000), p. 105.

27. Quentin Brown, *This Green and Pleasant Land: Chronicles of Cavan Township* (Millbrook: Millbrook & Cavan Historical Society, 1990), pp 34-38.

28. *The Mirror*, 8 March 1844.

29. *The Catholic*, 24 April 1844.

30. *The Cross*, 25 April 1846.

31. LAC, Colonial Office Papers, Report of the Colonial Land and Emigration Commissioners, 11845-1850, CO 384/78-83.

32. *The Irish Canadian*, 15 March 1876. Reprinted Eulogy of Power by Bishop Jean-François Jamot of Peterborough.

33. ARCAT, PP, Pastoral Letter, 13 May 1847.

34. Ibid.

35. Spelled Loretto Sisters in Canada.

36. Archives of the Archdiocese of Halifax, William Walsh Papers, vol. 2, Power to Walsh, 10 August 1847.

37. Archives of Ontario (AO), RG 11-3, Anthony Hawke Papers, copy, Quartermaster General, George Ryerson to Mayor William H. Boulton, 2 June 1847.

38. *The British Colonist*, 22 June 1847.

39. Mary Larratt Smith, ed., *Young Mr. Smith in Upper Canada* (University of Toronto Press, 1980), p. 111.

40. *The Globe*, 25 August 1847.

41. Stephen De Vere, cited in *Elgin-Grey Papers, 1846-1852*, vol. 4 (Ottawa: J.O. Patenaude, King's Printer, 1937), p. 1345.

42. *The British Colonist*, 20 August 1847.

43. *The Mirror*, 18 February 1848.

44. ARCAT, Special Collections, Holograph Collection, HO, Series 20.67, Father T. Kirwan, List of Farmers from Adjala Township Who Request Orphan Children, 18 April 1848.

45. Archives of the Institute of the Blessed Virgin Mary, Toronto, *Annals 1847-1870*, Teresa Dease, Book 1, transcribed by Maggie Lyons, 25 August 1875.

46. Ibid., p. 14.

47. Ibid.

48. Ibid., p. 11.

49. Ibid., p. 17

50. *The British Colonist*, 13 August and 14 and 21 September 1847; *The Mirror* 13 August 1847. LAC, Papers of the Provincial Secretary, Dominick Daly to Edward McElderry, 13 July 1847.

51. AO, MS 35 R 11, John Strachan Papers, LB 5, Strachan to Daniel Murray, 1 December 1847, p. 26; *The British Colonist*, 17 September 1847.

52. *The Mirror*, 24 September 1847.

53. *The British Colonist*, 5 October 1847.

54. Ibid., 8 October 1847 and *Nova Scotian,* 25 October 1847.

55. *Mélanges Réligieux*, 5 October 1847.

CHAPTER FOURTEEN

MONTREAL'S GREY NUNS, THE GREAT HUNGER MIGRATION AND THE MIRACLE OF ROSE'S MARBLE

Jason King

In 1847 and 1848, over 6,000 Famine Irish emigrants perished from infectious diseases such as typhus in the fever sheds of Montreal. They lie buried in North America's largest Irish mass grave. Among them was Michael Brown from Galway. The only archival record of his existence can be found in the Sisters of Charity or Grey Nuns' "Categories of the Orphans at Point St Charles," dated 19 March 1848.[1] It registers his children: Bridget Brown (9), Rose Brown (7), and George Brown as "brother and sisters," and notes that their "Father died in sheds." Under the "remarks" column, the document states, "Mother in sheds," and that her daughters, Bridget and Rose, were placed "at Grey Nunnery" with their mother. The Brown family was one of thousands from Ireland who were cared for by the Grey Nuns. Unlike most, the Brown family's surviving members joined the ranks of their rescuers to help shelter emigrant orphans. Their story attests to the Grey Nuns' courage, compassion and devotion, as well as to their extraordinary vulnerability to "ship's fever" or typhus, which afflicted both Irish emigrants and their caregivers alike.

This chapter explores the legacy of the Grey Nuns as "martyrs of charity" who cared for Montreal's Famine Irish emigrants through the Brown family case study.[2] Approximately 100,000 Irish people fled to British North America, or Canada, in 1847 to 1848 to escape from the Great Hunger, and over 70,000 of them arrived in Montreal, which had a population of less than 50,000 at the time. The most detailed and evocative eyewitness accounts of their suffering can be found in the French language annals of the Grey Nuns, who tended to the sick in Montreal's fever sheds.

The annals contain over 500 pages of first-hand testimonies relaying the agony of typhus-stricken fever patients. Yet, because they were unpublished and written in French, the annals remained largely unknown until they were digitized, transcribed, translated,[3] interpreted in scholarly publications,[4] and curated and displayed in the 2015-2020 exhibit "Saving the Famine Irish: The Grey Nuns and the Great Hunger."[5]

This chapter builds on that work by examining the Brown family case study that brings together and breaks down ethnic, linguistic, and social barriers between Irish emigrants and their Canadian caregivers, whose lives became increasingly intertwined in the aftermath of the catastrophe. More specifically, it is argued that their ultimately uplifting story of resilience and survival throws into sharp relief the recurrent "mortuary spectacles" found in the Grey Nuns' annals which compress countless Irish emigrants into an anonymous mass of stricken fever victims and stacks of corpses.[6] Yet, these mortuary spectacles also challenge interpreters to seek individual stories of Famine emigrants, such as the members of the Brown family, who survived the fever sheds to start new families overseas. Ultimately, tracking these stories can help put a face on the figure of an individual Famine migrant and inspire a sense of resilience in the midst of later crises.

Since Marie-Marguerite d'Youville founded the Sisters of Charity, or Grey Nuns, in 1738, and they had been led by a succession of strong women, including their Mother Superior Elizabeth McMullen in 1847.[7] The term "Grey Nun" (or *Soeurs Grise* in French), is derived from the color of their habit, but is also pejorative, implying "tipsy" or drunken women on account of the fact that their founder's late husband traded alcohol with native peoples, which was illegal at the time. By the nineteenth century, however, the Grey Nuns designation had become a badge of honor for the "Sisters of Charity." Under the leadership of Mother Superior Elizabeth McMullen, the Grey Nuns first entered the fever sheds of Montreal on 9 June 1847. They were summoned to the sheds by the city's mayor, John Easton Mills. The annals of the Grey Nuns reveal the considerable social distance between the predominantly French speaking, Roman Catholic, female religious community and the American born, English speaking, Protestant mayor. According to *The Typhus of 1847*:

> They were welcomed with great courtesy and deference by the government steward, who gave all authorization necessary to the Grey Nuns to visit and take care of the pestilent, authorizing them to engage faithful men and women. The venerated Mother superior [was] almost surprised by this cordial welcome.[8]

Mother Superior McMullen soon came to realize that "this steward was protestant; he knew little about catholic institutions," but "hastened to conduct them to a home almost in ruin by the river, under the name of the hospital."[9] The Grey Nuns were immediately confronted by a scene of mass suffering and death. As they recall in their annals:

> What a spectacle unravelled in the eyes of this good mother and her company! Hundreds of people were laying there, most of them on bare planks, pell-mell, men, women and children. The moribund and cadavers are crowded in the same shelter, while there are those that lie on the quays or on pieces of wood thrown here and there along the river.[10]

This mortuary spectacle would recur in Montreal's fever sheds throughout the summer of 1847. The Grey Nuns were, in fact, one of three orders of French-Canadian female religious who cared for the city's Famine emigrants. Two weeks after they entered the fever sheds, the Grey Nuns were forced to withdraw on 24 June 1847 because of illness and seven fatalities within their ranks. They were replaced by the Sisters of Providence, a female religious community founded only three years earlier by Émilie Tavernier Gamelin (1800-1851). The third order of nuns to care for the Famine Irish was the cloistered Religious Hospitallers of St. Joseph, who replaced the Sisters of Providence after they too succumbed to the epidemic. These three orders of nuns are depicted caring for Famine emigrants in Théophile Hamel's painting, *Le Typhus*, which provides the only eyewitness image of Irish death and suffering in North America in 1847.[11]

Relentless impressions of Famine Irish death and suffering are recorded in the annals of the Grey Nuns. From the moment of their arrival in the sheds, they repeatedly emphasized in their annals the degradation and mass mortality of Irish fever victims. In *Ancien Journal*, the Grey Nuns recalled:

> Words are lacking to express the hideous state in which the sick found themselves, up to three of them in the same bed, or cots to be more exact, that had been hastily fashioned and gave the impression that they were caskets. When touring the SHEDS, we would find cadavers exhaling an insufferable infection, lying in the same bed as those that still breathed; the number of sick was so considerable, that we at some point counted 1100 of them, some of whom had been dead for a few hours before we had noticed. One day, a Sister, passing one of those sheds, saw a poor afflicted that appeared restless; she came near his cot and saw that he was attempting to push off two dead bodies between which he was lying down. In spite of the delirium that deprived him of some of his faculties, the sight of those cadavers, one black as coal, the other, in contrast, yellow like saffron, caused him such fright that it momentarily brought him back to his senses; once delivered from his two companions, he fell back in his previous state of insensibility, and the next day, it was his turn to join the ranks of the dead ... we could cite a thousand traits of this kind; but it is impossible to report all of them.[12]

The annals dwell on such scenes of bodily suffering and putrefaction that afflicted emigrants and their caregivers alike. In *Ancien Journal*, it is noted that, "an insufferable odour emanated from the sick, that they were covered in vermin, and surrounded by the most repugnant dirtiness."[13] "Since we had not yet constructed a mortuary for the dead," recounts *The Typhus of 1847*, "the corpses were exposed in the outdoors, and once there was a great enough number of them, we made a cemetery for the bodies in the neighbouring fields. The odour that these cadavers produced and the horror they naturally caused add to the distressing picture of this situation."[14] These recurrent scenes and the stench of bodily decomposition define the mortuary spectacles in the Grey Nuns' annals. They capture the sense of immediacy and intimacy of death and physical decay within the sheds.

Nor were the Grey Nuns themselves spared these bodily indignities at life's end. Such was the case of Sister Alodie Bruyère, who "had but just arrived at the sheds and she caught the contagion almost immediately. Her illness was cruel, her poor body fell into a putrid state."[15] "Before dying, her entire body was but a wound which produced an insufferable infection," records the *Ancien Journal*.[16] Likewise, "our good sister JANE COLLINS, a novice for THREE months and EIGHTEEN (18) days, succumbed to the pestiferous disease following the cruellest of sufferance, accompanied by a near-continuous delirium."[17] Before they died, fever victims were often ravaged both in mind and body and seemingly deprived of any sense of consolation.

Montreal's "martyr mayor," John Easton Mills, suffered a similar fate. After summoning the Grey Nuns to the fever sheds in June of 1847, he presided over an increasingly acrimonious debate about whether they should be relocated from Windmill Point to the Boucherville Islands farther away from the city.[18] The question of whether the Sisters would venture beyond Montreal's perimeter to care for the sick was also raised. Mayor Mills paid tribute to them, insisting "they would go there... and would discharge their self-denying duties all the better ... in a healthy place."[19] Ultimately, he prevailed, but then succumbed to typhus as a result of his own ministrations. As William Weir recalled decades later: "I saw the Mayor (John E Mills) and Lord Elgin [the Governor General] visiting the ships on horseback, and afterwards riding towards the sheds. Later in the season the mayor fell a victim to the horrible disease."[20] Similarly, Bellele Guerin described Mills as a hagiographic figure who could often be seen:

> [In] the morning dawn, pursuing his weary march from one shed to another, soothing, consoling, cheering, and helping. Now he stops to take a last message from a dying father for those he left behind in the dear green land, and again, he lifts in his tender arms a little child who is unconsciously playing with her dead young mother's hand. His splendid health bore out during all these trying months.[21]

Indeed, Cecil Woodham-Smith notes that "John Mills regularly visited the sheds, but on the occasion which turned out to be his last and fatal visit his wife had a premonition of disaster, and as he left her she burst into tears."[22] Mills died on 12 November 1847 and was honored with the largest funeral in the city's history.[23] Like the Grey Nuns, Mills was venerated as a "martyr mayor" who perished from his ministrations to fever victims. His heroic self-sacrifice was defined against relentless impressions of Irish corpse-strewn fields and sheds that compressed them into an anonymous corporeal mass.

Despite these harrowing scenes, the Grey Nuns also recorded remarkable stories of resilience and survival. The most compelling is that of the dispersal and seemingly miraculous reunification of the Brown family. The earliest record of their arrival in Montreal is the aforementioned, "Categories of the Orphans at Point St Charles" document, dated 19 March 1848, in which Suzanne Brown and her three children Bridget, aged 9, Rose, aged 7 and George are listed. It stipulated that they were from County Galway and that their father died in the city's fever sheds. The document also noted that their "mother [was] in [the] sheds" and that both Bridget and Rose Brown had been placed at the "Grey Nunnery with mother." The document was compiled at the behest of Montreal's Bishop Ignace Bourget who, ten days earlier, had issued a pastoral letter on 9 March 1848 entreating his flock to take in the 99 emigrant orphans still being cared for in the city's fever sheds. He called on the clergy, religious communities, and laity in his diocese to provide homes for Irish children. Seven months earlier, on 11 July 1847, the Bishop had personally escorted hundreds of orphans from the sheds to shelters in the heart of the city. As he recalled in his pastoral letter:

> [T]hat [was]one of the most tender moments of our lives ... when, at the head of this numerous family of orphans, we walked the streets of this town, to lead them by the hand to the hospice which had been prepared for them. The sight of hundreds of these children ravaged by hunger, clothed in rags and suffering from the terrible disease which deprived them of their parents was too harrowing to ever forget.[24]

Bishop Bourget now sought to find shelter for the newly arrived emigrant orphans who had since taken their place. "Come communities dedicated to teaching or charity," he wrote, "adopt these poor orphans who are reaching towards you with their small, imploring hands." "Come pious and charitable laity," he added, "adopt these vulnerable children ... [and] show them all the tenderness that you would like to see in those who would receive your own children if they had the misfortune of losing you, and if consigned to a foreign land without family or friends, they were also subjected to such abject misery."[25] Among "these vulnerable children" removed from the fever sheds were Bridget, Rose and George Brown who were moved into the Grey Nunnery.

The Grey Nuns' annals also reveal the fate of their mother Suzanne. She was evacuated from the sheds with her children but she was in no condition to care for them. According to the *Foundation of St. Patrick's Asylum*:

> Very recently, an excellent widow named Suzanne Brown arrived in the country. Born in Ireland to an affluent family, who were stripped of their assets by misfortune, she was [left] widowed with her three children: George, Brigitte [sic] and Rose, and the courageous woman left her homeland to seek fortune abroad. She was travelling to Quebec with a group of Irish immigrants when she was struck down at sea by the contagion. From Quebec, she could nevertheless be transported to Montreal, but on her arrival she became so sick that, as it was unlikely she would recover and as she seemed unconscious, we entrusted her son George to the parish priest of Saint Hugues, her eldest daughter Brigitte to the Grey Nuns, and Rose, her youngest, was adopted by a courageous Irish woman whose name we unfortunately did not retain.[26]

The annal also states that her deceased "husband's name was Jeremy (Michael) Brown." The Brown children were thus placed with caregivers after their evacuation from the sheds as their unconscious mother seemed unlikely to recover.

Yet, Suzanne did survive and soon joined the ranks of her rescuers. "Having returned to health against all odds," the annal states, "Mrs. Brown was delighted to see her son in the parish priest of Saint Hugues' home and her eldest daughter with the Grey Nuns. But where to find her little Rose?"[27] While convalescing under the care of the Grey Nuns, she continued to search for her daughter, until "days and weeks passed with no clues to enlighten her." She was conspicuous because of her former affluence and education. According to the annal:

> One of her compatriots said of her: "If I dare to speak to Mrs. Brown today, it is because we are abroad. If I stayed in my country, I would not have dared, as she knew too much about my situation." In this way, misfortune was a great leveller of circumstance.[28]

More to the point, Brown was invited by the Grey Nuns to help care for other Irish orphans—"to spend the night with them and catechise them"—in a refuge they had established, the Franklin House, because she "was educated, pious and was ready and willing to devote herself."[29] Her role in educating Irish children is recounted in J.J. Curran's *Golden Jubilee of St Patrick's Orphan Asylum*. He recalled that:

> Mrs Brown, an Irish lady of good education and administrative ability, volunteered her services to teach these little ones the truths of religion and the rudiments of

learning. One room in the "House" was all that Mrs Brown occupied for her own use, whilst another had to be spared for the purpose of a school.[30]

In September 1848, she was joined by Father Patrick Dowd, who had "been appointed almoner of the poor, and, in that capacity, became Superior of the 'House.'"[31] Suzanne Brown remained the emigrant orphans' "first instructress"[32] until 17 November 1849, when she led "fifty children, barefoot and dressed in rags" from Franklin House to the new Perrault House shelter procured by Father Dowd.[33] Thus, after being carried unconscious from the fever sheds to the Grey Nunnery in March 1848, she became the "first instructress" of emigrant orphans in the year that followed.

Suzanne Brown found solace in caring for Irish children, but she continued to search for her missing daughter Rose. According to the *Foundation of St Patrick's Asylum*:

> When she found herself surrounded by the orphans who absorbed her teachings like thirsty earth absorbs the dew, she thought of her little Rose: "If I had her here with me, she said, I would teach her with all the others." With this weighing on her mind, one March evening, she attended a Lenten prayer service, or benediction of the Holy Sacrament in St Patrick's church. In the silence of the ceremony, she was disturbed from her contemplation by the sound of a marble rolling on the floor which came to rest in the folds of her clothes. She had barely raised her eyes when she saw a little girl aged three or four running to collect it. "Is this not my little Rose," she said trembling with emotion. Indeed, it was this child who she mourned and thought she had lost forever, now returned to her at this moment by our Lord, and by instinct, she reached out. However, her adoptive mother who had missed nothing of what happened, intervened and protested. Before the ceremony had even finished both women went to the sacristy to submit the case to Father Dowd. He did not delay in resolving the issue, and that very evening, Madame Brown triumphed, coming back to the refuge with little Rose.[34]

The Grey Nuns' annals make it clear that Suzanne Brown and her daughter were separated for approximately one year after they were evacuated together from the fever sheds to the Grey Nunnery in March 1848, and then reunited when Rose rolled her marble "one March evening" during a Lenten prayer service in St. Patrick's Church in 1849. It was fitting that Father Patrick Dowd presided over their reunification, as he had been the almoner and Superior of the refuge in which Suzanne Brown had taught since September 1848. The fact that the Grey Nuns had lost track of Rose Brown who "was adopted by a courageous Irish woman" attests to the chaotic circumstances of Rose's evacuation from the sheds with her unconscious mother. After a year of separation, Suzanne Brown "had now found... the whole of her family that remained in this land of exile."[35]

This story of the miracle of Rose's marble is both remarkable and historically verifiable from archival records and other sources. The vast majority of the Famine dead buried in a mass grave on the site of Montreal's fever sheds left no trace of their existence. That was the fate of Rose's father, Michael Brown. Yet Marie Rose Brown herself (mistakenly recorded as aged 5) and her elder sister Bridget (aged 14) can be found in the 1851 census for Canada East listed as "female orphans" (though they were half-orphans), still living under the care of the Grey Nuns.[36] Their elder brother, George, who had been "entrusted to the parish priest of Saint Hugues" in 1848, was raised to join the ranks of the clergy and minister to the same parish. He entered the seminary in St-Hyacinthe in Quebec's Eastern Townships and also studied in Sherbrooke and Montreal before he was ordained on 29 January 1860.[37] George was appointed vicar of Saint Hugues in 1860 and then parish priest of Compton, Quebec from 1860-1863.[38] The entry for "George Browne" in Jean Baptiste Arthur Allaire's *Dictionnaire Biographique du Clerge Canadien-Francais* (1910) notes that he was born in Galway on 17 July 1837, and he went on to serve as parish priest in Dunham and Sutton, Quebec (1863-1867), at a French-Canadian congregation in Troy, New York (1867-1875), in Syracuse, New York (1875-1877), back in Saint Hugues, Quebec (1877-1902), and that he died in St-Hyacinthe on 27 December 1902.[39] The "Rev. George Brown" (aged 24) is listed as a "minister" living with his mother Bridget Brown (aged 44, whom the Grey Nuns called Suzanne) and his younger sister Bridget (aged 21) in the 1861 census for Canada East in Compton, Quebec, where he served as parish priest.[40] In the 1891 Canadian census, the priest (aged 53) and his mother (aged 73) were still living in close proximity in Saint Hugues.[41] Ten years later, "Bridget Browne" (aged 83) was living near her daughter "Bedelia" (Bridget, aged 61) in Shefford in Quebec's Eastern Townships, as indicated in the 1901 Canadian census.[42] Bridget Browne's date of birth is recorded in that census as 16 October 1817, and her daughter Bedelia's birth-date as 4 March 1840. The mother, Bridget Browne, died at the age of 87 on 21 May 1905. Her daughter, Bedelia, lived until the age of 92 and died on 23 August 1930, in Valcourt, Quebec.[43] In short, the Brown family story reads like a fable, but it is a historically verifiable tale of dispersal and reunification from the Famine Irish migration.

The most poignant figures in that story are Bridget and Marie Rose Brown. After they were evacuated from the fever sheds in March 1848 and Marie Rose found her mother, both sisters lived for several years in the Grey Nuns convent. According to *The Typhus of 1847* annal: "BRIGITTE and ROSE entered the novitiate, but after a few months, it was quite visible that Brigitte was not being called to religious life; she returned to her mother and was properly married in the parish of her brother."[44] In fact, she met her fiancé Augustin Cousineau (born in Laval, Quebec, on 9 February

1839) while living with her brother in Compton and married Cousineau on 16 June 1863 in nearby Valcour, where she bore nine children.[45] In later life, Bridget yearned to find living relatives in her native Galway, but when she made the return voyage in 1885, she was bitterly disappointed to discover no trace of them in her ancestral home.[46] Her mixed marriage occurred on the threshold of a profound demographic and linguistic shift in Quebec's Eastern Townships when "the Irish were finally assimilated by the French Canadians."[47] Indeed, her French-Canadian great-granddaughter, Christiane Cousineau, and her husband, Bertrand Southière, discovered her Irish lineage through meticulous genealogical research. They learned that Christiane Cousineau is descended from her great-great-grandmother in Galway whose maiden name was Bridget O'Haverty, and that Bridget's husband who perished in the fever sheds was called Michael. According to family lore, Bridget and her husband had an eldest son also named Michael who did not survive their transatlantic voyage, though no archival trace of him remains.[48]

As for the youngest daughter, Marie Rose, or Rose Brown, she never left the Grey Nunnery. She took the veil and became a Grey Nun herself. "She persevered in holy vocation," notes the annal:

> [A]nd was professed under the name of the Sister Saint-PATRICE. God was happy with her sacrifice, she lived but a few years, dying at the age of twenty-two and some months, having passed close to SIX years in the Community where she truly was a little rose without thorns in her soft and pacific character, exhaling perfumes of a soft and solid piety.[49]

Like her mother, Sister Saint-Patrice found her vocation as an educator. In 1857, she helped establish a school for the poor in Sandwich (now Windsor), Ontario.[50] She was also one of the "foundresses" in 1863 of another parochial school in Montreal's Côte-des-Neiges area which became renowned for its "service to the poor and ... sick ... Parents and children venerated "their Grey Nuns" and the latter returned this love in affectionate service.[51] Sister Saint-Patrice died soon thereafter on 19 May 1865.[52] Ten months earlier, she had become the godmother for her sister Bridget's daughter, Marie-Rose Cousineau, who was born on 17 July 1864 and who kept alive the family name.[53]

Ultimately, the little girl who rolled her marble and found her mother in Saint Patrick's Church in 1849 became Sister Saint-Patrice and a godmother after she was rescued with her siblings from the fever sheds. If her mother was the "first instructress" of emigrant "orphans who absorbed her teachings like thirsty earth absorbs the dew," then Marie Rose followed in her mother's footsteps as the "foundress" of her own school. Like her mother, she joined the ranks of her rescuers and found solace in teaching the poor.

The miracle of Rose's marble attests to one family's story of resilience and survival in the midst of a mortuary spectacle. It contrasts with those of numerous families torn asunder by the Famine migration. Indeed, Rose Brown was but one of countless children plucked from the arms of their dying mothers by the Grey Nuns at the height of the typhus epidemic. The vast majority of them were never reunited with their families as their parents were buried in North America's largest Famine mass grave. The multitudes of Famine dead left no trace of their existence beyond the memory of mass mortality that is recalled in the Grey Nuns' annals. The annals represented the Sisters of Charity and other female religious orders with their compassion, devotion and self-sacrifice as caregivers who ministered to the sick and dying. They stood tall in the midst of a scene of mass death. It is also a story of rescue and recovery. Their legacy is to dispel impressions of Famine migrants as an anonymous mass, devoid of individual identities and stories of their own.

Ultimately, the miracle of Rose's marble provides a reminder that all 6,000 migrants who lie buried in Montreal's mass grave were individuals whose lives were cut short. Amongst them, Rose Brown survived and found her mother. She passed on her name to her niece whose godmother she became. As Sister Saint-Patrice, she carried on her mother's legacy to educate indigent children. She was honored by her fellow Sisters "as a little rose without thorns." Whether emigrant family trees were cut short or blossomed like the Browns after 1848, one respects their memory in seeking to find their stories. The Brown family story is just one that was passed on to subsequent generations. It inspires readers to look beyond the mortuary spectacles of the anonymous dead and learn more about the lives of the people who perished.

In conclusion, one of the last surviving Grey Nuns to serve in the sheds was Sister Martine Reid, who also worked alongside Bridget (Suzanne) Brown teaching emigrant orphans in 1848-49.[54] "We have spoken highly of Madam BROWN, who helped Sister Reid, as assistant and instructor of the FIFTY orphans that she had collected in the [Franklin] house," states the annal.[55] Sister Reid testified at the age of 80, on 13 November 1899, about her experiences in the fever sheds. These are her words:

> The terrible scenes that I have witnessed in these sheds made such an impression upon my mind that I can never forget them, nor the place where they occurred. I remember the cemetery very well. I have frequently passed there since, and I have never passed there and seen the stone without thinking of the scenes that I witnessed there in 1847 ...

Hundreds and hundreds of ship fever patients were buried in that enclosure where the monument now stands. I believe there were over six thousand. I saw numbers of bodies taken there to be buried ...

Each body was placed in a separate coffin.[56]

Sister Reid was haunted by the "terrible scenes" she had witnessed 50 years earlier. The stone and monument she referred to is the Black Rock Memorial erected on the site of the fever sheds mass grave in 1859, by mainly Irish workers engaged in building the city's Victoria Bridge. Although the "Black Rock" is the first memorial to be erected to victims of the Great Hunger in North America, it is relatively inaccessible and unknown. It is located in the median of a major traffic artery where most of the 6,000 Irish people who perished lie buried in derelict surroundings. In 2019, members of the Montreal Irish Memorial Park Foundation were invited to take part in an archaeological excavation of part of the site where some of the coffins observed by Sister Reid were respectfully and sensitively unearthed. It was a profoundly moving moment for those community members who will reinter their ancestors with full honors when a new memorial park is complete.[57] The new memorial park will create a more dignified setting for the Famine emigrants who succumbed by the thousand to ships' fever. The memory of such large "numbers of bodies taken there to be buried" weighed heavily on Sister Reid. One can only hope that she recalled no less vividly that March evening in 1849 when Bridget (Suzanne) Brown came home with her long-lost daughter, Rose.

NOTES

1. Anon. "Categories of the Orphans at Point St Charles" (19 March 1848), Archival Services and Collections, Maison de Mère d'Youville, Sisters of Charity of Montreal, "Grey Nuns."

2. The phrase is taken from Grey Nuns, *The Typhus of 1847*, *Ancien Journal*, vol. II. Translated by Philip O'Gorman. http://faminearchive.nuigalway.ie/docs/grey-nuns/TheTyphusof1847.pdf, p. 33.

3. Jason King (ed.), Irish Famine Archive, http://faminearchive.nuigalway.ie. It comprises Grey Nuns *Ancien Journal*, vol I. Translated by Jean-François Bernard. http://famine archive.nuigalway.ie/docs/greynuns/GreyNunsFamineAnnalAncienJournalVolumeI.1847.pdf; Grey Nuns, *The Typhus of 1847*; Grey Nuns, *Foundation of St. Patrick's Asylum*. Translated by Philip O'Gorman. http://faminearchive.nuigalway.ie/docs/grey-nuns/GreyNunsFamine AnnalFoundationofStPatricksOrphanAsylum.pdf .These records have also been excerpted in Jason King (ed.), *Irish Famine Migration Narratives: Eyewitness Testimonies*, vol 2, Christine Kinealy, Jason King, Gerard Moran (eds), *The History of the Irish Famine*, 4 vols (London: Routledge, 2019), pp 197-216.

4. See King, *Irish Famine Migration Narratives*, pp 21-27; Jason King, "The Famine Irish, the Grey Nuns, and the Fever Sheds of Montreal: Prostitution and Female Religious Institution Building," in Christine Kinealy, Jason King, and Ciarán Reilly (eds), *Women and the Great Hunger* (Hamden, Connecticut: Quinnipiac University Press, 2016), pp 95-108; Jason King, "The Remembrance of Irish Famine Migrants in the Fever Sheds of Montreal," in Marguérite Corporaal, Christopher Cusack, Lindsay Janssen and Ruud van den Beuken (eds), *Global Legacies of the Great Irish Famine: Transnational and Interdisciplinary Perspectives* (Brussels: Peter Lang, 2014), pp 245-266; Jason King, "Remembering and Forgetting the Famine Irish in Quebec: Genuine and False Memoirs, Communal Memory and Migration," *Irish Review* 44 (2012), pp 20-41; Jason King, "Remembering Famine Orphans: The Transmission of Famine Memory between Ireland and Québec," in Christian Noack, Lindsay Janssen, and Vincent Comerford (eds), *Holodomor and Gorta Mór: Histories, Memories, and Representations of Famine in Ukraine and Ireland* (New York: Anthem Press, 2012), pp 115-144.

5. The "Saving the Famine Irish: The Grey Nuns and the Great Hunger" exhibit, curated by Christine Kinealy and Jason King, was launched by Ireland's Great Hunger Institute and the Arnold Bernhard Library at Quinnipiac University where it ran from April 2015 – March 2016. The exhibit then transferred to the Centaur Theatre (April 2016) and the Grey Nuns' Hospital National Historic Site (September to December 2016) in Montreal and Dublin's Glasnevin Museum (September to December 2016). It was further exhibited in the National Famine Museum at Strokestown Park in Ireland from 2017-2020. Also see the short film *Montreal's Grey Nuns and the Great Hunger* (KM Productions, 2020), at: https://youtu.be/ndhO9fhvDss

6. See Jason King, "Mortuary Spectacles: The Genealogy of the Images of the Famine Irish Coffin Ships and Montreal's Fever Sheds" in Marguérite Corporaal, Oonagh Frawley and Emily Mark-FitzGerald (eds), *The Great Irish Famine: Visual and Material Cultures* (Liverpool University Press, 2018), pp 88-109.

7. Marie Maguerite d'Youville was canonized by Pope John Paul II in 1982, thus becoming the first Canadian-born saint. She was also a slave owner, as noted by Peter Tardif, "Quebec History X" (3 February 2021), www.cbc.ca/localinteractives/qc/quebec-history-x

8. Grey Nuns, *The Typhus of 1847*, p. 16.

9. Ibid.

10. Ibid.

11. See King, "Mortuary Spectacles," for a comprehensive analysis of Théophile Hamel's painting, *Le Typhus*. The painting features prominently in the "Saving the Famine Irish: The Grey Nuns and the Great Hunger" exhibit.

12. Grey Nuns, *Ancien Journal*, pp 6-7.

13. Ibid., p. 13.

14. Grey Nuns, *The Typhus of 1847*, p. 22.

15. Ibid., p. 42.

16. Grey Nuns, *Ancien Journal*, p. 18.

17. Ibid., p. 16.

18. See Dan Horner, "'The Public has the Right to be Protected from A Deadly Scourge:' Debating Quarantine, Migration and Liberal Governance during the 1847 Typhus Outbreak in Montreal," *Journal of the Canadian Historical Association / Revue de la Société historique du Canada* 2012, 23 (1), pp 65-100; Jason King, "'The Atrocious Avarice of the Irish Landlords': Canadian Public Sentiment and the Irish Famine Migration of 1847," in Marguérite Corporaal and Peter Gray (eds), *The Great Irish Famine and Social Class: Conflicts, Responsibilities, and Representations* (Oxford: Peter Lang, 2019), pp 237-256.

19. *Montreal Gazette*, 15 July 1847.

20. William Weir, *Sixty years in Canada* (Montreal: J. Lovell, 1903), p. 26.

21. Bellelle Guerin, *John Easton Mills — The Martyr Mayor of Montreal* (Montreal: 1911), p. 6.

22. Cecil Woodham-Smith, *The Great Hunger: Ireland, 1845-1849* (New York: Harper & Row, 1962), pp 235-236. She cites the *Montreal Gazette*, 15 November 1847 and 14 May 1855.

23. Bettina Bradbury, *Wife to Widow: Lives, Laws, and Politics in Nineteenth Century Montreal* (Vancouver: UBC Press, 2011), pp 225-29.

24. Bishop Bourget's pastoral letter of 9 March 1848 is reproduced and translated in Grey Nuns, *Foundation of St. Patrick's Asylum*, p. 5. Also see King, "Remembering Famine Orphans," pp 122-144.

25. Ibid., p. 6.

26. Ibid., pp 9-10.

27. Ibid., p.10.

28. Ibid., p. 9.

29. Ibid.

30. J.J. Curran, *Golden Jubilee of St. Patrick's Orphan Asylum* (Montreal: Catholic Institution for Deaf Mutes, 1902), p. 2.

31. Ibid., p. 3.

32. Ibid., p. 6.

33. Grey Nuns, *Foundation of St. Patrick's Asylum*, p.12.

34. Ibid., p. 10.

35. Grey Nuns, *The Typhus of 1847*, p. 108.

36. United Province of Canada, Canada East, *Census of 1851-1852*, District 37, Montréal, Montréal General Hospital, p. 4, Marie Rose Brown and Bridget Brown, lines 10 and 24, https://central.bac-lac.gc.ca/.item/?app=Census1851&op=&img&id=e002324165

37. Jean Baptiste Arthur Allaire, *Dictionnaire Biographique du Clerge Canadien-Francais*, vol. 1 (*Montréal* : Imprimerie de l'Ecole Catholique des Sourds-Muets, 1910), p. 86. https://numerique.banq.qc.ca/patrimoine/details/52327/2022769. I am grateful to Bertrand Southière for sharing his research with me.

38. Ibid.

39. Ibid.

40. United Province of Canada, Canada East, *Census of 1861*, District: Compton, p. 72, line 44. His mother Bridget Brown is line 45 and sister of the same name is line 46. https://central.bac-lac.gc.ca/.item/?app=Census1861&op=pdf&id=4108690_00162

41. Census of Canada, 1891, District 137, Bagot, St. Hugues, pp 16-17, family number 87. https://central.bac-lac.gc.ca/.item/?app=Census1891&op=img&id=30953_148187-00378

42. Census of Canada, 1901, District 192, Shefford, Ely South, p. 4, family number 34. https://central.bac-lac.gc.ca/.item/?app=Census1901&op=&img&id=z000170704

43. Bertrand Southière research. Unpublished correspondence with author, 8 August 2019.

44. Grey Nuns, *The Typhus of 1847*, p. 108.

45. Bertrand Southière, unpublished correspondence with author, 22 May 2019.

46. Ibid., 8 August 2019.

47. Marcel Bellavance, *A Village in Transition: Compton, Quebec, 1880-1920* (Hull, Quebec: National Historic Parks and Sites Branch, Parks Canada, 1982), pp 57-58. Also see Jason King, "The Genealogy of *Famine Diary* in Ireland and Quebec: Ireland's Famine Migration in Historical Fiction, Historiography, and Memory," *Éire-Ireland*, 47 (2012), pp 45-69, for an extended discussion of the cultural ramifications of this demographic and linguistic shift in Quebec's Eastern Townships.

48. *Bertrand* Southière, unpublished correspondence with author, 8 August 2019.

49. Grey Nuns, *The Typhus of 1847*, p. 108.

50. Clémentine Drouin, *Love Spans the Centuries: Origin and Development of the Institute of the Sisters of Charity of Montreal "Grey Nuns", 1853-1877,* vol 3, translated by Antoinette Bezaire (Montreal: Meridian Press, 1990 [1933]), p. 65

51. Ibid., p. 132.

52. Bertrand Southière, unpublished correspondence with author, 22 May 2019.

53. Ibid.

54. Grey Nuns, *Foundation of St. Patrick's Asylum*, pp 7-12; Grey Nuns, *The Typhus of 1847*, p. 103, pp 106-108.

55. Grey Nuns, *The Typhus of 1847*, p. 106.

56. Sister Martine Reid, deposition (13 November 1899), "Typhus 1847 46." Archival Services and Collections, Maison de Mère d'Youville, Sisters of Charity of Montreal, "Grey Nuns."

57. See *Montreal Gazette* (24 June 2020): https://montrealgazette.com/news/local-news/irish-community-denounces-naming-of-rem-station-after-landry

Irish Involvement

CHAPTER FIFTEEN

ARTHUR EDWARD KENNEDY (1810–1883)

Kilrush Poor Law Inspector

Ciarán Ó Murchadha

Captain A.E. Kennedy is a minor figure in the narrative of the Great Famine, yet one who carries a powerful charge, largely on account of the famous 1849 sketch in *The Illustrated London News* in which he figures. From this and the handful of other sources through which we know him, we imagine the captain to be still young, but wise and mature beyond his years. We imagine him energetic and decisive, yet reserved and austere. And we imagine him compassionate towards the poor and courageous in confronting their landlord oppressors. In many ways, it is a satisfying portrayal, and one that has survived even the stringent scholarship of Ignatius Murphy, the first professional historian to draw attention to Kennedy.[1]

But nothing human is quite so simple and, as we re-evaluate Kennedy through further interrogation of the evidence, much of which was unavailable in Monsignor Murphy's time, serious discrepancies come to light. On one level, Captain Kennedy was almost a caricature of the class structure that produced him, and his controlling temperament and social prejudices made him, in a number of respects, a carbon copy of some of the worst evicting landlords of his time; on the other hand, he was often troubled, and he struggled with a conscience that told him the horrors he daily encountered held a very different causation than what the official culture ascribed to the actual victims. That his conscience prevailed was not a foregone conclusion and that it did lends the inspector a credibility that is more impressive than the simple heroic image could ever be.

Even as we absorb this evidence of fraud-hunting zealotry, insensitivity and prejudice on the part of the Kilrush inspector, we never quite lose sight of the other

Kennedy who was indeed emotionally affected by what he witnessed and who felt compassion towards famine and fever victims. At the height of his tirades against them, there was never a time when such feeling was entirely absent. This contradiction suggests that, for much of the time, Kennedy was at war with himself, and that his escalating anti-poor rhetoric in early 1848 reflects an internal struggle of conscience that was approaching a crisis point. This chapter explores the complexity of this flawed famine hero.

Kennedy spent two years and eight months at Kilrush in west Clare, a short sojourn that proved life-changing for him, as for the many thousands he encountered, from landlords to the starving poor, and for thousands he never met. Without the Kilrush interlude, it is doubtful whether the distinguished career that came afterwards would have happened. But that was for the future, and none of it was remotely predictable when he arrived in Kilrush in November 1847, a solitary military man adapting to civilian life as a temporary Poor Law union inspector, at a time when another horrifying famine crisis was unfolding.

Arthur Edward Kennedy was the fourth son of a well-connected County Down landlord, Hugh Kennedy of Cultra.[2] He was a career officer who saw service in several British army regiments over two decades. It was his lot during that time to serve in a succession of garrison postings in Britain, Ireland and Canada, although he never saw combat. All of Kennedy's commissions were purchased, including his captaincy in 1840, fairly late in his career. Kilrush was his second appointment with the Poor Law; earlier he had served as inspecting officer in the Kells Union in County Meath, administering the Soup Kitchen Act.[3] To this point, Kennedy's *curriculum vitae* was very similar to those of scores of temporary inspectors appointed under the amended 1847 Poor Law. Among his colleagues, the youngish captain's (he was 38) values of duty and discipline or his perspective on the poor did not stand out.

A generous salary of £439 per annum, added to his own private income, afforded Kennedy a lifestyle in Kilrush commensurate with his breeding and background.[4] Renting a house at Cappagh, a hamlet south-west of the town, he filled it with good furniture, china, glassware, drapes, clocks and books, and sent for his wife Georgina and his young daughter, Elizabeth, who arrived within weeks.[5] In a short time, his spare figure, attired in frock coat and tall hat, became a familiar sight in and around Kilrush, either with his family in a horse-drawn vehicle, or more often riding alone between Cappagh and the workhouse. As he became acquainted with the town, he would have taken note of many good buildings and some really elegant streets, a surprise in such a remote location. Kilrush was a fine town although, for gentlefolk of late, enjoyment of its better precincts had been marred by the slow-moving presence of ragged crowds of the hunger-worn poor, who listlessly wandered the streets; individual corpses were not infrequently found on the footpaths in the morning, like discarded litter. Such sights would not have shocked Kennedy; several years of famine had rendered those scenes familiar in most Irish towns, although the sheer volume of the famine-afflicted in this urban center might have surprised him.

One street Kennedy traveled frequently led eastwards from the square, away from the waterfront, before shortly coming up against the high stone walls enclosing the wooded demesne surrounding Kilrush House, the home of Colonel Crofton Moore Vandeleur, the town's owner. By virtue of their respective Poor Law offices as chairman of the Board of Guardians and union inspector, Vandeleur and Kennedy were thrown together immediately and, from their earliest meetings, an easy cordiality developed born of mutual admiration and similar backgrounds—they were nearly the same age and had both served in the army.[6] Almost certainly social visits were exchanged between the Kennedy and Vandeleur families, who would also have worshipped on Sundays together in Kilrush's Anglican parish church. For the inspector, whatever difficulties he might have expected to encounter in his work, the friendship and support of Vandeleur promised to make them more manageable.

The day after arriving in Kilrush, Captain Kennedy inspected the union workhouse and made the acquaintance of the guardians, the *ex-officio* or landlord guardians and those who had been elected and who were for the most part farmers, middlemen and shopkeepers. His first two reports to the Irish Poor Law Commissioners, brisk documents designed to impress, show him launching vigorously into his responsibilities: identifying problems, imposing solutions and making forceful recommendations as to how matters might be resolved.[7] Kennedy found the guardians to be congenial and encouraging, yet they and the rate collectors displayed a "want of activity and energy" in their respective duties. The workhouse master was elderly and incompetent, and his neglect was the cause of "numerous and culpable" irregularities within the house. Blunders had been made in collecting the Poor Law rate, the paupers were undisciplined and unclean and, in one serious lapse, a side-gate to the adjoining fever hospital had been left open, allowing visitors access to afflicted patients, thereby facilitating the spread of contagion. Almost as an afterthought, Kennedy told the commissioners that 21 persons had died in the workhouse of small-pox and fever in his first week as inspector.[8]

Regarding the rural hinterland surrounding the workhouse, it would be a long time before Kennedy was able to find his way around its enormous geographic sprawl, and a claim made in February 1848 that he had already "acquired an intimate personal knowledge" of the union's "people and localities" was premature and not a little arrogant.[9] The Kilrush Union comprised perhaps one-fifth of County Clare's land mass, much of it road-less terrain through bog and poor land, as the county road system had been wrecked during the public works phase of famine relief. The union had already suffered atrociously through starvation, its teeming pre-Famine population of 82,000 souls had been much reduced by hunger and fever mortality but very little by emigration. In these early weeks, therefore, Kennedy concentrated on policing the workhouse and addressing irregularities and inefficiencies wherever he found them. For perhaps a year after his appointment, his knowledge of the union's wider geography was a superficial matter of villages, squalid hamlets and isolated crossroads where the indigent poor assembled for relief assessment. Daily, in this early period, he inspected the workhouse, arranged for additional accommodation and tightened up the collection of the rate. He had pauper labor mobilized in making a garden of the land about the workhouse and the yards covered with gravel. Rate collectors and workhouse staff were called to account.[10]

Twice in his first two reports, Kennedy mentioned that 6,000 notices to quit had been recently served in the union, but these references were as oddly offhand as those related to workhouse mortality.[11] The same lack of curiosity on his part was evident when he was first presented with the human fallout from evictions and clearances, as well as a puzzling inability to connect consequences with causes. In his second report, for example, he described the condition of about 200 persons applying for admission to the workhouse as "a tangled mass of poverty, filth and disease," the sufferers being "in all stages of fever and small-pox mingling indiscriminately with the crowd, and all clamouring for admission."[12] How strange then that he made no comment as to what or who could have been responsible for such "an appalling sight." A diligent inquiry of the kind—for which he would later become noted—would have revealed that the only relevant ejectment notices, those in respect of townlands in and around Kilrush town, related to properties owned by Vandeleur, the genial chairman of the Board of Guardians. Instead, Kennedy praised the chairman who had stood with him in the workhouse all day, along with one or two guardians, and had "regardless of personal danger, examined and admitted [the applicants] to the house or hospital."[13]

Trivial though they appear at first, these apparent failures of discernment are bothering, and they would be followed by others until finally an unmistakeable pattern emerged. This was not a case of initial confusion but suggested a pre-existing prejudice with a pronounced hostility towards the poor whose misery he had been appointed to relieve. It is this attitude, perhaps, that most clearly defined Kennedy as a servant of the Poor Law, and a holder of a belief found everywhere among his colleagues, namely, that the poor were degraded persons, who observed few moral standards and whose innate failings included dishonesty, passivity and a high level of craftiness. Unless rigorously challenged, these vices would lead to a massive, and unnecessary, expenditure on relief, permanent habits of social dependency and a ruinous level of taxation. Kennedy, like all Poor Law inspectors, was resolutely determined to prevent this.

Kennedy's anti-poor attitude became even more pronounced as he began to travel along the seaboard of the Kilrush Union and become aware of the depths of the poverty of its people, "a turf-digging, seaweed-gathering, fish-catching, amphibious population; as bad fishermen as they are agriculturists." In such contemptuous terms he described them to the Poor Law commissioners in November 1847—people who were without "any regular mode of gaining a living," and were "inert, improvident, and utterly without foresight."[14] Had he been more aware, Kennedy would have realized that none of this was true, and that the combination of turf-digging, seaweed-gathering and fish-catching represented an extremely resourceful adaptation by the poor to the conditions of their existence, and that, far from displaying inertia, they were exceptionally active. Contrary to being irregular, their "mode of gaining a living" formed an endless, regular and repetitive cycle of backbreaking work, all of it dictated by the need to survive. Without the exceptional variety of survival techniques displayed in pre-Famine times, they would have perished. That their activity yielded such poor results was a function of their poverty, illiteracy and exclusion from the technical knowledge and resources that might have improved their lives. Neither were the poor, as Kennedy declared elsewhere, "content on the lowest scale of existence," they were merely accepting a reality they could not change.[15] The collapse of their modes of subsistence after 1846 meant that by the time he encountered them, large numbers had already died.

To this anti-poor prejudice was added exceptional bureaucratic rigidity in Kennedy's early investigations into the deaths of persons for whom the Poor Law held responsibility. He insisted, doggedly, often against the evidence, that such persons had died of causes other than Poor Law negligence—usually their own foolishness. Thus in December 1847, regardless of a police inspector's report, the certification of a physician and the verdict of a coroner's court, Kennedy concluded that 50-year-old John Reidy of Kilmacduane, had not died of starvation, but was a long-ailing "delicate" man, who died of disease, "aggravated by want."[16] Likewise, Denis Clohessy of the same parish who died in January 1848, "was constantly destitute of most of the necessities of life," yet was "undoubtedly in possession of sufficient [means] to prevent death."[17] Sixty-year old Timothy O'Keeffe of Bresla, who died in February, after being struck off the relief lists for fraudulently claiming rations for his two children, might well have died of starvation but, because of the fraud, the Poor Law was not accountable.[18] At times, Kennedy's concern with exculpating the Poor Law authorities became a reflex that led him into circular reasoning and absurd distinctions. The best example dates from January 1848 when, after encountering an emaciated man bringing his two dead daughters in a cradle to a cemetery (whose family had been in receipt of outdoor relief) Kennedy rationalised their situation to the Poor Law commissioners. Reflecting on the undeniable fact of the dead children and the physical condition of the father, who had made "no claim of a want of food," Kennedy held that neither starvation nor disease was in question, but rather "a protracted insufficiency of food."[19] There was no questioning the monstrous nature of a system purporting to relieve the destitute but under which such atrocities proliferated.

Kennedy's attitude towards evicted persons was no different—his anger at the ragged and filthy family groups and other parties arriving at the workhouse gates mounting with the increasing frequency of the arriving groups. In describing the first evicted party he met, Kennedy referred to the parents as being possessed of the "sagacity of animals" in allowing their children to descend to such a level. Subsequent accounts would replicate over and over his biting denunciation of parents, and the accounts frequently would feature animal comparisons. In March 1848, after another clearance resulted in the dumping of "three cart-loads of half-comatose creatures" outside the workhouse on one day, many of whom could not walk, "some in fever, some suffering from dysentery, and all from want of food," the "most appalling cases of destitution and suffering," his response mingled his pity with exasperation and absolute contempt.[20]

Kennedy's greatest frustration with the occupants of the three carts lay in the fact that regardless of their physical state, when they realized they had been brought to a workhouse, many refused to enter, despite his encouragement to take a look inside first so he could "demonstrate the utter groundlessness of the prejudice against it." He was careful, however, neither to inquire into the "prejudice" nor make any comment on it in print: his reticence is understandable given that both he and the Poor Law commissioners shared an unstated awareness of the extent to which the Poor Law depended on the Irish poor's dislike of the institution in order to keep inmate numbers at manageable levels. Kennedy's prejudicial commentary on the poor peaked in April when, on one board day, the workhouse was engulfed with a wave of destitution as some 300 persons arrived at the gates. As before, his words of sympathy were laced with revulsion for the "mass of helpless, hopeless and revolting misery" he was gazing upon, among whom there abounded "impostors" who "came dressed for the occasion"—that is, relatively well-off persons who supposedly attired themselves in rags in the hope that outdoor relief was about to be granted.

Kennedy was as vocal in regard to "imposture," "imposition" or "abuse" as any other official, and he pursued it with the zeal of a medieval cleric in search of heresy and heretics. He discovered it among relief applicants and among those admitted to the workhouse—most often by humiliating body searches—which revealed pitiful sums of money secreted about their persons in the forlorn hope of future independence from the Poor Law. In one case, Kennedy commented with mingled triumph and indignation on an illiterate fisherwoman who was found to have woven a string of dried mackerel into a belt around her waist for consumption later. Kennedy's abuse-phobia was most pronounced in regard to outdoor relief, that is assistance afforded to needy persons either in cash or cooked food, without them being obliged to enter the workhouse. Under the extended Poor Law Amendment Act of 1847, such assistance could only be offered to able-bodied persons when workhouses were overcrowded and then under the most stringent conditions. By November 1847, the aged and infirm were being allowed outdoor relief, as were disabled persons and dependent widows with children. In December, Kennedy advised the commissioners that it would soon be necessary to extend outdoor relief to the able-bodied, a suggestion that was not favorably received.[21] However, he refrained from pursuing the matter, even when sealed orders arrived just before Christmas, his reason being that a demonstration outside the workhouse convinced him that the demand for outdoor relief was artificially stimulated.[22]

Christmas came and went and, in the misdst of what he acknowledged were catastrophically deteriorating conditions, Kennedy still withheld approval for outdoor relief to the able-bodied. He held out for two months more, until finally the commissioners themselves stepped in to remind him that, "one of the main objects of a Poor Law is the preservation of human life, and the Commissioners rely on you making such arrangements as will prevent the possibility of death from starvation in Kilrush Union."[23] Though gently phrased towards an officer in whom the commissioners held particular trust, Kennedy was very definitely being given an instruction. Thus Kilrush, the most afflicted union in County Clare, became the last one to sanction outdoor relief to the starving, so-called able-bodied, class of pauper.

These months featured other instances of insensitivity, even inhumanity, on Kennedy's part towards the starving. In January and February 1848, while inspecting recipients of outdoor relief in coastal parishes, he forced these sick and infirm people to parade before him in all their misery. Of the several thousand he saw, those "whose state would admit of their attending" constituted a "fearful array" who must have endured much just to be present. "Their constitutions," he wrote, "are irretrievably broken by protracted privation, and the most trifling ailment will bring them to the grave." He expected one-third to be dead by the summer.[24] Did he not realize that his mode of inspection caused great additional suffering to these unfortunate people, many of whom had traveled long distances to be present? His letters reveal no such realization. Instead, through it all, he expressed astonishment at "the lying and deception" among the people—innate traits, he believed, rather than stratagems resorted to in their struggle for survival. Aged and infirm parents, sent by their families to the workhouse to take the pressure off the remainder, were "abandoned" by their children; wives whose husbands had gone to America to make money to send home for their families were "deserted" by them.[25] Instances of cruelty or callousness were seized on as indications of inherent tendencies, and isolated occurrences taken as typical: the man, for example, who would not go near his seriously ill wife for fear of catching fever, or the woman in fever who was thrown out of her lodging along with her illegitimate child.[26] His comment on the latter incident was a simplistic generalization that "the inhuman conduct of the poor towards each other when stricken by fever or dysentery is incredible."[27]

Since Kennedy's Poor Law correspondence survives in excerpted form only for the summer and autumn of 1848, we cannot determine what processes were in use long term. But these extracts, and further materials published afterward, are notable for a striking change in tone—the level of sympathy expressed for the poor significantly increased while anti-poor rhetoric and the shibboleths of abuse and imposition, so evident previously, vanished. The patience of the poor despite their many afflictions appears increasingly as a motif in Kennedy's writings and, by January 1849, he concedes that men "are called able-bodied here who would not be so designated elsewhere."[28] Thus, 18 months later when he came to give evidence to searching parliamentary investigation into Kilrush Union chaired by George Poulett Scrope, almost nothing remained of his earlier attitudes.

This change on Kennedy's part is traceable to four main developments: the absence of Vandeleur from the Kilrush boardroom beginning in late January 1848, and his subsequent departure from the town; the dissolution of the Board of Guardians in March; the granting of outdoor relief to the able-bodied in April and, at about the same time, the decision to collect eviction statistics. Vandeleur, who had been ill for much of January, left Kilrush for Dublin along with his family, "to recuperate from his travails as Chairman of the Kilrush Board of Guardians," according to one partisan source. The family stayed away until June. When they returned, the Board of Guardians no longer existed.[29] Very soon afterwards, Vandeleur decamped once again.

According to Kennedy, the immediate effect of Vandeleur's departure was that union business fell apart and disorder reigned supreme. More significantly for the inspector, however, was that henceforth he was liberated—permanently as it turned out—from the chairman's insidious influence.[30] As guardian performance deteriorated, Kennedy acted decisively in March to have the board dissolved for gross neglect of its responsibilities, a fate that had already befallen one-third of all Irish Poor Law boards. Two paid vice-guardians replaced the dissolved Kilrush board and, until November of the following year, ran the union as a three-man team in conjunction with the inspector.[31] During this period, the union was managed efficiently for the first time in its short history, even if in many respects the poor did not feel the benefit of the change.

Now that it was safe to leave workhouse management to others, Kennedy began to travel deeply into the union's hinterland for the first time, his main task being the policing of outdoor relief to the able-bodied, the introduction of which he had so vigorously resisted. More than anything else, his travels through a clearance-scarred landscape made him realize their full horrific extent, and he began to come to terms with the fact that men known to him and liked by him were centrally involved in this hideously omnipresent destruction of lives and property. A precise knowledge of the dynamics of clearance was thus forced on Kennedy, making it impossible for him to ignore landlord culpability any longer. The main outcome of this new knowledge was the compilation of an exhaustive catalogue of evictions throughout the union. It is impossible to tell from the documentation whether the proposal originated with Kennedy or with the commissioners, but the purpose of the exercise was clear—to determine if landlords were illegally dumping their evicted tenantry on the union.[32] Whatever humanitarian impulse was involved, it was not the first priority. Moreover, the decision to collect statistics was fraught with the danger of antagonizing powerful and politically influential magnates who owned much of the land, in the persons of Colonel Crofton Vandeleur, the Marquis of Conyngham and Colonel George Wyndham. It was, therefore, carried out in the most tentative and careful manner.

It was about this time that Kennedy began to appear in the newspapers as a benefactor. On 30 March 1848, *The Clare Journal* told its readers that the "philanthropic exertions of this gentleman in the cause of suffering humanity were deserving of the highest praise," while on 5 April, *The Limerick Chronicle* was referred to the "great improvements" already visible at Kilrush workhouse under Kennedy and the vice-guardians.[33] Henceforth, praise would be showered on the Kilrush inspector from all directions, initially in the provincial papers and then the national prints, regardless of the papers' individual political stance. Newspaper coverage of the guardian or vice-guardian meetings where Kennedy features is not that extensive; there are long gaps, reflecting times when he was in the field or temporarily seconded to other unions. Each reference, however, is laudatory and suggested a wider knowledge and appreciation of the inspector's humanity. Much of the evidence was anecdotal and emphasized Kennedy's generosity towards afflicted persons on the one hand and his fearlessness for his own personal safety on the other.

Incidents in the first category featured Kennedy at eviction sites, giving sums of money, invariably silver rather than copper, to evicted families. He opened his purse also to the relatives of deceased destitute persons at coroners' inquests, and he distributed money liberally to poor people he met in the street. Late in October 1848, for example, when faced by a great crowd of starving young women and men, he placed as many as he could on the relief lists and emptied his pockets to those remaining, all of them persons outside the Poor Law's legal definition of relievable destitution.[34] In December, he gave a seller of goats' milk a loan of ten shillings to clear a debt for which his goats had been seized. When the man repaid the money, Kennedy was so struck by his honesty that he declined to take it.[35] In May 1849, before questioning an evicted woman during a clearance investigation in Killofin, Kennedy first handed her "some silver" to enable her to buy milk for her skeletal infant, who appeared as if "sent forth from the grave for human commiseration." At the sight of the money, the woman "burst into a flood of tears."[36] On hearing her story, Kennedy gave her more money for her children. Anecdotes of a similar kind and testimonials to his kindness by reporters, local correspondents, the Society of St. Vincent de Paul, coroners and even policemen followed Kennedy down to his last days in Kilrush.[37]

Kennedy's fearlessness was evident from the time he took office. He was constantly in the midst of fever-ridden crowds, ignoring the very serious health dangers this posed. In April 1848, during a fever outbreak which killed 63 persons in the workhouse in a single week, *The Limerick Chronicle* praised the courage and composure he displayed by his daily fever hospital visits, which calmed the nurse tenders who otherwise "would before now be frightened away by the awful mortality."[38] In acting thus, Kennedy exemplified the general run of union inspectors, who, whatever their other faults, were notably courageous. In the winter of 1848-1849, two successive temporary inspectors at the Ennis Union had died at their posts within weeks of each other, of typhus, with Kennedy substituting for both on a temporary basis.[39] His own behavior, however, went far beyond what was expected of Poor Law officers, even reaching a level of recklessness which had him regularly approaching fever-stricken persons in the street, touching their bodies or physically lifting them onto carts for transportation to the workhouse.

The earliest example of this tendency came in May 1848 when he rescued a recently evicted woman named Nancy Hoare and her child from their pestiferous roadside shelter where they lay. Climbing down to reach the comatose pair, he came into close physical contact with both and, the accounts suggest, lifted them out of their shelter before sending them to the workhouse. In the previous two months, he was reported to have rescued 39 people in similar circumstances.[40] The following April, while inspecting cholera hospitals at Carrigaholt and Kilkee at the height of the epidemic, both he and the union physician, the equally self-careless Dr. William Foley, were "all but obliged to place a poor man in his coffin" when his widow and son understandably hesitated to endanger the remainder of the family with this dreadful disease.[41] "I candidly acknowledge," wrote a reporter some months later, "I have shrunk from approaching some of the hospital huts this gentleman has been seen to enter for the purpose of examining the condition of the fevered and deserted inmates."[42] One Sunday afternoon in spring 1849, when promenading along the Square Road, Kennedy came upon a young man who had collapsed from hunger and cold and was being ignored by those passing by.[43] Placing "his hand on the poor man's bosom to try to find whether there was action in the poor man's heart," he had him sent to the workhouse. In June of the same year, he rescued a dysentery-afflicted woman named Ellen Lynch from a cowshed where she and her young son had lain after eviction from the adjacent cabin, while Kennedy stood, "ankle deep in manure" as he tended to her.[44] In August, he came across another recently evicted widow, this time with seven children, five with fever, lying together in a hollow near a bank outside Kilkee. Placing three of them in his own carriage, he had the remainder removed "from the unwhole-some couches and the exposed position on which they were remaining."[45]

In June, *The Limerick and Clare Examiner*, which credited Kennedy with saving hundreds of lives, paid him a tribute that provided some idea of the esteem in which he was held, and something of the self-destructive impulses inherent in his actions:

> He has often raised the diseased starveling in his own arms from the ground; he has handled corpses that no other man but the physician and himself would venture to approach. He has examined the bodies of the destitute, though infected with cholera and other dangerous maladies, and has habitually visited the wards of the hospitals when most crowded, and most filled with the vitiated atmosphere exhaled from the poor. If ever the purest and most exalted benevolence were personified in a layman, it is in this officer ....and a manliness of spirit that disdains modifying the truth in deference to anyone, constitutes him the ablest, most effective, and yet the most charitable officer connected in any rank with the administration of the Poor Law.[46]

Can we see in the extravagance of the alms-giving of this "most charitable officer" and the recklessness of his physical-touch an expiation of the guilt generated by his earlier anti-poor rhetoric and behavior? Does it represent to any extent the hidden internal turmoil of a loyal Poor Law officer who was unable to admit to himself that, far from addressing the needs of the poor, the organisation he served was the major contributor to their suffering, and was an active as well as indirect cause of mass death by fever, starvation or clearance? We can only speculate about such things, and all we can say definitely is that the evidence points to a considerable level of inconsistency in Kennedy's behavior.

The notion is strengthened by the manner in which Kennedy exposed not just himself but those he loved to the same risks—his wife and, even more so, his 7-year-old daughter, Elizabeth. "Miss Kennedy" is first mentioned by *The Limerick and Clare Examiner* in October 1849 as being of a similar character to her "excellent" father, despite her youth. She is reported as giving "practical effect to the parental inculcations and the example she is set." Under her "immediate and attentive superintendence," 200 suits of clothing were "purchased and made up" for distribution "among the ragged, thinly vested poor."[47] According to another report, Miss Kennedy had traversed the union, aided:

> by the amiable and charitable mother whose virtues she inherits ... conveyed from house to house ... and hut to hut, by a father who never wearies in the service of the poor ... distributing her bounties; carrying comfort to the trembling; virtually bestowing life to infancy and age.[48]

Inevitably, Elizabeth Kennedy became part of her father's growing legend.[49] When 33 starving persons who had just been rejected by a cost-cutting Kilrush workhouse regime, were drowned while crossing Poulnasherry Bay late in November, the bodies were recovered days later in a naked state, with the exception of one dead child who wore a dress given her a few days earlier by Miss Kennedy. In Kells, County Meath, a poet was moved to apostrophize her in verse:

> Fair Child, and is it left to Thee,
> Young as thou art in years
> To soothe the pangs of Misery,
> And dry the mourner's tears?[50]

A few days before Christmas, Miss Kennedy acquired brief international celebrity when *The Illustrated London News* published a sketch which showed her dispensing clothing under her father's watchful eye to a group of ragged women and children from a cart. More than any other document, it is this drawing, combining a philanthropic father with his charitable daughter, that has fixed the image of Captain Kennedy as a significant figure in the Famine landscape.[51]

Elizabeth makes a lonely little figure in the drawing. The sketch was accompanied by text informing readers that the misery of destitute children had so affected her that "with the consent of her parents, she gave up her time and her own little means to relieve them," giving away her own clothes and purchasing materials with which she "made up clothing for children of her own age." The reporter hoped that the drawing would "immortalize the beneficent child, who is filling the place of a saint, and performing the duties of a patriot."[52] So, indeed, it has done. A degree of media flummery attaches to this saintly portrayal of Miss Kennedy. Despite its undoubted poignancy, the drawing has more than a hint of Victorian sentimentality about it: no observer had the poor taste to point out that no matter how precocious a 7-year-old might be, she could not have been anything but a disastrous hindrance to any relief operation. Nor did anyone posit a level of parental irresponsibility in the placing of a vulnerable child in such proximity to fever-ridden persons. In any case, Elizabeth's celebrity was a thing of a few months only and, after *The Illustrated London News* sketch, there are only a handful of further references to her, making us suspect that she had perhaps been whisked away to safety by a mother finally gripped with terror and desperate to preserve her little girl's continued health.

At the time Elizabeth and her father posed for the sketch by the Cork-born artist James Mahony, Captain Kennedy was coming to the end of his great project for recording all evictions that had taken place in the Kilrush Union since November 1847, the date he had assumed the role of inspector. By this time, however, the Kilrush board of guardians had been restored, and the union was again under the control of landlords, their middlemen client-tenants, and the compliant business folk of Kilrush town. Kennedy might have expected antagonism from the board, which he had not spared in his correspondence and reports, and no doubt certain guardians were seething at the stream of well-connected visitors he had conducted through the union who had carried away very negative impressions from the experience.[53] In any event, union business was resumed tranquilly. The absence of Vandeleur from the early meetings was undoubtedly a contributing factor, combined with a very poor attendance on the part of *ex-officio* guardians. The residue of elected members was so inept—a "body of farmers and shopkeepers", as Kennedy had once described them, people of "presumption and absurdity"—that they welcomed direction from the inspector.[54] At the first meeting of the restored board, Kennedy, knowing well those with whom he had to deal, gave a patient assurance "of his ready and earnest assistance if the Board would only help themselves."[55] Neither was this situation immediately affected when Vandeleur returned to Kilrush in December. He signalled his resumed control by immediately proceeding to dismantle the relief structures erected during his absence. Kennedy did not rise to the provocation and, over the successive weeks, strove to maintain a working relationship with Vandeleur. So carefully did he hide his feelings that, a year later, when Vandeleur himself declared his relationship with Kennedy had been one of occasional differences of opinion but had been generally a cordial one, he was not necessarily being untruthful.[56]

Of course, Vandeleur was also being disingenuous since, behind the scenes, he had actively sought to subvert Kennedy's authority and to use his political connections to scheme for the removal of the inspector. An attack on Kennedy by the Tory *Dublin Evening Mail* in late December was probably instigated by Vandeleur, who traveled to Dublin shortly afterwards in order to "work heaven and earth" to get rid of the troublesome inspector.[57] Despite Kennedy's efforts through the winter and into the first six months of 1850, relations with the board became increasingly frayed and, after the Poulett Scrope hearings, severed beyond repair, as were Kennedy's cordial connections with the union's landlords in general.

Kennedy had been the first witness called in the hearing, and he was recalled repeatedly to the committee room, elaborating on his previous answers and fielding queries based on the testimony of others. The entire investigation came to revolve around his evidence. Its proceedings were marked throughout with the imprint of his personality, all the more so in that, unlike the landlord witnesses, he did not seek to impose himself on the committee. His answers were unhesitating except where he paused to consult or present a document. In his testimony, Kennedy did not condemn the philosophy behind mass eviction, and he made no general criticism of the Poor Law system. These omissions, suggestive of a still-conflicted attitude on his part, do not at all redound to his credit, but had the effect of simplifying his testimony to the level of factual statement and information, delivered without heat or vituperation. Because he spoke without apparent emotion or passion, as other witnesses did, his testimony and rebuttal of his opponents' justifications were powerfully authoritative. As the hearings went on, Kennedy's testimony accumulated into an immensely detailed and complex body of data about the Kilrush Union, which remains a monument to his engagement with every aspect of his duties. As we survey it in its totality, we realize why his mind should have been so troubled, since it reveals an understanding of affairs in Kilrush on his part to which, try as he might, he failed to shut his mind and conscience as so many of his colleagues had succeeded in doing elsewhere.

If Kennedy's testimony enraged the Kilrush landlords, it was deeply embarrassing to the Irish Poor Law commissioners and, beyond them, to the Whig-Liberal government in London. In the aftermath of its delivery, it was obvious that Kennedy could not continue at Kilrush or, indeed, remain in Poor Law employment for any length of time. Vandeleur's machinations, such as they were, now became redundant. Within weeks of Kennedy's triumphal return from London to his Cappagh home, the news came that he was to be promoted to assistant commissioner and transferred to the management of two unions in Kilkenny. Within months of his transfer, he was quietly eased out of service with the Poor Law.[58] It may be that Kennedy was not reluctant to leave Kilrush, given all he had experienced and witnessed and the strains on his family life that his work produced. The Kilrush poor, for their part, were under no illusions as to what his departure portended and, as he and his wife and children took their leave in early September 1850, tattered crowds followed their party to the quay where the Shannon steamship awaited.[59] In the wake of Kennedy's departure, no check was placed on exterminating landlords who continued to evict until their campaigns exhausted themselves. Vandeleur was allowed reign supreme in the Kilrush boardroom, and with the compliance of a timid new inspector to oversee an even tighter restriction of the parameters of relief.[60] As mismanagement and abuse of the workhouse inmates became ever more wanton, the death toll from fever and starvation began to rise catastrophically again.

A reporter who had watched the Kennedys leave and the crowd shuffle sadly away, wrote: "I cannot conceal the gloomy conviction that the departure of this officer seals the fate of a multitude."[61] It was a prescient comment. No reform at all emerged from the deliberations of the Scrope Committee, whose report was soon buried in the graveyard of unread parliamentary papers, where it lay entombed for over a century until rediscovered by modern Famine scholars

NOTES

1. Ignatius Murphy, "Captain A.E. Kennedy, Poor Law Inspector and the Great Famine in Kilrush Union 1847-1850", in *The Other Clare*, vol. 3 (1979).

2. Burke, *Landed Gentry of Ireland* (London, 1912), under "Kennedy of Cultra."

3. Jennifer Harrison, "Old World Famine, New World Plenty: The Career of Sir Arthur Edward Kennedy," in *Journal of the Royal Historical Society of Queensland*, vol. xvii (no.4), November 1999, pp 155-171; Peter Connell, *The Land and People of County Meath, 1750-1850* (Dublin: Four Courts Press, 2004), pp 206-208.

4. For Kennedy's salary see *Return of All Persons ... receiving Salaries, Pensions, Pay, Profit, Fees, Emolument, Allowances or Grants of Public Money in the Year 1848* (London 1849), p. 264.

5. For house fittings see auction notice, *The Limerick and Clare Examiner,* 28 August 1850.

6. Kennedy's ancestral property, at 4,000 acres, was smaller than Vandeleur's estate, Fionuala Carragher, "The Kennedy Family of Cultra," in *Ulster Folklife*, vol. xxxvii (2001), p. 54.

7. Kennedy to Irish Poor Law Commissioners, 11 and 18 November 1848, *Papers relating to Proceedings for the Relief of the Distress and State of the Unions and Workhouses in Ireland,* BPP, Fourth Series (London, 1847), pp 155-158.

8. Ibid., Kennedy to Commissioners, 11 November 1847, p. 155.

9. Kennedy to Commissioners, 24 February 1848, *Papers relating to Proceedings for the Relief of Distress and State of the Unions and Workhouses in Ireland*, BPP, Sixth Series (London, 1848) p. 796.

10. Kennedy to Commissioners, 18 November 1847, *Papers relating...*, Fourth Series, p. 157.

11. Ibid., pp 155, 157.

12. Ibid., p. 156.

13. Ibid.

14. Kennedy to Commissioners, 25 November 1847, *Papers relating to Proceedings for the Relief of the Distress and State of the Unions in Ireland*, BPP, Fifth Series (London, 1848), p. 381.

15. Ibid.

16. Ibid., Kennedy to Commissioners, 24 December 1847, p. 392.

17. Letter from Captain Kennedy, 18 January 1848, National Archives of Ireland, Outrage Reports, Clare, No. 3183/48.

18. Kennedy to Commissioners, 11 February 1848, *Papers relating...*, Sixth Series, p. 789.

19. Kennedy to Commissioners, 29 January 1848, *Papers relating...*, Fifth Series, p. 402.

20. Kennedy to Commissioners, 16 March 1848, *Papers relating...*, Sixth Series, pp 803-804.

21. Kennedy to Commissioners, 1 December 1848, *Papers relating...,* Fifth Series, p. 383; Commissioners to Kennedy, 3 December 1848, *Papers relating...,* Fifth Series, pp 383-384.

22. Kennedy to Commissioners, 2 December 1847, *Papers relating...*, Fifth Series, pp 386-387; Ibid., Commissioners to Kennedy, 21 December 1847, pp 388-389. See also pp 397-398.

23. Commissioners to Kennedy, 4 April 1848, *Papers Relating...*, Sixth Series, p. 813.

24. Ibid., Kennedy to Commissioners, 11 February 1848, p. 790.

25. Ibid., p. 796. See also p. 808.

26. Ibid., Kennedy to Commissioners, 24 February, 26 March 1848, pp 797, 807.

27. Ibid.

28. Kennedy to Commissioners, 22 January 1849, *Papers Relating to Proceedings for the Relief of the Distress and State of Unions and Workhouses in Ireland*, BPP, Eighth Series (London, 1849), p. 82.

29. *The Limerick Chronicle.*, 2 February, 7 June 1848.

30. Kennedy to Commissioners, 5 January 1848, *Papers relating ...*, Sixth Series., p. 396.

31. Ciarán Ó Murchadha, "The Years of the Great Famine," in Matt Lynch and Pat Nugent (eds.), *County Clare: History and Society* (Dublin: Geography Publications 2008), pp 256-257; Christine Kinealy, *This Great Calamity: The Irish Famine 1845-1852* (Dublin: Gill & Macmillan, 1994), pp 210-216.

32. *Reports and Returns*, pp. 4-6; Kennedy to Commissioners, 13, 15 April 1848, *Papers relating...*, Sixth Series, pp 820-821.

33. *The Clare Journal*, 30 March 1848; *Limerick Chronicle,* 5 April 1848.

34. *The Limerick and Clare Examiner*, 1 November 1848.

35. Ibid., 9 December 1848.

36. Ibid., 15 May 1849.

37. See, for example, *The Clare Journal,* 2 February 1849; *The Limerick and Clare Examiner*, 28 February, 15, 19 December 1850.

38. *The Limerick Chronicle,* 22 April 1848.

39. Ciarán Ó Murchadha, *Sable Wings over the Land Ennis, County Clare and its Wider Community during the Great Famine* (Ennis: CLASP, 1998), p. 187, 195.

40. *Clare Journal,* 18 May 1848; *The Limerick Chronicle*, 20 May 1848.

41. *Clare Journal*, 9 April 1849. See also *The Limerick and Clare Examiner,*19 May 1849.

42. Ibid., 18 August 1849.

43. Ibid., 8 April 1849.

44. *Reports and Returns*, p. 47; *The Limerick and Clare Examiner,* 9 June 1849.

45. *The Limerick & Clare Examiner*, 15 August 1849.

46. Ibid., 16 June 1849.

47. Ibid., 31 October 1849.

48. Ibid., 24 November 1849.

49. *The Illustrated London News*, 22 December 1849.

50. *The Limerick and Clare Examiner,* 28 November 1849.

51. For more on the role of artist, James Mahony, and *The Illustrated London News* see the chapter by Niamh Ann Kelly.

52. *The Illustrated London News*, 22 December 1849.

53. See, for example, *The Limerick and Clare Examiner*, 13 October 1849.

54. Kennedy to Commissioners, 18 February 1848, *Papers relating...*, Sixth Series, p. 793.

55. *The Limerick and Clare Examiner,* 10 November 1849.

56. *The Clare Journal*, 11 November 1850.

57. *The Limerick and Clare Examiner,* 5, 12 January 1850.

58. Ibid., 31 July 1850; Murphy, "Captain Kennedy," p. 23.

59. *The Limerick and Clare Examiner*, 4 September 1850.

60. See letter by Sidney Godolphin Osborne in *The Limerick and Clare Examiner*, 20 August 1851.

61. *Limerick & Clare Examiner*, 4 September 1850.

CHAPTER SIXTEEN

JAMES MAHONY (c.1816–1859)

The Illustrated London News

Niamh Ann Kelly

On the night of 7 September 1860, a collision with a schooner following a "violent squall of wind and rain" caused the steamer *Lady Elgin* to sink in Lake Michigan.[1] Among the 300 who died were Herbert Ingram, founder and proprietor of *The Illustrated London News* (ILN) and his teenaged son. Born in England, in Boston, Lincolnshire, Ingram rose from working as an apprentice printer to founding, in 1842, the world's first pictorial weekly newspaper. He was also elected a Liberal MP in 1856. The ILN was hugely successful and, on his death, Ingram's estate was valued at £90,000, with the paper selling 300,000 copies a week.[2]

In its first issue on 14 May 1842, Ingram's savvy at prioritizing pictorial representations of disaster was evident as the only front-page news-story was about a fire in Hamburg in Germany. Ingram had no time to send anyone to Germany: instead, an artist copied a print of Hamburg from the British Library and added flames.[3] Clearly, Ingram's alertness to the commercial potential of visual impact was not curtailed by a need for directly witnessing all events reported.[4] The launch issue consisted of 16 pages, 32 wood engravings and 48 columns of text. It reached a circulation of 21,000. An extensive front page "Address" proclaimed that the "public will have henceforth under their glance, and within their grasp, the very form and presence of events as they transpire, in all their substantial reality, and with evidence visible as well as circumstantial."[5] As a newsvendor, Ingram had observed that when an edition of any newspaper, such as *The Weekly Chronicle*, included illustrations, usually of crimes, catastrophe or tragedies, it sold more copies.[6] He had also noted that customers regularly asked for a newspaper with London news, so Ingram put

London in the title and on the masthead and made the news pictorial.[7] News media was changed forever.

Five years later, on 13 and 20 February 1847, the ILN published a shocking two-part eye-witness account of the Great Hunger in Ireland.[8] "Sketches in the West of Ireland, by Mr. James Mahony," was a proto-type of a journalistic approach developed by the pictorial weekly. It was also one aspect of Mahony's complex artistic engagement with Ireland and its position in the British Empire, in which narratives of modernity became entangled with sustained mechanisms of colonialism. Mahony's 1847 image-text reports on the devastation of famine within the empire were read by a growing middle-class readership whose interests, in the midst of industrial expansion, variously reflected shifting political debates on private property and workers' rights.[9]

As the original pictorial newspaper, the ILN was the first to mine a new expanding market—middle-class, literate and largely beholden to empire. Peter W. Sinnema suggests that:

> Engraved images in the ILN function to *implicate* the reader as a willing receiver of the world(s) pictorially configured and validated; an image is acceptable to the reader, or makes sense as a valid representation, when the propositions it offers as 'true' adequately align themselves with the reader's own assumptions about the 'way things are.'[10]

The propositions offered in the pages of the ILN were, broadly, expressive of imperial perspectives on collective identity, such as class and nation, framed by attendant narratives of presumed progressive modernity.

From the outset, the rhetoric of the ILN touted a marriage for the dawn of a new modern age between sentimental appeal—"a family pictorial weekly"—and intellectual address—"Clasping Literature and Art together in the firm embrace of Mind."[11] In its successful visual focus, the weekly was instantly distinct from its nearest market competitors and imitators swiftly followed, including the *Pictorial Times* and *Illustrated Weekly Times*. Michael Foley notes contemporary tax reductions were an incentive for start-up newspapers and periodicals.[12] The satirical paper *Punch* had launched the previous summer; its appeal driven by pithy lampooning in images and text and a small but focused circulation giving it political weight.[13] The publisher, Henry Vizetelly, is credited with tailoring the tone of the ILN to adroitly address a middle-class readership, with a focus on making news appear accessible and relevant.[14]

Through the 1840-1850s, the weekly became, in James Loughlin's terms, "the representative organ of British middle-class opinion."[15] Indicative of the economic status of Ireland within the British empire, pictorial newspapers were read, notes Niamh O'Sullivan, "as avidly by the middle-classes in Ireland as in England."[16] Ingram's use of images and spectacle in targeting this consumer market was pursued through three key strategies: a large detailed masthead image of London; promotional image-based offers for subscribers and, with most lasting resonance, the presentation of news as a series of pictorial fragments narratively bound by accompanying text. For its first image-based promotion a six-month subscriber would receive a large format print (3 x 4 feet) of London called "a colosseum." This image was produced with significant investment: "Three artists and eighteen engravers worked night and day for more than two months to produce the sixty box-wood engravings required for the complete print, which was stereotyped on a steam press."[17] By December 1842, the ILN's circulation had tripled to 66,000.[18] Sinnema observes that in the colosseum the reality of labor "disappears in the wonder of the spectacle," with the city presented as a sight open for viewing; an image available for individual possession. Similarly, the tranquility of toil suggested weekly by the masthead image—the Thames populated by processional barges with St. Paul's Cathedral defining a London skyline in the background—belied the lived reality of grinding labor throughout the length and breadth of the British Empire that sustained its political and commercial center.

The ingenuity of Ingram and his colleagues was at its most vivid, however, in the visual and textual representations of the news itself, what Paul Fyfe describes as a "hybrid journalistic form."[19] Termed by Sinnema as "linguistic-pictorial moments," the signifying relations between words and images were often elucidated by editorial text.[20] Though many such "moments" were so implicated in the wider ideological train of the ILN, not all contributions can be thus reduced. Furthermore, how the images were realized was complex and varied in terms of commission and highly mediated in practical realization. Vizetelly recounts how editors of the illustrated weeklies would scan morning newspapers for stories before requesting their own draftsmen and engravers to generate images for print.[21] Thus Lorraine Janzen Kooistra describes illustrated news as a "mix of on-the-spot coverage and imaginative composition."[22] During the 1840s, how printed images looked was significantly dictated by the process of wood-block engraving used.[23] Each sketch was worked up by house draftsmen for transfer to woodblocks. Patrick Leary points out how studio staff "finished the drawings" and, much like in an artist's studio, would specialize in different aspects of expertise.[24] Engravers then worked further on each image, the number depending on the scale or intricacy indicated by the sketch, with potential for further "monotonous" specialization.[25] This laborious, pressured process has been described by O'Sullivan:

> As fast as the draftsman finished a section, it was assigned in individual portion to the jobbing engravers, who never saw the whole of the drawing together... The master engraver guided the tone and texture, with the jobbing engravers concentrated on the centre sections ... This collaborative technique resulted in a house style that harmonized various contributions.[26]

From the 1830s, there was a network of wood engraving workshops. In London, for example, some became like factories, as image-making began to follow an assembly line model and authority replaced artistic autonomy.[27] Though the ILN set up its own engraving workshop, under master engraver Ebenezer Landells, founder of *Punch*, it continued to use other workshops "in urgency."[28] This process of image-making lends complexity to inferring authorship of printed images based on stylistic characteristics, with literally several hands involved from sketch to print. Printed images sometimes included the engraver's name. Clarifying authorship of images or texts was also complicated by a trend of anonymity, or near anonymity, in reporting.

In light of its readership and the technicalities shaping image-text reports, how the ILN presented what was in the 1840s commonly termed "the condition of Ireland" is intriguing for its multifariousness. The weekly's approach is also noteworthy given that across many British pictorial newspapers, "representations of a massive social calamity such as the Famine were framed in such a way as to attract the target audience without overly disturbing it," remaining checked by readers' "own self-interests" and in line with "wider interests of Empire."[29] In reflective mode by 1849, for example, the ILN proffered divergent emphases on repercussions of the Great Hunger. On 4 August 1849, just prior to Queen Victoria's first visit, the weekly suggested that one effect of the Famine was to prepare the country to receive the Queen: "Hence it is that the visit of Her Majesty to Ireland is calculated to do more good than enactments which a populace might demand or a Parliament devise" and that "famine and plague have taught all classes that the real evils of Ireland are social and not political."[30]

Later that same year, the ILN began a set of seven substantial reports called "Condition of Ireland—Illustrations of the New Poor-Law." In the first of these, on 15 December 1849, the following passage appears:

> The present condition of the Irish, we have no hesitation in saying, has been mainly brought on by ignorant and vicious legislation. The destruction of the potato for one season, though a great calamity, would not have doomed them, fed as they were by the taxes of the state and the charity of the world, to immediate decay; but a false theory, assuming the name of political economy, with which it has no more to do than with the slaughter of the Hungarians by General Haynau, led the landlords

and the legislature to believe that it was a favourable opportunity for changing the occupation of the land and the cultivation of the soil from potatoes to corn ... The Poor-law, said to be for the relief of the people and the means of their salvation, was the instrument of their destruction. In their terrible distress, from that temporary calamity with which they were visited, they were to have no relief unless they gave up their holdings. That law, too, laid down a form for evicting the people, and thus gave the sanction and encouragement of legislation to exterminate them ... through the slow process of disease and houseless starvation, nearly the half of the Irish.[31]

These illustrated reports are usually attributed to James Mahony and their text and visual representations much cited across famine historiography.[32]

The passage quoted above is striking in its clarity of blame and seeming ideological contradiction to the quotations from 4 August of the same year. These text representations operate both in their singularity and in tension within the ideological framework of the ILN. Mahony's images of Ireland from the mid-1840s to the mid-1850s can each be read in their singularity; but when considered in comparable tension, they can be seen as a constellation of correlated works that reflect a range of aspects of the island's unstable status in a changing empire. Mahony's artistic vision and political leanings were presumably imbued by his economically privileged and culturally complex status as a man from Cork, a gentleman and a successful artist. His mode of working for the ILN in particular was shaped by developing conventions for commissioned pictorial journalism.

On 13 February 1847, the ILN informed its readers:

The accounts from the Irish provincial papers continue to detail the unmitigated sufferings of the starving peasantry. Indeed, they are stated to be on the increase, notwithstanding the very great exertion of public bodies and individuals to assuage their pressure.

With the object of ascertaining the accuracy of the frightful statements received from the West, and of placing them in unexaggerated fidelity before our readers, a few days since, we commissioned our Artist, Mr. James Mahony, of Cork to visit a seat of extreme suffering, viz., Skibbereen and its vicinity; and we now submit to readers the graphic results of his journey, accompanied by such descriptive notes as he was enabled to collect whilst sketching the fearful incidents and desolate localities; premising merely, that our Artist must already have been somewhat familiar with such scenes of suffering in his own locality, (Cork), so that he cannot be supposed to have taken an extreme view of the greater misery at Skibbereen.[33]

Across his work for the ILN, Mahony was consistently referred to as "our Artist." While he had already produced several images of Ireland, this two-parter was his first commissioned image-text report. The paternalistic editorial tone of this introductory content was typical for feature reports. At this time, the ILN's inaugural editor, F.W.N. Bayley, was still in post.[34] In drawing attention to Mahony as a commissioned artist and a Cork man, Bayley lays claim to the veracity of what followed. Aspects of these reports bear resemblances to the modus operandi of later special correspondents.

In his 1885 book, Mason Jackson described the "special artist" as a hero in his work and virtue:

> Wherever there is any moving accident by flood or field the "special artist" of the illustrated newspaper is found "takin' notes." No event of interest escapes his ever ready pencil, he undergoes fatigues, overcomes formidable difficulties, and often incurs personal danger in fulfilling his mission. On the eve of a battle he will sleep on the bare ground wrapped in a blanket or waterproof sheet, and he will ride all night through a hostile country to catch the homeward mail, he is equally at home in the palace and the hovel, and is as ready to attend a battle as a banquet ... In pursuing his vocation the special artist has to encounter the perils of earth, air, fire, and water. Now he is up in a balloon, now down in a coal-mine; now hunting tigers in India, now deer-stalking in the Highlands ... in peace or war the special artist pursues his purpose with stoical self-possession in spite of cold, hunger, and fatigue.[35]

Jackson was art editor for the ILN from 1860 to 1895.[36] Kooistra notes the "special artist emerged as a professional category when the ILN (which coined the term) and other papers began sending their own graphic journalists to the front during the Crimean War (1854-56)," and that later this role was more generally applied to a graphic journalist who would travel "to record events as they happened," producing "visual reportage."[37]

Kooistra discusses the "heroic" aspect of such occupation as suggested by Charles Baudelaire in his 1863 text, *The Painter of Modern Life*. This was inspired by the art of Constantin Guys, including his images and texts for the ILN from the Crimean War front, published under the monogram "CG."[38] For Baudelaire, the heroism of the "painter of modern life" was in his humble alliance with, and immersion in, the lives of the subjects he portrayed. With Guys, that humility was further expressed in the diminishing of self that came with his (near) anonymity in print, and Baudelaire sustains this with use of "MG" ("Monsieur G") in discussing his works and work ethic.[39] Such was the extent of the ILN's interest in this type of reportage, it sent six special correspondents to the Crimean conflict and five to the Franco-Prussian War in 1870-71.[40] These were most likely the first war correspondents to report in both images and text directly from fields of conflict.[41] Catherine Waters writes of the distinction between the foreign correspondent, who was "based in one place," and that the more peripatetic "special," noting the common byline "from Our Own Correspondent" was used for both.[42] She cites Alfred Baker writing in 1890 on varieties of special correspondents: the "travelling correspondent," the "special commissioner" and the "war correspondent."[43] While the first and last of these are self-evident, the special commissioner covered events deemed by the editor to be in the public's interest.

Graphically written eyewitness accounts of events were intended to rivet readers and transport them to the scene depicted. Some special correspondents re-published their journalism as books, positioning their writing "in between literature and journalism—in the print culture of their day."[44] Even within the pages of the ILN, reports routinely coexisted with poetry and overtly creative forms of narrative writing.[45] A common trait of a special correspondent's writing was that the text was "centred incorrigibly upon himself" through use of the first person with the reader occasionally addressed in the second person.[46] Mahony's February 1847 commission fits many aspects of these descriptors: a traveling correspondent, he could just as easily be described as a foreign correspondent for the same work, while the combined text and visual reportage produced from both traveling and embedding himself in the location of catastrophe casts him as a forerunner of the commissioned special artist/correspondent. While drawing on eye-witnessing, interviews and local guides, Mahony, relative to many special correspondents, restrained from self-dramatization.

Born in Cork city c. 1816, Mahony studied art in Rome and traveled across continental Europe as a young man.[47] In 1841, he returned home and set up the Cork Art Union with Samuel Skillen, though he traveled intermittently and spent considerable time in Dublin. He exhibited at the Royal Hibernian Academy as early as 1844 and was a regular contributor throughout the 1850s, becoming an associate member from 1856 until 1859.[48] He died in Cork later that year. Mahony's social circle in Dublin was an elite one with socially fashionable and international diplomatic connections.[49] Accomplished across the media of drawing, oil painting and watercolor, he was professionally and commercially successful.[50] A watercolor by him was one of the few Irish works owned by the National Gallery of Ireland when it opened in 1864.[51] However, Mahony's key visual legacy has been his affecting work for the ILN in the 1840s.

The significance of Mahony's 1847 work, the breadth of his illustrations and artistic oeuvre bears consideration. Like many of his contemporaries, he documented industrialized dominion epitomized by the building of railways, erection of monuments and the launch of big ships, such as *The Kingstown and Dalkey Atmospheric Railway—Starting of the Train* and *Geo. IV. Obelisk—The Atmospheric Railway Kingstown Station and Club-house*, 6 January 1844. As fascinating as the heralds of triumphant modernist progress were conceived to be, the thrall of modernism up-ended was borne out in disaster journalism, reported when ships sank, bridges collapsed and trains derailed.[52] On this topic, Mahony made a series of sketches for the report "The Wreck of the 'Sirius' Steamer," 30 January 1847. Mahony also illustrated for the ILN on abiding cultural customs including a moralistic assemblage promoting temperance, *Saint Patrick's Day*, on 13 March 1847 and a lively scene in *Procession of the Wren Bush and Wren Boys,* 21 December 1850.

In addition to these strands, Mahony provided a nuanced visual log of Ireland in the mid-nineteenth century that mapped the faltering continuity of empire in the face of famine. In the spirit of Ariella Aïsha Azoulay's call to re-look and re-read images, a visual literacy of human rights is proposed.[53] Specifically, this is directed toward "unlearning the imperial mode of bearing witness premised on recognizing violence in the bodies of the victims and dismissing it in the bodies of white men in civilized halls."[54] In this way, Mahony's affecting visual reportage on the Great Hunger in February 1847 is integral to his broader imaging of Ireland under British rule recorded across his images of the lived realities and mechanisms of colonialism. Sites of political violence are made apparent in the apparatus of spectacle and the banality of administration, as well as in fields of conflict and at locations of starvation.

James Mahony, Conflict at Ballinhassig – sketched by Mr. Mahony, Cork – *The Illustrated London News*, 12 July 1845. All images courtesy of Ireland's Great Hunger Museum, Quinnipiac University, Hamden, CT.

On 5 July 1845, the ILN reported "The Fatal Collision between the Police and Peasantry of the County Cork" describing the violent death of eight and the wounding of 25 civilians on 30 June as "a melancholy collision."[55] Police who opened fire on a crowd may have been drafted into the market town in anticipation of a possible scheduled faction fight on a fair day.[56] An informant described the incident as the response to a group protesting a man's arrest earlier that day.[57] In Parliament on 4 July, it was referred to it as an "affray."[58] Mahony's front-page image of terror and dramatic suspense was printed on 12 July, when the ILN reported that two more had died from their wounds.[59] Officers were depicted shooting as a crowd of men, women and children dispersed in panic. The figure of a man lying slain in the foreground, "the first man who was shot," acted as a visual foil to the image's action.[60] The bare ground on which he lay was contrasted by deep shadows cast by a looming cloud over the officers, the dispensary building and the landscape. On the following page, Mahony presented a much stiller image of the site, post-conflict, *The Dispensary*. The reader was informed: "The sketches have been made by our artist on the spot, who had the incidents described to him by eye-witnesses." A lithograph pictorial-map of the area, produced for the *Southern Reporter and Cork Commercial Courier*, suggests that officers blocked off roads from the town's center green.[61] This implied that as people fled the first scene of shooting, they ran toward more armed officers and Mahony may have drawn on such visuals for his front-page composition.

The text of the ILN report is tri-part. A substantial passage quoted from *The Cork Constitution* is followed by one from *The Cork Examiner*. These newspapers were vitriolic in articulating their counter-positions on the events of 30 June.[62] The ILN concludes its 12 July report with a lengthy unattributed poem, under the heading "The Cork Tragedy," *The Fair of Ballinhassig*. In this text context, Mahony's pictorial emphases run distinctly against the grain of the report to provide an unambiguous image of colonial conflict. The images resonated further when, in December 1845, the ILN reported an inquest verdict of "justifiable homicide" in the death of one of the men shot by police.[63]

Mahony's iconic images of suffering produced amid the Great Hunger have transcended that era, functioning as "proto-documentary," described by Linda Nochlin as "early attempts to capture the effects of hunger, poverty, uprooting and alienation before the existence of the coherent genre of documentary photography."[64] A presentation of their original printed context, in series format with accompanying text, highlights their contemporary potential as pictorial-linguistic moments that were intrinsic to the broader fragmentation of first-person news narratives in the work of commissioned correspondents.

SKETCHES IN THE WEST OF IRELAND.—BY MR. JAMES MAHONY.

Unconfin'd, unshrouded, its bleak corpse
    they bore,
From the spot where he died on the
    Cabin's wet floor,
To a hole which they dug in the garden
    close by ;
Thus a brother hath died,—thus a Chris-
    tian must lie!

'Twas a horrible end and a harrowing
    tale,
To chill the strong heart—to strike po-
    verty pale,
No disease o'er this Victim could mastery
    claim,
'Twas Famine alone mark'd his skeleton
    frame !

The bones of his Grandsire and Father
    too, rest
In the old Abbey-yard, by the holy rites
    blest;
Their last hours were sooth'd by affec-
    tions fond cares,
Their last sighs were breath'd 'midst their
    Friends tearful prayers !

Unshriven, untended, this man pass'd
    away,
Ere Time streak'd one hair of his dark
    locks with gray,
His requiem the wild wind, and Ilen's
    hoarse roar,
As its swollen waves dash on the rock-
    girded shore.   C. C. T.—

THE accounts from the Irish provincial papers continue to detail the
unmitigated sufferings of the starv-
ing peasantry. Indeed, they are stated to be on the increase, notwithstanding the very great exertion of public bodies and individuals
to assuage their pressure.

With the object of ascertaining the accuracy of the frightful statements received from the West, and of placing them in unexaggerated
fidelity before our readers, a few days since, we commissioned our

FUNERAL AT SHEPPERTON LAKES.

Artist, Mr. James Mahony, of Cork, to visit a seat of extreme suffering,
viz., Skibbereen and its vicinity ; and we now submit to our readers
the graphic results of his journey, accompanied by much descriptive
notice as to was enabled to collect whilst sketching the fearful incidents and desolate localities ; premising merely, that our Artist must
already have been somewhat familiar with such scenes of suffering in

his own locality, (Cork), so that he
cannot be supposed to have taken an
extreme view of the greater misery
at Skibbereen.

"I started from Cork, by the mail
(says our informant), for Skibbereen,
and saw little until we came to Clonakilty, where the coach stopped for
breakfast ; and here, for the first
time, the horrors of the poverty became visible, in the vast number of
famished poor, who flocked around
the coach to beg alms : amongst
them was a woman carrying in her
arms the corpse of a fine child, and
making the most distressing appeal
to the passengers for aid to enable
her to purchase a coffin and bury
her dear little baby. This horrible
spectacle induced me to make some
inquiry about her, when I learned
from the people of the hotel that
each day brings dozens of such applicants into the town. (See the
Sketch.)

"After leaving Clonakilty, each
step that we took westward brought
fresh evidence of the truth of the reports of the misery, as we either met
a funeral or a coffin at every hundred yards, until we approached the
picturesque country of the Shepperton Lakes. (See the Sketch.) Here,
the distress became more striking,
from the decrease of numbers at the
funerals, none having more than eight or ten attendants, and many
only two or three.

"We next reached Skibbereen, a general view of which I send you
from Clover Hill House, the residence of J. Macarthy Downing, Esq. ;
and, it being then late, I rested until Monday, when, with the valuable

LD CHAPEL-LANE, SKIBBEREEN.

aid of Dr. D. Donovan, and his assistant, Mr. Crowley, I witnessed such
scenes of misery and privation as I trust it may never be again my
lot to look upon. Up to this morning, I, like a large portion, I fear, of
the community, looked on the diaries of Dr. Donovan, as published
in *The Cork Southern Reporter*, to be highly-coloured pictures, doubtless,

intended for a good and humane purpose ; but I can now, with perfect
confidence, say that neither pen nor pencil ever could portray the misery
and horror, at this moment, to be witnessed in Skibbereen. We first
proceeded to Bridgetown, a portion of which is shown in the right
hand distance of the sketch ; and there I saw the dying, the living, and
the dead, lying indiscriminately upon the same floor, without anything
between them and the cold earth, save a few miserable rags upon them.
To point to any particular house as a proof of this would be a waste of
time, as all were in the same state ; and, not a single house out of 500
could boast of being free from death and fever, though several could be
pointed out with the dead lying close to the living for the space of three
or four, even six days, without any effort being made to remove the
bodies to a last resting place.

"After leaving this abode of death, we proceeded to High-street, or
Old Chapel-lane (See the Sketch), and there found one house, without
door or window, filled with destitute people lying on the bare floor ; and
one, fine, tall, stout country lad, who had entered some hours previously
to find shelter from the piercing cold, lay here dead amongst others
likely soon to follow him. The appeals to the feelings and professional
skill of our kind attendants here became truly heart-rending ; and so
distressed Dr. Donovan, that he begged me not to go into the house,
and to avoid coming into contact with the people surrounding the doorway.

"We next proceeded to the Chapel-yard, to see the hut, of which Dr.
Donovan gives the following graphic account in his diary :—

'On my return home, I remembered that I had yet a visit to pay ;
having in the morning received a ticket to see six members of one
family, named Barrett, who had been turned out of the cabin in which
they lodged, in the neighbourhood of Old Chapelyard ; and who had
struggled to this burying-ground, and literally entombed themselves
in a small watch-house that was built for the shelter of those who
were engaged in guarding against exhumation by the doctors, when
more respect was paid to the dead than is at present the case. This
shed is exactly seven feet long, by about six in breadth. By the side
of the western wall is a long, newly-made grave ; by either gable are
two of shorter dimensions, which have been recently tenanted ; and
near the hole that serves as a doorway is the last resting-place of two or
three children ; in fact, this hut is surrounded by a rampart of human
bones, which have accumulated to such a height that the threshold,
which was originally on a level with the ground, is now two feet beneath
it. In this horrible den, in the midst of a mass of human putrefaction, six individuals, males and females, labouring under most malignant fever, were huddled together, as closely as were the dead in the
graves around.

'At the time (eleven o'clock at night) that I went to visit these
poor sufferers, it was blowing a perfect hurricane, and such groans of
roaring wind and rain I never remember to have heard.

'I was accompanied by my assistant, Crowley, and we took with us
some bread, tea and sugar ; on reaching this vault, I thrust my head
through the hole of entrance, and had immediately to draw back, so
intolerable was the effluvium ; and, though rendered callous by a com-
panionship for many years with disease and death, yet I was completely unnerved at the humble scene of suffering and misery that
was presented to my view ; six fellow creatures were almost buried alive
in this filthy sepulchre. When they heard my voice, one called out, 'Is
that the Priest?' another, 'Is that the Doctor?' The mother of the
family begged in the most earnest manner that I would have them

HARRINGTON'S HUT.

WOMAN BEGGING AT CLONAKILTY.

James Mahony, Sketches in the West of Ireland – by Mr. James Mahony, *The Illustrated London News*, 13 February 1847.

SKETCHES IN THE WEST OF IRELAND.—BY MR. JAMES MAHONY.

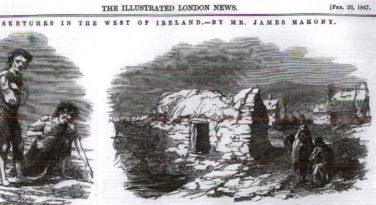

BOY AND GIRL AT CAHERA.   THE VILLAGE OF MIENIES.

MULLINS'S HUT, AT SCULL.

We resume from our Journal of last week our Artist's Sketches of Scenes and Incidents from the distressed district of Skibbereen, and its neighbourhood; premising that our main object in the publication of this Series of Illustrations is to direct public sympathy to the suffering poor of those localities, a result that must, inevitably, follow the right appreciation of their extent and severity.

We left our Artist, last week, on the road to Droundaleague, to inquire into the horrible circumstances of Leahey's death.

The first Sketch is taken on the road, at Cahera, of a famished boy and girl turning up the ground to seek for a potato to appease their hunger. "Not far from the spot where I made this sketch," says Mr. M., "and less than fifty perches from the high road, is another of the many sepulchres above ground, where six dead bodies had lain for twelve days, without the least chance of interment, owing to their being so far from the town. After leaving this fearful dawn, we soon reached Droundaleague, where I called upon the Rev. J. Creedon, and inquired of him as to the fate of Leahey. 'Not only do I know the statement to be true,' replied the reverend gentleman,' but also prepared the man for death, and am ready to accompany you to the spot.' We, accordingly, started; and, within half an hour's drive, reached the village of Meinies, where the houses of Leahey is situated, and of which I send you a sketch. Whilst making this, I learned from Mr. Creedon, and one of the villagers, that not only was the account of Leahey's house in the Diary true, but the case

was even more disgusting than there stated; and, horrifying as it was, the man's mother, who found the dogs about him, after having first lain him across the few remaining sparks of fire upon the floor, went out to beg as much as would purchase a coffin to bury him in."

"Having heard much of the wants of Dunmanway, I proceeded thither, and am delighted to say that this large and thriving town (of which I send you a sketch, taken from the bridge on the Cork road) seems to be the barrier to the dreadful want further west. Not, at the same time, but that much want does exist here, though nothing beyond what may be expected upon land where nature is not bountiful. The worst feature presenting itself, at this moment, all through the West, is the entire abandonment of agricultural occupation; and, during my entire excursion from Clonakilty round to Dunmanway, not more than ten or a dozen fields seemed to have been prepared for the spring; and the answer of all those to whom I addressed myself on the subject was, that if they put down, they did not know who would reap; and that, in case the crops were sown, the poor famished wretches would be there to eat them up long before they had time to grow.

"Again, all sympathy between the living and the dead seems completely out of the question; and the revolting practice will, doubtless, go on until it works its own remedy. I certainly saw from 150 to 180 funerals of victims to the want of food, the whole number attended by not more than 50 persons; and so hardened are the men regularly employed in the removal of the dead from the workhouse, that I saw one

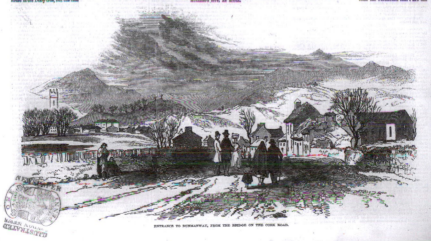

ENTRANCE TO DUNMANWAY, FROM THE BRIDGE ON THE CORK ROAD.

James Mahony, Sketches in the West of Ireland – by Mr. James Mahony, *The Illustrated London News*, 20 February 1847.

The first image in the two-part series sets a desolate tone. *Funeral at Shepperton Lakes* depicts a small forlorn group walking behind a coffin on a horse-drawn cart. The picture is in contrast to the highly social, organized and celebratory conventions of wakes, common in pre-Famine rural Ireland.[65] Mahony wrote that there was "either a funeral or a coffin at every hundred yards" and the "distress became more striking" as the journey progressed. A subdued melancholy atmosphere pervades the images printed on 13 February of shadowy streets and emptied cottages and houses. The figuration of *Woman Begging at Clonakilty* gives desperation a face—its statuesque serenity is altered as the reader learns of the woman's "distressing appeal" to Mahony for money to bury the dead infant in her arms.[66]

The images published a week later, reflecting the direction of Mahony's journey further west, are more abrasively expressive. The first image, *Boy and Girl at Cahera*, is of two children raggedly dressed and emaciated searching for potatoes. The girl is crouched while the boy stands, pausing to look directly at the reader. Mahony wrote of a "fearful spot" nearby: "another of the many sepulchers above ground, where six dead bodies had lain for twelve days, without the least chance of interment, owing to their being so far from the town." Beneath it is *Mullin's Hut, at Scull*. The editorial text informed the reader that Mullins, "lay dying in a corner on a heap of straw, supplied by the Relief Committee, whilst his three wretched children crouched over a few embers of turf, as if to raise the last remaining spark of life. This poor man had buried his wife some five days previously."[67]

The man with the top hat seated amid this heart-breaking scene is the local vicar, Rev. Robert Traill. Traill was active in local famine relief and would die of "famine fever."[68] Mahony accompanied him for his research into the appalling conditions of the area. In the previous week's report, Mahony recounted the work of Dr. Daniel Donovan, who was a guide on his journey around Skibbereen, of which Mahony wrote: "I witnessed such scenes of misery and privation as I trust it may never be again my lot to look upon." Donovan worked tirelessly in the area to relieve suffering and raise public awareness, publishing "Diaries of a Dispensary Doctor" on the cataclysmic effects of famine in *The Southern Reporter and Cork Commercial Courier* in 1846-47.[69] Mahony supported the veracity of Donovan's harrowing accounts: "I can now, with perfect confidence say that neither pen nor pencil could ever portray the misery and horror, at this moment, to be witnessed in Skibbereen."[70]

Other visuals on 20 February comprise detailed vignettes of townlands and streets, with the subdued desolation of the previous week's images replaced with more rugged-looking scenes of depletion and devastation. Across the two reports, Mahony eschewed Victorian models of presenting palatable accounts of poverty through sentimentalizing aesthetics or moralizing observation. Though teetering close to an "othering" of his subjects and a sense of distancing by way of the beautiful vistas of landscapes, his insistence on the specificity of suffering, stated in his alternate attention to place-names and family names, maps the dissolution of townlands wrought by a colonially-conditioned humanitarian catastrophe.[71]

In Mahony's words:

I have thus ... been lengthy in my details in order that you may be as well informed upon the subject as I can enable you to be; and, bearing in mind the horrifying scenes that I have just witnessed, I entreat you to do the best you can for so much suffering humanity; as this visit to the West will, I trust, assist in making this affliction known to the charitable public.[72]

James Mahony, The Funeral Procession in Westmoreland-Street, Dublin, *The Illustrated London News*, 14 August 1847.

In the summer of 1847, the death of the former MP for Kerry, Daniel O'Connell, was marked in the public sphere by elaborate mourning ceremonies. Known as "The Liberator" for his work towards the Catholic Emancipation Act of 1829, O'Connell died in Genoa, Italy, and his body transported back to Ireland for burial. On 14 August 1847, the ILN devoted several pages to coverage of various aspects of the return home of the body, and related obsequies, including a public procession in Dublin. Leslie A. Williams suggests Bayley's interest in O'Connell may have been as a controversial figure who might sell newspapers. She writes:

> The contrast of the *Illustrated London News'* coverage of O'Connell with those of *The Times* and the *Standard* is striking. The ILN pointed out the Liberator's strengths and successes; *The Times* concentrated on what it considered his many failures. While *The Times* could only portray O'Connell as an Irish demagogue fixated on his parochial issues, the ILN placed him within the broader context of British politics: "After he entered the House of Commons, he by no means confined himself to Irish affairs. His speeches on the Reform Bill were among the best of that memorable period; he assisted in carrying Corporation Reform, and he took part in the discussion of the Anti Corn-Law League." (29 May 1847, 338) ...*The Illustrated London News* ... treated O'Connell with sympathy and dignity.[73]

Mahony provided a series of large-scale images for the report, including formal spectacular aspects of the funeral and more intimate family-oriented moments with the coffin en route from Genoa.

A sense of scale and solemnity is imparted in his rendering of *The Funeral Procession in Westmoreland Street, Dublin*. A detailed street scene, its execution was evidently overseen by ILN engraver H. Harrison, whose pride in the image is indicated by his signature. A focal point of the image is "the 'triumphal car' that had been used on the occasion of O'Connell's release from Richmond Jail three years earlier."[74] The splendor of the funeral procession—"horses pulling the hearse were draped in velvet banners"—was reflective of O'Connell's own deployment of spectacle, which was as effective as his legendary oratory skills.[75] His so-called "monster meetings" were defined by elaborate rituals and parades to produce visual and emotive impact: O'Connell was a "master of the dramatic public gesture."[76] Mahony's visual interest in the ceremonial chair and the banners paraded at the funeral procession may well reflect on his design of the visual settings of a similar parade chair and car for a monster meeting in June 1845, which *The Cork Examiner* termed a "gorgeous and imposing spectacle."[77] As O'Sullivan notes, that 1845 design work signals Mahony's politics as supporting a repeal of the Act of Union.[78]

James Mahony, *Delivery of Dispatches at Lismore Castle, The Illustrated London News*, 12 August 1848.

ENCAMPMENT AT EVERTON NEAR LIVERPOOL.

harvests of grain known for many years. Everywhere it is luxuriant. But since I came here the weather has been often wet, always cloudy.

Of the potatoes I read bad accounts, and occasionally hear people's fears, and see their heads shake with doubts: but I never saw a better growth, or a healthier bloom than potato fields. Than I have seen throughout the eastern and central counties. In no market-place, in no shop, at no dinner-table have

SEARCHING FOR ARMS.

I yet seen a diseased potato, though frequently inquiring for them. On some of the earlier sorts in gardens I have seen withered leaves, and in the fields where the seed failed I have seen blanks; but if there be disease, it is but imperfectly developed.

The State trials in Dublin are now in progress, and cause much public anxiety.

The accompanying Illustrations, by another artist, Mr. James Mahony, show some of the precautionary measures, as the *Posting of Proclamations*, and the *Search for Arms*. Next, we have the porch of *Lismore Castle*, with the delivery of despatches for the officer in command of the troops stationed there.

Of the *Encampments* we have a series of Sketches, commencing with that in the *Phoenix Park, Dublin*. Next are two scenes from the *Encampment of the 74th Highlanders*; one representing the performance of the *Church Service*, and the other *Major Ansel and the Officers at Mess*, the appointments of the mess-table being void of all ceremony, each officer being obliged to provide his own knife, fork, plate, and drinking vessel.

The next sketch shows the *Watch-fires, with Sentinels of the 81th on duty*.

Soon after our Artist was there an express arrived from Thurles, less than a mile distant, with the account of O'Brien's arrest.

For the remaining Illustration, *the Camp at Everton*, with the following, we are indebted to a Correspondent.

The force at present encamped at Everton consists of a demi-battery of artillery, under Captain Mitchell; the 46th Regiment, under Colonel Garret; and the head-quarters of the 81st, under Colonel Willcocks; the whole camp being

MAJOR ANSEL AND THE OFFICERS OF THE 74TH AT MESS.

who flock to see the camp: not even the heavy rains which have prevailed of late have prevented thousands from visiting the ground; and the audience at tattoo is enormous. The vendors of Everton toffee and Ormskirk gingerbread make a rich harvest. By-and-bye, when all gets square, and bands playing, parades and reviews take place, the worthy Liverpoolonians may be rewarded for the violent admiration they entertain for red coats. But is it admiration or curiosity which prompts them to risk drenchings, and craftily to evade sentries, in order to get into the heart of the camp?

The accompanying diagram may assist in explaining. The black O are soldiers' circular or bell tents, of which there are six to every company; the officers' bell tents (O) being in the rear of their respective companies. Field officers are allowed marquees, as may be seen by the mark ——." Each of the

under the charge of Deputy-Assistant-Commissary-General Crookshank; and numbering about 1150 souls.

On the north side of the ground is the demi-battery of artillery, sheds having been erected for their horses and those of the field and staff officers. On the south side, parallel with the Black-road, are the cooking-grates; whilst the whole of the ground in front of the camp is devoted to parade and drill purposes.

Greenwich Fair Primrose Hill on a Sunday, would give no idea of the crowd

ENCAMPMENT IN PHOENIX-PARK, DUBLIN.

James Mahony, Illustrations for 'Insurrection in Ireland', *The Illustrated London News*, 12 August 1848.

One year later, on 12 August 1848, Mahony's images in the ILN make apparent the sites of colonial violence. By mid-1848, tensions surrounding increased land agitation led to rough suppression, State Trials in Dublin and a general climate of fear. William J. Smyth points out that between 1843 and 1849 the number of troops stationed in Ireland nearly doubled (from 15,046 to 29,500).[79] An extensive report entitled "Insurrection in Ireland" began on the front page with three engravings of the conflict at Mrs. McCormack's House in Ballingarry, County Tipperary. "Mr James Mahony" is cited as the artist for a number of illustrations. On one page, *The Arrest of Smith O'Brien at the Railway Station at Thurles*, *Delivery of Dispatches at Lismore Castle*, *Posting Proclamations*, *Camp Fire and Sentinels* are dramatically portrayed through strong use of light and shadow with active figuration adding exigency. As Mahony did not witness the arrest, or presumably the delivery of dispatches, imaginative renderings supplement information to augment the text reports.

On the following page, a set of large images resonate forcibly in their pictorial interplay. The barbarous invasion of privacy delineated in *The Search for Arms* is bolstered by the sheer banality of the administrative forces of political suppression going about the business of empire. Officers depicted on the previous page on watch and sending and receiving messages are here portrayed at rest in *Major and the Officers of the 74th at Mess*; and lastly, all individuality disappears into the vista of an orderly military camp on armed stand-by during the State Trials, *Encampment at Phoenix-Park, Dublin*.[80] The writer commented that the trials underway in Dublin "cause much public anxiety."[81]

Mahony's skill in portraying crowds in large interior spaces was notable in several large-scale paintings focused on the dual themes of the significance of ritual and the outward symbolism of spectacle trained upon two towering institutions in colonial Ireland, the Roman Catholic Church and British royalty. The monumental magnificence of the scene painted in his *Consecration of the Roman Catholic Church of St. Mary's, Pope's Quay, Cork*, c. 1842, which suggests Mahony's awareness of the importance of the Catholic Church, is also a virtuoso depiction in oils of both a crowd and a complex interior architecture.[82] Over a decade later, Mahony matched this religious focus with a royal one in three large watercolor paintings documenting the visits of Queen Victoria and Prince Albert to the Irish Industrial Exhibition in 1853.[83] In Mahony's first watercolor, he detailed a relief medallion of Dargan with an inscription underneath: "The darkest hour is before the dawn." Nancy Netzer links this to the "social outlook of an elite" for whom the event "signified the regeneration of Ireland."[84] In his second image, *Queen Victoria and Prince Albert in the Paintings and Sculpture Hall of the 1853 Irish Industrial Exhibition, Dublin*, c. 1853, Mahony depicted the royal couple centrally positioned on a dais in the early morning light-soaked splendor of the vaulted Paintings and Sculpture Hall.[85] Netzer suggests that Mahony's focus on the exhibition room may have reflected a generalized perception that Ireland's cultural strength was to be found in the arts.[86]

Mahony's watercolors document the constructed splendor of the occasion and the "exhibitionary complex" that underpinned it.[87] The grandeur of John Benson's building, a sense of the exhibition content, the society fashions paraded and the imperative of the exhibition to place Ireland on an international economic platform seem in Mahony's image harnessed to the pageantry of empire and the event redirected onto an elaborate stage for royal endorsement.[88] When contemplated in light of his earlier illustrative work for the ILN, the clash between the symbolism pictured in the 1853 watercolors and the struggles for "livable lives" delineated in his earlier works echo far beyond the beautiful frosted glass panels in the pavilion ceiling.[89]

Illustrated news media began just prior to the Great Hunger. The ILN led the charge of this new news media, which sought out disaster to sell issues: first famine, then war. Subtly subverting the medium's commercially oriented paradigm of selling spectacle, Mahony's February 1847 pictorial-linguistic moments of suffering do not make for easy viewing. In his geo-specificity, his visual reportage in ILN of the devastation of the Great Hunger resisted prevailing reductive journalistic forms. Regarding, in retrospect, Mahony's images of the administration of colonial power in a similar view renders them, potentially, as disturbing and informative as the images of the experiences of social injustice that in turn emanated from the politics they represent.

Mahony's is a layered visual legacy that persistently elicits emotive responses: a privileged painter of modern life who nonetheless casts his eye across the social and cultural spectrum of colonial Ireland. In both the popular medium of the day and on artistic circuits, he deployed his artistic skills, social advantage and Irish identity to portray a complex picture of entangled cultural and political tensions that attended Ireland as part of the British empire. It is with lasting effect that, in his recounting of an imperially conditioned horror of modern life—famine—he did not look away.

NOTES

1. "The Late Herbert Ingram, P.P., Proprietor of the 'Illustrated London News'," *Scientific American* 3, no. 13 (22 September 1860), p. 202.

2. Peter W. Sinnema, "Constructing a Readership: Surveillance and Interiority in the Illustrated London News," *Victorian Review*, 20, no. 2 (Winter 1994), p. 142.

3. Paul Hockings, "Disasters Drawn: *The Illustrated London News* in the Mid-19th Century," *Visual Anthropology*, 28, no. 1 (2015), p. 22.

4. Lorraine Janzen Kooistra recounts Charles Knight, publisher of the *Penny Magazine*, watching artists take "visual notes" in a criminal court for a report in the ILN's first issue. Lorraine Janzen Kooistra, "Illustration," in Joanne Shattock (ed.) *Journalism and the Periodical Press in Nineteenth-Century Britain* (Cambridge University Press, 2017), p. 111.

5. *The Illustrated London News* (ILN), 14 May 1842.

6. Hockings, "Disasters Drawn," p. 22.

7. Patrick Leary, "A Brief History of the Illustrated London News," *The Illustrated London News Historical Archive 1842-2003*, www.gale.com/intl/essays/patrick-leary-brief-history -illustrated-london-news.

8. Between 1845 and 1852, a clear impact of food shortages was a population decline of over 25 percent. Christine Kinealy, *Apparitions of Death and Disease: The Great Hunger in Ireland* (Hamden CT: Quinnipiac University, 2014), p. 29.

9. Michael Foley, *Death in Every Paragraph: Journalism and the Great Irish Famine* (Hamden CT: Quinnipiac University, 2015), p. 17.

10. Sinnema, "Constructing a Readership," pp 143-144.

11. ILN, 14 May 1842.

12. Foley, *Death*, p. 21.

13. Peter Gray, "Punch and the Great Famine," *History Ireland*, 1, no. 2 (Summer 1993), pp 26-27.

14. Thomas Seccombe, "Vizetelly, Henry Richard (1820-1894)," *Oxford Dictionary of National Biography*, online.

15. James Loughlin, "Allegiance and Illusion: Queen Victoria's Irish Visit of 1849" *History*, 87, no. 288 (October 2002), p. 499.

16. Niamh O'Sullivan, *The Tombs of a Departed Race: Illustrations of Ireland's Great Hunger* (Hamden CT: Quinnipiac University, 2014), p. 19.

17. Peter W. Sinnema, "Reading Nation and Class in the First Decade of the Illustrated London News," *Victorian Periodicals Review* 28, no. 2 (Summer 1995), p. 143.

18. Leary, *A Brief History*.

19. Paul Fyfe, "Illustrating the Accident: Railways and the Catastrophic Picturesque in The Illustrated London News," *Victorian Periodicals Review*, 46, no. 1 (Spring 2013), p. 64.

20. Sinnema, "Reading Nation," p. 136.

21. Kooistra, "Illustration," pp 118-119.

22. Ibid., p. 109.

23. *The Observer* was the first newspaper in the nineteenth century to revitalize this form of printing images. O'Sullivan draws attention to the "pioneering work of Thomas Bewick who reclaimed wood engraving to a fine art." O'Sullivan, *The Tomb*, p. 19.

24. Leary, *A Brief History*.

25. Michèle Martin, "Nineteenth Century Wood Engravers at Work: Mass Production of Illustrated Periodicals (1840-1880)," *Journal of Historical Sociology* 27, no. 1 (March 2014), p. 140.

26. O'Sullivan, *The Tombs*, p. 20.

27. Martin, "Nineteenth Century," p. 145.

28. Ibid., p. 140.

29. O'Sullivan, *The Tombs*, p. 21.

30. Cited in Loughlin, "Allegiance," p. 499. This visit was covered extensively by the ILN, 11 August 1849. Discussed in: Margarita Cappock, "Pageantry or Propaganda?: The Illustrated News and Royal Visitors in Ireland," *Irish Arts Review*, 16 (2000), pp 86-93.

31. *The Illustrated London News*, 15 December 1849.

32. The ILN does not retain records as to who was commissioned for the reports. The visually arresting image of *Bridget O'Donnel and Children* and her extraordinary printed first-person narrative have become widely recognizable testimonial tropes of the Great Hunger.

33. ILN, 13 December 1847.

34. John Timbes took over as editor in 1848; he was succeeded by Charles Mackey in 1852, who remained in post until 1859.

35. Mason Jackson, *The Pictorial Press: Its Origin and Progress* (London: Hurst and Blackett Publishers, 1885), pp 328, 330.

36. Anita McConnell, Jackson, Mason (1819–1903), *Oxford Dictionary of National Biography*, online.

37. Kooistra, "Illustration," p. 109.

38. Ibid, pp 105-106.

39. Charles Baudelaire, "The Painter of Modern Life" in Jonathan Mayne (ed.) *The Painter of Modern Life and Other Essays by Charles Baudelaire* (London: Phaidon Press, 1995) pp 6-7.

40. Leary, *A Brief History*.

41. Hockings, "Disasters," p. 37.

42. Catherine Waters, "'Doing the Graphic': Victorian Special Correspondence," in Joanne Shattock (ed.) *Journalism and the Periodical Press in Nineteenth-Century Britain* (Cambridge University Press, 2017), pp 165-166.

43. Ibid., p. 170. Alfred Baker's book was *The Newspaper World: Essays on Press History and Work, Past and Present* (Bath: Isaac Pitman and Sons, 1890).

44. Ibid., p. 181.

45. Charles Mackey was known as a poet-editor.

46. Waters, "Doing the Graphic," p. 171. Though the work of the early special correspondents was considered, by dint of its potential perils, best suited to men, that convention was contravened by Frenchwoman Harriet Martineau in her 1852 work in Ireland for the *Daily News*. The "conventional anonymity of foreign correspondence" enabled Martineau's writing, with Martineau even utilizing a male persona in some reports. Teja Varma Pusapati, "Going Places: Harriet Martineau's 'Letters from Ireland' and the Rise of the Female Foreign Correspondent," *Women's Writing*, 24, no. 2 (2017), p. 209.

47. Julian Campbell, "James Mahony," in Andrew Carpenter, Nicola Figgis, Maria Arnold, Nesta Butler and Elizabeth Mayes (eds), *Art and Architecture of Ireland Volume II: Painting 1600-1900* (Dublin: Royal Irish Academy/Yale University Press, 2014), p. 361.

48. John Turpin, *History of the Royal Irish Academy of Arts, Volume One 1823-1916* (Dublin: Lilliput Press, 2018), p 109; Ibid., *Volume Two 1916-2020*, p. 631.

49. Niamh O'Sullivan, "James Mahony, ARHA (c. 1810-59)," in Niamh O'Sullivan (ed.) *Coming Home: Art and the Great Hunger* (Hamden CT: Quinnipiac University), p. 151.

50. Julian Campbell, "The Artists as Witness: James Mahony," in John Crowley, William J. Smyth and Mike Murphy (eds.), *Atlas of the Great Irish Famine, 1845-52* (Cork University Press, 2012), p. 475.

51. Turpin, *History,* vol. 1, p. 183.

52. The "industrial picturesque" and "its uncanny after-image" are discussed in Fyfe, "Illustrating," pp 61-91.

53. Ariella Aïsha Azoulay, *Potential History; Unlearning Imperialism* (London/New York: Verso, 2019), pp 501, 520.

54. Ibid. p. 522.

55. ILN, 5 July 1845.

56. *The Cork Examiner*, 16 July 2019.

57. The Schools' Collection, vol. 0349, National Folklore Collection, University College Dublin, pp 276-280.

58. Sir T. Fremantle replied to a question: "that he had received an account of the affray at Ballinhassig, in the neighbourhood of Cork," "Affray at Ballinhassig" *Hansard Debates,* 4 July 1845, vol. 82, cc.14-514.

59. ILN, 12 July 1845.

60. Ibid.

61. *View of the Village of Ballinhassig, where eight persons were shot by the police on the 30th June 1845, Lithographed for the Cork Southern Reporter by O'Driscol, Pembroke St.,* Prints and Drawings Collection, National Library of Ireland.

62. *Cork Examiner*, 4 July 1845.

63. ILN, 27 December 1845.

64. Linda Nochlin, *Misère: The Visual Representation of Misery in the 19th Century* (London: Thames and Hudson, 2018), pp 9, 42-43.

65. Discussed in Niamh Ann Kelly, *Ultimate Witnesses: The Visual Culture of Death, Burial and Mourning in Famine Ireland* (Hamden, CT: Quinnipiac University, 2017).

66. ILN, 13 February 1847.

67. Ibid., 20 February 1847.

68. Traill was grandfather of Irish playwright, John Millington Synge. Kate Newman, "Robert Traill (1793-1847)," *Dictionary of Ulster Biography* (2020): www.newulsterbiography.co.uk.

69. See chapter by Marita Conlon-McKenna.

70. ILN, 13 February 1847.

71. On a reading of Mahony's figurations as "othering" and his landscapes as "pleasingly picturesque," see: Charlotte Boyce, "Representing the 'Hungry Forties' in Image and Verse: The Politics of Hunger in Early-Victorian Illustrated Periodicals," *Victorian Literature and Culture* 40, no.2 (2012) pp 421-449.

72. ILN, 20 February 1847.

73. Leslie A. Williams, *Daniel O'Connell, the British Press, and the Irish Famine: Killing Remarks* (Burlington VT: Ashgate, 2003), pp 238-239.

74. Michael Laffan, "Commemorating O'Connell" paper, *The Daniel O'Connell Summer School* (2018), p. 3.

75. Ibid.

76. Gary Owens, "Hedges Schools of Politics: O'Connell's Monster Meetings," *History Ireland*, vol. 2, no. 1 (Spring 1994), p. 38.

77. *The Cork Examiner*, 9 June 1845.

78. O'Sullivan, "James Mahony," p. 152.

79. William J. Smyth, "The Long Durée: Imperial Britain and Colonial Ireland," in John Crowley, William J. Smyth and Mike Murphy (eds), *Atlas of the Great Irish Famine, 1845-52* (Cork University Press, 2012), p. 57. He notes that the cost of maintaining the "police and military presence in Ireland was greater than the monies spent on famine relief between 1846 and 1852." Ibid., p. 54.

80. The top image is a camp at Everton from "a correspondent."

81. ILN, 12 August 1848.

82. Oil on canvas, 37 x 43 inches. Collection: Ireland's Great Hunger Museum.

83. The exhibition was initiated and bankrolled by Irish railway engineer, William Dargan, who had extensive infrastructural contracts across the island of Ireland: he "built most of Ireland's railway system." Nancy Netzer, "Picturing an Exhibition: James Mahony's Watercolours of the Irish Industrial Exhibition of 1853," in Adele M. Dalsimer (ed.), *Visualizing Ireland: National Identity and the Pictorial Tradition* (Boston & London: Faber and Faber, 1993), p. 89. In its six-month run, the exhibition, organized by the Royal Dublin Society, had 1.1 million visitors and cost Dargan £21.000 in losses. Fergus Mulligan, "William Dargan: An Honourable Life," *An Irish Quarterly Review*, 104, no. 413 (Spring 2015), pp 46-47. When the National Gallery of Ireland opened in 1864, a wing was named in his honor and a statue by Thomas Farrell unveiled in front of the building. Dargan refused a baronetcy from Queen Victoria. Irish Architectural Archive, "Dargan William, 1799-1867," *Dictionary of Irish Architects*, online.

84. Netzer, "Picturing," pp 89, 94.

85. Watercolor, gouache and graphite on paper, 62.8 x 81 cm. Collection: National Gallery of Ireland.

86. Ibid., p. 95. While fine arts were excluded from the 1851 Great Exhibition of the Works of Industry of All the Nations, in London, their inclusion in Dublin was hard worn where there were only three other categories: raw materials, machinery and manufactures. Ibid., pp 94-95.

87. Tony Bennett, "The Exhibitionary Complex," *New Formations* 4 (Spring 1988) pp 73-102.

88. Benson received a knighthood for his design of the exhibition pavilions at the exhibition opening on 12 May 1853. G.V. Benson, "Benson, Sir John (1812–1874)," *Oxford Dictionary of National Biography*, online.

89. The term "livable lives" is adapted from Judith Butler, *Precarious Life: The Powers of Mourning and Violence* (London: Verso, 2004), pp 146-147.

Reflections

CHAPTER SEVENTEEN

THE CHOCTAW GIFT

Thoughts on 21st Century Choctaw-Irish Relations— A Reflection of Our Past

Padraig Kirwan and LeAnne Howe

In the winter of 1847, as the people of Ireland were stricken by a devastating famine, members of the Choctaw Nation met in a small town in Indian Territory called Skullyville, which is in current-day Oklahoma. Members of the tribe discussed the plight of the Irish poor, and it was proposed that they would gather together what monies they could spare. Founded as the first Choctaw agency in the West in 1832, the booming town was an altogether apt place to gather and collect money. Muriel H. Wright notes that "The word iskvlli means a 'small piece of money or coin,' in [the] Choctaw" language, and that "[t]he name 'Skullyville' was given the village that grew up around" the agency itself. According to Wright, the town's name arose because of "a corruption and a combination of the word iskvlli and the English suffix ville, literally meaning 'money town.'"[1] Crucially, Wright also notes that the Choctaw "themselves probably spoke of the agency as 'Iskvlli ai ilhpita,' meaning 'the place where money is donated or presented.'"[2] It is entirely fitting, then, that the donation was gathered at this site. The town was also a site of intercultural exchange, and its very name reflected such mingling in post-contact America.

Other complexities associated with the site perhaps made it even more fitting. Beyond its significance as a growing commercial site, the founding of Skullyville spoke to other, darker realities within the tribe's recent experience. As well as being associated with Choctaw trading, the town—and the agency, which was under the governance of Major F.W. Armstrong—had come into being primarily because the tribe had been forcibly removed from their homelands in western Alabama and eastern Mississippi and into lands then known as Indian Territory. The relocation of people, which took place following the Indian Removal Act that President Andrew Jackson signed into law on 28 May 1830, led to untold death and loss amongst the Choctaw. Indeed, just 16 years earlier in 1831, before their generous donation to the people of Ireland, the tribe had endured what the French diplomat, political scientist and historian Alexis de Tocqueville had described as "frightful sufferings." In his work *Democracy in America,* de Tocqueville wrote about witnessing the terrible anguish and distress that befell the tribe because of the "forced migration" of the Choctaw people.[3] This mass movement of people occurred largely because of the expansionist policy adopted by the U.S. government during the early years of the nineteenth century. Historian Clara Sue Kidwell (Choctaw) has written about the "new economic opportunities for trade along the Mississippi River" that opened up after the "defeat of the British in the War of 1812." [4] In many respects, Skullyville represented and reflected both the effects of colonization and the new movement of capital in the young republic. Accordingly, the tribe's recent experience of removal and hardship would have meant that many who gathered in that small town would have deemed themselves bonded with the poor, the landless, the dispossessed and the dying in Ireland—a country that had witnessed the machinations and effects of colonial settlement in the seventeenth century, the Act of Union with Great Britain in 1801 and multiple famines. On one level, the fact that Choctaw people took Ireland's starving poor into consideration and decided to send a donation to people thousands of miles away, is illustrative of their history as powerful negotiators, traders and politicians. The Choctaw are a proud people and those gathered in 1847 knew that their ancestors had often helped others. On another level, the turmoil created because of Jackson's law and the tribulations of the Choctaw who traveled to Indian Territory would have served to underline the extent to which national and international events had shaped the lives of the people, and the various ways in which the tribe's contact with missionaries, traders and various government agents had often led to truly poor outcomes. It is possible to see, then, how the town's genesis and development reflected both the continuation of indigenous strength and reciprocal responsibilities on one hand, and the tribe's experiences of dislocation, death and destruction at the hands of the U.S. government on the other. In total, $710 was collected at Skullyville on 23 March 1847.[5]

That money was badly needed. In the years from 1845 to 1849, the worst famine to befall any European country in the nineteenth century devastated the population of Ireland. The blight that decimated the potato crop in 1845 was a calamity of huge proportions, and the "Great Irish Famine killed at least one million people and led more than that number to emigrate."[6] The story of *An Gorta Mór*, as it is often referred to in Ireland, is an appalling tale of death and depopulation, and it is an event that historians have sought to understand ever since. The quest to reach such understanding means that there have been numerous debates about the sources of that inequality within the political and social structures of Irish society during the nineteenth century. The legacy of English colonial practices in Ireland, and British responses to the news of famine during that period, have also come under increased scrutiny. Some commentators have argued, along rather Malthusian lines, that the Irish population had grown rapidly in the decades leading up to 1845 and was, therefore, likely to undergo a sharp reduction in numbers.[7] Others have provided altogether more sophisticated—and convincing—analyses of the complex connection between rising poverty levels, landlessness, inequality and the blight that struck the potato in 1845 and later.[8] There now seems to be some consensus that a deadly mixture of "providentialism, stadialism and neoclassical economics" ultimately came to inform what has been described as the British state's "catastrophic failure" to tackle the causes of the Famine.[9] Regardless of how one seeks to parse historical events and political machinations, the simple fact remains that the population of Ireland declined from over eight million people in 1846 to 6.6 million in 1851. Accounts from that time are similar in their gravity and their horror to those told by witnesses of the Choctaw removal. The testimony of William Forster, an English Quaker who visited Ireland in 1846 to survey the country's need for famine relief, included an agonized portrayal of children who "were like skeletons, their features sharpened with hunger and their limbs wasted, so that there was little left but bones."[10] His account invites comparison with the depth of suffering outlined in another well-known account—a letter which appeared in *The Times* on Christmas Eve, 1846. Penned by Nicholas Cummins, a justice of the peace from County Cork, that correspondence recounted the author's sense of complete dismay and mounting shock during a visit to Skibbereen. Cummins wrote of "scenes that ... no tongue or pen can convey the slightest idea of."[11]

Rather than use what money they had to buy badly-needed resources in the new territory—land, food, housing, and so on—the tribe made the altogether remarkable decision to send a goodly portion of their money to those who were starving and destitute in Ireland. Although the international dimension of this charitable aid is itself notable, it is the fact that the Choctaws had themselves endured displacement, poverty and untold hardship that makes this donation particularly marvelous. Countless commemorations, celebrations and acknowledgements of the gift are testimony to the extent to which the people of the Choctaw Nation are regarded as Famine heroes in Ireland. The esteem that the Irish hold the Choctaw in has been expressed in myriad ways, ranging from Don Mullan's pilgrimage to Doolough in County Mayo (1990) and official visits by Presidents Mary Robinson and Mary McAleese (1995 and 2011), to the unveiling of Alex Pentek's "Kindred Spirits" (2015) and the Irish government's decision to offer a scholarship to Choctaw scholars studying in Ireland (2018). The people of Ireland will be forever grateful to those who showed remarkable compassion, generosity, and kindness to their ancestors. This fact was most recently reflected in the outpouring of affection and empathy witnessed during the 2020-2021 pandemic, when innumerable Irish donors called to mind the Choctaw gift while donating funds to the Navajo and Hopi Families COVID-19 Relief Fund. Time and time again, Irish and Irish-American donors cited the Famine relief sent from Skullyville in 1847, and thousands of online messages on the GoFundMe page have referred to an enduring sense of connectedness between Ireland and indigenous communities in the U.S. Crucially, virtually all of them cited the historical gift as the vital originary moment in the ongoing relatedness.[12]

Where there are heroes, there are sometimes villains too, especially in terms of popular narratives surrounding the tragedy of the Famine. For instance, there is in Ireland, in terms of cultural memory, contemporary discourse and global relations, a propensity to recall two donations above all others: the Choctaw gift and the donation made by Queen Victoria. Given the moniker "the Famine Queen" by Maud Gonne, Britain's monarch contributed £2,000 to relief funds established in the early years of the Great Hunger.[13] It is not all that difficult to see how or why these two gifts might appear to crystallize vital strands of the historical narratives that replay various accounts of Ireland's relationship with its nearest neighbor, as well as bringing to mind the suffering experienced during the Famine itself. A comparative assessment of the Queen's donation and that made by the tribe brings a number of previously disparate political and cultural agents into contact with one another. In this context, the oppressor's rather benign benevolence stands radically opposed to the altogether more affecting munificence of a recently dispossessed and migratory minority group: old enemies and new friends. This standpoint is, in Edward T. O'Donnell's opinion, also reflected in the views of "contemporary Choctaw" who "note that both groups were victims of conquest that led to loss of property, forced migration and exile, mass starvation, and cultural suppression (most notably language)."[14] The memory of that form of "cultural suppression" that lives on within both communities, and, we would add, results in there being far more to the story than questions of politics alone. Although the donation may have initially served as a means to acquire "moral and political capital" by engaging in a form of "politicized philanthropy," it has come to symbolize something much bigger than a mere tool in the political armory of the Choctaw.[15] By realizing the connection between the experiences in our two cultures—including the loss of land, life and language, the $710 does not just offer us a means to consider, comprehend and bear witness to the horrors of our collective past, it also underlines the similarities that existed *prior* to colonization *and* the enduring nature of both communities as well as the cross-cultural connection(s) between them. So, beneath that essential story of subjugation and sympathy—which has been co-opted by various groups in a number of ways—there are possibly far more complicated and compelling stories to be told about both the historical circumstances surrounding the Choctaw donation itself, and the complete range of energies framed not only by the gift itself, but also by perceptions of its meaning and import.

Here, Padraig Kirwan asks LeAnne Howe how she came to know of the Irish Famine and the Choctaw gift to the Irish in 1847:

Padraig Kirwan [PK]: *You have spoken about the Choctaw concept of* ima *(giving) over the past few years. Could you possibly say a little more about that?*

LeAnne Howe [LH]: For the past 25 years, maybe longer, I have written about what I determined was a core belief of the Choctaws, their sense of "giving" or *Ima*. While I was working on my first novel, *Shell Shaker* I spent ten years reading through the Mississippi Provincial Archives, French Dominion (MPAFD), Vols. 1-V. For me, they were an amazing source of information, from the lack of nails needed by the French to build Fort Rosalie, to weather patterns in the gulf that affected Choctaw corn crops. Other subtleties emerged for me, which could be seen in the repeated habits of the Choctaw people. Their propensity for "giving" to other tribes meant that there would be a cycle of giving and receiving. That cycle included the French, whom I have argued the Choctaws saw as merely another "tribe" they could trade with. The cycle of reciprocity between the Choctaws and French can be traced in the MPAFD historic records. *Ima*, giving, was a basic, fundamental practice and a way to survive for Natives and newcomers in the lean times, and times of abundance. Today, the Choctaws continue to give to other tribes and communities in need. In 2017, during the South Dakota pipeline fiasco, the Choctaw Nation gave bedrolls, firewood, water and much more to help out the Dakota water protectors.

So how does giving, *Ima* continue today at the community or family level? My answer is through the mothers and their sisters. Regularly, when my mother and aunts were alive, they would cook together for people in their community that were in need. And so *ima* continues.

LH: *When you were growing up, did you know, or had you been told the story of the Choctaw-Irish gift exchange of 1847?*

PK: Yes, I certainly did know. I seem to remember hearing about the gift when I was still at primary school in Rathdrum, County Wicklow, and the very idea of it seemed epic, almost folkloric, to me then. That is one aspect of this story that is really notable: there's a great awareness of the general facts of the story in Ireland, and most Irish people recognize the bare elements of this great tale immediately when it is mentioned. I think for many people this is a story that they will have heard at a young age; people often have a loose idea of the facts themselves. In many ways, that is a glorious thing in and of itself—just knowing the bare bones of the story. Later, in my teens and early twenties, when I began to investigate the circumstances surrounding this truly amazing act of generosity, I realized that the real story was, in fact, more impressive and awe-inspiring than I had first thought.

PK: *The extent to which the story of the gift is generally known in Ireland always strikes me as amazing. Can you remember the first time you heard about it?*

LH: Like everything else about the Choctaws . . . that story came from my mother. I think she was baking bread in the kitchen, and it must have reminded her about the story. She told me that in the 1800s the Choctaw sent money to the Irish because they were starving. From there, I looked up the details.

LH: *Where in Ireland do you think the story of the gift exchange resonates most powerfully? In a particular city, or town, on the coast or inland in Ireland?*

PK: That is a great question! As you know, Ireland is not a huge place: Oklahoma is 100,000 kilometers bigger than the island of Ireland (even if Ireland does have just a little over one million extra people living there – just under five million as opposed to Oklahoma's population of four million). So, we both come from small but proud nations. An effect of that, I think, is that any one site's special connection to the Choctaw ultimately reverberates and ripples out, touching all other parts of the island. For instance, the decision made by the local authorities in Midleton to commission a sculpture to memorialize the connection between our two peoples is one that has been celebrated and saluted in every part of the country. And I'd wager that Irish people all over the country—and the world—have shown their delight at Alex Pentek's glorious "Kindred Spirits." By the same token, the famine walks undertaken in Mayo, Donegal and Tipperary have included participants from all over the country. With that, I believe that there is a great awareness of how the gift speaks broadly to many of the cultural, social, historic and even civic aspects of contemporary Irish identity; the people of Ireland, including those who have recently settled there, and the Diaspora abroad, see shadows of loss, immigration and death in the gift on one hand. That undoubtedly resonates deeply, and I believe that it leads to a particular form of groundedness that is to be found in many communities in Ireland. That being said, it is surely no coincidence that some of the most hard-hit parts of Ireland are among the ones that have commemorated the Choctaw gift in really innovative and exciting ways: Cork is now home to Alex's sculpture as well as welcoming a Choctaw student at University College Cork each year, and Mayo was the location of the first famine walk. Both of those counties saw some awful suffering during the famine. There is also a Famine graveyard in my hometown—Rathdrum, County Wicklow—and my teachers made us aware of that fact and the fact that Wicklow Gaol (jail) held its largest number of prisoners ever in 1848. The majority of those incarcerated were found guilty of crimes related to theft of livestock or other food items. The memories endure in those places, for sure, but they resonate all over Ireland, really.

PK: *News of recent events in the Navajo and Hopi Nation has been heart-breaking. The Choctaw experience of the Covid-19 pandemic has been quite different, I know, but it is the case that all Native communities continue to feel the effects of historic injustices and continued inequality, isn't it?*

LH: I think it is the historic grief and trauma that Native people all still feel. Maybe it is passed down in the blood, I simply don't know, but we carry these stories in our bodies—we can relate to one another through these stories. We know we must survive these stories.

LH: *In the writing of the book, Famine Pots, and all the research you have done about the 1847 gift exchange, what has surprised you most or moved you during this process?*

PK: Undoubtedly, it has been the global response to the story. Responses to the story have been incredibly heartfelt and people's faith in the strength of the connection has been amazing. Even though I *shouldn't* have been surprised by the outpouring of amity that the story generates, it is nevertheless the case that I have found the level of interest in the Choctaw gift staggering. Time and again, I have been touched by the delight that accompanies a remembrance of the connection in both communities. And, if I may say so, working with you and the Choctaw contributors to our book *Famine Pots* has, in and of itself, been a moving experience. To be part of an ongoing conversation about what this gift means, and how it might offer us a path to a shared future, has been a real delight.

PK: *Shall we talk about the Irish response to the Navajo & Hopi GoFundMe page? What did that story mean to you personally, and have you heard much about the response to it amongst citizens of the Choctaw Nation?*

LH: For me it means that the 1847 Choctaw gift exchange is still talking. It is overwhelming that an event that happened 174 years ago still calls out people to give what they can. That powerful spirit is still moving between our two peoples, *and, she* has now added the Navajo and Hopi in the giving circle. Good things are happening. Remarkable, isn't it?

LH: *What ignites your imagination about the history of the gift in 1847? What do you see when you think of the event?*

PK: That is such a great question! I see the deserted and empty homesteads: tiny stone cottages on an outcrop of rock in the Wicklow Mountains, or sidled into a hollow in the land between a stream and the road. Many of those structures became vacant during the Famine years, and there is a real poignancy about seeing their roofs open to the elements; where there was once a laneway or a path to the door there is usually an unpassable tangle of grass and rushes. Those covered, now invisible, pathways and silent cottages are heavily freighted symbols of loss that put me in mind of desolation and death on one hand, but also emigration, movement and hope on another. I imagine some of those hardy rural dwellers and envisage them starting anew, making meaningful connections and leading good lives owing to the support given to them by the Choctaw and many others.

PK: *The story of the Choctaw gift continues to resonate in all kinds of exciting and positive ways in our own times. Do you think we need this story now more than ever?*

LH: Yes, I think that spirit has always been with us. We only have to call on it. For example, the Choctaw Nation's newspaper *Biskinik* just reported that a total of 716 staff members volunteered 5497.8 hours (about seven and a half months) in 2020 in response to the COVID-19 pandemic. Our tribe was known as givers in the lower Mississippi Valley, and we are continuing that tradition in the 21st century. That is continuity.

LH: *What part of the story do you take into your body and mind? Where do you carry this story?*

PK: The very idea of hunger itself has become the predominant element for me. I think of the part played by the unimaginable hunger felt by those who experienced the Famine, as well as the suffering and forms of destruction that flowed from starvation. But I also think of the hunger that the Choctaw had to help others, the hunger for survival, and the hunger that our communities have in terms of sharing this narrative; the passion to learn more about the affinity that exists between us, and to find comfort and solace seems very deep rooted. In the first instance, as an academic, I am driven to find new ways of keeping the story in mind—to ruminating on the various facts and circumstances that inform our understanding of the gift and the era that it was made in, as well as the political and cultural contexts. In the second instance, as someone who is Irish, I will confess to being quite receptive to the notion that the story of the Famine is in our soul somehow; it is part of what Angela Maye-Banbury describes as a "continuum of memory which foregrounds the corporeal and spiritual dimensions."[16]

The gift of the Choctaw community in 1847 indicates how even small communities in far-away places contributed to the relief efforts, and how the crisis in Ireland resonated with their own experiences.

NOTES

1. "Organization of Counties in the Choctaw and Chickasaw Nations" Chronicles of Oklahoma 8, no. 3 (September 1930): p. 318.

2. Ibid., p. 319.

3. Alexis de Tocqueville, *Democracy in America,* vol. 1, translated by Henry Reeve Esq., third edition (New York: George Adlard, 1839). Online: www.gutenberg.org/files/815/815.txt

4. Clara Sue Kidwell, *Choctaws and Missionaries in Mississippi, 1818-1918* (Norman: Oklahoma University Press, 1995), 26.

5. Reports of this amount have been corroborated by several commentators, including Anelise Hanson Shrout and Mike Ward ("'Voice of Benevolence from the Western Wilderness:' The Politics of Native Philanthropy in the Trans-Mississippi West," *Journal of the Early Republic* 35, no. 4 (2015), pp 553-578, 563; "Irish Repay Choctaw Famine Gift: March Traces Trail of Tears in Trek for Somalian Relief." It is not possible to know what source(s) Ward is quoting, but he is possibly citing Carolyn Thomas Foreman's entry in "Organization of Counties in the Choctaw and Chickasaw Nations." *Chronicles of Oklahoma* 8, no. 3 (1930), p. 318, in which Foreman writes "In 1847 a meeting was held at Skullyville where a collection of $710 was taken up for the relief of victims of the Potato Famine in Ireland. Agent William Armstrong presided, and contributions were made by traders, agency officials and missionaries, but the Indians gave the largest part of the money." Ward might also be referring to Angie Debo's famous historical work, *The Rise and Fall of the Choctaw Republic* (Norman: University of Oklahoma University Press, 1934), p. 59.

6. Timothy W. Guinnane, "The Great Irish Famine and Population: The Long View," *American Economic Review* vol. 84, no. 2 (1994), p. 303; Cormac Ó Gráda, *Black '47 and Beyond: The Great Irish Famine in History, Economy, and Memory* (Princeton: Princeton University Press, 2000), p. 110; David Dickson, "Famine and Economic Change in Eighteenth-Century Ireland," in *The Oxford Handbook of Modern Irish History*, ed. Alvin Jackson (ed.), (Oxford University Press, 2014), p. 432.

7. Mary Daly, who taught Padraig Kirwan as an undergraduate at University College Dublin in the 1990s, was one such historian. For a synopsis of the general opinion of Daly and others, see Patrick Brantlinger's essay "The Famine," *Victorian Literature and Culture* vol. 32, no. 1 (2004), pp 193-207.

8. Thomas Malthus was of the opinion "that land in Ireland is infinitely more peopled than in England." It was Malthus's conviction, as a result, that "to give full effect to the natural resources of the country, a great part of the population should be swept from the soil." See Patrick Brantlinger's *Dark Vanishings: Discourse on the Extinction of Primitive Races, 1800-1930* (Ithaca: Cornell University Press, 2003). Readers wishing to explore the various arguments surrounding the ideologically bound perspectives that shaped, and even governed, responses to the Famine in Ireland would do well to start with Christophe Gillissen's useful survey of the field, "Charles Trevelyan, John Mitchell and the Historiography of the Great Famine," *Revue Française de Civilisation Britannique*, vol. 19-2 (2014).

9. Kevin Whelan, "The Long Shadow of the Great Hunger," *The Irish Times,* 1 September 2012.

10. The English novelist, Anthony Trollope, drew on Forster's accounts of his time in Ireland when writing his final novel, *The Landleaguers* (London: Trollope Society, reprinted edition, 1905), p. xi.

11. Christine Kinealy, "The British Relief Association and the Great Famine in Ireland," *Revue Française de Civilisation Britannique* vol. 14, no. 2 (2014), p. 49.

12. *Forbes* Magazine reported that "The Navajo & Hopi Families COVID-19 Relief Fund went viral in Ireland, where donors were eager to repay a donation by Native Americans to Irish suffering from the Great Famine or Hunger in 1872." Online: www.forbes.com/sites/oliverwilliams1/2020/12/11/the-worlds-most-generous-countries-in-2020/?sh=561f-7c7f29fa), and *Time Magazine*, CBS News, the *New York Times*, Vox.com and several other international news corporations and websites reported on the Choctaw gift during the pandemic.

13. Christine Kinealy, "The Real Famine Queen? Maud Gonne and Famines in the 1890s," in Christine Kinealy and Gerard Moran (eds), *Irish Famines before and after the Great Hunger* (Hamden: Quinnipiac University Press, 2020), pp 239-260.

14. Edward T. O'Donnell, "Hibernian Chronicle 154 Years Ago: The Choctaw Send Aid," *The Irish Echo*, 16 February 2011. Online: www.irishecho.com/2011/02/hibernian-chronicle-154-years-ago-the-choctaw-send-aid-2/

15. Shrout, "Voice of Benevolence," pp 554, 565.

16. Angela Maye-Banbury, "The Famished Soul: Resonance and Relevance of the Irish Famine to Irish Men's Accounts of Hunger Following Immigration to England during the 1950s and 1960s," *Irish Studies Review* vol. 27, 1-22 (2019), p. 3.

CHAPTER EIGHTEEN

AFTERWORD

Caroilin Callery

In early 2020, bushfires raged in Australia and spread out of control, creating, literally, a "wild" fire. Similar to 9 /11, people fled for their lives as fire-fighters headed into danger. Little did we know then that a micro-organism was about to spread, like wildfire, across our planet, causing rampant disease and death and putting immense pressure on health systems worldwide. There were strong echoes of Ireland in the 1840s when the workhouse system was creaking at its seams, "famine fever" was rife, and the ships people hoped would bring them to a new life became vessels of disease, endangering all passengers and transporting not only people, but lethal organisms across the Atlantic to the new world.

In times of such disasters, humanity is called on in unparalleled ways and many "heroes" step forward and run straight into the flames. According to one definition, a hero is a person of distinguished courage or ability, admired for his or her brave deeds and noble qualities. Heroes are often unsung and forgotten when the crisis passes. How do we value our heroes then and now? What conditions do such extraordinary humans work under and is their pay commensurate with their sacrifice? What acknowledgements do they receive for their selfless deeds?

This book honors a number of relatively unknown heroes of the Great Irish Famine—there are 15 individual passengers and two groups of travelers on our "Famine Heroes" ship. They are, of course, representative of numerous other heroes, or, in Fintan O'Toole's words: "The famine reminds us of the terrible truth that our humanity isn't something that we own ourselves; it is something that we depend on each other for."[1] In times of disaster, there are always cohorts who are marginalized and vulnerable, most often the poor, the elderly, and women and children, as was the case in the Great Famine. The journey of these people is often dependent on the charity and humanity of others, as through their suffering, they have lost agency themselves. Those who stepped up to the mark are the antithesis to "man's inhumanity to man:" those heroes selflessly devoted themselves to alleviating the pain and suffering of others.

Famine has been defined as resulting "from a triple failure—in food production, access to food and response."[2] The biggest failure during the Irish Famine was not the failure of the potato crop, but the failure to provide access to other foodstuffs and the failure in the response of the authorities and the British government of the day. Our Famine heroes attempted to fill this gaping hole. The heroes can be broken into three broad categories—the medical professionals, those with a religious vocation and a miscellaneous grouping of courageous individuals. Two groups can be classified as first responders, whose jobs entailed them being the first at the scene of disasters and devastation. Six of our heroes are from the medical profession, five doctors and the Order of Grey Nuns who offered their services as nurses—all devoted to curing and caring for others in their hour of need. This group represents the thousands of medical staff who risked their own lives daily—including doctors working in three continents—Ireland and Liverpool in Europe, Canada in North America, and Australia. Across these continents, these responders struggled in a variety of contexts, usually with inadequate supplies. We can only imagine their stress and fear as they collectively saved lives and gave thousands of poor souls something more— dignity. Undoubtedly, they had the same concerns as current-day pandemic medics, highlighted in an article in the *Irish Independent*:

> I definitely had a huge amount of fear and anxiety going to work, and guilt. I suppose, about the possibility of bringing it back to my family. But you just have to get over that. I think that's inbuilt in us, as health workers and front-line workers. There's a level of challenge that you tend to rise to, but that's not to say it doesn't take its toll.[3]

Challenging it was for our heroes and take its toll it did—for some, the ultimate toll.

Dr. Daniel Donovan of Skibbereen was one of an estimated 2,600 doctors in Ireland during the Famine. Dealing with a workhouse "full to suffocation" and a "fever hospital sleeping three to a bed," he was also a great humanitarian who, as a landowner, forgave rent for his own tenants. All the while, he carried out autopsies, recording that he was shocked by the absence of any sign of food in their bodies. One hundred and seventy miles away, Dr. Richard Grattan in Kildare, an ardent political lobbyist and prolific writer, exerted his boundless energy locally and nationally in bringing about legislative change for the benefit of the poor and labouring classes.

Also amongst these remarkable medical professionals was Dr. Duncan of Liverpool, a pioneer of public health reform, whose persistent lobbying aided in the enactment of the 1848 Public Health Act, while he simultaneously worked at the coalface of the colossal influx of Famine poor into Liverpool—up to 13,000 emigrants a day.[4] Unusual in the 1840s, Duncan was an advocate of following the scientific evidence and, similar to Dr. Anthony Fauci in the United States and Dr. Tony Holohan in Ireland during the COVID-19 crisis, he sought to stand above political divisions. On another continent, Dr. Charles Edward Strutt was fastidious in ensuring that the Earl Grey orphan girls were treated with dignity and respect. Meanwhile, as famine fever crossed the Atlantic, the cities of Montreal and Toronto were seized by typhus. The Grey Nuns—martyrs of charity—saw 70,000 Famine emigrants flood into Montreal, a city of 50,000 residents.[5] Their eyewitness accounts provide a rare 500 pages of first responders' testimonies about the agony of typhus-stricken fever patients.

In 2020, images of the ExCEL Exhibition Centre in London being turned into a makeshift hospital abounded, mirroring the description of the 125-bed Emigrant Hospital in Toronto in 1847, overrun with over 800 patients, necessitating dining rooms being converted into wards. Similarly, both reported on the chaos of the early months of the epidemics, and on the disruption of persistent illness amongst the hospitals' physicians and staff. In Toronto, a patient-nurse ratio of 70 to one was quoted—an unimaginable and almost unmanageable ratio for the medical superintendent, Dr. George Grasett and his team. Reports from Montreal were equally dire, with one of the Sisters witnessing a patient "attempting to push off two dead bodies between which he was lying."[6]

In 2021, one respiratory consultant in Ireland noted, "there is a generous amount of luck involved in not picking up the infection because, in the nature of our work, we have to work closely together."[7] In 1847, it was no different. A number of our heroes died from disease themselves, including seven of the Grey Nuns who passed away within two weeks of entering the Montreal fever sheds. The city's mayor John Easton Mills followed them to the grave in November. Dr. Grasett died one month after the opening of the Emigrant Hospital in Toronto, along with his Head Nurse Susan Bailey and eight other medical workers before the summer of 1847 was over. Edward McElderry, an emigration agent in Toronto who toiled all summer, lost his life on 29 October, leaving behind a pregnant wife and seven young children. Dr. Donovan, Count Pawel de Strzelecki and James Hack Tuke caught typhus fever but recovered, albeit with lingering health issues.

The second cohort of our Famine Heroes is those with a religious vocation, that is, "a call from beyond oneself to use one's strengths and gifts to make the world a better place through service, creativity, and leadership."[8] This is true of the group of exceptional people included in this volume. They were diametrically opposed to the religious groups on the Famine landscape who used the horrific conditions to proselytize, entice or bribe the starving poor to turn their backs on Catholicism in exchange for sustenance, thus becoming "Soupers." Their actions were also in marked contrast to providentialists like Charles Trevelyan, who suggesting that the calamity was "Divine Intervention" to teach the Irish a lesson.

Asenath Nicholson made it clear that she believed that the Famine was not a Divine judgment but "the failure of man to use God's gifts responsibly."[9] Nicholson and Mary Ann McCracken represent our first independent women, two fearless, selfless females who following their humanitarian convictions toiled endlessly for the betterment of others. With little thought for her own well-being, Nicholson, an arthritic widow in her 50s, carried out three tours of duty in Ireland between 1844 and 1852. Her initial impetus was Bible reading, which quickly turned to relief work and championing the poor. It is hard to imagine this "teacher, reformer, abolitionist, vegetarian reformer" hiking thousands of miles on the highways and byways of Ireland. Moved deeply by all she experienced, she found time to record, publicize and lobby for change. In an ironic twist of fate, after returning to the United States in 1852, Nicholson contracted typhus in 1855, which was the cause of her death.

Mary Ann McCracken was central to the Famine work of the Belfast Charitable Society. Like Nicholson, she worked tirelessly to assist those less well-off, especially women. She was involved in setting up the Ladies' Industrial School in 1847. Influenced by Frederick Douglass's 1845 and 1846 Belfast visit, she was actively involved with the Belfast Ladies' Anti-Slavery Committee. She was also a champion of a wide range of charitable endeavors, including feeding and clothing the hungry and destitute during the Great Famine. These two female heroes' paths crossed, with Nicholson regarding the older woman as indefatigable.

The work of the Quakers has been well-documented, highlighting their commitment to the golden rule: "Do unto others as you would have them do unto you." The Quakers worked tirelessly, setting up soup kitchens and tending to the needs of the desolate poor. The English Quaker, James Hack Tuke, stands out among the other heroes in that he returned time and again to Ireland, decade after decade, food shortage after food shortage, right up to the 1890s. The Tuke Emigration Scheme of 1882-1884, assisted around 9,500 people in an exemplary model of how an emigration scheme should be run. He was back in County Mayo during the 1885–1886 food shortages to distribute seed potatoes. In line with Quaker practice, he used pamphlets, publicity, parliamentary pressure and patience to highlight the deplorable conditions that were endemic in the west of Ireland. His patience paid off, resulting in the establishment of the Congested District Board in 1891, thus bringing long-term improvements to the west of the country.

Within the religious cohort are two men who rose to the rank of bishop in the Catholic Church. Bishop Edward Maginn in Derry and Bishop Michael Power in Toronto lobbied, raised funds and administered daily to the sick and dying. Power would never have considered himself a hero. This would be true of all those aboard our Famine Hero ship. Maginn wrote in despair of the Famine suffering—God only knows where it will end. His end came all too soon as he succumbed to typhus at only 47 years of age in January 1849. Meanwhile, Bishop Power visited Ireland in June 1847 and, on his return to Toronto, prepared for the deluge he knew would come. When Power's four priests who worked in the Emigrant Hospital in Toronto fell sick to typhus, he single-handedly made the daily trek to the sheds. The four priests recovered but Power would follow Maginn and, on 1 October 1847, at just 42 years old, another great humanitarian was lost.

Our final group to board the Famine Heroes ship consists of six individuals and one Native American nation. This cohort was not composed of first responders in the traditional way, nor was it linked by a profession or sense of religious vocation, so their benevolence was unexpected. Indeed, some are unlikely heroes. Lady Sligo, an atypical aristocrat, Captain Arthur Edward Kennedy, a Poor Law inspector who had a change of heart, James Mahony, an artist, and Count Pawel de Strzelecki, a Polish count, all worked diligently on the ground in Ireland. On the other side of the Atlantic, Captain Robert Bennet Forbes, a ship captain, Mayor John Easton Mills, a politician, and the entire Choctaw Nation, showed compassion for the stricken Irish. These heroes are connected only by the golden thread of their deep humanity. Lady Sligo, the third female hero on our ship, was not a typical representative of the roughly 8,000 Anglo-Irish landlords who owned 95 percent of the land in Ireland. She and her son represented a small number of benevolent landowners whose contributions are sometimes overlooked. Lady Sligo's letters show how this widow cared and fought for her tenants in the face of disappearing income from the estate. Like many of our heroes, her humanity was global and extended to the abolition of slavery. Sligoville in Jamaica was named in the family's honor. James Hack Tuke and, our most unlikely hero, Count Strzelecki, were also based in the impoverished County Mayo. Strzelecki, who volunteered with the British Relief Association, reported in March 1847 that words were inadequate to describe the distress surrounding him. Strzelecki, with no previous connections to Ireland but with a humanitarian heart so large that he set his own life plan and scientific explorations to one side, emerges as a giant of heroes. His schools' scheme was simple and ingenious and saved thousands of lives at a minimal cost, but was cruelly shut down by Charles Trevelyan. In 2020 and 2021, another unlikely hero emerged in Britain during the COVID-19 crisis—Marcus Rashford, a soccer player for Manchester United, initiated a campaign to demand that the British government provide vulnerable schoolchildren with free school meals during the holidays. Unlike Strzelecki, he was successful, winning him praise in many parts of the world.[10]

Captain Kennedy, a Poor Law inspector in Clare, at first behaved like many arrogant officials. He is unusual among our heroes as his compassion came later in the Famine when he called out the injustices of his superiors despite the repercussions for himself. Meanwhile, in counties Cork and Clare, the accomplished artist, James Mahony, redirected his skill to providing illustrations of the unspeakable. Endangering himself, he accompanied Dr. Donovan to visually record the graphic scenes of Famine horror. These illustrations have become iconic, especially the image of Captain Kennedy's daughter—Miss Kennedy—distributing aid from a cart.

It is not unusual for a captain to charter a ship, but it was rare in the mid-nineteenth century for a captain to commandeer a war ship, fill it with grain and a volunteer crew, and sail half-way round the world on a mission of mercy. Along with ensuring its efficient distribution, Captain Forbes of Boston brought life-saving aid to thousands. Meanwhile, in the Montreal fever sheds, despite the efforts of care-givers, mortality resulted in the creation of one of the largest Famine mass graves anywhere. Politicians are not often known for front line work, but Mayor Mills, who set up the fever sheds and called on the Grey Nuns, himself ministered to the pitiful emigrants. He, too, would pay the ultimate price—becoming known as the "martyr mayor" when he lost his life to typhus in November 1847. Our final Famine hero may be the best known and comes in the form of a whole nation—the Choctaw Nation. The Indian Removal Act of 1830 had resulted in dislocation, death and destruction, and the Choctaw Nation empathized with the Famine Irish as they suffered similarly under a government that failed to protect them. The Choctaw principle of *Ima*—giving—came full circle in 2020 as Irish donations flooded to the Navajo and Hopi pandemic appeals, with many Irish donors citing the Choctaw Gift as their reason for giving.

This is the full crew of our Famine Heroes ship—five male doctors, one order of nursing nuns, five individuals of multidenominational religious vocations, six random individuals and one nation, all bound together by their great humanitarian hearts. Heroes who we learned not only gave relief, but lobbied vociferously and devoted time to other humane causes. Their one common characteristic was humility.

This motley Famine hero crew fared much like many nineteenth-century coffin ships—seven succumbed to typhus, five of whom did not survive the disease. Those who survived continued as champions of the poor but remained haunted. On 13 November 1899, Sister Martine Reid of the Grey Nuns testified at the age of 80 about her experiences in Montreal's fever sheds: "The terrible scenes that I have witnessed in these sheds made such an impression upon my mind that I can never forget them, nor the place where they occurred."[11] Today, we would call this post-traumatic stress disorder, which, undoubtedly, all of our surviving heroes and indeed our entire nation would have suffered from. With no support therapies available then, they would have had little relief from nightmares, flashbacks and anxiety. We hope that today's governments will fund therapies for the inevitable trauma that will occur in our COVID-19 front line workers. This comes back again to how we value those who lay their lives on the line for us. It was difficult to learn that in Toronto in 1847, "nursing wages were low at approximately £1-15s a month," while simultaneously watching BBC reports in March 2021 about British nurses battling for more than the meager one percent pay rise proposed by the government.

Many of our heroes were honored before they slipped from memory—Power, Maginn and Mills each had the largest funerals ever in their respective locations. Dr. Donovan received a plate and a purse and his wife, on his death, received a Royal Bounty for his humane acts. Captain Forbes refused to accept any official honors for his "mission of mercy" to the Irish poor. Count Strzelecki was knighted for his tireless work with the British Relief Association, but so also was Charles Trevelyan. These forgotten heroes are again resurfacing in a number of projects—Toronto's Canada Ireland Foundation (formerly Ireland Park Foundation) is in the final stages of creating the Dr George Robert Grasett Park to memorialise the doctor and his medical staff who lost their lives caring for disease-stricken Famine immigrants. The magnificent Kindred Spirits sculpture in Midleton, County Cork, honors the Choctaw gift. A recent plaque to Strzelecki in Clifden was erected by the Polish, and not the Irish, community. Many more projects, such as the Mary Ann McCracken Foundation launched in January 2021 and publications like this book, once again honor those who came to the aid of the starving Irish, in our worst hour as a nation. The final words belong to Mary Ann McCracken in a letter written when she was in her 80s:

> This world affords no enjoyment equal to that of promoting the happiness of others, it so far surpasses mere selfish gratification from its not only being pleasant at the time but from affording agreeable recollections afterwards.[12]

NOTES

1. Fintan O'Toole, Launch of Inaugural Irish Famine Summer School, Percy French Hotel, Strokestown, 16 June 2015.
2. https://localnews8.com/news/2021/02/21/famine-fast-facts-2/
3. *Irish Independent*, 6 March 2021.
4. "Irish Paupers," *Liverpool Mercury,* 30 April 1847.
5. The phrase is taken from the Grey Nuns, *The Typhus of 1847*, *Ancien Journal*, vol. ii. Translated by Philip O'Gorman. http://faminearchive.nuigalway.ie/docs/grey-nuns/TheTyphusof1847.pdf, p 33.
6. Grey Nuns *Ancien Journal*, vol. i. Translated by Jean-François Bernard. http://faminearchive.nuigalway.ie/docs/greynuns/GreyNunsFamineAnnalAncienJournalVolumeI.1847.pdf pp 6-7.
7. *Irish Independent*, 6 March 2021.
8. See: www.dbq.edu/CampusLife/OfficeofStudentLife/VocationalServices/WhatisVocation/
9. See: www.rte.ie/history/famine-ireland/2020/0820/1160364-asenath-nicholson-the-american-who-described-the-great-famine/
10. "This Manchester United footballer is helping feed U.K.'s hungry schoolchildren. His opposition: Boris Johnson," *America. The Jesuit Review,* 30 October 2020, at: www.americamagazine.org/politics-society/2020/10/29/manchester-united-footballer-feed-uk-hungry-schoolchildren-boris-johnson
11. Sister Martine Reid deposition (13 November 1899), "Typhus 1847 46." Archival Services and Collections, Maison de Mère d'Youville, Sisters of Charity of Montreal, "Grey Nuns."
12. See chapter by Peter Murphy.

ABOUT THE CONTRIBUTORS

REBECCA ABBOTT is Professor Emerita of Communications at Quinnipiac University and an Emmy-award winning independent filmmaker whose films have explored aeromedical rescue in the U.S. Air Force; the history of jazz music in New Haven, Connecticut; the impact of war on Veterans and the role of arts in healing; and the life of humanitarian Albert Schweitzer. *Ireland's Great Hunger and The Irish Diaspora*, narrated by actor Gabriel Byrne, is her most recent full-length documentary.

CAROILIN CALLERY has lifetime associations with the National Irish Famine Museum at Strokestown Park in Co. Roscommon. She is a Director of the company who own the property and is also a Director of the Irish Heritage Trust. She has a Masters' Degree in Modern Drama Studies and has devoted much time to a number of *Making History Visible* projects including the National Famine Way.

MARITA CONLON-McKENNA is an award-winning Irish writer of both adult and children's fiction. Her books include the children's classic *Under the Hawthorn Tree* and *The Hungry Road*.

LEANNE HOWE, an enrolled citizen of the Choctaw Nation of Oklahoma, is the Eidson Distinguished Professor of American Literature in English at the University of Georgia. Her newest books in 2020 are: *Famine Pots: The Choctaw Irish Gift Exchange 1847-Present*, MSP Press, co-edited with Irish scholar, Padraig Kirwan; and, *When The Light of The World Was Subdued, Our Songs Came Through: A Norton Anthology of Native Nations Poetry* edited by U.S. Poet Laureate Joy Harjo, Howe, and Jennifer Elise Foerster.

ROBERT G. KEARNS was born in Dublin and emigrated to Canada in November 1979. He is the owner and founder of an Insurance Firm advising successful Canadians. He is the Chair and Founder of Canada Ireland Foundation. His philanthropic interests include History, Archaeology and the Arts.

NIAMH ANN KELLY lectures in contemporary visual culture and the history of art at Technological University Dublin. She has published on contemporary art, art histories and commemorative visual culture and is author of *Imaging the Great Irish Famine: Representing Dispossession in Visual Culture* (Bloomsbury Academic, 2018) and *Ultimate Witness: The Visual Culture of Death, Burial and Mourning in Famine Ireland* (Quinnipiac University/Cork University Press, 2017).

CHRISTINE KINEALY was appointed founding Director of Ireland's Great Hunger Institute at Quinnipiac University in 2013. She has published extensively on nineteenth-century Ireland including, *Charity and the Great Hunger. The Kindness of Strangers* (2013) and *Black Abolitionists in Ireland* (2020).

JASON KING is Academic Coordinator of the Irish Heritage Trust and National Famine Museum, Strokestown Park, and a member of the Government of Ireland National Famine Commemoration Committee. His recent publications include Irish Famine Migration Narratives: Eyewitness Testimonies, vol II, The History of the Irish Famine (4 vols with Christine Kinealy and Gerard Moran, Routledge, 2019.)

PADRAIG KIRWAN, Senior Lecturer in the Literature of the Americas at Goldsmiths, University of London, specializes in Indigenous literatures and contemporary Native American and Irish fiction. He has published articles in *NOVEL*, *Comparative Literature*, and the *Journal of American Studies*. He is co-editor (with LeAnne Howe) of *Famine Pots: The Choctaw–Irish Gift Exchange, 1847–Present* (2020).

Buncrana-born **TURLOUGH MCCONNELL** is a writer, playwright and producer specializing in Irish-American topics of historical significance, including numerous special features published in *Irish America* Magazine and the *Irish Voice* newspaper and many museum exhibitions across the U.S. and Ireland. Turlough's pre-pandemic stage productions include *The Land of Promise: A Celebration of the Scots-Irish* in partnership with Carnegie Hall's *Migrations The Making of America--A City Wide Festival*; in 2020-21, his virtual productions for the New York Irish Center won the 2021 Spirit of the Festival Award from the Origin 1st Irish Theatre Festival.

MARK G. MCGOWAN is Professor of History at the University of Toronto and is Principal Emeritus at St. Michael's College. He has published extensively on the Catholic Church and the Irish in Canada and is currently completing a monograph on Irish Famine orphans in Canada, which includes the chronicle of 271 assisted migrant families from Strokestown, County Roscommon.

GERARD MORAN, a senior researcher at the Social Science Research Centre at NUI Galway, has lectured in the History Department at NUI Galway and at Maynooth University. He has written extensively on nineteenth-century Ireland, most recently, *Fleeing from Famine in Connemara: James Hack Tuke and his Assisted Emigration Scheme in the 1880s* (2018).

MAUREEN MURPHY, Joseph Dionne Chairholder and Emerita Professor at Hofstra University, is the Past President of the American Conference for Irish Studies and the Past Chair of the International Association for the Study of Irish Literatures. The author of *Compassionate Stranger. Asenath Nicholson and the Great Irish Famine,* she is the recipient of honorary degrees from the State University of New York and the National University of Ireland and well as the recipient of the 2015 President's Award for Distinguished Service Abroad.

With and a lifelong passion for History, **PETER MURPHY** has an undergraduate degree in European History from the University of California, San Diego, and a Masters' degree in American History from Trinity College (Connecticut). His current interest is Ireland in the eighteenth century, with a particular focus on the Emmet family of Cork and Dublin.

SANDY LETOURNEAU O'HARE holds a Master of Library Science degree and is currently Head of Access and Document Services at the Arnold Bernhard Library at Quinnipiac University. In addition to her regular duties, Sandy participates in Informational Literacy Instruction, serves as the Library liaison to the English and First Year Writing departments, is the personal librarian to all student veterans on campus, collaborates with Ireland's Great Hunger Institute on various projects and exhibitions and has previously been an adjunct professor in the First Year Seminar Program.

CIARÁN Ó MURCHADHA lectured in the Department of History at NUI Galway. He has published extensively on the Great Famine including *Sable Wings over the Land: Ennis, County Clare and its Wider Community during the Great Famine* (1998), *The Great Famine: Ireland's Agony, 1845-1852* (2013) and *Figures in a Famine Landscape* (2016).

CIARAN REILLY is an historian of nineteenth and twentieth century Irish history based at Maynooth University. His publications include, *Capard: An Irish Country House & Estate* (Dublin, 2019); *The Irish Land Agent, 1830-60: the case of King's County* (2014); *Strokestown and the Great Irish Famine* (2014) and *John Plunket Joly and the Great Famine in King's County* (2012).

CATHERINE B. SHANNON is Professor Emerita of History at Westfield State University whose publications include studies of the roles of Arthur J. Balfour and Lord Randolph Churchill in Irish affairs. She has published on the role of women in the Northern Irish conflict and peace process. Her recent publications focus on the response of Boston's Irish-American community to Irish famines.

LAURA J. SMITH is a university administrator and a historian of the Irish in early nineteenth century Canada.

ACKNOWLEDGEMENTS

In summer 2020, as the world sought to understand and combat the COVID-19 pandemic, a glimmer of hope was provided by the emergence of a group of heroes—the front-line workers who, in any crisis, risk their own lives in order to save the lives of others. They are often nameless, faceless and low waged. To historians of the Great Hunger, there were many parallels. It is to these heroes—historic and contemporary—that this book is dedicated.

As the publication began to take shape, it became obvious that there were many more heroes and heroines than could fit into one volume, and that many will forever remain invisible. This book, however, examines the contributions of 15 individuals, and two groups—the Grey Nuns of Montreal and the Choctaw Nation. Their diverse stories are a reminder that heroes come in many guises. The one thing that they each have in common is their role in helping to save lives during the dark years of the Irish Famine.

Despite lockdowns, travel restrictions, library and archive closures, the demands of home-schooling and of becoming familiar with new forms of communication platforms, the contributors to this volume have each demonstrated their professionalism—and often their passion—when delivered their chapters on their particular hero to us. We thank them for their dedication and their scholarship.

Finally, we would like to acknowledge the Government of Ireland Emigrant Support Programme for funding the "Famine Heroes" season of the Great Famine Voices Roadshow, hosted by the National Famine Museum, Strokestown Park and Irish Heritage Trust in partnership with Ireland's Great Hunger Institute at Quinnipiac University, which inspired this book.

The Editors

INDEX

**IRELAND'S GREAT
HUNGER INSTITUTE**

Quinnipiac University
275 Mount Carmel Avenue
Hamden, CT 06518-1908
203-582-7809
qu.edu/ighi

*Photo courtesy of
Ireland's Great Hunger
Museum, Quinnipiac
University, Hamden, CT*

The tragedy that struck Ireland between 1845 and 1852 is often viewed through the lens of cold-hearted bureaucrats, greedy merchants or indifferent landlords who put profit, principles of political economy, and prejudice against the Irish poor above the need to save lives. This groundbreaking volume examines the contributions of the numerous men and women who risked their lives – and sometimes their livelihoods – to care for the sick and the starving.

This publication examines the uplifting contributions of numerous individuals who combatted hunger, famine and disease in the mid-19th century to save the lives of strangers. At a time when the world is struggling with the deadly COVID pandemic and its aftermath, these stories are a tribute to all forgotten or nameless caregivers and front-line workers.